Key ground-floor plan (Scale 1:200)

Chapters 3, 4 and 5 (16th and 17th century)
G1 Low parlour
G2 Kitchen
G3 Hall
G4 High (linenfold) parlour
G5 Inner parlour
G6 South-west room

Chapter 6 (mid-18th century)
G1 Georgian parlour
G2 Kitchen/Breakfast parlour
G3 Georgian hall
G4 Linenfold parlour
G5 & G6 Georgian kitchen

Chapter 7 (late 18th and 19th century)
G1 Georgian parlour
G2 Entrance hall
G3 Library
G4 Linenfold parlour
G5 & G6 Kitchen

Chapter 8 (early 20th century)
G1 Parlour (Secretary's room)
G2 Lavatories
G3 Library
G4 Linenfold parlour (Committee room)
G5 Inner hall
G6 Dining room

Chapter 11 (modern)
G1 Georgian parlour
G2 Tudor kitchen
G3 Shop
G4 Linenfold parlour
G5 Staircase lobby
G6 Dining room

Sutton House

Sutton House

A Tudor Courtier's House in Hackney

Victor Belcher, Richard Bond, Mike Gray and Andy Wittrick

with contributions by
Emily Cole, Richard Griffiths and Carole Mills

THE NATIONAL TRUST

ENGLISH HERITAGE

Published by English Heritage at the National Monuments Record Centre, Great Western Village, Kemble Drive, Swindon SN2 2GZ.

First published 2004

ISBN 1 873592 56 6
Product Code 50210

British Library Cataloguing in Publication Data
A CIP catalogue record for this book is available from the British Library.

Brought to publication by Rachel Howard, Andrew McLaren and
    René Rodgers, English Heritage
Edited by Kate Fielden
Designed by George Hammond
Indexed by Susan Vaughan
Printed in Ghent by Snoeck-Ducaju & Zoon

Frontispiece
Conjectural reconstruction drawing showing Sutton House from the north-east as it might have appeared when first built c 1535, *prior to the removal of the gables.*
The form of the chimneys, doorcase, dormers and gables is conjectural. (Not to scale)
[*Richard Bond/The National Trust*]

Contents

Foreword

London has no building quite like Sutton House. This early Tudor brick house, altered from time to time by a succession of occupants, has long fascinated people living nearby as well as artists and architects from further afield. Yet in 1936 it was at risk of being demolished for the value of its site and its panelling before being taken on by the National Trust. In 1987, when no tenant could be found, it was again at risk, left empty, a prey to vandals and about to be converted into flats.

These crises might not have occurred had more been known of the history of the house. There was, however, little information: there were no accounts or plans, no inventories, and its occupants had left few personal papers. Much of the evidence to be found within and around the house was concealed by later work.

Painstaking investigations of the building itself and of remaining archives have now shed light on the people who lived in the house and of what it looked like over the centuries. As this monograph records, the initial documentary research found that the house had been built, not by Thomas Sutton as had been supposed, but by Ralph Sadleir, an influential official at the Court of Henry VIII. The analysis of the building has revealed 16th-century windows, vividly painted decorative schemes and other features, some of which can now be seen by opening hinged panels. Archaeologists have discovered the ground plan of earlier outbuildings and of the terraced garden. Among the accumulated debris under floorboards and behind panelling were odds and ends discarded by children who went to school in the house during the 19th century.

The authors describe how the National Trust came to own the house, the wartime experiences when fortunately it suffered relatively little damage, and the care taken over repairs until the trade union tenant unexpectedly gave up its lease in 1982. At that stage the Trust hoped that the Hackney Borough Council or some local organisation would lease the house, but negotiations fell through and meanwhile valuable fittings were stolen and squatters moved in.

Urgently in need of a solution, the Trust decided to lease the house to a developer for conversion to flats. When this proposal became known there was an explosion of local anger and a 'Save Sutton House' campaign was organised, calling on the Trust to restore the house as a museum and community centre.

It was at this point that I first saw it. I was immediately persuaded that division into self-contained units would damage the building's integrity and atmosphere as well as limiting public access. More difficult was to judge whether the alternative proposals would provide a secure long-term future. Working together, the Trust and the campaign group have shown that it could. The building has been restored and new facilities designed in a contemporary style have been fitted in. The house is alive with school children, visitors to the café and people attending weddings, concerts or other functions.

Sutton House demonstrates that it is possible for a 16th-century building to be intensively used while the fabric is preserved. Its historic character has been the key to its success in attracting a wide range of activities and is greatly appreciated by the local community.

Dame Jennifer Jenkins
CHAIRMAN, NATIONAL TRUST 1986–90

Preface and Acknowledgements

After many years of neglect, the future of Sutton House is well assured. Situated in the London Borough of Hackney, this 16th-century courtier's residence stands as a model of what we believe to be good conservation practice. The process by which the building was understood, rehabilitated, and carefully brought back into sympathetic use was very much guided by a well-planned programme of investigations into its history and architectural development. In short, the future of Sutton House is informed by its rich past.

Apart from acknowledging the success of the conservation scheme itself, this book might be said to represent the 'added value' from the investment put into the various research investigations. The work was largely carried out by the four principal authors over a period of almost fifteen years. To begin with, the documentary research into the history of Sutton House was initiated by Mike Gray in 1987. His findings were the basis of a more expansive account of the history of the building and its owners by Victor Belcher. Meanwhile, under the auspices of English Heritage, a painstaking analysis of the fabric of the house was carried out by Richard Bond and Andy Wittrick from 1988 to 1990, their findings being periodically updated as the restoration of the building produced fresh revelations. Later, when it became clear that the new building works associated with the conservation process would involve ground disturbance, a limited archaeological investigation was seen as a priority. This was undertaken by a team from the Museum of London Archaeological Unit, headed by Chris Philpotts. His report is one of several which deserve to be mentioned here for their contribution to our fuller understanding of the history of Sutton House, along with Ian Tyers' report on the dendrochronological analysis of the structural timbers and panelling and Lucy Medhurst's report covering the wall paintings. Full details of all these reports are found in the bibliography.

As the four authors' various studies progressed, their interdependence upon one another became increasingly apparent. It was clear that the history of the house was helping to elucidate the archaeology of the building. Similarly, it was impossible to divorce the below-ground archaeology from the analysis of the standing building. Thus, when it came to a decision on synthesising the various studies for publication, we chose to adopt a broadly chronological approach. For each of the major periods of change in this much altered Tudor house, we were agreed that the history, the structural analysis, and results of the archaeological investigation should as far as possible be integrated. This was in preference to each of us presenting a study which would stand alone, with its own dedicated authorship. In presenting the material in this way, we believe that the reader will have a greater chance of understanding how the house would have looked and functioned in each phase of its complex history. Moreover, the approach was considered to have the added benefit of extending the appeal of the work. We hope, of course, to move beyond the specialist in each area of study to a broader readership, embracing, for instance, local people who seek a wider understanding of one of the outstanding historic buildings in east London, as well as the many visitors to the house who want more information about one of the National Trust's more remarkable urban properties.

It might fairly be said that the text represents a mutual collaboration between the four principal authors over the entire course of the project. Each chapter has benefited from the constant discussions which have taken place along the way. The historical content was for the most part written by Victor Belcher and Mike Gray, and the accounts of the fabric and its architectural analysis were drafted and illustrated by Richard Bond and Andy Wittrick. In addition, we are very happy to acknowledge the specific contributions made by several other colleagues involved with the project at various stages: Emily Cole (with Richard Bond) for the concluding section of Chapter 3 on 'The architectural and social context of Sutton House'; Carole Mills for Chapter 10; and Richard Griffiths for Chapter 11. The job of collation and the preparation of the entire text for publication has been undertaken by Victor Belcher.

A full list of all those who have contributed to our understanding of Sutton House since the mid-1980s would be very long indeed. But for assistance during the historical and architectural research we would specifically like to thank the staff of the following institutions: the British Library, Charterhouse, the Clothworkers' Company, the College of Arms, the Drapers' Company, English Heritage London Region, the Guildhall Library, Hackney Archives Department, the Huguenot Society, London Metropolitan Archives, the Museum of London Archaeology Service, the Public Record Office (now National Archives), the Royal Historical Society, the Survey of London (now part of English Heritage) and the Trustees of the History of Parliament.

We would also like to extend our warm appreciation and gratitude to a number of individuals who offered advice and assistance of various kinds in the course of our preparing the material for publication. In particular, we are grateful to Jan Cummings, the late Marie Draper, Joan Hardinges, Julian Harrap, David Mander, Hilary Marshall, Robin Mills, the late Stan Piesse, Pauline Rothschild, Ralph de Ste Croix, Professor Arthur Slavin, Dr David Starkey, Dr Andrew Thrush, Jean Wait, Gayne Wells and Margaret Willes. The work was read in manuscript by Professor Maurice Howard and

Dr David Robinson; the final text is much the better for their care and attention and we are especially indebted to them for the valuable suggestions they made for improvements.

Within English Heritage, among those who were kind enough to assist with specific aspects of the editing, illustration, and production of the monograph itself, we would particularly like to mention Nigel Corrie, Karen Dorn, Rachel Howard, Pam Irving, Andrew McLaren and René Rodgers. The task of copy editing was completed on our behalf by Dr Carol Davidson Cragoe.

Moreover, we must extend a sincere note of gratitude to Emily Cole for her efforts in ensuring that the final stages of the work were brought to a successful conclusion.

Finally, we are most grateful to Dame Jennifer Jenkins for agreeing to contribute a foreword to the volume.

Victor Belcher
Richard Bond
Mike Gray
Andy Wittrick

Illustration Credits

Unless otherwise specified below or in the captions, illustrations are either © Crown copyright. NMR or © English Heritage. The negative numbers are given in brackets at the end of the captions to assist with the ordering of prints from the National Monuments Record.

We gratefully acknowledge permission from the following individuals to reproduce illustrations: Richard Bond: 3.21, 4.13, 6.3 and 6.4; Grace Bryan-Brown: 11.15; Mike Gray: 1.1, 1.6, 1.7, 3.2, 3.15, 3.32, 3.33, 3.37, 3.56, 3.64, 3.66, 3.68, 3.88, 3.89, 4.1, 4.3, 5.2, 5.11, 6.25, 7.3, 7.5, 8.17, 10.2, 10.3 and 11.6; Jim Holland: 8.5; Ken Jacobs: 4.15, 5.14, 10.1, 10.4, 10.7, 10.8 and 11.7; James Morris/Axiom: 3.25, 5.9, 6.29, 8.1, 11.2, 11.5, 11.8 and 11.13; The Rector and Churchwardens of the parish of St John at Hackney: 8.11, 8.12 and 8.13; and Colin Stuart and Grace Bryan-Brown: 2.2 and 2.3.

The following institutions, organisations and record offices gave permission to reproduce illustrations: Bristol Record Office: 3.5; British Library: 3.3; Caroe & Partners: 6.13, 6.31 and 7.14; The Governors of Sutton's Hospital in Charterhouse: 2.8; Guildhall Library, Corporation of London: 3.1; Hertfordshire Archives and Local Studies: 3.4; Historic Royal Palaces:

3.90; Julian Harrap Architects: 11.11; Loe & Co: 10.5; London Borough of Hackney Archives Department: 2.4, 2.6, 2.9, 7.6 and 8.16; London Metropolitan Archives: 3.11, 3.44, 3.94, 4.17, 4.18, 4.20, 5.8, 6.7, 6.9, 7.8, 7.9, 8.9, 8.10, 8.14 and 8.18; Museum of London Archaeology Service: 3.20, 3.36, 3.51, 6.33, 6.35, 6.36 and 6.37; National Portrait Gallery: 7.2; National Trust: 9.2; 3.8 (Richard Bond); 3.17, 3.49 and 6.11 (John Bethell); 3.74 (Duncan Murray); 5.13 (Engineering Surveys Ltd); 9.3 (MSF Union); 10.6 (Martin Shortis); 10.9 (Chris King); and 3.26 and 8.2 (Sutton House archive); Public Record Office (now National Archives): 6.39; and the *Sunday Times*: 9.1.

The following drawings were produced by Andy Wittrick, English Heritage: 1.3, 1.4, 1.5, 3.6, 3.10, 3.13, 3.19, 3.22, 3.23, 3.24, 3.27, 3.29, 3.31, 3.34, 3.35, 3.38, 3.40, 3.41, 3.42, 3.47, 3.53, 3.57, 3.58, 3.65, 3.67, 3.70, 3.75, 3.76, 3.78, 3.80, 3.82, 3.84, 3.85, 3.86, 4.2, 4.16, 5.3, 6.5, 6.8, 6.10, 6.12, 6.15, 6.19, 7.4 and 8.22. The following drawings were produced by Richard Bond, English Heritage: 3.50, 3.54, 3.59, 3.60, 3.61, 3.81, 3.83, 6.6, 6.17, 6.26, 6.30, 6.32 and 6.38.

Every effort has been made to trace copyright holders; we wish to apologise to any who may have been inadvertently omitted from the above list.

1
A House is Saved

By the time I first visited it early in 1987, this surviving fragment of the ancient hamlet of Hackney seemed to be at the end of its days. The makeshift sheds of a troublesome-looking car mechanic were built right up against its west wall; the Georgian front was boarded up, and a passing vandal with a spraycan had added humiliation to the injury of the peeling notice announcing that the building had come to the National Trust through the benevolence of one W A Robertson, who had made his gift in the memory of two brothers killed in the Great War. Recent 'repairs' to upstairs windows and brickwork only added to the sense of dereliction; although carried out by the National Trust, they made Hackney DIY look positively refined. Inside, the story was far worse. The enclosed courtyard was full of junk. Damp and rot were creeping through the structure. Ancient fireplaces had been stolen or shattered and left lying around in pieces. The linenfold panelling had also disappeared. Thieves had ripped it out of the empty building a year or so earlier and sold it for £1 per foot to the London Architectural Salvage and Supply Company in Shoreditch, the proprietors of which recognised its exceptional rarity and saw that it was returned to the National Trust.

Thus Patrick Wright, journalist, author and sometime resident of Hackney, described Sutton House in his book, *A Journey through Ruins* (1991)[1] (Fig 1.1). In the four years between his visit and the appearance of the book, much had happened. The visit had been made in the company of the developer chosen by the National Trust to convert the house into flats and the chairman of the Save Sutton House Campaign, which had been formed by a group of concerned local residents to persuade the Trust to change its mind and restore the house as a community resource and open it to the public. By 1991 not only had the campaign group succeeded, probably beyond their wildest expectations, but the restoration of the house had also begun.

The story of their campaign is told later in this volume. From the start, however, they realised that the key to success was knowledge. Sutton House had been described as a Tudor manor house 'built of brick in the first half of the C16', which later became the home of Thomas Sutton,[2] but very little was actually known about it. Rumour and legend abounded, but hard facts were in short supply. Even such essential information as when it was actually built and by whom was completely lacking.

Antiquarian interest in the house had been aroused in the 1890s when it was adapted for use as a young men's institute under the auspices of the parish church. When its fate hung in the balance in the 1930s, it was sufficiently highly regarded as a historic building to have been purchased by the National Trust. After World War II, John Summerson, in the book edited by James Lees-Milne to celebrate the first fifty years of the National Trust, wrote that though the house as a whole was perhaps of 'no great artistic merit', it nevertheless formed a 'composition of fragmentary beauties welded together in the course of time'.[3] A few years later, Nikolaus Pevsner, in one of the earliest volumes in his *Buildings of England* series, *London except the Cities of London and Westminster* (1952), not only provided a fairly lengthy description of the house but also included a photograph of the linenfold-panelled room.[4] Subsequently, however, several decades of its use as offices virtually removed the building from national consciousness. Thus, one of the first decisions of the campaigners was to fill some of the gaps in the knowledge of the house by archival research. Most of this work was undertaken by the chairman of the Save Sutton House Campaign, Mike Gray, although he would readily acknowledge the help given him by others. Some of the early results were disappointing, especially as it soon became apparent that the name Sutton House was a misnomer; Thomas Sutton had, in fact, lived in the now-demolished house next door.

Despite this apparent setback, the names of other important occupants soon began to emerge from the records and the breakthrough came with the discovery of both the name of the builder of the house, Ralph Sadleir, and an approximate construction date of 1535. Sadleir was secretary to Thomas Cromwell (c 1485–1540) and later Secretary of State to Henry VIII (1509–47). Thus, at a stroke, the importance of the house was magnified. It could not only be closely dated and therefore confirmed as a remarkably early example of a brick-built house, but it could also be shown to belong to an important group of courtier's houses built within easy reach of London and the court.

The research has continued to the present day, but several gaps remain. There are no building accounts or plans relating to the construction of the house; no inventories from any period; very little in the way of diaries, letters or any personal papers of its occupants; and virtually no record of life in the house before the 20th century. The historical record for Sutton House remains sparse, but much more is known now than in 1987.

While the archival research was in progress, English Heritage decided to make a detailed record of the fabric of the building.

Two of the current authors, Andy Wittrick and Richard Bond, made a minute study of the historic fabric of the house over the period from 1988 to 1990. As it happens, this work was undoubtedly aided by the parlous state of the building which revealed normally hidden details of construction. Fallen ceilings enabled floor constructions to be carefully examined, and areas of missing plaster and ripped-off panelling facilitated the study of the Tudor brickwork beneath (Fig 1.2). The degree of destruction wrought by the passage of time, while the house had been empty, squatted in and vandalised, enabled a non-destructive survey to be much more informative than would otherwise have been the case (Figs 1.3, 1.4 and 1.5).

In addition to the main survey of the structure, a painstaking sifting of the accumulated debris of centuries, which had collected under floorboards and elsewhere, was also undertaken, chiefly by Ken Jacobs, one of the campaigners for the community scheme (Fig 1.6). It revealed a remarkable array of ephemera, mainly dating from the years when the building was used as both a boys' and a girls' school.[5] For a building which had produced relatively little record of the activities within it, these were priceless additions to its own archive.

The building analysis informed the documentary research and vice versa, and many discoveries were made. Some were momentous, such as the opening-up of a long-blocked garderobe and the location of the Tudor kitchen with most of the large timber bressumer which had spanned the range still intact in the brickwork. Others were more minor, including the discovery of an 18th-century dado rail reused as packing to level the floor (Fig 1.7) and the location of a stone lintel in a later hearth, but all of these discoveries contributed to the overall picture of the history of the house.

The building analysis also informed proposals for the restoration of the house, for, by the time the English Heritage work was underway, the National Trust had accepted the merits of the community scheme even if a formal decision to implement it had to await the approval of various committees. By 1990, however, the Trust had come to enthusiastically embrace the principle of the restoration of the house for public use and, as a further strand in the process of discovering more about it, had commissioned an archaeological investigation by the Museum of London Archaeology Service (MoLAS).

This investigation took place in three stages ahead of building work, in the summer of 1990, February 1991 and September 1992, and was inevitably constrained by the presence of the standing building. Excavation was confined to areas where new floors were to be laid or runs of service pipes and new drainage introduced; this was mainly on the parts of the site occupied by Edwardian additions and the courtyard, but also embraced the ends of the wings and some other parts of the older structure. Among the features revealed by the excavations were a well to the southwest of the house which still had water in the bottom and the remains of a wide garden terrace on the south side of the house.[6]

As part of the Museum of London work, a dendrochronological analysis was performed on a number of the structural timbers in the house and on its panelling. The principal revelation was that one of the structural timbers had sufficient bark edge to be dated with precision, indicating that the tree from which the timber had been cut was felled in the winter of 1534–5.[7] Several separate pieces of documentary evidence were increasingly pointing to the year 1535 as the date of construction of the house, and the independent evidence from the dendrochronology that one of the main beams of the house could also be dated

Figure 1.2
Room G3. South wall showing the substantial brick relieving arch of the original 16th-century fireplace. The fireplace opening was reduced in size in the 18th and 19th centuries and a smaller cast-iron firegrate later inserted.

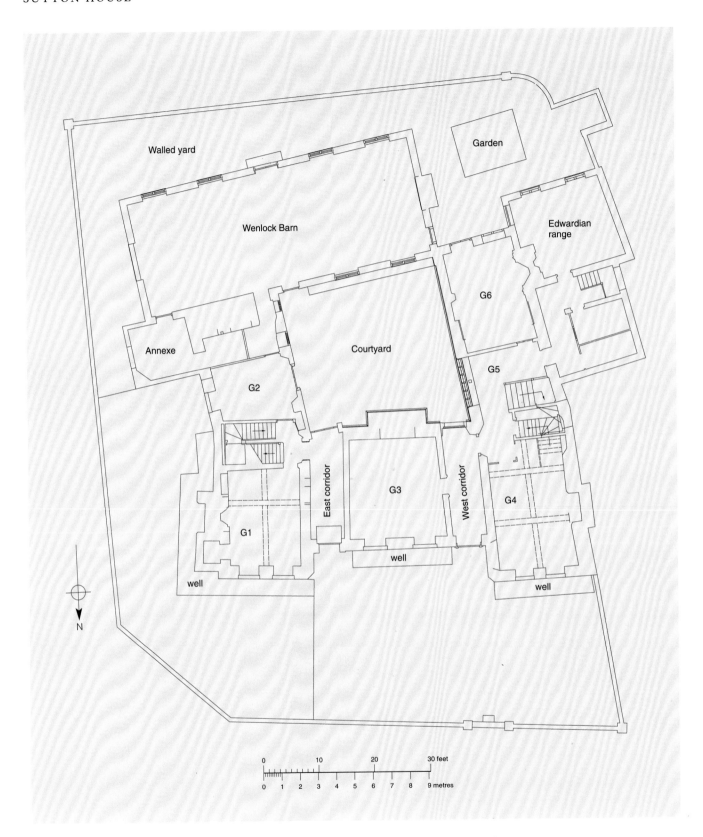

Walled yard

Garden

Wenlock Barn

Edwardian range

Annexe

Courtyard

G6

G2

G5

East corridor

West corridor

G3

G1

G4

well

well

well

N

0   10   20   30 feet

0 1 2 3 4 5 6 7 8 9 metres

Figure 1.3
A ground plan of the site as
existing in 1990.
(Scale 1:200)

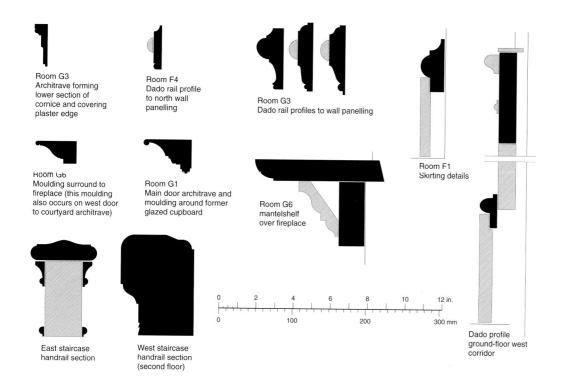

Room G3
Architrave forming
lower section of
cornice and covering
plaster edge

Room F4
Dado rail profile
to north wall
panelling

Room G3
Dado rail profiles to wall panelling

Room F1
Skirting details

Room G6
Moulding surround to
fireplace (this moulding
also occurs on west door
to courtyard architrave)

Room G1
Main door architrave and
moulding around former
glazed cupboard

Room G6
mantelshelf
over fireplace

East staircase
handrail section

West staircase
handrail section
(second floor)

Dado profile
ground-floor west
corridor

0   2   4   6   8   10   12 in.
0   100   200   300 mm

Figure 1.4
Mouldings recorded during
the investigation of Sutton
House. These are largely
18th-century, but the
handrail section from the
west staircase is late
17th-century.
(Scale 1:5)

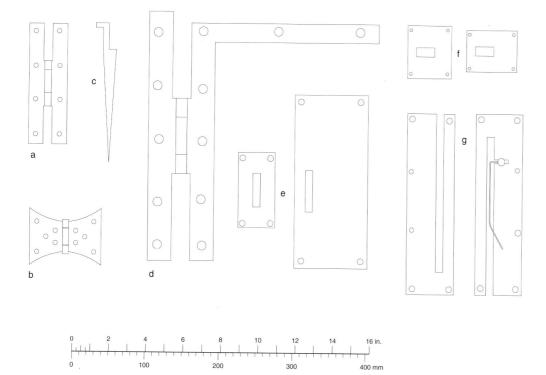

a

b

c

d

e

f

g

Figure 1.5
Examples of ironmongery
recorded during the
investigation of Sutton
House (Scale 1:5):

a) 18th-century shutter
hinge from rooms G1
and G3

b) 'butterfly' cupboard
hinge from room S2

c) iron cramp nail used to
fix wainscot to wall in
room F2

d) 18th-century cranked
hinge from room G3
(east corridor)

e) 19th-century shutter bar
fixings within sash boxes
from room G1

f) early 19th-century
shutter bar fixings from
rooms G3, G4 and F3

g) 19th-century shutter bar
locking plate assembly
for fixed pivot bar from
rooms G3, G4, F3 and
F4.

0   2   4   6   8   10   12   14   16 in.
0   100   200   300   400 mm

Figure 1.6 Ephemera collected from under floorboards and elsewhere. The finds date mainly from the years when Sutton House was in use as a school.
[Mike Gray]

Figure 1.7 18th-century dado rail with applied plaster decoration reused as packing to level the floor of room S2.
[Mike Gray]

to that year was almost, but not quite, suffi-cient to remove the historian's endemic caution in dating the house to *c* 1535. By no means do all the findings of the building analysis and the archaeological excavation fit so neatly with the documentary evidence and in some cases there are significant problems in arriving at the conclusions of each field of study. These are discussed in succeeding chapters.

With the restoration of the house now complete (and inevitably more was learned about the history of the structure during the restoration work), this book synthesises the results of the documentary research, the analysis of the fabric and the archaeological excavations. A chronological approach has been adopted, so that an impression can be gained of the appearance of this much-altered house at key periods in its history. For the most part, it is the story of the occu-pants of the house and how it would have looked when they lived there. From the mid-20th century, however, a different tale unfolds of the decay of the building and its resurrection (Fig 1.8). Thus, this is the story not only of a remarkable house but also of its remarkable rescue.

Figure 1.8
Sutton House today.
Interior of the great
chamber (F3), looking
east. At the far end hangs
a full length portrait
thought to be of Ralph
Sadleir, grandson of
Sir Ralph.
[B000342]

2
Tudor Hackney:
The Setting of Sutton House

By the time Sutton House was built in the early 16th century, Hackney had become a prosperous country satellite of London, some 5km to the north of Bishopsgate (Fig 2.1). The centre of the village lay around the street then called Church Street (the northern end of Mare Street, known locally as the 'Narroway'), with the medieval church of St Augustine, of which only the tower now survives, as its focal point (Fig 2.2). There were a number of other hamlets in the large parish of Hackney, but large tracts of meadow and pasture interspersed with market gardens lay between most of the settlements except for Homerton (also known as Humberton or Humberston) which lay so close to the east of the village centre that the two settlements almost merged. Farmers and gardeners both enjoyed the benefits of easy access to the lucrative markets of London, where their dairy products were particularly highly valued.[1] Sutton House itself stood slightly to the east of the village centre on Humberston Street, which led to Homerton.

Although it was a large parish of over 1,335ha in extent, Hackney was originally part of the bishop of London's vast manor of Stepney. It only gradually achieved independent manorial status, being accounted for separately from the late 14th century and having its own courts by the late 16th century. The main manor of Hackney came to be known as Lordshold, to distinguish it from a number of sub-manors which developed in the late Middle Ages. These included the rectory manor of Grumbolds, which consisted of some 20ha around the parish church and was apparently so named after a family which had farmed the manor, for a John Grumbold of Hackney is recorded as having made a will in 1452. A third so-called manor, that of Kingshold, seems to have originated in land once owned by the Knights Templar and later transferred to the Knights Hospitaller, which reverted to the king at the dissolution of the monasteries, thus acquiring its later name.

The manor of Grumbolds extended eastwards as far as Homerton, so that although the land on which Sutton House was built was in Lordshold manor, the adjacent property to the west was in Grumbolds, the manorial boundary in effect passing between them. Ralph Sadleir later acquired land in Grumbolds and for a time part of this land was included in the estate attached to Sutton House. Hackney Brook ran a short distance to the south of Sutton House, and some of the land on the

Figure 2.1
Detail of John Norden's Map of Middlesex *(1610), showing Hackney in relation to London.*
[A copy of this map can be found in the Sutton House archive]

8

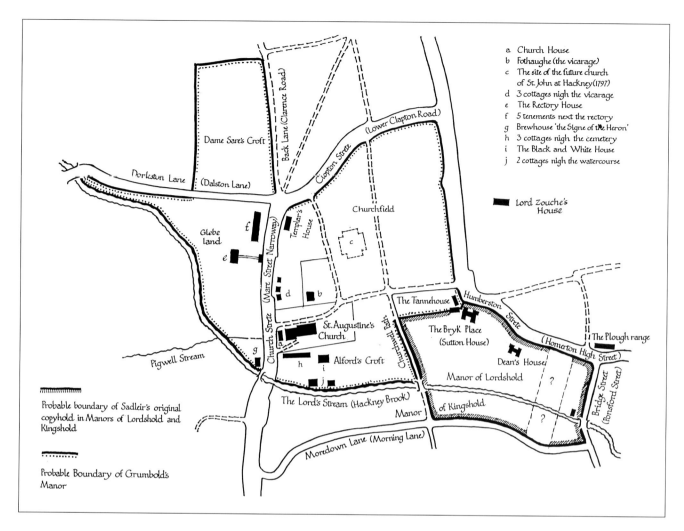

a Church House
b Fothaughe (the vicarage)
c The site of the future church
   of St. John at Hackney (1797)
d 3 cottages nigh the vicarage
e The Rectory House
f 5 tenements next the rectory
g Brewhouse 'the Signe of the Heron'
h 3 cottages nigh the cemetery
i The Black and White House
j 2 cottages nigh the watercourse

■ Lord Zouche's House

Dame Sare's Croft
Back Lane (Clarence Road)
(Lower Clapton Road)
Clapton Strete
Norleston Lane
(Dalston Lane)
Churchfield
Glebe land
Marc Street Narroway
Templar's House
St. Augustine's Church
The Tannehouse
Humberston Strete
The Bryk Place (Sutton House)
The Plough range
(Homerton High Street)
Dean's House
Church Strete
Pigwell Stream
Churchwell Bach
Alford's Croft
Manor of Lordshold
Bridge Street (Ponsford Street)
The Lord's Stream (Hackney Brook)
Manor of Kingshold
Moredown Lane (Morning Lane)

▭▭▭▭▭
Probable boundary of Sadleir's original
copyhold in Manors of Lordshold and
Kingshold

▬▬▬
Probable Boundary of Grumbold's
Manor

south side of the brook which also belonged
to Sadleir lay in Kingshold. Thus, land
which was at one time associated with
Sutton House was situated in three manors,
and the elucidation of the complex descent
of these parcels of land is hampered by the
varying degrees of survival of the manorial
records.[2]

Hackney gained a reputation among
Londoners for the wholesomeness of its air
and in the 16th century it seemed miracu-
lously free of the plagues which constantly
racked London and Westminster. Because it
was regarded as having such a salubrious
aspect and was so close to the city and the
court, noblemen, courtiers and rich merchants favoured Hackney as a place of
residence from an early date, either for their
principal homes or in many cases as a place
of retreat from their houses in the City. In
1537 Ralph Sadleir, the builder of Sutton
House, wrote from Hackney to explain that
the reason for his absence from the court
was that 'the plague reiynese in dyvers p'tes

of London and in dyvers villages about
London but thankes be to God – Hackeney
was never clerer than it is at this present'.
Over a century later Pepys frequently re-
sorted to Hackney 'to take the ayre', and in
1720 John Strype praised its 'healthful air'.[3]

Prominent residents: Urswick and Heron

Christopher Urswick was one of the wealthy
and prominent people who made their
home in the village of Hackney. In the
early years of the reign of Henry VII (1485–
1509), Urswick undertook several important diplomatic functions for the new king
and, in 1502, when he was already Dean of
Windsor and Lord High Almoner, he
accepted the additional benefice of the
rectory of Hackney. Unlike most incum-
bents of this usually sinecure rectory,
Urswick chose to live in Hackney and played
a significant part in the life of the parish.

Figure 2.2
*Map of Hackney village in
the 16th century. Sutton
House, then known as the
Bryk Place, lay to the east
of the village centre within
the manor of Lordshold.
[Colin Stuart/Grace
Bryan-Brown]*

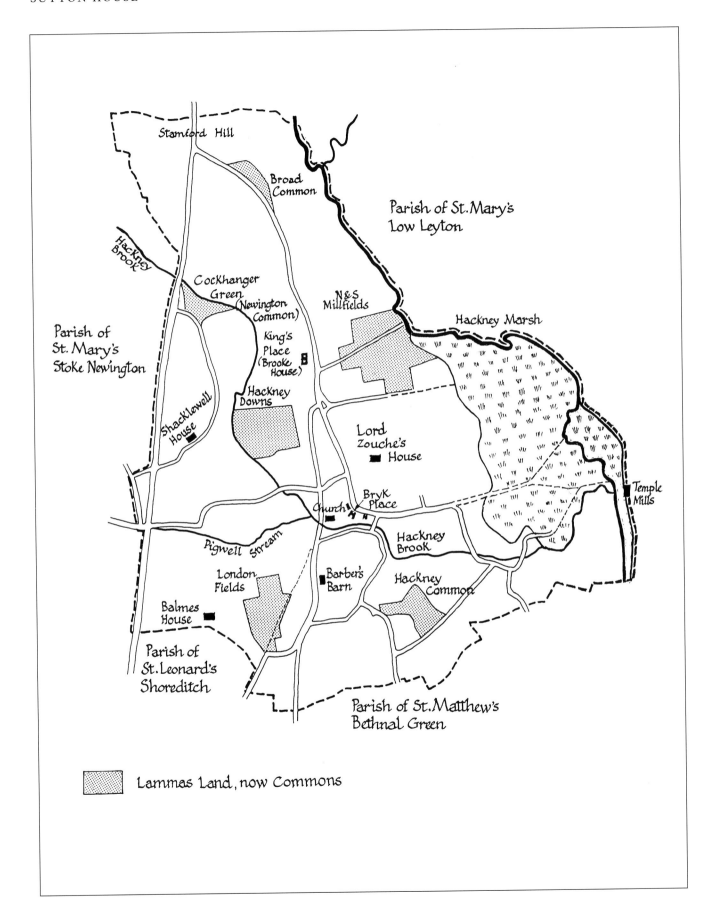

Stamford Hill

Broad Common

Parish of St. Mary's Low Leyton

Hackney Brook

Cockhanger Green (Newington Common)

N & S Millfields

Hackney Marsh

Parish of St. Mary's Stoke Newington

King's Place (Brooke House)

Hackney Downs

Lord Zouche's House

Shacklewell House

Bryk Place

Church

Temple Mills

Pigwell Stream

Hackney Brook

London Fields

Barber's Barn

Hackney Common

Balmes House

Parish of St. Leonard's Shoreditch

Parish of St. Matthew's Bethnal Green

Lammas Land, now Commons

He resided in the rectory house which stood in spacious grounds on the west side of Church Street opposite the church. He became close friends with Sir Thomas More and entertained the humanist Erasmus in his house in 1505, presenting him with the gift of a horse. The modern Urswick Road, historically known as Upper Homerton, is named after him.[4]

Sir John Heron was another important figure at court who lived in Hackney. He held the post of Treasurer of the Chamber between 1492 and 1521, under both Henry VII and Henry VIII (1509–47), administering vast sums of money on behalf of the king. In the latter reign he was also appointed Clerk of the Jewel House, Chamberlain of the Exchequer, Supervisor of Customs in London and Clerk of the Hanaper (the treasury of the Chancery), thus combining a range of financial control functions.[5] Heron lived in a mansion in the hamlet of Shacklewell about a mile to the north-west of Hackney (Fig 2.3), but he also owned property in and around the village centre and was a major benefactor to the parish.

In 1520 Heron was appointed financial administrator for the Field of Cloth of Gold, the elaborate pageant near Calais created for the meeting of Henry VIII and Francis I of France. The spectacle involved the construction of a temporary palace and other buildings in wood and canvas. The man employed as 'parvenour of canvas and buckram' was Henry Sadleir, then steward to Sir Edward Belknap, who, as the king's chief butler, was closely involved in the planning of the spectacle. Shortly after Belknap's death in 1521, Henry Sadleir said that he had bought a house in Hackney.[6] Its whereabouts are not known, but Sutton House, built by Henry Sadleir's son, Ralph, was on a site immediately adjacent to property which had been bought by Heron and was at that time still owned by his descendants.[7]

The village centre

The parish church lay at the centre of Hackney village. Thought to have been founded by the Templars in the 13th century, it was originally dedicated to St Augustine, apparently in honour of St Augustine of Hippo whose rule the Templars followed. On their suppression in the 14th century, their land and property were transferred to the Hospitallers, or Order of St John, from which the later dedication of the church to St John is thought to derive, although the change of name did not apparently occur until the 17th century. The church was substantially rebuilt c 1519 at the expense of Christopher Urswick and Sir John Heron.[8] Although the medieval church has largely been demolished, its appearance can be judged from later engravings.

Built mainly in Kentish ragstone, it consisted of a nave with north and south aisles, a north porch and a chancel, as well as a prominent tower. The aisle roofs were low-pitched, giving the body of the church a rather squat and box-like appearance, despite the clerestory windows in the nave. In 1614 a mortuary chapel was built on to the south side of the chancel by Sir Henry Rowe, who was then living in Heron's former house in Shacklewell, to commemorate his father, Sir Henry Rowe, and his grandfather, Sir Thomas Rowe, both Lord Mayors of London.[9] After the completion of the new parish church of St John at Hackney to the north-east in 1798, the main body of the old church was demolished, but the Rowe chapel was allowed to stand until the late 19th century and the tower still stands. A number of Tudor and Jacobean monuments, including one to Urswick (d 1522), were moved into the new church (Fig 2.4).[10]

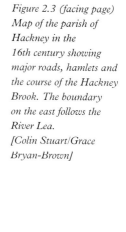

Figure 2.3 (facing page) Map of the parish of Hackney in the 16th century showing major roads, hamlets and the course of the Hackney Brook. The boundary on the east follows the River Lea. [Colin Stuart/Grace Bryan-Brown]

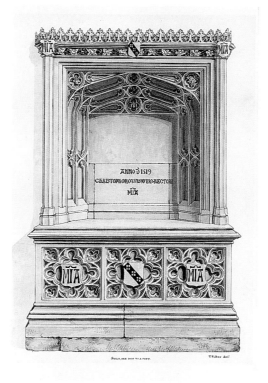

Figure 2.4 Monument to Christopher Urswick (1448–1522) in the church of St John at Hackney, from a late 18th-century watercolour by T Fisher. [London Borough of Hackney Archives Department P12982.4]

Figure 2.5 (above, left) Church House and the church tower as seen from Church Street (now Mare Street) in the late 18th century. [Published 1798 by J P Malcolm]

Figure 2.6 (above, right) The Black and White House, shown from the rear in a print of c 1780, artist unknown. [London Borough of Hackney Archives Department WP4439.1]

Among the buildings clustered around the churchyard were the vicarage on the north side (until 1821 Hackney had both a rector and a vicar), standing in about an acre (0.4ha) of land, and an irregularly shaped building of brick in front of the church tower known as Church House (Fig 2.5). The latter was said to have been built by Urswick in 1520, possibly for his own residence. Subsequently meetings of the parish vestry were held there, and it also housed at times the village lock-up and the church charity school.[11] To the south of Church House and the churchyard, three cottages stood at right angles to the road. They were owned until 1507 by the prior of the Hospital of St Mary without Bishopsgate (St Mary Spital) and later by Sir Roger Chomley, sergeant-at-law. In 1533 they were held by one Richard Hawkes at 'a rent of 3s 4d, a capon and a man by the day in autumn'.[12]

Near these cottages, on the south side of the churchyard, a substantial timber-framed house that became known as the Black and White House was built in the 1570s (Fig 2.6). It was said by local tradition to have later been the residence of Princess Elizabeth of Bohemia on the strength of a coat of arms displayed in stained glass and, in the 17th century, it was the home of Sir Thomas Vyner, a Lord Mayor of London who chose to live in Hackney, and his son, Sir George. It was demolished in 1796 to make way for Bohemia Place.[13]

A short distance to the south, the watercourse, which went by various names but was eventually known as Hackney Brook, formed one of the principal geographical features of the village. It rose in the hills of Hornsey and flowed south-eastwards through Stoke Newington, passing through Shacklewell in the north of Hackney parish and skirting Hackney Downs, before crossing Church Street (where there was a watersplash) about 50m to the south of the church. It then flowed in an easterly direction, passing to the south of Sutton House on a line now formed by the gardens of the houses on the south side of Mehetabel Road, through the hamlet of Homerton, before turning southwards to empty into the River Lea at Old Ford. The brook was progressively culverted during the 19th century and now runs underground as a sewer.[14]

Where the brook formed a watersplash as it crossed Church Street, a wooden bridge was provided for pedestrians on the west side. Near this bridge was a brewhouse and inn known by 1591 as The Signe of the Hearne, possibly through an association with the Heron family. In 1487 the tavern with its garden, orchard, barn and stable was conveyed to Robert Nederton, whose family held it until 1533. By 1568 it was in the possession of Henry Herne [sic], who may have been Henry Heron, the fourth son of Sir John Heron. On the surrender of Herne in 1676, John Katcher of London, pewterer, was admitted as tenant. The inn survived into the 19th century, when illustrations show it to have been a jettied, weather-boarded building with an M-shaped roof, known at that time as The Eight Bells (Fig 2.7).[15]

To the north of The Signe of the Hearne, Urswick's rectory house was set back some distance from the west side of Church Street, where it had a gatehouse. It stood in a 'great garden' of 5½ acres (2.2ha) stretching from Hackney Brook on the west to Church Street on the east and extending north as far as Dalston Lane. In the 1540s it was occupied by Elizabeth, Countess of Shrewsbury, as farmer to the then absentee rector, John Spenlowe.[16] An inventory made in 1601, after the arrest of the then tenant John Daniell for blackmail, provides evidence of its accommodation. On the ground floor there was a hall with two trestle tables, five stools and an old straw bed; a parlour comfortably furnished with a wickerwork chair and a fireplace with a pair of andirons; and a kitchen, buttery and milkhouse. On the first floor Mr Daniell's chamber was furnished in the manner of a great chamber with a table, three covered stools, a court cupboard, a cabinet to display plate, and four pictures; Mrs Daniell's chamber, however, was a bedroom with a 'standing bedsted of waynscote' and curtains and covers of 'green stuff', another court cupboard, stool and table, a window curtain and two bibles; there were also two other chambers and a study.[17]

Apart from the gatehouse, the grounds of the rectory house did not extend to the Church Street frontage. Beside the gatehouse to its north stood 'a cottage with a barn and a garden' which was surrendered to Thomas Sunnys in 1488.[18] By the 17th century, a house of the same description (although the 'cottage' had become a 'messuage') was owned by several generations of a family by the name of Macro. From later evidence it was a substantial house, with a parcel of land some 6½ acres (2.6ha) in extent on the north side of Dalston Lane known as Dame Sares Croft.[19] Opposite this house, on the east side of Church Street, stood a 'customary house called a barn' which was said to be 'ruinous and unrepaired' in 1525, when it was owned by Robert Elrington. This seems to be the house traditionally known as the Templars' House (although unlikely to have been associated with the Templars themselves) and sometimes as the Blue Posts or

Bob's Hall. Later illustrations suggest that it may have been of ancient origin, though much altered,[20] and the house may have been included in a group of five cottages on the east side of Church Street to the north of the churchyard owned by the family of the courtier, Sir John Elrington, who had been a prominent resident of Hackney in the late 15th century. By the mid-17th century, the southernmost of these had become the Mermaid tavern, where Pepys played shuffleboard in 1666.[21]

The Tanhouse

From the church a path ran eastwards towards the hamlet of Homerton between Churchfield to the north, consisting of some 13 acres (5.26ha), and Alford's Croft, some 5½ acres (2.2ha) in extent, to the south. Where it joined Humberston or Homerton

Figure 2.7
Engraving of c 1800 showing Church Street (now Mare Street) looking north towards the church tower. On the left is The Signe of the Hearne, known in the 19th century as The Eight Bells. [Drawn by Schnebbelie, engraved by Warren, for Dr Hughson's Description of London, *published 1805]*

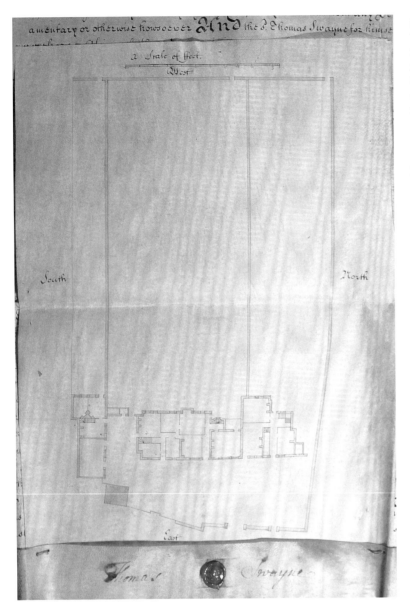

resumé of the ownership and occupancy of the house is pertinent at this point because its history was typical of that of Hackney in general and Homerton in particular, and because the most famous early 17th-century occupant of the Tanhouse lent his name to Sutton House.

Sir John Heron acquired the Tanhouse along with Churchfield and Alford's Croft in 1511–13, and when he died in 1522, his property passed to his sons. One of them, Giles, sold the house and its accompanying land in 1537 to Ralph Sadleir, whose own 'capitall mansion house' (Sutton House) had been built some two years previously on an adjacent site to the east. At that time the tenant of the Tanhouse was Robert Heneage, a member of an important family of office-holders who owned land in various parts of Hackney.[23] In 1550 the house passed, along with most of Sadleir's extensive property holdings in Hackney including Sutton House, to John Machell, a cloth merchant, who had been Master of the Clothworkers' Company and was subsequently an alderman. In 1573 Francis Bowyer, a leading merchant who pioneered the development of trading links with new areas like Russia, Spain and Morocco, purchased the Tanhouse from Machell's son, and in 1605 his own son, Sir William Bowyer, sold it to Thomas Sutton who lived there until his death in 1611.[24]

Sutton was said at the time to be the richest commoner in the country, having made a fortune from coal mining in Durham and money-lending in the City. Just before his death he founded Charterhouse hospital and school, and he left the Tanhouse and its walled garden and orchard to the governors of Charterhouse.[25] An inventory of the Tanhouse's contents, drawn up after Sutton's death in 1611, shows that it consisted of Sutton's chamber, a wainscot chamber, a great chamber with a closet, a wardrobe containing among other items 'olde hangynges of ymagery', a chamber at the stairhead next to Sutton's chamber, a little garret chamber, a chamber over the larder, a chamber which was probably the steward's, a garret near the turret, a great hall, a parlour, a kitchen, wet and dry larders, a wash-house, a stable, a bakehouse, and a house next to the stable.[26] The tenant after Sutton's death was Sir John Peyton, Governor of Jersey,[27] and it continued to have prosperous occupants throughout the 17th century. In the 18th century, however, it was converted into three residences before

Figure 2.8
Plan of Tanhouse, c 1741.
The building stood adjacent to Sutton House.
[The Governors of Sutton's Hospital in Charterhouse]

Street, a building stood on the south side. Described at the end of the 15th century as 'formerly a tannehouse but now a dwelling house', it was known as the Tanhouse and had an acre (0.4ha) of garden which had apparently been carved out of Alford's Croft. It appears to have been a substantial two-storey, timber-framed house with brick cellars and a turret (Fig 2.8).[22] In terms of present-day topography, the eastern end of the path now forms the roadway of Sutton Place, and the houses and their gardens on the south side of that road occupy the site of the Tanhouse and its garden. The Tanhouse was next door to Sutton House and at times its history impinged closely on that of Sutton House. These episodes are described in more detail in later chapters, but a brief being demolished in 1806 to make way for the building of the present late-Georgian terrace on the south side of Sutton Place which remained in the freehold ownership of the governors of Charterhouse until the 1930s.

While it was well known that Thomas Sutton had lived in the area, after the demolition of the Tanhouse the precise location of his residence was lost. Thus, in the 1890s when antiquarian interest arose in the old house with the fine interior features standing at the east end of Sutton Place, it was understandable that this house was thought to have been Sutton's former home. So, the name Sutton House came to be informally applied to it and was later officially adopted by the National Trust in 1953 at the request of the trade union acquiring a tenancy of the house (see p 216). By the time historical research had shown that Sutton had, in fact, never lived there but had occupied a now demolished house next door, the name had become so ingrained in local consciousness that it was considered undesirable to impose a change.[28]

Homerton

An indication of the standing of Homerton at the end of the Tudor period can be gained from the names of the residents who were assessed for contributions towards the repair of Hackney parish church in 1605. They included the third Lord Cromwell (d 1607), Lord Rich (created Earl of Warwick in 1618), Lord Zouche, Sir James Deane, Sir Edward Holmeden, Sir William Hynde, Sir Thomas Leighton, Sir John Peyton, Sir Marmaduke Wyvell, Roger Clarke, alderman, and Humphrey Smythe, merchant.[29] Few of the actual locations of their residences, which may in some cases have been occupied only occasionally, are known, but a number of houses of some consequence existed in Homerton in the Tudor period.

Ralph Sadleir accumulated several properties in the area. One such property, on the south side of Homerton Street, was a house with 'three days' work' of land (about 2 acres (0.8ha)) attached.[30] Later evidence from maps and rate books suggests that a substantial H-shaped house stood a short distance to the east of Sutton House, at the point where the present-day Link Street joined Homerton High Street, and this may be the house in question. By the late 16th century this house was owned by Sir James Deane, a merchant who was later also

to acquire Sutton House. Thereafter, as detailed in subsequent chapters, for much of the 17th century the histories of the two houses were to be closely, sometimes inextricably, linked.

Another house which belonged to Sadleir on the north side of Homerton Street may have been the antecedent of a 'great house' which stood back from the high road. The house had a garden of 1½ acres, with 5½ acres of arable land and 4½ acres of meadow attached (a total of 11½ acres (4.7ha)) and, in the late 16th century, this house was owned by Rowland Beresford. This may be the Hackney house which is subject to an inventory once thought erroneously to be of Brooke House, for the inventory refers to the 'chamber of Rowland Beresfourd'; if so, it had a great and little parlour, a great chamber, about seven bedrooms, a kitchen, buttery, larder, still house, press chamber and wash-house, as well as a lead cistern in the garden, a stable, hen-house and corn-loft.[31]

In 1595 Beresford sold the house and grounds, with other land, to Edward, Baron Zouche (1556?–1625), later to become President of Wales and Lord Warden of the Cinque Ports. While living in Homerton, Zouche cultivated a physic garden which was superintended by the celebrated botanist Matthias L'Obel, after whom the lobelia plant was named.[32] Zouche sold the house and garden to a barrister, Paul Ambrose Croke, son of the prominent judge Sir John Croke, who in turn sold it in 1620 to Sir Julius Caesar, Master of the Rolls and son of the physician to both Queen Mary and Elizabeth I. The house was later adopted as his manor house by Sir Thomas Cooke, a goldsmith, after he purchased a share of the Hackney manors in 1675. It was apparently demolished in the early 18th century to make way for the grand Palladian house and grounds, known as Hackney House, designed by Colen Campbell for Sir Stamp Brooksbank.[33]

During clearance work in the 1970s, for the development of the Jack Dunning Estate on the east side of Urswick Road, underground vaults (or cellars), built in Tudor brickwork similar to that found at Sutton House, were uncovered. The vaults were known about in the 19th century and may have given rise to persistent stories about underground tunnels in the area.

There were other large houses situated along Humberston or Homerton Street as it stretched eastwards to Hackney Marshes

and the River Lea. No record has survived of the appearance of most of these, but a substantial timber-framed, gabled range on the north side of the street, opposite the present junction with Ponsford Street, remained long enough to be photographed (Fig 2.9). It was later divided into the Plough Inn and other tenements. Another building of 16th-century appearance, known from 19th-century engravings, stood on the site of the present Hackney Hospital and served as the parish workhouse before being rebuilt in the 19th century.[34]

Farther afield

On the east side of Church Street to the south of Hackney Brook, where Darnley Road stands today, and a short distance from the village centre and Homerton stood the Elizabethan house known as Barber's Barn. Apparently built of brick with four gables and pedimented windows, it was said to have been the home of Lady Margaret Douglas, Countess of Lennox. She was the mother of Lord Darnley, who was the second husband of Mary, Queen of Scots, and the father of James I of England. However, if she did live here, she also later lived at Brooke House. In the 1780s it was acquired by one of Hackney's most famous nurserymen, Joachim Conrad Loddiges,

who demolished it to make way for extensive nursery fields and hot-houses.[35]

By far the largest and most significant house in Tudor Hackney, however, was the one known as the King's Place for much of the 16th century, but better known by its later name of Brooke House. Standing about 1km to the north of Sutton House (near the present Lea Bridge Road roundabout) and directly linked to it by Lower Clapton Road and Upper Homerton (the present Urswick Road), the King's Place was largely constructed of brick on the ground floor with timber-framing on the upper storey (Fig 2.10).[36] Much altered at various times, the house was probably built by William Worsley, later Dean of St Paul's Cathedral, who acquired the land in 1476. By the 1530s it was in the possession of Henry Percy, Earl of Northumberland, but in 1535 the impoverished and out-of-favour earl conveyed it to the king. He in turn granted it to Thomas Cromwell who undertook the first of the major building campaigns which transformed the house.

Whether Cromwell refashioned the house for his own or the king's use is unclear, but he does not appear to have lived there. In 1536 it was the venue for a meeting between the king and his estranged daughter, Mary, who 'was brought rydynge from Hunsedonne secretly in the nyght to

Figure 2.10
Brooke House, the largest
and most significant
property in Tudor
Hackney, stood about half
a mile north of Sutton
House. This photograph
shows the courtyard as it
appeared in the early
20th century.
[AA009974; © Crown
copyright.NMR]

Hacknaye, and . . . the King and Queene [Jane Seymour] came theder'.[37] It appears that Cromwell's building work was in progress at about the same time that his secretary, Ralph Sadleir, was constructing Sutton House nearby. The relationship between these two events is discussed in the next chapter. Sadleir later owned, but did not live in, King's Place. In the later 16th century its owners included Sir Rowland Hayward, twice Lord Mayor of London, and Elizabeth, Countess of Oxford whose husband, the poet Edward de Vere, Earl of Oxford, said by some to have written plays attributed to Shakespeare, lived there from 1596. The countess sold the house to another poet, Fulke Greville, later Baron Brooke, who provided the house's later name. After being damaged by bombing in 1940, it was demolished in 1954–5.

Hackney and the East India Company

As the merchant community of London grew in the second half of the 16th century, so an increasing proportion of the prominent citizenry of Hackney came to be merchants, the village being conveniently close to the City where their places of business, and often their principal residences, were located. A high point of England's development as a trading nation in the reign of Elizabeth came in 1599 with the founding of the East India Company. At least four of the members who were named in the charter of incorporation which was granted in the following year lived in Homerton, and others lived elsewhere in Hackney.[38]

The history of Hackney in general, and Sutton House in particular, can be seen as a microcosm of the nation in the 16th century. During the political instability and the forging of a modern state in the earlier part of the century, courtiers and office-holders tended to form the dominant elite. However, as the reign of Elizabeth generated greater stability and opportunities for the expansion of overseas trade, merchants increasingly took on this role. As the 16th century gave way to the 17th, the East India Company emerged as a major trading force, and it is perhaps no coincidence that it was members of the Company who played a very large part in the history of Sutton House in the first half of the 17th century. Their role is discussed in Chapter Five.

3

A 'Capitall Mansion House'

Date of construction

The evidence revealed by the documentary research, the detailed survey of the physical fabric of the house and the more limited archaeological investigation all strongly suggest that the house now called Sutton House was built in or about 1535. Nevertheless, a number of questions remain unanswered and it is unlikely that the full circumstances surrounding the building of the house will ever be known.

The most compelling evidence for the dating of the house derives from the dendrochronological analysis carried out on a number of structural timbers in 1991. Although complicated by the absence of full sapwood from most of the samples, there was a strong correlation between all of the timbers, except for one joist from the great chamber (F3) which was of an earlier date and may have been reused from an older building on the site or elsewhere. The remaining joists sampled were felled between 1527 and 1560 and those of the large transverse ceiling beams between 1532 and 1564. One of the joists from room F5 had full sapwood and a bark edge and, consequently, could be accurately dated to the winter of 1534–5. It was quite common, indeed often considered necessary, for unseasoned timber from recently felled trees to be used in the construction of timber-framed buildings at this period.[1] Although Sutton House was of brick construction, it is likely that the carpenters who assembled its floors would have followed this tradition. Thus the presence of a structural timber from a tree that had been felled in 1534–5 is entirely consistent with a building date of 1535.

The extensive fabric survey of Sutton House carried out between 1988 and 1990 led specialists to conclude that the plan form, materials used, method of construction and general appearance of the structure were also compatible with a date of erection for the whole house of 1535. The 1990–2 archaeological excavation by MoLAS, although restricted in scope by the presence of the standing structure, revealed no evidence of any earlier buildings, indicating that the original H-shaped house was all of one contemporary build on a site which had previously been an arable field. There are one or two pieces of the jigsaw puzzle which do not quite fit in with this overall picture but the general conclusions of the physical evidence are remarkably firm.

'A Brewhouse and afterwards a dwelling house'

The documentary evidence presents the possibility of a slightly different scenario. The building now known as Sutton House was first mentioned in 1537 in connection with the sale of the Tanhouse, the immediately adjacent property to the west (see p 13). The Tanhouse was conveyed by Giles Heron to Raff [Ralph] Sadleir and is described as being 'next adjoinyng to the capitall mansion house of the said Raff'.[2] The contiguity of the two properties and the configuration of the surrounding fields and roads mentioned in the document mean that this can only be a reference to Sutton House, by then clearly in Sadleir's occupation.

When Sadleir sold Sutton House in 1550, it was described in the deed (Fig 3.1) as 'that capitall messuage or tenement with the appurtenancies of old tyme called a Brewhouse and afterwards a dwelling house . . . and nowe called the bryk place'.[3] The record of the same transaction in the court rolls of Lordshold manor described the property as 'one tenement a brewhouse and another small tenement attached to the same called from of old a dwellinghouse'. A slightly later reference in the court rolls called it 'one tenement sometime a brewhouse and other small tenements attached to the same called from of old a dwellinghouse',[4] while a 1612 lawsuit described it as 'one capitall messuage or tenement customarie . . . which premises were then in times past surrendered and known by the name of one tenement sometymes a brewhouse and of three other little tenements to the same

18

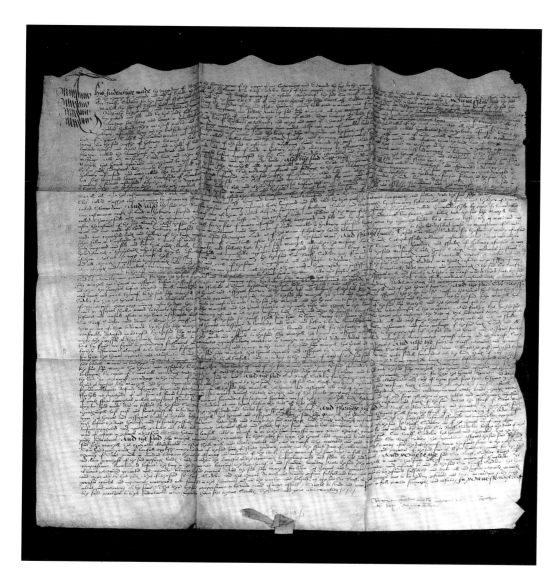

Figure 3.1
The deed of sale for 'the
bryk place' and most of
Ralph Sadleir's other
landholdings in Hackney
purchased by John Machell
in 1550.
[Guildhall Library Ms
1594, Corporation of
London]

annexed caulled of ancyent time a dwelling house'.[5] At a time when estate maps or plans were rare, it was usual to continue to cite ancient descriptions of a property and its former uses, especially in court rolls, to provide continuity and confirm the descent of a title to the land. These descriptions appear to indicate that there were former buildings on the site, however modest and insubstantial, and that the house may not have been constructed anew.

The Sadleir family

The association of the Sadleir family with Hackney has long been recognised by historians. In the mid-17th century, Thomas Fuller claimed that the most notable member of the family, Tudor courtier, politician and diplomat Sir Ralph Sadleir (Fig 3.2), was born in Hackney, where he was 'heir to a fair inheritance'. Later historians accepted Fuller's words at their face value and, in his biographical note to the *Sadler State Papers* compiled by Arthur Clifford in 1809, Sir Walter Scott claimed that Sadleir's family had been 'for some time settled in Hackney'.[6] Research, especially that of A J Slavin, has questioned this version of events. Despite exhaustive research, Slavin was unable to find any evidence of the Sadleir family's presence in Hackney before the 1520s. He concluded that the Sadleirs came from Warwickshire and did not settle in Hackney until Henry Sadleir, Ralph's father, purchased a house there in about 1521.[7] The crucial piece of evidence for his argument was a letter from Henry Sadleir to Thomas Cromwell asking him to intercede in obtaining some money which was owed to him in order that he could complete the purchase of the house:

Figure 3.2
Detail of the effigy of
Sir Ralph Sadleir in the
chancel of the Church of
St Mary, Standon.
[Mike Gray]

Syr, I shoyd your Maistr'ship howe I have boughte a howse in Hackeney, it is xlˢ a yere to be lett, and the quytrent is viiiᵈ by the yere. And I thanke Almyghty God I have payed for hit with yn viiiˡ iiˢ with ought eny daynger of my frynds; and within the Vtas of the holy Trenyte next I am bound to paye the sayed viiiˡ iiˢ. That payd, I trust I, my wyff, and our chyldryn shall injoye the saied howse with the apportenaunce, to Godds pleasure.⁸

In the *Calendar of Letters and Papers, Foreign and Domestic, of the Reign of Henry VIII*, this letter, which is undated, was assigned to 1531,⁹ but Slavin argued convincingly that from internal evidence it must be earlier and assigned it to 1521.¹⁰

Whatever the actual date of the letter, it is the earliest evidence of a Sadleir living (or

at least intending to live) in Hackney. As far as Henry Sadleir is concerned, much of the immediately succeeding period of his life was spent at Tiltey, Essex in the service of the Marquis of Dorset. However, in another letter, probably of the early 1530s, he asked his son to try to procure him a post nearer to London, where, by implication, his wife was then living.¹¹ All that is known for certain is that Henry Sadleir next appears in a definite connection with Hackney in 1540 when he was renting a house there (at 26s 8d per annum) from his son Ralph, who was by then in a far more exalted position in the land than his father had ever reached.¹²

Ralph Sadleir

Ralph Sadleir, Henry Sadleir's eldest son, was born in 1507 and entered the household of Thomas Cromwell at an early age.¹³ As Cromwell rose in the king's service, Sadleir rose in Cromwell's, becoming his trusted clerk and confidante, and by 1529 he was on sufficiently close terms with his master to be appointed an executor of his will. In the 1530s he gravitated to the royal court, still essentially as Cromwell's man but gaining increasing respect for his abilities as an administrator. In May 1534 he was granted the reversion to the post of Prothonotary in Chancery. Although only a minor clerkship, it was a vital first rung up the ladder of royal preferment. To this post was added in the following year the important administrative position of Co-keeper (with Cromwell) of the Hanaper, the treasury of the Chancery. This was a life tenure and brought with it the added emoluments of a major office. By 1535, then, Sadleir had truly arrived in the royal service.

The early 1530s were an important period in Sadleir's private life as well. In about 1534 he married a woman, also employed by Cromwell, whom he thought to be a widow. There is some confusion about her name: that her maiden name was Mychel (Mitchell) is generally agreed, but she is sometimes referred to as Margaret, though more frequently as Ellen, Helen, or even Eleanor. An early pedigree of the Sadleir family, which is backed up by some 19th-century antiquarian research, suggests that she was a first cousin of Thomas Cromwell. If this is correct, it might help to explain Ralph Sadleir's interest in her at this crucial period in his life. Ellen had been married before, to a man named Mathew Barre who proved to be a ne'er-do-well and deserted her.

Believing him to be dead, she married Sadleir. However, Barre was still alive and reappeared in 1545 to Sadleir's great consternation. He hurriedly obtained a special Act of Parliament in December of that year to legitimise his children, in the course of which he declared that his marriage had taken place 'eleven years past and more', which would make the date about 1534.[14]

This discovery was, of course, in the future, and one of Sadleir's first tasks in his new-found state of matrimony would have been to acquire or build a home, as his wife displayed an immediate propensity for child-bearing. His choice of Hackney as its location may have been related to his father's residence there, then or earlier, or it might have been owing to the association of Thomas Cromwell with the suburb, especially at that precise time. Cromwell appears to have owned some property in Hackney before 1534, although its whereabouts are unknown, but in 1535 he set his sights on the large house in Clapton, later known as Brooke House (see Fig 2.10). It had come into the king's hands as a result of the failure of Henry Percy, Earl of Northumberland, to honour his mortgage commitments.

In May 1535 a royal order was given to the keepers of Enfield Chase and Park to deliver fifty oaks from each place to the Surveyor of the King's Works, James Nedeham, 'to be employed towards our buyldynges At our place of Hakney'.[15] Several letters to Cromwell from his servants during the course of the year provide information about the progress of building operations which were taking place at a number of his houses, including extensive works at a house in Hackney.[16] That this was Brooke House is suggested by the physical evidence that substantial additions were made to the house at about this time, and by the king's grant of the house and its surrounding estate to Cromwell in September 1535.[17]

There is no evidence that Cromwell ever lived in the house and, in May 1536, he surrendered it back to the king. Whether the house was always intended for the king's use (although the grant to Cromwell, and the tone of the letters from his servants, would suggest otherwise); whether he did not find the house to his liking, despite the large-scale improvements; or whether he thought it politic to surrender the aggrandised house to the king can only be conjectured. What is significant about this puzzling episode is that it indicates that Cromwell had considerable interests in Hackney in 1535, and

where Cromwell went, Sadleir was likely to follow. Moreover, it is certainly conceivable that some of the large supply of timber which was directed to Hackney in that year by royal command could have found its way to Sutton House and could have been used for the structural woodwork there.

Sadleir in Hackney

Several of Sadleir's letters to Cromwell have survived and provide firm evidence for his residence in Hackney from the mid-1530s. One letter sent from Hackney is assigned in *Letters and Papers* to the year 1534, but no date is given in the letter and the dating of letters in the calendar is frequently unreliable.[18] As the letter is addressed to Cromwell as 'Chief Secretary', it must have been written between April 1534, when Cromwell was appointed to the office of Principal Secretary, and July 1536, when he was made Lord Privy Seal and created a baron. Another, addressed to 'Maister Secretarye' and therefore dating from the same period, asks Cromwell to be godfather to Sadleir's newly born son, whom he proposes to name Thomas after his master. As the letter makes clear, Sadleir had already had a son, who had died in infancy and to whom Cromwell had also acted as godfather. Thomas had been born in Hackney, where the christening was to take place on the following day.[19] He matriculated in Trinity Hall, Cambridge, at Easter 1554, along with his younger brother Edward, making it likely that he was born in 1535 or 1536.[20] On the evidence of these letters, written before Cromwell was ennobled, Sadleir and his family must have been settled in Hackney by July 1536, and most probably earlier.

By this time Sadleir was well established at court. He had recently been appointed as a Gentleman of the Privy Chamber and so was admitted to the charmed inner circle of courtiers who surrounded the king. This advancement probably occurred in May 1536 when the ousting of the Boleyn faction after the trial and execution of the queen left a number of vacancies which Cromwell took care to fill with his own supporters.[21] With a major role in the service of Cromwell and increasingly important duties at court, Sadleir had to keep living quarters in a number of places, including the royal palaces.[22] He also began to acquire a number of properties, including some former monastic land at Lesnes in Kent which he was given by royal grant in 1536.[23]

Figure 3.3
Extract from the account
book kept by Ralph
Sadleir's steward Gervase
Cawood in 1540–1,
detailing Sadlier's holdings
in Hackney.
[By permission of
The British Library, Add
Ms 35824 f.23v]

Here he had a farm which seems to have been a favourite rural retreat. In October 1537 his wife was lying-in there when, one of his servants having fallen ill with what looked suspiciously like the plague, the king ordered Sadleir to stay away from the court and advised him not to go to his wife. Instead he went to Hackney, which had been largely free of the plague.[24]

The number of letters sent from Hackney, the allusions to it in other letters, and his 1537 acquisition of property adjoining his 'capitall mansion house' (see p 18), leave little doubt that Hackney was Sadleir's principal residence at this time. His apparently dismissive reference to 'my poore howse at Hackeney',[25] is probably no more than the self-effacement necessary when writing to someone in a higher position.

In a 1540 grant of lands formerly belonging to the monastery of Selby in Yorkshire, Sadleir is described as 'of Hackney',[26] and it may have been this and other references from the period when he was at the height of his political powers that persuaded Fuller and later commentators that he came from a prominent Hackney family.

In the 1530s and 1540s, Sadleir assiduously built up a substantial landholding in Hackney parish. An account book (Fig 3.3) kept by his steward, Gervase Cawood, recorded that in 1540–1, besides his own house, he also owned a tenement with garden, orchard and pond on the south side of Homerton Street in the tenure of his father, Henry Sadleir (possibly the Tanhouse which he had acquired in 1537 and which is not otherwise identifiable in the account); another tenement on the south side of the street; one more on the north side; and a large house and land at Shacklewell which, like the Tanhouse, had formerly belonged to Giles Heron.[27] He may have held this property in trust for the Heron family who were in political difficulties at that time (Giles Heron later suffering the fate of execution all too common in Henry's reign), and were in some way dependent on Sadleir. In 1547 Sadleir also purchased Brooke House but perhaps not with any intention of living there, for he sold the house at a modest profit in the following year.[28]

Figure 3.4
Sadlier built Standon
Lordship in 1545–6.
This view of c 1700 from
an engraving by Drapentier
appeared in Chauncy's
The Historical Antiquities
of Hertfordshire.
[Hertfordshire Archives and
Local Studies D/EHX Z15]

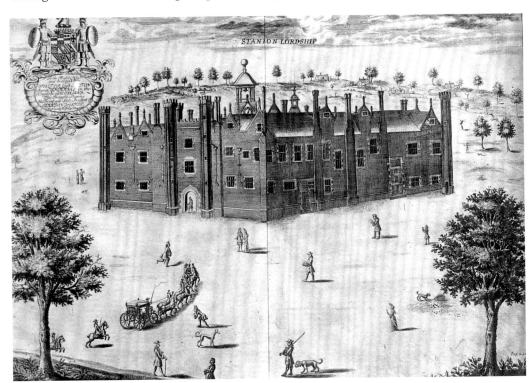

Ralph Sadleir's later years

Sadleir rose rapidly in the king's favour. In 1537 he was entrusted with delicate diplomatic missions to the dowager Queen Margaret in Scotland and to her estranged son, James V, then in France. Thereafter regarded as an expert on Scottish affairs, he was sent on further missions by the king in 1540 and 1543–5, and possibly at other times too. In April 1540 he was appointed principal Secretary of State jointly with Thomas Wriothesley, and was knighted. He survived the fall of Cromwell in 1540, though not without some alarms, and retained the secretaryship, which was one of the major offices of state, until April 1543. He lost that office, ostensibly on the grounds of his prolonged absences in Scotland, but in reality because he fell victim to the faction-fighting which characterised the last years of Henry VIII's reign. He was compensated, however, with the highly profitable post of Master of the Great Wardrobe, a major position in the royal household. Nominally concerned with clothing and materials, as the name would suggest, it involved the administration of vast stores and large-scale contracts.

Sadleir used his power and influence to amass a considerable fortune in this period. He benefited from the profits of office and from astute land dealings buttressed by the gift of former monastic lands from a grateful monarch for services rendered. In his now celebrated article of 1941, R H Tawney singled out Sadleir as an example of the new gentry whose rise during this period resulted in a vast transfer of wealth and power.[29] Certainly, within a very few years Sadleir became an extremely wealthy man.

Among several landholdings which Sadleir acquired in 1539–40 was the manor of Standon in Hertfordshire, where he built up what has been termed 'a small empire'.[30] Standon replaced Lesnes, which he sold in 1541, as a favoured retreat, and in 1545–6 he built a substantial house there (Fig 3.4). Thereafter he had less need of the Hackney house and in 1550 he sold it and the surrounding property he had acquired for £500 to John Machell, a cloth merchant.[31]

To conclude Sadleir's story, he remained a Privy Councillor during the reign of Edward VI (1547–53) and was Treasurer for the war against Scotland, in which he fought with great distinction at the Battle of Pinkie in 1547. For his services there he was created a knight banneret and was also given land by

the same monarch (Fig 3.5). Nevertheless, there is a sense in which he failed to reach the great heights that might have been expected from his meteoric rise in the 1530s and early 1540s, and it may be that the peculiar circumstances of his marriage, which became public knowledge in 1545, militated against him. Forced into virtual retirement during the reign of Mary (1553–8), his political career revived on Elizabeth's accession and he resumed his seat on the Privy Council. He was appointed Chancellor of the Duchy of Lancaster in 1568 and once again played a role in Anglo-Scottish affairs. He was custodian of Mary, Queen of Scots, from 1584 to 1585 and one of his last public acts was to participate in her trial. He died at Standon on 30 March 1587, some six weeks after Mary's execution.

Sadleir and Sutton House

The connection of Sutton House with Sadleir at a pivotal point in his career gives the house a particular significance as the base from which a rising courtier-politician could launch his assault on the fastnesses of power. It was of some pretension, being built of brick, but was relatively modest in size, as befitted the purse of a man whose office-holding was still in its infancy and whose status was still essentially that of a servant, however favoured, of one of the great men of the realm. There was a thin line to be trod

Figure 3.5
Ralph Sadleir receiving a grant of land from Edward VI (1547–53). [Bristol Record Office AC/AS/1/2]

between living in sufficient grandeur to emphasise current rank and future aspirations, and affecting such ostentation that it seemed to threaten those in higher positions. Sadleir was doubtless careful that he should not be accused of over-reaching himself through his 'poore howse'. The house was conveniently placed for access to most of the royal palaces which were the peripatetic centres of government and, while he lived there, his career reached its peak. Within a relatively short time, he outgrew the house in both wealth and status and replaced it with the more opulent, but less central, Standon, where a successful grandee could live in state when he no longer needed or wished to be at the very heart of power.

The deed confirming Sadleir's sale of Sutton House in 1550 (*see* Fig 3.1) gives limited information about the house itself. Apart from the comment that it was formerly a brewhouse, we learn that it was called 'the bryk place', as much, perhaps, because it stood out as one of the very few brick buildings in the locality as through deliberate choice, and that it had 'appurtenancies': all manner of lands, tenements, meadows, pastures and feedings. The entries in the court rolls are slightly more forthcoming, listing barns, stables, garden, dovehouse, and lands stretching as far south as Hackney Brook (approximately on the line of the present Mehetabel Road).[32] Virtually all traces of this complex of outbuildings, formal gardens and additional land have now disappeared, but these may hold the clue to the whereabouts of the enigmatic brewhouse and tenement or tenements which might have been elsewhere on the site and demolished after the new house was built or even utilised as part of the small estate attached to it.

When Sadleir sold Sutton House in 1550 it was only one, though undoubtedly the most important, of several buildings and parcels of land in Hackney, including the Tanhouse (*see* Fig 2.8) and another house to the east of Sutton House with three days' work of land attached to it, which Machell purchased as part of the same transaction. The overall price of £500 seems low, but it should be remembered that Sadleir had sold the very much larger Brooke House, with a considerable estate surrounding it, for £1,200 some two years previously.

There is little direct evidence of Sadleir's personal life at Sutton House: no memoirs, diaries, or family letters, nor much in the way of gossip. There is some indication that he was a private man who valued family life and was not much given to the frivolities or the gregariousness of the court. A serious man, in both politics and religion, he was a staunch defender of the Protestant cause, very able and astute enough to have a long and relatively trouble-free political career. If this did not bring the rewards which might have been expected, such as a peerage, the reason may have been his concern to protect his domestic life, especially in the peculiar circumstances of his marriage. He was highly protective of his wife, on one occasion declaring that he was unable to undertake a mission to Scotland because she was ill.[33]

Ellen Sadleir rarely if ever attended court and when, in 1543, there was some suggestion that she might be appointed a governess to the infant Mary, Queen of Scots, Sadleir excused her on the grounds of her lack of experience of court matters. During the period when the Sadleirs lived there, Sutton House was likely to have been dominated by domestic routine. Between their marriage *c* 1534 and 1545, the Sadleirs had nine children, seven of whom, four girls and three boys, survived infancy. Two girls from Ellen Sadleir's former marriage probably also lived with them. There were other residences (Lesnes, for instance, apparently favoured for lying-in), but Sutton House was the family's main home for some ten or so years after the marriage and the children would have been brought up there. The increasing financial security which Sadleir enjoyed during these years would have enabled him to employ the number of servants judged necessary by the standards of the time and to meet the demands of such a rapidly growing family. Despite the relatively generous provision of accommodation in its three storeys, Sutton House must at times have been stretched to cope with such a large household.

Sutton House was not intended to be a great house of state and would never have been a stopping point on a royal progress. That role was reserved for Standon, but when he built Sutton House, Sadleir must have anticipated that entertaining and the holding of ceremonial functions (albeit on a lesser scale) would be part of life there. The house had both a large hall and a great chamber, and from the outset there was a clear distinction between the lower, or service, end of the house on the east side, and the upper end on the west; provision was also made for the creation of guest suites when necessary (*see* p 37).

The fabric of the house

Sutton House has been subjected to many alterations over its long history, but sufficient remains or was discovered in the course of the detailed survey carried out from 1988 to 1990 and during subsequent building works, to reconstruct both the original appearance and plan, and much of its appearance throughout its history.

When it was built c 1535, Sutton House was a compact, H-plan house of three storeys. It was constructed of brick, a comparatively novel material still largely reserved for the grandest homes, and made a bold show of status with a considerable degree of diaper and other patterning, especially at first-floor level, where the principal rooms were located (Fig 3.6). Its design retained some elements of the medieval tradition, such as an asymmetrical entrance into a screens passage flanking a ground-floor hall, but it is more notable for the way it looked forward, especially in its nascent centralised planning, use of full-storeying throughout and shifting of the principal focus of the household to the great chamber: all features much more commonly found in houses built forty or more years later.

Modifications to the fabric and especially to the interior decoration were introduced at an early date, probably soon after Ralph Sadleir sold the house in 1550, and by the later 17th century the building housed a girls' school. In the mid-18th century, Sutton House underwent at least two phases of significant upgrading, the second of which was probably the result of its division into two residences. Then, in the late Victorian period, both houses were purchased by the rector of Hackney church and converted into the St John's Institute, a recreational centre for young men. In 1904 a substantial programme of restoration and adaptation was undertaken in an essentially Arts and Crafts style by the architects Lionel Crane and Sydney Jeffree.

In 1938 the house was purchased from the Institute by the National Trust, which let it to various institutions, but by the 1980s it was vacant and being vandalised. A major programme of building recording and analysis, largely by two of the present authors, was undertaken from 1988 to 1990; the results form the basis for the discussions of the house in the following chapters. A programme of conservation and restoration was carried out by the architect Richard Griffiths from 1990 to 1994 and further building analysis was conducted in tandem with this work. The fully restored building was opened to the public in

Figure 3.6
Reconstruction drawing of Sutton House, based on evidence discovered during the investigation of the building, indicating how the main (north) elevation might have appeared when built c 1535. The form of the chimneys, doorcase, dormers and gables is conjectural.
(Scale 1:200)

February 1994 (Fig 3.7). The guiding principle of the restoration was to present some aspects of all phases of the house's history.

In its discussion of the fabric of Sutton House, this monograph presents the evidence for each phase in turn. For those areas of the house where no significant alterations appear to have taken place in a given period, or where the evidence does not survive, the reader is referred back to the preceding chapters. For ease of reference and to enable comparisons across periods, each room is given an alpha-numeric reference which appears on the plans in addition to labels giving an approximate use of that room in the appropriate period (*see* Key Plans).

The exterior

The way in which Sutton House (Fig 3.8) must have stood out among the gaggle of timber buildings around the stone church which then made up the village of Hackney is suggested by the contemporary epithet applied to it: it was 'the bryk place', and a survey by Ralph Sadleir's steward described it as *construct est cum pulcr. edificiis* (built with beautiful buildings).[34] In 1535 the erection of a wholly brick, medium-sized house by a man of still modest, albeit rising, social standing, was innovatory and even a bit pretentious. As Malcolm Airs has noted, 'the use of brick . . . was no longer a novelty by the 16th century', but 'few houses of a social level below that of the country house were built solely of brick during this period'.[35] As is discussed below (*see* pp 82–5), Ralph Sadleir would have been familiar with the use of brick for large scale buildings from the royal palaces at Richmond, Greenwich, Bridewell, Whitehall and St James's; the Bishop of London's palaces at Fulham and Lambeth; and especially from Hampton Court. Perhaps as

Figure 3.8
Conjectural reconstruction
drawing showing Sutton
House from the north-east
as it might have appeared
when first built c 1535,
prior to the removal of the
gables. The form of the
chimneys, doorcase,
dormers and gables is
conjectural. (Not to scale)
[Richard Bond/The
National Trust]

importantly, his master Thomas Cromwell had made extensive use of brick during the alterations and additions to Brooke House in 1535 (*see* p 21)[36] and his plans may have encouraged Sadleir to use brick for his own house under construction at much the same time.

Brickwork

Sutton House was built of reducing, load-bearing brickwork laid in English bond (Fig 3.9). It lies on the fringe of the eastern counties in which pioneering brick buildings were concentrated in the later Middle Ages and the early Tudor period.[37] There is evidence that brick earth was present nearby, and unnatural declivities in the ground a short distance to the east of Sutton House suggest that the bricks for its construction could have been made locally.[38]

Structural openings in the brickwork were largely supported by the door and

Figure 3.9
The exterior of Sutton
House was originally
extensively decorated with
face-patterning using
vitrified bricks. Some of
the best examples of this
survive on the west
elevation of the west wing,
shown here before
restoration.
[87/2011; © Crown
copyright.NMR]

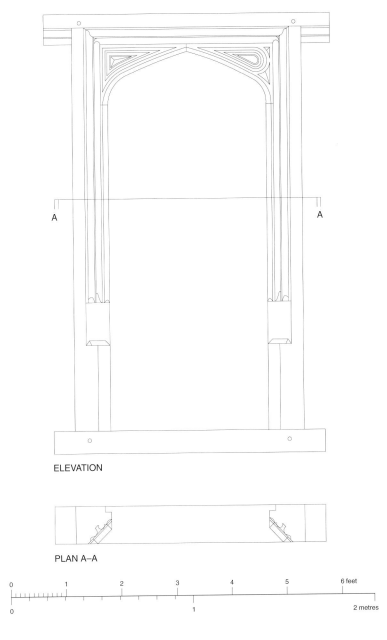

ELEVATION

PLAN A–A

0   1   2   3   4   5   6 feet

0   1   2 metres

Figure 3.10
Plan and elevation of early
16th-century door case.
(Scale 1:20)

window frames (Fig 3.10), which were prefabricated in oak, with the remaining brickwork supported on flat timber lintels. The orange-red bricks varied in size, with average dimensions of 2in. by 4in. by 9in. (51 × 102 × 230mm). Apart from obvious areas of repair and rebuilding using different sized bricks, more than one type of brick was found in the early fabric. It is unclear whether this was the result of bricks having been reused during the original construction or, as seems more likely, repairs having been carried out at a relatively early date. The quality of the brickwork was high, both in manufacture and bonding. The original mortar was of lime and coarse sand, soft on

exposed surfaces but remaining hard internally, and generally struck flush with the outer surface of the bricks. Later sand and cement repointing has, however, obscured much of the original work.

The brick foundations, exposed during excavations, have survived remarkably well with little deterioration or damage. The quality of the material used below ground was the same as that above and bricks were not purposely manufactured for foundation work. There are a number of vitrified bricks in the foundations, but this was almost certainly the result of a desire to use misfired or misshapen examples out-of-sight, rather than their deliberate inclusion to aid impermeability.

The amount of reconstruction, particularly on the north elevation, has obscured what appears to have been an extensive and complex use of diapering. Some of the best remaining indications are on the west elevation, sadly the least readily visible side of the house owing to the proximity of the adjoining property. Nevertheless, a degree of survival occurs on most elevations, in a mixture of patterns including a diamond lozenge with variations, a vertical chequer board pattern and, most commonly, parallel bands of zigzag. The diamond lozenge patterns, frequently joined and interlaced, were haphazardly placed, usually on large, exposed areas such as external chimney breasts. The chequer board pattern appears mostly in the rear courtyard and has a strong vertical emphasis. The parallel bands of zigzag occur, almost without exception, along the same horizontal course lines around the building at first-floor level. Unfortunately, as a result of the major reconstruction of the north front *c* 1740, no evidence survives of the pattern there, but it can be confidently assumed to have existed originally.

The majority of the bricks used for diapering appear to have been intentionally vitrified. There is ample evidence of a number of bricks having only one header face glazed, while some had half of their stretcher face glazed, indicating a consciousness on the part of the brickmaker of the need for such bricks to complete patterns. The loss of some of these vitrified faces as a result of weathering has contributed to the poor rate of survival of the diaper patterns.

The most intricate areas of surviving diapering occur between the levels of the first and second floors. There are remnants on the ground floor but none on the second storey, although the diapering may well have extended there originally. Despite the substantial losses, it appears that, in face-patterning, a deliberate emphasis was placed on the first floor, which contained the most important chambers internally and the largest windows externally.

Apart from the face-patterning or dia-pering, which although fragmentary in its survival was clearly originally extensive, little ornamental brickwork appears to have been used for decoration. Some moulded bricks with 'wire-cut' marks were found during excavations in a back-fill made in the 18th century, but it is the general absence of such bricks, rather than the existence of this small sample, that is notable. Even the cut or moulded bricks used around openings, or to fit the awkward angles of the building, appear to have been kept to a minimum. Such an emphasis on flat surfaces decorated only with diaper patterning, deliberately eschewing the prominent moulded brick-work used in 15th-century brick buildings, reflected a change in fashion which occurred in the early Tudor period.[39]

Windows

Only one complete window, situated at ground-floor level on the west side of the rear courtyard (Fig 3.11), remains from the

Figure 3.11
This photograph, taken c 1920, shows the exterior of the early 16th-century twelve-light window in the east wall of the west wing (detail of Figure 8.9). [London Metropolitan Archives]

original construction. A rare complete survival of a large timber window frame from the early 16th century, it is of twelve-light, mullion-and-transom form, with a substantial carved oak frame (Fig 3.12; *see also* Fig 8.9). The traditional mortise and tenon method was adopted for the assembly of the frame, the joints being held fast with oak pegs. No two mullions were exactly the same, having been fairly crudely carved by

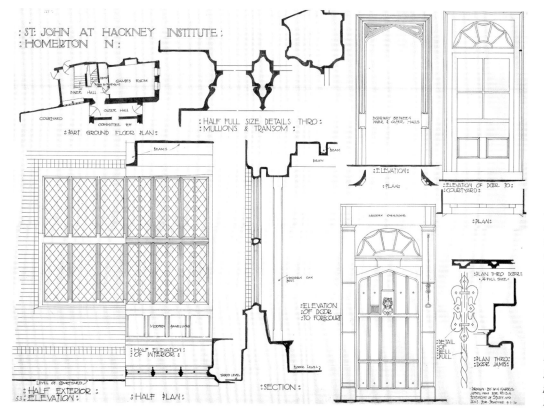

Figure 3.12
Drawing by architectural student W H Harris, made in 1904 around the time of the Crane and Jeffree restoration of the house. The drawing shows assorted architectural details, including the twelve-light window from the west wing and a moulded doorcase. [96/01262; Reproduced by permission of English Heritage.NMR]

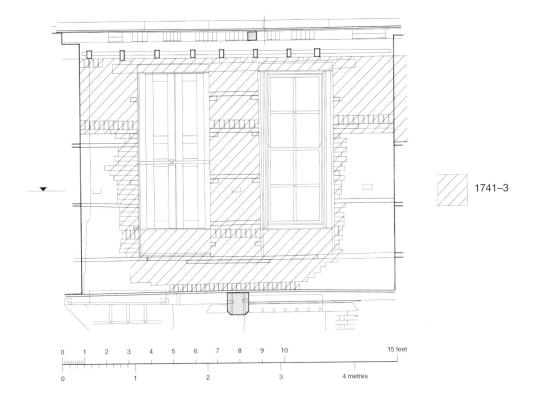

1741–3

0 1 2 3 4 5 6 7 8 9 10   15 feet

0   1   2   3   4 metres

hand, and there is evidence for some repair internally and much externally, where a new projecting sill has been attached and the upper moulding of the transom refaced. The vertical iron glazing bars appear to be original, but the leaded lights are replacements, mostly following blast damage during World War II. From the evidence of this window and the structural remnants of other original openings, it is possible to reconstruct the original pattern of fenestration with a reasonable degree of conviction.

Most of the windows on the ground floor were single units set at a high level, much wider than they were long and with mullions but no transom. The only certain exceptions were on the inner façades of the rear courtyard, where the extant window on the west side lit the inner parlour (G5), and a similar (though perhaps ten-light) example on the opposite side of the courtyard lit the kitchen (G2). The use of windows at such a high level on the outer façades seems to have been the result of a conscious decision to sacrifice light, and an outward view, for privacy and security. Such high-level openings were apparently also used at Sir Ralph Sadleir's great house at Standon, built c 1545–6, only ten years after Sutton House (see Fig 3.4). Even though alterations may have been made and perhaps more windows inserted at Standon by the time Drapentier

engraved it c 1700, it is clear that many of the openings in the ground-floor façades were set well above eye level. In fact, the general disposition of the windows shown in this illustration may well provide a pointer to the arrangement at Sutton House.

It is possible that there was one other large ground-floor window opening: a tripartite window with the central lights extending down to a lower level, on the north front of the west wing, lighting the high (linenfold) parlour (G4). The arrangement of the panelling in this room supports such a configuration, but the almost complete reconstruction of this wall to accommodate new windows c 1740 removed most of the structural evidence. What remains (Fig 3.13) shows that there were high-level windows, possibly continuous, extending to the edges of the room. When the existing window openings were made in the 18th century, the whole of the central section of the wall was removed and rebuilt with reused 16th-century bricks, so that all trace of the original form of the window in this area has been lost.

The continuous lintel beam carrying the first-floor wall above the openings, now supported by a series of small timber props embedded in the rearranged brickwork, is very slender and would probably originally have needed some additional support midway along its length (as is now provided by the brick pier between the 18th-century openings). This support could have been supplied by additional framing or even brick piers built around a long central light, but it is just as likely that the original opening was a pair of four-light windows set high in this wall with a brick pier between them (*see* Fig 3.8). The use of such relatively small windows, despite the high status of the room, may explain why it was considered necessary to insert a new high-level opening in its east wall shortly after the house was completed (*see* Fig 4.8).

Structural evidence for the window openings at first-floor level survives in the east and west wings. They were of double height with a central transom, and probably very similar to the surviving window in the courtyard at ground-floor level (*see* Fig 3.11). An original window opening at this floor level on the west elevation, which had been blocked up (*see* Fig 3.9), was reopened during the restoration of 1994–5.

The complete rebuilding of the central part of the north front removed most of the evidence for the original first-floor fenestration there (*see* Fig 3.38), but splayed brick jambs surviving internally in both the east and west walls of the great chamber (F3) indicate that it had double-height windows extending to the extremities of the room. These probably comprised three double-height, ten-light windows across the north front, with one double-height, probably eight-light window overlooking the court-yard at the corner. The size and structural function of these windows probably dictated the wholesale rebuilding of the north wall when sash windows were introduced.

Only two window openings survive from the original build on the second floor, though constructional joints indicate the possibility of a third towards the rear of the east elevation. This last would appear to have been a dormer from the height of its sill. There were undoubtedly others of which nothing now remains, and the evidence suggests that the windows on this floor were of the same type as those on the ground floor.

It appears from the rebates that the windows were originally designed to receive glass, as would be expected in a house of this status at the date of its construction; indeed, a fragment of early glass was found near the blocked window (now reopened) in the bedchamber (F4). The remains of early paint applications found on a window sill, reused as a joist in the cellars, suggest that a maroon colour was applied initially to the frames, perhaps to match the colour of the brickwork, and that this was later repainted cream, possibly to imitate stone.

Entrance

The Tudor entrance to the house was in the eastern half of the central section of the north front. This area was comprehensively reconstructed between 1741 and 1743 and the door here dates from the remodelling. The original form of the doorcase is not known but the original door may survive, albeit repositioned in the new entrance to the west created when the house was divided into two in the 18th century. This door (Fig 3.14; *see also* Fig 3.12) consists of five oak planks about 25mm thick, loosely held together by strap hinges bolted on to its back at the top and bottom; it appears to be of the 16th century but has undergone substantial repair. Some at least of the applied mouldings to the external face may be original and there is evidence on the back for at least three surface-mounted locks, but the present door furniture dates to the 19th century. Traces of maroon and cream paint on the edges, under the applied mouldings, match similar paint fragments found on a window sill (*see* p 41) and on a carved oak barge board (*see* p 32).

Figure 3.14
Early 16th-century front door prior to repair. The door appears to have been removed from its original position on the east side of the house to its current position in the west entrance when the house was divided in the 18th century.

Figure 3.15
*View of the present roof
arrangement of the north
elevation. Evidence would
suggest that originally this
façade was topped by a
series of gables, hipped back
and replaced by a parapet
between 1741 and 1743.
[Mike Gray]*

Cellars

The discovery of what appears to be part of a retaining wall for the steps to the east cellar indicates that the cellars of the house were at first entered from the outside via short stairways down from the front garden or courtyard (*see* Fig 3.8). These were probably blocked up during the large-scale alterations of the first half of the 18th century. The cellars were lit by small windows, the opening to that of the west cellar having survived, with the sockets to receive iron bars still visible in the soffit of its extant lintel.

Roofline

Except for the north front, Sutton House's roofline has changed little since the 16th century. Originally the main north façade was topped by a series of gables, but these were hipped back and replaced by a parapet

*Figure 3.16
South elevation during
restoration. Exposed
timber-framing of original
16th-century gable
overlooking the courtyard.*

(Fig 3.15) during the remodelling of 1741–3 and all evidence for reconstructing their former appearance has been lost. It is not known whether the gables were of brick or timber-framing, or a mixture of both, as at Compton Wynyates, Warwickshire. Perhaps there were brick gables over the projecting wings and timber-framed gables over the central range; the surviving rear gables of the latter were certainly both timber-framed (Fig 3.16). These gables were rendered over at some time, but the weathering of the surfaces of the timbers beneath the render suggests that they were once exposed. The gable enclosing the chimney stack at the rear of the east wing was of necessity built of brick, but the rear wall of the west wing with its gable may have been entirely timber-framed. It was demolished in the 18th century, although the insubstantial brick footings uncovered in the excavations in the 1990s suggest that the whole wall may have been timber-framed, not brick, odd as that may have looked.

Lengths of carved bargeboards, presumably taken from the demolished gables, were reused as hip rafters in the alterations to the central range. They were removed during restoration work in the 1960s and two of the best examples were put on display in the house but were subsequently stolen (Fig 3.17). One other, which was discovered during the restoration work, is currently exhibited in the house (Fig 3.18).

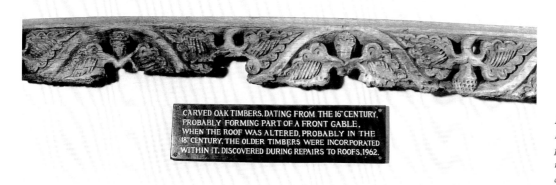

Figure 3.17 (left)
16th-century bargeboards
were reused as hip rafters in
the roof over the hall range
in the 18th century. They
were placed on display in
the house following repairs
carried out in 1961–2.
[John Bethell/The National
Trust]

Figure 3.18 (below)
Display in the west cellar,
principally of building
materials and finds made
during investigations of the
house. [B000347]

The plan

Sutton House was built on an H-plan with a relatively short east–west range flanked by longer north–south ranges which projected at the back to form a courtyard (Fig 3.19). The plan is somewhat irregular, with the rear parts of both wings being skewed to the east. One suggestion that has been made is that the building consists of the remains of a medieval courtyard house on to which a new front was grafted, with an alignment more closely following that of Homerton High Street.[40] This interpretation is supported by the documentary evidence (*see* p 18), but during the very detailed survey carried out between 1988 and 1990, no direct evidence was found of any fabric pre-dating the early Tudor period. The house appeared to be of one build, and where it was necessary to accommodate the angular plan in the construction of the walls, specially moulded bricks were used.

It seems likely that the irregularity was a result of the constricted nature of the site. Although Ralph Sadleir subsequently owned land to the east of Sutton House, a later document suggests that this may not have been contiguous.[41] To the west of Sutton House, Sadleir only acquired the neighbouring property, the Tanhouse (*see* Fig 2.8), some two years after the completion of Sutton House. The archaeological investigations uncovered the footings of a substantial wall running north–south, a short distance to the west of and parallel to the skewed southern half of the west wing (Fig 3.20). This wall and the building to which it was presumably attached may have been part of the Tanhouse complex and so not in Sadleir's ownership at the time Sutton House was built. The presence of the wall

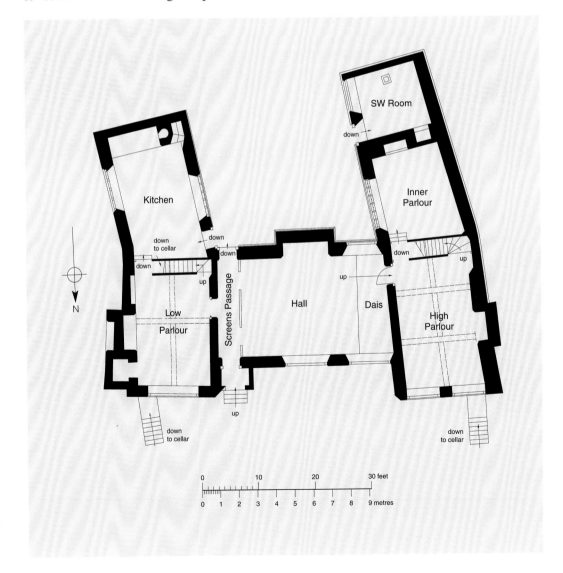

Figure 3.19
Reconstructed plan of the ground floor c *1535.*
(Scale 1:200)

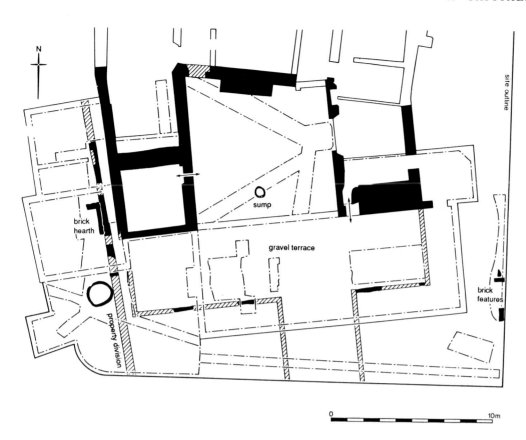

N

brick
hearth

sump

gravel terrace

property division

site outline

brick
features

0   10m

Figure 3.20
Plan of the southern (rear)
half of the site showing the
location of features revealed
by archaeological
excavation in 1990. (Note
the different orientation of
this plan.) The hatched
lines show the assumed
layout of former walls. The
north–south wall, a short
distance from the side of the
west wing, may predate the
building of Sutton House
and account for the
irregularities of its plan.
[Museum of London
Archaeology Service]

probably determined the angularity of
the plan of Sutton House, as there was
just enough space between it and the west
wing to enable scaffolding to be erected.
Today the site is part of Sutton House and
is occupied by the west wing additions, but
the boundaries here, which have always
been somewhat complex, may have been
rationalised after Sadleir purchased the
Tanhouse in 1537.

The internal arrangement of Sutton
House was strongly influenced by the fact
that it had three full storeys throughout,
unlike a medieval house, which would have
had an open hall rising to the roof flanked
by storeyed wings. The development of fully
storeyed houses has been traced in timber-
framed buildings to the end of the 15th
century, but the form was only adopted for
greater houses in the early Tudor period.
The architectural context of Sutton House
is discussed in the concluding section of this
chapter, but it is worth noting here that
the house, now known to have been built
c 1535, was an important and unusual early
example of this type.

Because Sutton House was fully
storeyed, it provided a greater variety of
flexible accommodation and a wider grad-
ation of rooms than might have been

expected in a house of relatively modest size.
The hall (G3) was still a dominant feature of
the house, as reflected in the survey by
Sadleir's steward in 1540 in which the hall
was the only room specifically mentioned,
with spaces left (but not filled in) for its
dimensions. However, the form of construction of the house meant that rather than
being open to the roof, as would have been
the case a few years earlier, the hall had a
ceiling. Above the hall was a room of equal
dimensions and possibly equal importance,
which could serve as a great chamber (F3).
The importance of the first-floor rooms was
emphasised visually on the exterior by the
size of their windows and by the apparent
concentration of diaper patterning in the
brickwork (*see* pp 28–9).

The front of the west wing is wider than
that of the east wing (excluding the projecting chimney stack). The difference, most
noticeable on the exterior, is less than
a metre, but it is sufficient to give rise to
the possibility, reinforced by the surviving
structural evidence, that there were two
horizontal windows on the ground floor at
the front of the west wing and only one in
the east wing (*see* Fig 3.6). This additional
width is likely to be a reflection of the higher
status of the west wing.

Figure 3.21
Exploded perspective
drawing showing the
plan layout and room
functions within the early
16th-century house.
There is still some doubt as
to the original status and
function of G1 and the
rooms on the second floor.
G1 (low parlour) may
have had a part-reception/
part-service function that
made it of somewhat lesser
status than G4 (high
parlour) and the second
floor may have been used
mainly as living quarters
for the household servants.
[Richard Bond]

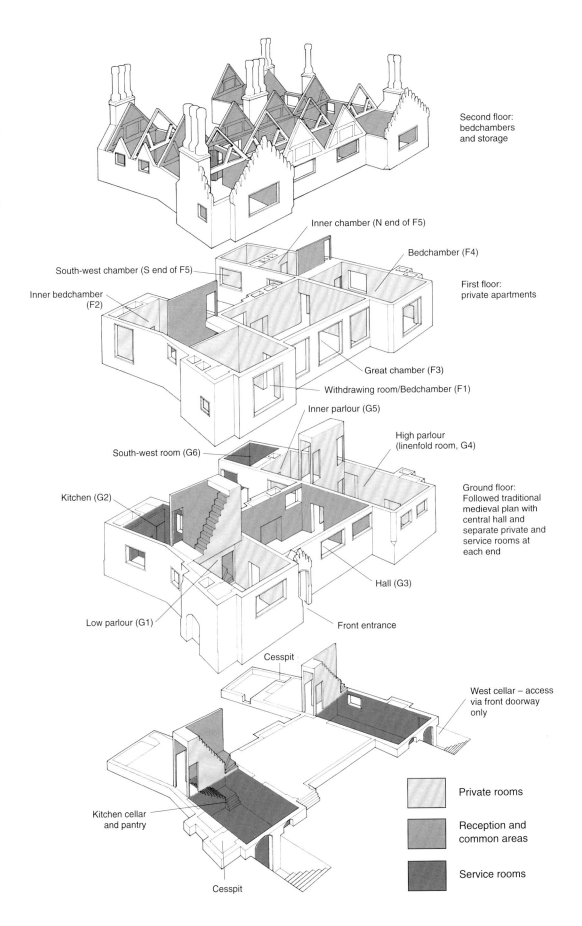

Second floor:
bedchambers
and storage

Inner chamber (N end of F5)

Bedchamber (F4)

South-west chamber (S end of F5)

First floor:
private apartments

Inner bedchamber
(F2)

Great chamber (F3)

Withdrawing room/Bedchamber (F1)

Inner parlour (G5)

High parlour
(linenfold room, G4)

South-west room (G6)

Kitchen (G2)

Ground floor:
Followed traditional
medieval plan with
central hall and
separate private and
service rooms at
each end

Hall (G3)

Low parlour (G1)

Front entrance

Cesspit

West cellar – access
via front doorway
only

Kitchen cellar
and pantry

Cesspit

Private rooms

Reception and
common areas

Service rooms

That the house had 'upper' (private) and 'lower' (service) ends, on the west and east respectively, is abundantly clear but the division in social functions that this encompassed was quite complex. An exploded perspective drawing (Fig 3.21) provides a conjectural reconstruction of how the house functioned when it was first built. The entrance was situated at the lower end of the hall, close to the service accommodation. At ground-floor level in the east wing (*see* Fig 3.19), there was a kitchen (G2) to the south and what appears to have been a parlour (G1) to the north, in the position traditionally occupied by the buttery and pantry, which at Sutton House appear to have been in the cellar. A screens passage in line with the entrance separated the latter room from the hall and, between the kitchen and parlour, a staircase provided access to the east cellar and the upper floors.

On the west side of the house, there is evidence of a raised dais at the western end of the hall (G3), lit by a window in the south wall as well as one on the north front. The dais communicated directly with a parlour (G4) at the front of the west wing, which,

from the quality of its decoration, was always a room of high status. A narrow, single-flight staircase led from this room to the first floor only, while to its south was another important room (G5) which may have been used as a summer parlour, as at that time of the year it would have been flooded with light from the large window overlooking the courtyard. Both the status and function of the remaining room (G6) on the ground floor, at the rear of the west wing, are unclear, but it was almost certainly only accessible from the courtyard.

The first floor (Fig 3.22) was dominated by the great chamber (F3), measuring some 9×5.5m, above the hall in the central range. The remaining rooms in the east and west wings were family and guest chambers, but here the division between the upper and lower ends of the house becomes less clear. The front chamber of the east wing (F1) was certainly a room of distinction and had the benefit of a garderobe.

In the west wing the plan form reflected the arrangement of the rooms on the ground floor, although in this case the southernmost room appears to have been only accessible

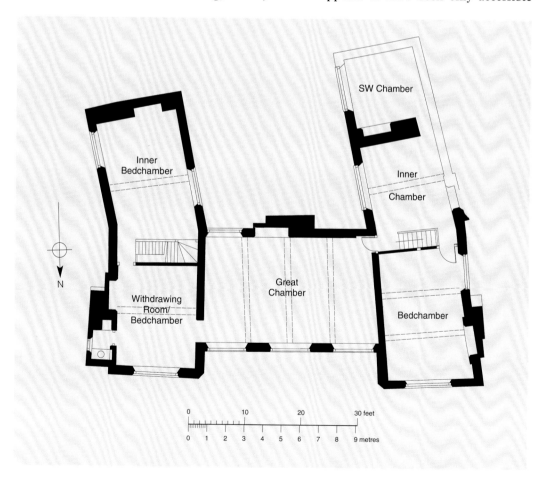

Figure 3.22
Plan of the first floor
c 1535. Much of the
evidence for the south end
of the west wing has been
lost through structural
failure and later alterations.
(Scale 1:200)

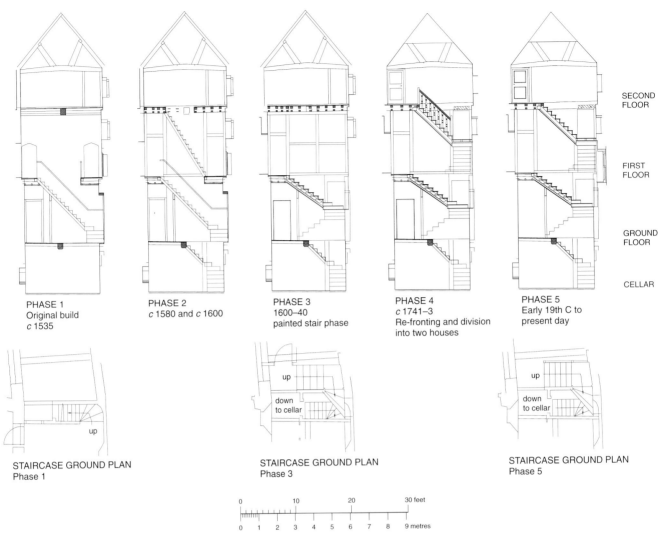

PHASE 1
Original build
c 1535

PHASE 2
c 1580 and c 1600

PHASE 3
1600–40
painted stair phase

PHASE 4
c 1741–3
Re-fronting and division
into two houses

PHASE 5
Early 19th C to
present day

SECOND
FLOOR

FIRST
FLOOR

GROUND
FLOOR

CELLAR

STAIRCASE GROUND PLAN
Phase 1

STAIRCASE GROUND PLAN
Phase 3

STAIRCASE GROUND PLAN
Phase 5

Figure 3.23
Phased reconstruction drawings showing the evolution of the west staircase. The new work carried out in each phase is shown in red. (Scale 1:200)

Phase 1 c 1535: Original build. The second floor was open to the roof with the staircase lit by an existing window on the west wall. No access was provided to the second floor. It is unlikely that internal access was provided to the west cellar in Phase 1, although it had been by Phase 2. External access could be gained to both cellars by doors in the north wall (see Fig 3.6).

Phase 2 c 1580: The original screen/partition on the south side of the staircase was demolished and the staircase area became part of the room arrangement within the inner chamber (F5). This alteration also involved the rebuilding of the floor and ceiling construction above the staircase, in order to maintain the appearance of a flush ceiling. c 1600: A new access was provided to the second floor by the installation of a ladder-type staircase. The construction of this staircase may have involved the building of a new enclosing partition to the south. The position of this new partition may have rendered the fireplace on the west wall of room F5 redundant. Internal access to the cellar was provided by this phase.

Phase 3 1600–40: The steep and uncomfortable ladder staircase to the second floor was removed and the floor closed to provide a ceiling above the new staircase. A new grand staircase was installed from ground to first floor, with access reoriented from the north to the south side to accommodate a greater stair width. Elaborate and rich strapwork decoration was applied across the new plasterwork and framing of the new assembly. Original doorcases from elsewhere in the house were resited into the north and south partitions at first-floor level.

Phase 4 c 1741–3: To accommodate a new staircase from the first-floor southern chamber, the second floor was reopened and cut back. This involved the breaking through of the 17th-century partition wall to accommodate the lower flight of the new stair, which partly covered the previously blocked 16th-century fireplace. A ceiling was installed to the second floor with a new door access provided to the second-floor south room. The new staircase was reduced in width to allow the passage of light to the existing stair from ground to first floor, following the replacement of the second-floor window. The majority of the earlier strapwork decoration was left exposed.

Phase 5 Early 19th century to present day: There were minor changes and repairs to the previous phases including the removal of the 17th-century partitioning around the staircase. On the ground floor the lower flight was renewed, incorporating a further tread and balustrade. The light-well was sealed after the removal of the balustrade and repair of the treads etc was undertaken to the staircase to the second floor. A window was installed to offer light to the staircase from ground to first floor.

38

from the room immediately to its north (F5) and must have served as an additional withdrawing chamber. The staircase in the west wing originally extended only from the ground to the first floor, while the west cellar could only be entered from outside the house, thus enhancing the private nature of the rooms on the ground and first floor of this wing. It is possible that when important guests stayed in the house, the rooms in the west wing were given over to them while the family used those in the east wing. Despite this, the original west staircase was not particularly grand, or even distinguishable from that in the east wing; however, this may be due to the fact that the concept of a great staircase was a later architectural development, as it was in Sutton House itself (Fig 3.23).

The second floor was originally only approachable via the staircase in the east wing. There is some indication that on this floor only the rooms in the east wing were originally heated and that these may have been used as bedchambers. The rest of the floor was probably used as storage or lesser accommodation, a conjecture supported by the relative inaccessibility of many of the rooms on this floor.

The interior

This account of the interior of the house as it would have appeared when built, based on the evidence of surviving fabric, proceeds from the cellars to the upper floors and in general from east to west. The rooms are named and, except in the cellars, are also given the numbers that appear on Figures 3.27, 3.57 and 3.84. A full analysis of the structure of the house was possible only in those rooms in which features such as decorative panelling or ceilings were missing or had been removed, and this is reflected in the relative comprehensiveness of such accounts in the descriptions of the rooms which follow. The accounts of alterations in subsequent chapters will deal only with changes made in the period under discussion.

The cellars

West cellar
The west cellar (Fig 3.24), considerably less altered than that to the east, was primarily designed for storage, and could only be accessed via the external door at the front. The floor, almost certainly of brick, was originally some 240mm higher than at

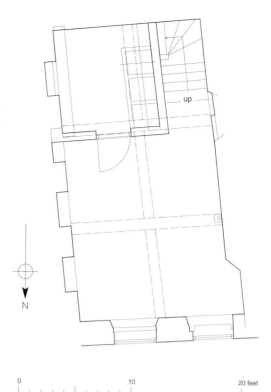

present, leaving head room of 1.8m. Part of this floor may survive, or have been relaid, in the brick enclosure in the south-east corner created in the 18th century. Here the bricks are of the type, colour and texture of the Tudor bricks used elsewhere in the house, but are harder and were probably designed as paviours. They are laid with staggered joints parallel to the east wall on fine sand covering a sandy river gravel containing pebbles and tumbled flints and have been pointed with a mixture of brick dust and sand, now contaminated with coal dust.

In addition to the floor of the small enclosure, the exposed brickwork of the walls is mainly of the original build, laid in English bond with a sand and lime mortar. The west wall contains the remains of an original splayed window opening in the southern half of the room, which would have looked out on to the adjoining property. It was blocked at an early date, possibly because of a design fault in the original construction. A beam supporting the floor of the room above bears on the slender timber lintel of this opening approximately at its midpoint, and failure may have threatened or actually occurred here. No trace of the

Figure 3.25
West wing. View to north
from west cellar showing
original 16th-century floor
construction with room G4
above. Taken in 1991
following the temporary
removal of part of the floor.
[© James Morris/Axiom.
London]

opening remains at ground-floor level. Further along the west wall, at its junction with the north wall, there is a splayed recess. This undercuts the brickwork of the high (linenfold) parlour (G4) above, which has been built up on floorboards spanning the recess. The recess accommodated the inward-opening external door to the cellar so that it could be swung back fully to facilitate the passage of stores and provisions.

This cellar doorway was blocked and partially converted into a window opening, probably between 1741 and 1743 when the major re-fronting took place, a new internal access having already been created by that date. The timber lintel for the doorway, however, is still in position in the north wall and

has always had a structural function. It is very substantial, measuring 350 × 170mm with a span of 1.42m; its lower inside edge is rebated 35mm to receive the door and on the underside at each end are double mortises, now filled with lime plaster, which took the tenons of the jambs of the door frame. The jambs, which have been replaced with brickwork, would have been of similar proportions to the lintel, the whole frame forming a structural unit. The original sill would have been some 160mm above the floor level, but even when the latter was lowered the sill remained *in situ* for a while, as there is evidence of notches in the brickwork beneath to receive the frame of a ramp or steps.

The north wall also contains an original splayed window opening. Here also the timber lintel remains and supports the brickwork above. The north–south floor beam for the high (linenfold) parlour (G4) above was cut to fit around the lintel at its west end, and is thus partially supported by the lintel and held in position by the brickwork built up around it. Much of the original fabric around this opening has been cut away or destroyed during subsequent alterations and the window replaced.

The most notable feature of the east wall is the presence of four original arched recesses (*see* Fig 3.82), one of which is now concealed in the bins of the later small enclosure. They are of similar dimensions (910 × 320mm) and were probably all originally of the same height from the sill to the apex of the intrados of the arch. The apex of each arch follows the same horizontal course and the arches are evenly spaced along the east wall. Only one retains an original timber sill but there is evidence for timber sills on two of the others, although the northernmost recess may have had a brick sill. (Since the restoration in the 1990s all four now have timber sills.) The gauged brick arches supporting the brickwork above are four-centred and, although smaller, are identical in construction to the relieving arches over the 16th-century fireplaces elsewhere in the house. All brickwork around these recesses has been 'closed' with no sign of alteration apart from the sills.

The function of these recesses, which are also found in the east cellar, is a matter of conjecture as they appear to serve no structural purpose; they are too small and inconvenient to act as seating but too large and elaborate for candles or other lighting. There are similar recesses in the Guildhall at

Lavenham in Suffolk, where it has been suggested that they may have been constructed to house butts of wine. Those in Sutton House may have had a similar purpose, the rear bases of the barrels resting on the sills of the recesses and the fronts supported on trestles. It may be that they were designed to take account of the degree of entertaining that might fall to the lot of a rising courtier-politician like Ralph Sadleir.

The ceiling construction of the cellar and the floor construction (Fig 3.25) of the high (linenfold) parlour (G4) comprise two transverse east–west oak beams dividing the ceiling into three equal bays, with bridging beams spanning north–south and mortised and tenoned into the east–west beams at their midpoints. The cross-sectional dimensions of the beams are approximately 300 × 350mm. No timber bearers were found at their points of entry into the walls (Fig 3.26) and the beams have been positioned directly on to the brickwork. Most of the 16th-century joists are still in position but now only provide partial support for the floor above. Those to the east, which are more complete, have scribed carpenters' marks in a sequence I–XIII from south to north; similar scribed marks occur on the remains of the original joists to the west. The majority of the 16th-century joists are reused timbers that have been reworked to suit and this is one of the few areas within the building where it can be clearly demonstrated that the reuse of timbers occurred during the original construction.

All the joists appear to have been built into the brickwork as it rose, but the need for substantial repair and additional support as a result of decay at the edges has obscured the evidence. A row of large, iron, hook nails indicates that at one time a timber plate may have been introduced as a secondary support at the eastern end of the joists, perhaps when damp penetration had begun to cause decay. At the junction of the joists and beams with the western wall there is evidence of several stages of additional support having been provided, including wall plates for the joists, substantial timber posts under the beams and, finally, steel corbel plates. Although the evidence is somewhat ambiguous, it seems likely that the cellar ceiling, of which fragments remain, was erected *c* 1700 and that the beams and joists were not ceiled originally.

One of the replacement joists which was inserted just to the north of the northern transverse beam in the north-west bay was a

reused 16th-century window sill, part of the original fenestration and presumably removed when the house was re-fronted. The surviving length of this timber sill, which was removed during the restoration in the 1990s and displayed elsewhere in the house, is approximately 1.9m and the window from which it came was at least five lights in width. There are layers of paint remaining, those on its external face suggesting that the first colour applied was maroon and that this was subsequently covered with cream paint. Internally, it appears that the sill was originally unpainted and that a creamy-white colour was later applied.

There are remnants of ironwork fittings which were built into the brickwork during the construction of the cellar. Those which

Figure 3.26
Room G4. View to south-west showing original Tudor floor construction with west cellar below.
[From the National Trust collection at Sutton House]

survive and are recognisable take the form of hooks and eyes and are mostly flattened against the walls.

East cellar

The east cellar was extensively altered when it was converted into a chapel for St John's Institute in 1914 (see Fig 8.14), but sufficient remains of its original fabric to be reasonably certain that it had a similar form and function to the west cellar. Like the latter, it was entered externally through a doorway in the north wall, but it also appears to have had an internal entrance via a staircase from the kitchen (G2).

No trace of the original floor remains, but the evidence of brick courses on the east wall suggests that it was originally higher than the present arrangement. The majority of the brickwork of the walls survives from the construction of the house and is, like that of the west cellar, well coursed and laid in English bond. The north wall apparently had the same type of window and door openings as observed in the west cellar. Evidence of an opening for the doorway and part of its frame were discovered during restoration, and construction lines indicate that it had a high brick sill similar to that of the west cellar. In this case the opening appears to have been slightly wider, eliminating the need for a recess in the east wall. The present windows date from 1914 but were inserted into the 16th-century door and window openings.

The east wall has the remains of three brick recesses with four-centred heads which are almost identical to the four in the west cellar (see Fig 6.6). The northernmost recess appears to have been little altered and to have had a brick sill, but close examination of the brickwork was not possible because of a covering of white paint. The central recess was cut away to the south when a new external access was formed to the cellar in the 18th or 19th century and the remains of the opening sealed with brick (see Fig 3.65). Little remains of the third recess, the area of walling in which it was situated having been almost completely rebuilt in 1914.

Above this recess the remains of a major, four-centred, chamfered brick arch were uncovered high on the east wall during the restoration of the building in the 1990s. The arch spanned an opening some 1.5m wide and 600mm deep, coming to within a half-brick thickness of the external plinth. During the restoration work, the arch was extended to the outside of the building, and at first sight it appears that an external opening must have originally been formed here. When the arch was exposed from the outside, however, the crude construction techniques and poor quality bricks used, together with the bonding pattern and the presence of original mortar, suggested that the arch may never have extended to the external face.

The floor level of the low parlour (G1) above corresponds with the springing line of this arch, and original brickwork continuing under the arch beyond its southern jamb suggests that it had a high sill, almost certainly at the floor level of the low parlour, where the floor construction extended into the opening. Plaster has been found within the opening, indicating that the recess was probably plastered internally. It might thus have functioned as a large, deep recess for the ground-floor room although no parallels for such a feature are known to the authors. Moreover, the present partition between the low parlour and the staircase cuts through this opening, but it is possible that the partition itself may not be in its original position. Whether this peculiar feature was a secondary feature or the result of a change of plan during the construction of the house can only be surmised, but it is yet another element of mystery in its building.

What survives of the original brickwork on the south wall is now hidden behind a stud-and-plaster partition. The majority was cut away to accommodate the present staircase access and what is left, mostly at the west end, is a brick-and-a-half thick. No remains of openings are apparent, but the layout of the cellar and the need to avoid the beam supporting the floor above means that the original staircase from the ground floor would have entered in the south-west corner (as it does presently in the west cellar).

The construction of the east cellar ceiling and the floor of the low parlour (G1) above consists of a transverse east–west oak beam located centrally, with independent bridging beams of the same section spanning north–south and mortised and tenoned and pegged into the east–west beam at its midpoint. The dimensions of the beams are identical to those of the west cellar. The north–south beam was truncated at its southern end either during the alterations of 1914 or earlier and supported by a timber column, to allow for the present arrangement of the staircase into the cellar.

A cantilevered, pre-cast concrete padstone buried in the wall now also supports the north end of this beam. Most of the joists date from the construction of the house with the exception of those above the later cellar access on the east wall, which have been renewed. It is unlikely that a plaster ceiling existed before the 18th century.

The ground floor (Fig 3.27)

Low parlour (G1)

This room, which has been heavily Georgianised, was in the position frequently occupied by a buttery in a conventional hall-house plan though here the east cellar may have served such a function, for certain features suggest a higher status from either the time of the original build or very soon afterwards. There was a steward's room next to the hall in Sadleir's later house at Standon and the Sutton House room may similarly have served as a parlour for Sadleir's steward, Gervase Cawood, who was a man of some substance himself and occupied an important position in Sadleir's household.

The room communicated directly with the hall (G3) through a doorway in its west wall to the south of its midpoint, but central to the hall itself (*see* Fig 3.42). Its position is still evident in the odd, larger panel which disturbs the symmetry of the Georgian

Figure 3.27
Ground plan of Sutton House prepared in 1989, prior to the detailed investigation of the fabric. The reason for the irregular shape of the building remains unclear.
(Scale 1:200)

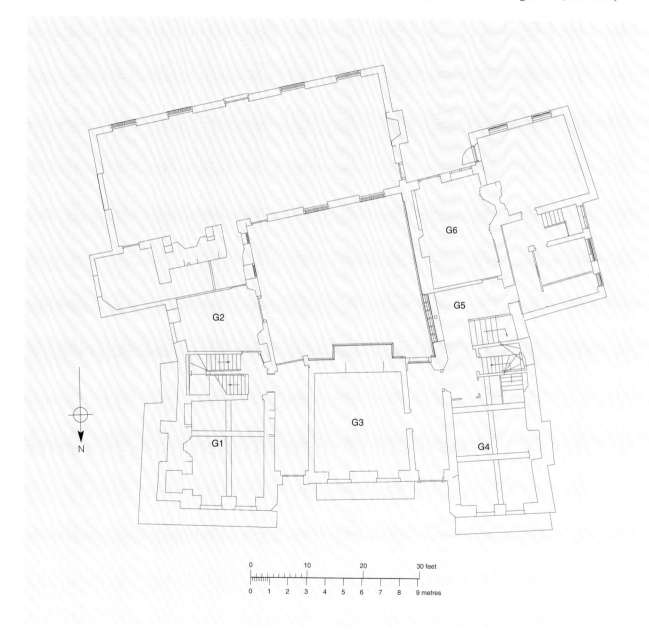

Figure 3.28
Room G1. South end of west wall with blocked 16th-century entrance to the hall and remains of a scheme of probably 16th-century wall painting, seen following temporary removal of the 18th-century panelling during restoration.

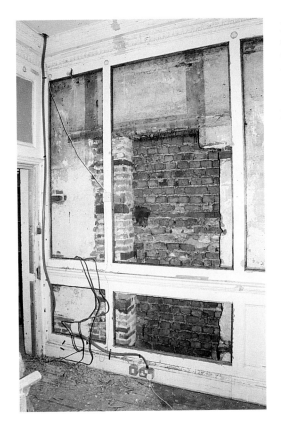

panelling now covering this wall (Fig 3.28; *see also* Fig 3.59). There were probably two openings in the south wall: one at the east end, for which evidence survives, providing access to the kitchen and the staircase to the east cellar, and another at the west end (as at present) leading to the staircase to the upper floors (Fig 3.29; *see also* Fig 3.58). The north wall, which has been substantially rebuilt and refenestrated, probably originally had a single high-level window (Figs 3.30 and 3.31), as discussed in the description of the exterior of the house (*see* p 30). The floor and ceiling levels have not been changed, but the ceiling plaster and most of the floor-boards date from the 18th century.

An interesting feature of the room is the 16th-century stone fireplace formerly hidden behind the 18th-century panelling on the east wall (Fig 3.32; *see also* Fig 7.11). Its carving, consisting of grape vines in the spandrels and decorative shields in the corners, is more elaborate and of a higher quality than that on the remaining fireplaces in the house; other, similarly elaborate fireplaces may have been lost. The siting of such a decorative fireplace in the 'lower' end

Figure 3.29
Room G1. Cross-section as existing in 1991 illustrating the arrangement of the panelling and the original timber wall framing of the south wall (shown in dashed lines).
(Scale 1:50)

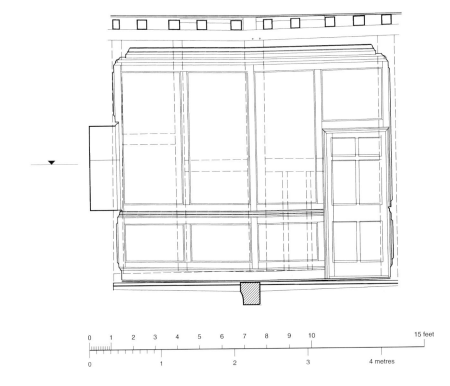

Figure 3.30
Room G1. Section of 18th-century wall panelling removed to reveal brick jamb of original 16th-century window opening.

of the house is unusual, but there is no evidence that it was installed later or moved from elsewhere in the house. A brick relieving arch supports the 16th-century brickwork above the opening, potentially allowing for the fireplace below to have been changed though any such replacement could only have been installed at the same time as, or before, a thin layer of early plaster was applied to the walls, the remnant of which above the fireplace has been little disturbed. Later alterations to the fireplace, including the reduction in the size of the opening by bricking up from the south end, have destroyed some of the detail and made it structurally weak. Ironically, however, what remains of the carving has been well preserved because at one time a crude rendering was applied over the mouldings to 'square off' the reveals. A series of graffiti incised into the stonework of this fireplace include the letters 'SS', and a small figure who might have been intended to be a good luck charm to ward off evil spirits with a gridiron (Fig 3.33).

The arched recess, which originally existed at a low level to the south of the fireplace, has been discussed in the description of the east cellar. As a recess in this room it would have measured 1,520 × 250 × 450mm. The floor joists appear to have been laid on its sill and the floorboards are carried into the opening. The present timber-framed south partition wall of the room would have interrupted the span of this opening, however, and, although of 16th-century date, it may not be of the original build. The partition is crudely assembled, with pegless joints and reused timbers, and later brick infilling with a different mortar type used.

Figure 3.31
Cross-section through the east wing showing the inside of the main north wall and the original garderobe arrangement. (Scale 1:100)

Figure 3.32 (above, left) Room G1. Carved decoration in spandrel of 16th-century fireplace. [Mike Gray]

Figure 3.33 (above, right) Room G1. Graffiti on 16th-century stone fireplace, including the letters 'SS' and a small figure in what appears to be Tudor dress. [Mike Gray]

If the partition had formerly been located further to the south, in line with the southern jamb of the arched recess, it would have provided support for the original east staircase and allowed adequate access to the recess. There is no direct evidence to support this hypothesis, but it fits in with what has been conjectured about the development of the east staircase and consequent alterations elsewhere.

This is the only ground-floor room in the house that appears to have had a thin layer of a lime-based plaster applied to the walls in a single coat at an early date. Evidence of the plaster survives under the extant 18th-century panelling, and what remains is in good condition, largely because it appears to have been covered over relatively soon after being applied (*see* Fig 3.28). The presence of bond timbers, coursed in to the brickwork under the extant plaster, suggests that the room was originally intended to be panelled, but the absence of any regularly spaced nails or nail holes in the bond timbers may mean that it was never panelled. Two shelves 15mm thick were fixed along the northern half of the west wall. The impressions of these shelves remain on the wall, as does part of one of the brackets supporting them and rebates for them in the brickwork of the north wall. The plaster covering was applied after the shelves had been installed.

In the north-east corner of the room is the lower stage of a garderobe or privy 'tower' on the north end of the chimney stack. It measures approximately 1,180 × 920mm and may have functioned as a privy here, as it did for the chambers on the first and second floors above, but no remains of an opening to light the chamber have been found. It is plastered internally and partially covered with a later timber lining. The floor is paved with brick and slopes down to a brick vaulted culvert leading into a cesspit, which was presumably accessible from outside the building to enable it to be cleaned out.

East staircase

The east staircase and staircase compartment have been very substantially altered several times and in their present form date from the 18th century (*see* Fig 6.6). Originally this was the only staircase that provided access to all the floors of the house, as that in the west wing only extended from the ground to the first floor.

The exploded perspective drawing (*see* Fig 3.21) illustrates the original configuration of this staircase. As first built, the southern wall of the staircase compartment rose on the brick south wall of the east cellar. Within the cellar a right-angled stair led from the south-west corner up to the ground floor. Directly above this a single-flight staircase rose eastwards up to the first floor, beginning with two or three winders with their ends accommodated in a recess in the west wall of the east wing. The position of the north partition wall of the staircase compartment (the south wall of room G1) has been discussed above. Another single-flight steep staircase then rose westwards from the first floor to the second. The stairs were lit by high-level windows in the east external wall, for which two splayed openings have been identified.

Kitchen (G2)

This room was originally the kitchen, but its form is not easily discernible as it has been greatly altered at various periods (Figs 3.34 and 3.35; *see also* Figs 6.12 and 6.15). There was a substantial range in the south wall,

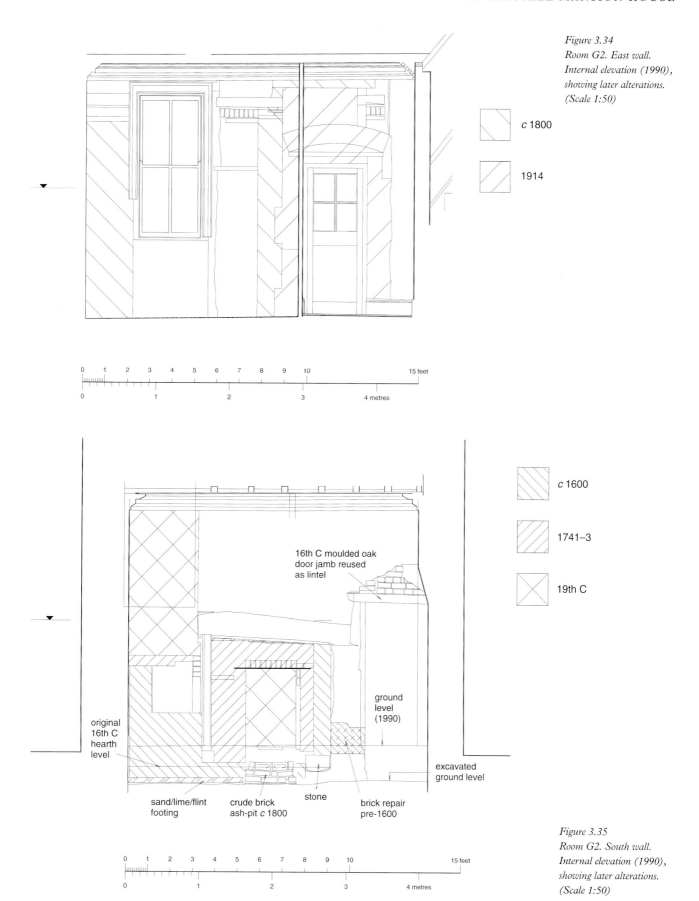

Figure 3.34
Room G2. East wall.
Internal elevation (1990),
showing later alterations.
(Scale 1:50)

c 1800

1914

16th C moulded oak
door jamb reused
as lintel

ground
level
(1990)

original
16th C
hearth
level

excavated
ground level

sand/lime/flint
footing

crude brick
ash-pit *c* 1800

stone

brick repair
pre-1600

c 1600

1741–3

19th C

Figure 3.35
Room G2. South wall.
Internal elevation (1990),
showing later alterations.
(Scale 1:50)

Figure 3.36 (above, top) Room G2. South wall during restoration, showing the remains of the large timber bressumer that formerly spanned the cooking range. [Museum of London Archaeology Service]

Figure 3.37 (above, bottom) Room G2. South wall following restoration, showing carefully reconstructed storage area to the right of the fireplace. [Mike Gray]

measuring some 2.75m across (Fig 3.36), with an additional small bread oven on its west side; its large timber bressumer survives *in situ*, although cut back at its eastern end. An obliquely splayed opening in the south-west corner of the room, restored in the 1990s (Fig 3.37), may have contained a storage larder or a way out to the gardens through a back door. Although there is no physical evidence for it, reference was made in the early 17th century to a back door through which entry was gained into the kitchen. This may have been the door in question, although there was also another door from the kitchen into the courtyard.

The floor was approximately 250mm below the existing level and appears to have been paved with clay tiles measuring approximately 300mm square. Because of the low level of the floor it would have been necessary to step up to gain access to the

east cellar and low parlour (G1) through an opening at the east end of the north partition wall. The kitchen was well lit by a high window in the east, external wall, near its south end, and a double-height window (possibly of ten lights) in the west wall overlooking the courtyard. The opening for the latter window was in the same position as the present doorway and the position of its sill is visible on the right side of the door. To the north of this window, near the corner of the room, a door led out into the courtyard. Part of the lintel of this doorway with a lath-and-plaster infilling below has been exposed.

During the restoration of the building, irregularities were discovered in the construction of the east wall of this room at its northern end which cannot be easily explained. The brickwork recedes at a low level beneath a built-in timber wallplate, and above this there is embedded timber-framing or propping. There are no obvious reasons for such features and, like the nearby low-level niche in the low parlour, they are minor elements of the construction of the house which defy explanation.

Hall (G3)

It is difficult to envisage the appearance of the early Tudor hall, divided as it now is into two corridors and a heavily Georgianised room between them. The north wall was rebuilt with new fenestration *c* 1741–3 with little of its earlier fabric remaining (Fig 3.38). The brickwork of the south wall, however, is original and contains part of the wide, four-centred, relieving arch that was constructed over the hall fireplace. During the restoration in the 1990s the panel above the fireplace was hinged for outward opening, enabling the arch to be seen. The fireplace itself, which would have been by far the largest in the house, is now lost and the opening for it severely cut down (Fig 3.39; *see also* Fig 1.2). To the west of the fireplace, there was a splayed window opening looking out into the courtyard and lighting the dais. This was at the same high level as the windows on the north front even though it faced on to the courtyard. The window opening has been extended downwards to form the doorway existing at the south end of the west corridor, but the original lintel remains. The present southern doorway of the east corridor represents a widening of an original doorway which led out into the courtyard at the south end of the screens passage. The presence of horizontal bond timbers in the brickwork

Figure 3.38
Central hall range.
Internal elevation of
the main north wall as
existing in 1990.
(Scale 1:80)

1741–3

1752

Figure 3.39
Room G3 to south-east in
1989. The metal pole
shown in the foreground
was inserted during the
restoration works carried
out by Pamela Cunnington
in the 1960s.

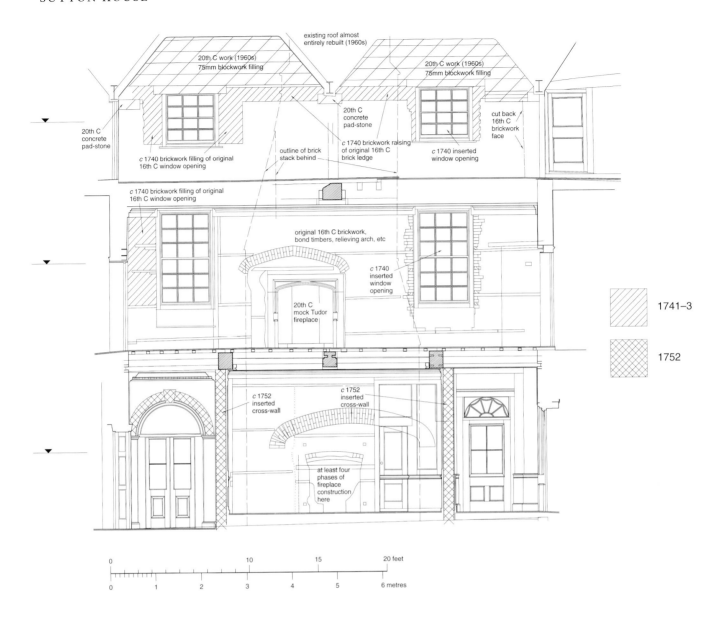

existing roof almost
entirely rebuilt (1960s)

20th C work (1960s)
75mm blockwork filling

20th C work (1960s)
75mm blockwork filling

20th C
concrete
pad-stone

20th C
concrete
pad-stone

c 1740 brickwork raising
of original 16th C
brick ledge

cut back
16th C
brickwork
face

c 1740 brickwork filling of original
16th C window opening

outline of brick
stack behind

c 1740 inserted
window opening

c 1740 brickwork filling of original
16th C window opening

original 16th C brickwork,
bond timbers, relieving arch, etc

c 1740
inserted
window
opening

20th C
mock Tudor
fireplace

c 1752
inserted
cross-wall

c 1752
inserted
cross-wall

at least four
phases of
fireplace
construction
here

1741–3

1752

0   10   15   20 feet

0   1   2   3   4   5   6 metres

Figure 3.40
Central hall range. Internal elevation of the main south wall as existing in 1990. (Scale 1:80)

suggests that the hall was intended to be panelled (Figs 3.40 and 3.41).

The extant east wall of the east corridor was the original east wall of the hall (Fig 3.42), possibly with a passage in front occupying the site of the present corridor, although no direct evidence of the screen has been found. Access to the hall from the low parlour (G1) was gained through a doorway which was centrally located in this wall. There is evidence of this opening in the low parlour and inspection behind the plaster of the east wall of the corridor prior to its restoration showed that the 16th-century brickwork of the wall was 'closed' around an opening which was of the right size to contain a moulded doorcase similar

to that surviving in the west corridor. When the doorcase was removed in the 18th century, the size of the opening was adjusted to accommodate the new panelling in the parlour, and a reused timber was inserted to support the brickwork above. Sixteenth-century tiles, which probably came from the original floor of the hall, were used as packing above this lintel.

Changes in the floor levels indicate that there was a dais at the west end of the hall. This would have been raised above the level of the hall floor by about 300mm, the approximate difference between the present floor levels of the low parlour (G1) and the high (linenfold) parlour (G4). The west wall of the west corridor is, like its counterpart in

Figure 3.41
Reconstructed elevation of
the central hall range
showing internal elevation
of main south wall as it
may have appeared when
first built c 1535.
(Scale 1:100)

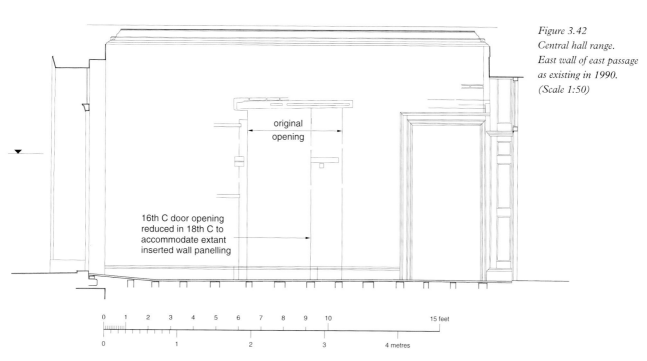

Figure 3.42
Central hall range.
East wall of east passage
as existing in 1990.
(Scale 1:50)

original
opening

16th C door opening
reduced in 18th C to
accommodate extant
inserted wall panelling

the opposite corridor, the end wall of the Tudor hall. Access from the hall to the private chambers in the west wing was through a doorway, very nearly, but not quite, in the position of the present door in the south-west corner of the west corridor (Fig 3.43). A vertical joint in the exposed brickwork of the wall, visible at the time of the survey, marked its original position. The asymmetrical head of the four-centred, moulded oak doorcase shows that it once formed a handed pair with the similar doorcase in the south wall of the high (linenfold) parlour, but it was reversed and moved marginally further south during the large-scale reconstruction that took place between 1741 and 1743.

Like the others in the house, this doorcase originally consisted of four main pieces – head, jambs and threshold – mortised, tenoned and pegged together, with the asymmetrical sunk spandrels mortised and tenoned into the head and upper jambs (see Fig 3.10). Although the frame has been altered, the original decoration and door hanging can still be determined. The earliest door, which opened on to the hall, was hung on hook hinges hammered into the frame. Traces of paint remain on the rear of the frame, and the local historian Benjamin

Clarke, writing c 1894, thought the doorcase to be of stone which had been painted over.[42] When the paint was removed shortly afterwards, channels were revealed in the surface of the timber, probably caused by wood-boring beetles tunnelling under the layers of paint. Now left exposed, these channels could almost be mistaken for a decorative enhancement of the ancient woodwork.

The hall floor, like some of the other floors at ground level, was originally covered with clay floor tiles measuring 300mm square and 30mm thick, remains of which were found below the floorboards. Where alterations were made in the 18th century, these tiles were reused as packing and filling in the walls and as coping tiles on the parapet of the raised north front (see Fig 3.15). This suggests that the present suspended timber floor was first constructed in the hall at this time. The original floor tiles were bedded on sand and brick dust and impressions of them can still be found under the floorboards of the east corridor. As indicated above, the hall floor up to the dais was on a level with that of the low parlour (G1) where the level has remained little altered. Consequently, when a timber floor was laid in the east corridor, the joists were buried in the bedding of the 16th-century floor.

Three large beams spanning north–south, originally 310 × 340mm, provide the main structural components of the hall ceiling and the floor of the great chamber (F3) above. Remains of the original ceiling survive in the present west corridor. The plaster is made up of a hard, dense, grey-coloured base, consisting of lime, sand and charcoal, with a skim finish of lime plaster; there is no visible binding material such as hair. Elsewhere the former hall ceiling has been renewed but at the same level. It was hung from separate small section joists with tenons which slotted into slip mortises cut into the sides of the main beams near their bottom edges. When the original ceiling was replaced, probably in the 18th century, substantial repairs were made to the central beam; these are described in Chapter 6.

High (linenfold) parlour (G4)

The principal function of this room was probably as a parlour and private dining chamber for the owner of the house and his family. It was always a room of high status but its present appearance, although largely of the 16th century (apart from the 18th-century fenestration), is almost certainly not

Figure 3.43
16th-century doorcase at the south end of the west entrance passage, recorded in a watercolour by F C Varley.
[AA009975; Reproduced by permission of English Heritage.NMR]

Figure 3.44
View of linenfold parlour
(G4), from a photograph
of c 1920.
[London Metropolitan
Archives]

as it would have looked when first built. In particular, there is considerable evidence that the very fine linenfold panelling which is now its dominant feature was, despite being roughly contemporary with the house, introduced from elsewhere and adapted to fit this room (Fig 3.44). It is possible that Ralph Sadleir may have been responsible for this change but it seems unlikely that he would have allowed such high quality panelling to remain when he sold the house, for it could have been readily reused at Standon. A late 16th-century inventory of Standon shows that the interior of that house was much more notable for the quality of its tapestries and other hangings than for its panelling.[43]

The presence of 50mm wide bond timbers built into the walls indicates that the room was designed to receive panelling but, as in the case of the low parlour (G1), there is some doubt whether it was decorated with panelling initially. For instance, wool fibres which were trapped beneath some iron nails in the brickwork of the west wall may be from the hem of a square-shaped wall hanging fixed centrally above the fireplace. It seems much more likely, therefore, that the

panelling in Sutton House was installed by the Machell family, some time after 1550, and so it is discussed in more detail in the next chapter.

The north wall, although substantially altered during the refenestration of 1741–3 (Fig 3.45; *see also* Fig 3.13), had one continuous or, more likely, two separate high-level windows (*see* pp 30–1), and the continuous timber lintel beam which carried the first-floor wall above the openings remains. The stone fireplace itself is original though the

Figure 3.45
Room G4. North wall and
18th-century fenestration
following temporary
removal of the linenfold
panelling during the
investigation of the fabric.

Figure 3.46 (right)
The stone fireplace in room
G4 dates from the original
construction of the house,
although the central section
of the top has been repaired.
This photograph was taken
during the restoration.

Figure 3.47 (below)
Room G4. West wall.
Cross-sectional elevation
as existing in 1990.
(Scale 1:50)

broken central section of the top has been repaired (Fig 3.46). A row of empty spaces within the brickwork of the west wall may be putlog holes for the fixing of the timber scaffolding used during construction or for the fixing of decorative panelling (Fig 3.47).

The existing partition wall at the south end of the room is a later insertion, but the timber-framed partition wall on the far side of the closet, which has been formed by the addition of this later partition, is the original south wall of the room (*see* Fig 3.78). In the south-east corner of the room there was a pair of doorways set at right angles communicating with the remainder of the west wing and the hall (G3) as described above (*see* p 52). A doorway (now blocked) at the west end of this wall opened on to a steep staircase which provided access to the first floor only. The outer ends of the winders at the bottom of this staircase were accommodated within a recess (Fig 3.48) built into the thickness of the exterior west wall using shaped bricks. A vertical timber in the middle of the recess may be part of the original door jamb.

At the time it was surveyed, the high parlour provided particularly good evidence for the construction of the house, because the panelling had been removed and the structure of the walls exposed. In addition, much of the ceiling plaster had broken away, revealing the construction of the ceiling and

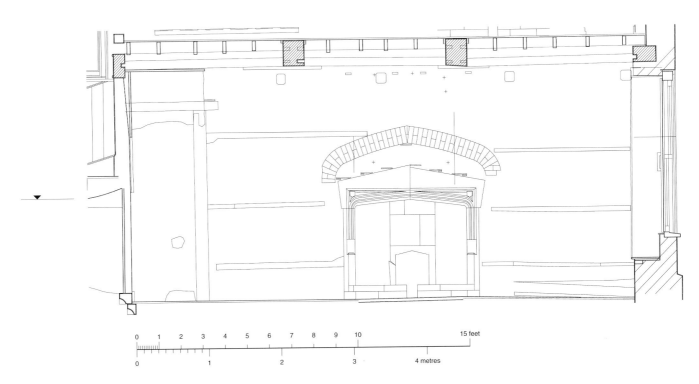

the floor of the room above. There is a double-floor arrangement with two 300 × 330mm transverse beams running east–west between the side walls of the wing, supporting three equal bays of floor and ceiling joists. The surviving floor joists measure approximately 120 × 135mm. The joist mortises on each side of the northernmost beam were numbered by the carpenters with large inscribed Roman numerals and corresponding marks were made on the ends of the joists, but the southernmost beam has no marks other than the normal setting out marks for cutting the mortises. The plaster ceiling of the room was carried on smaller 80 × 100mm joists running directly beneath the floor joists. They were jointed to the main beams by tenons which were fixed into continuous slip mortises. Similar mortises were cut into the beam set into the brickwork of the north front, which also served as a lintel to the window openings beneath, and into the girding beam of the original timber-framed partition on the south side of the room built into the brick side walls of the wing. The respective north and south ends of the floor joists in the outer bays rested on the top faces of these beams, which were correspondingly of lesser depth than the transverse floor beams.

Inner parlour (G5)

The historical integrity of this room has now been completely lost through later alterations. Both its timber-framed north wall, which probably rose off the brick end wall of the cellar beneath to enclose the south side of the narrow staircase compartment, and its south wall, a massive brick cross-stack, have been demolished (*see* Fig 3.51). The ceiling and ceiling joists have also been removed, perhaps as recently as 1904, exposing the floor construction of the room above. The extant structural east–west bridging beam would have been central to the room and helps to define its original proportions. The floor was lower, probably by as much as 300mm, and there would have been steps down into the room from the single entrance in the north-east corner. It may have been paved with floor tiles in a similar manner to the hall.

The twelve-light window in the east wall (Fig 3.49; *see also* Figs 3.11 and 3.12), discussed in the account of the exterior of the building (*see* pp 29–30), is a remarkable survival and, along with the bond timbers for panelling coursed into the brickwork, indicates that this was a high-status room. Shortly after the house was built, linenfold

Figure 3.48
Room G4. Recess in south end of the west wall, which probably housed the lower winding treads of a steep staircase giving access to the great chamber and adjoining first-floor rooms.

Figure 3.49
Original 16th-century window in the east wall of the west wing, as viewed from room G5.
[John Bethell/The National Trust]

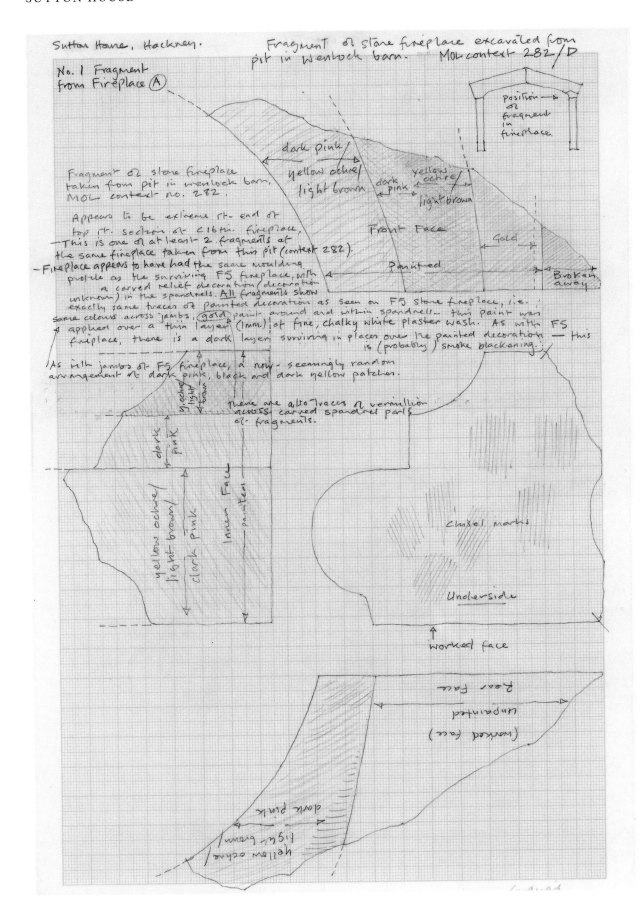

Sutton House, Hackney.   Fragment of stone fireplace excavated from pit in Wenlock barn.   MOL context 282/D

No. 1 Fragment from Fireplace Ⓐ

position of fragment in fireplace.

Fragment of stone fireplace taken from pit in wenlock barn, MOL context no. 282.

Appears to be extreme rt. end of top rt. section of C16th. fireplace. This is one of at least 2 fragments of the same fireplace taken from this pit (context 282).

Fireplace appears to have had the same moulding profile as the surviving F5 fireplace, with a carved relief decoration (decoration unknown) in the spandrels. All fragments show exactly same traces of painted decoration as seen on F5 stone fireplace, i.e. same colours across jambs, gold paint around and within spandrels — this paint was applied over a thin layer (1mm.) of fine, chalky white plaster wash. As with F5 fireplace, there is a dark layer surviving in places over the painted decoration — this is (probably) smoke blackening.

As with jambs of F5 fireplace, a now-seemingly random arrangement of dark pink, black and dark yellow patches.

There are also traces of vermillion across carved spandrel parts of fragments.

dark pink
yellow ochre
light brown
dark pink
yellow ochre
light brown

Front Face

Gold

Painted

Broken away

y. ochre / light brown
dark / pink

yellow ochre / light brown / dark pink
Inner Face painted

Chisel marks

Underside

worked face

Rear Face

unpainted

(worked face)

dark pink
light brown
yellow ochre

Figure 3.50 (facing page)
Survey note of fragments of
painted masonry, probably
from a fireplace, discovered
inside the Wenlock Barn
during the MoLAS
excavation of 1990.

Figure 3.51 (left)
Brick foundations of former
cross chimney stack in room
G6, as revealed during the
MoLAS excavation. To the
left of the former hearth can
be seen the square cesspit
forming the base of a
garderobe closet, which
opened into the south room
of the west wing.
[Museum of London
Archaeology Service]

panelling was apparently installed here, as in the high (linenfold) parlour (G4) to the north (*see* Chapter 4). The inner parlour would have been heated by a fireplace located centrally in the brick cross-stack which formed its south wall. The archaeological investigations in the 1990s revealed not only what appear to be the foundations for its hearth, but also the broken pieces of an elaborate painted fireplace (Fig 3.50), possibly from this room, reused in the foundations of the 18th-century buildings which occupied the site of the present Wenlock Barn.

South-west room (G6)

This room has also been very substantially reconstructed, largely because of a structural failure in this part of the house. Although there is sufficient evidence to indicate the original form of the room, its function is less clear, especially as it appears to have been isolated from the rest of the west wing and accessible only from the courtyard. It was separated from the inner parlour (G5) to its north by a wall formed by the now-demolished cross-stack (Fig 3.51), referred to above, but there is no evidence of any opening in this wall communicating with the room to the north, nor of any fireplace on the south side of the stack which would have heated the south-west room. Thus,

the door to the courtyard in the east wall, long blocked up but reopened during the restoration, provided the only access to the room. There is also vestigial evidence of a high-level window opening towards the south end of the east wall but the extent of repair in the wall makes its Tudor appearance difficult to determine.

A deep, brick-built chamber (Fig 3.52) in the western half of the cross-stack, measuring 820 × 550mm and extending 985mm below the original floor level, was discovered

Figure 3.52 (above)
Room G6. 16th-century
cesspit at the western end of
the cross chimney stack.
The pit is now visible
beneath a trap door which
has been created in the
present floor.

during the excavations. Remains found within it suggest that it was used as a cess and rubbish pit and probably housed a privy or garderobe built into the stack. During the restoration a trap door was made in the new floor construction to allow access to the pit.

The south wall of this room, like the north wall, has been entirely demolished, although in this case it was rebuilt in the 1740s out of reused 16th-century bricks (Fig 3.53). Excavations revealed that this wall had the type of narrow footings more usually associated with a timber-framed wall than a brick one, and that these footings had had to be substantially renewed when the wall was rebuilt. However, if a brick wall was originally constructed on these footings, it might account for the major structural collapse which seems to have occurred when, or shortly after, the substantial brick cross-stack was demolished.

The earliest floor construction, approximately 485mm below the extant skirting level, appears to have consisted of layers of mortar compacted on to a base of disturbed earth; later layers may represent the renewal of what would have been an unstable floor finish (Fig 3.54). Near the south end of the room a small square pit measuring 250mm square and 360mm deep, pierced the surface of the floor (Fig 3.55). When excavated it was found to be filled mainly with ash; decayed wood and charcoal were discovered in the ground around it. Glass remains (Fig 3.56) from the cesspit of the cross-stack (*see* Fig 3.52) have been linked with a distilling process and the weight of evidence suggests that this room, accessible only from the outside, may possibly have served as a brewhouse or still room for the making of beer, medicines and spirits for the use of the household.

Figure 3.53
West wing. Internal elevation as existing in 1990, showing the arrangement of the main south wall.
(Scale 1:80)

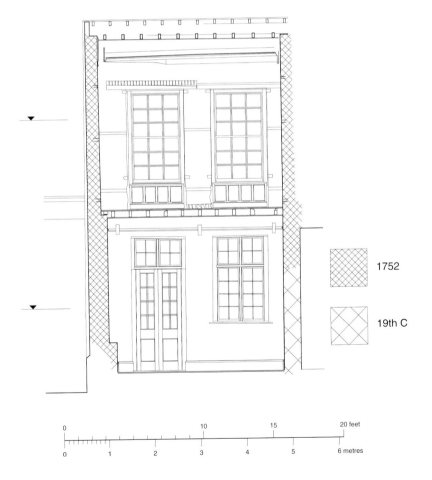

1752

19th C

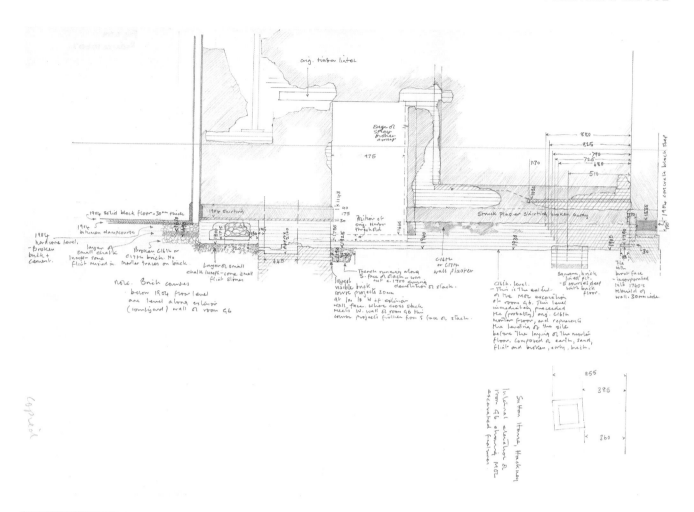

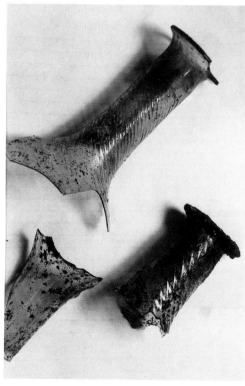

*Figure 3.54 (above)
Room G6. East wall.
Survey note showing the
relationship of the aboveground brickwork to the
below-ground archaeology.*

*Figure 3.55 (far left)
Room G6. Brick-lined pit
at the southern end of the
room, uncovered during the
MoLAS excavations.
The precise function of the
pit remains unknown.*

*Figure 3.56 (near left)
Tudor glassware found in
the base of the 16th-century
cesspit at the western end of
the cross chimney stack in
the rear of the west wing.
[Mike Gray]*

The first floor (Fig 3.57)

Withdrawing room or bedchamber (F1)

This room, which now has a largely Victorian character, is likely to have been one of the principal bedchambers of the house. It was entered directly from the great chamber through a doorway in the west wall, and a doorway in the south-east corner would have given access to the inner bedchamber (F2) via a landing on the east staircase (Figs 3.58 and 3.59). The room was heated by a large fireplace in the southern half of the east wall, for which the brick relieving arch survives (Fig 3.60), and lit by a double-height mullioned-and-transomed window in the north wall. The presence of bond timbers in the original brickwork indicates that the room was intended to be panelled.

Although the room now bears little resemblance to its original appearance, the 16th-century floor construction has survived in a remarkably complete condition. In a double-floor arrangement, a 355 × 400mm beam spans the room from east to west, and supports a north–south run of floor and ceiling joists on either side. The north side of the floor beam is marked with a series of Roman numerals, similar to the carpenters' marks found elsewhere in the house, which

Figure 3.57
Plan of the first floor as existing in 1990.
(Scale 1:200)

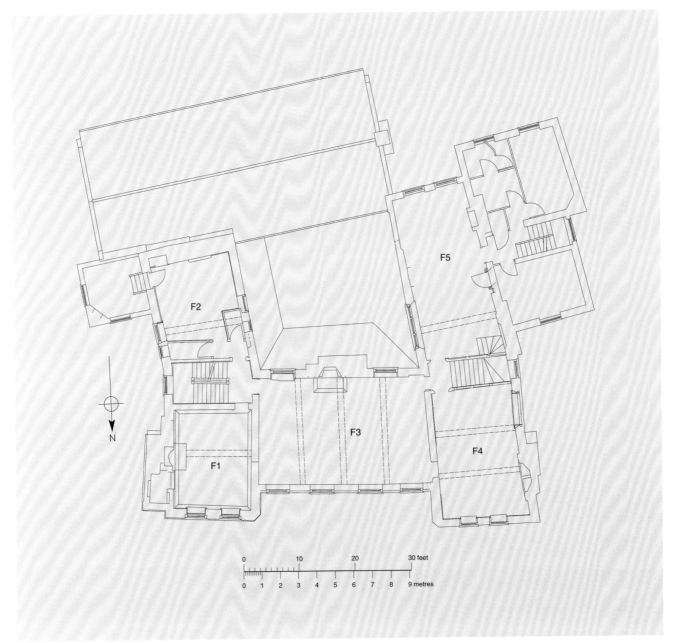

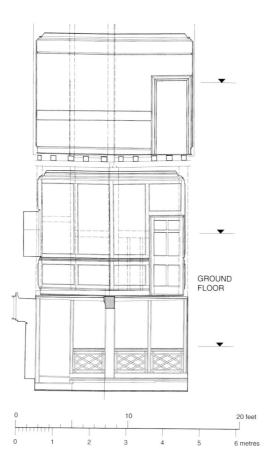

Figure 3.58
East wing. North elevation
of north staircase partition
wall as existing in 1990.
(Scale 1:100)

GROUND
FLOOR

correspond with numbers on the northern run of floor joists. There is no equivalent numbering on the south side of the beam or the southern joists.

The form of the garderobe closet in the north-east corner of the room, corresponding with that of the room below, is clearly visible on this floor (Figs 3.61 and 3.62). It was rectangular in plan, measuring 1.543m north–south and 1m east–west, and was lit by a window opening situated centrally in the east wall. It was originally ceiled by the floorboards and joists of the closet above on the second floor and a plaster wash was applied to the full height of the walls up to these floorboards. This wash appears to have been renewed several times prior to the insertion of the present ceiling, probably in the 18th century. A tall and deep arched recess with a raised, plastered floor in the south (chimney stack) wall to the right of the entrance into the closet may

have originally housed washing facilities (Figs 3.63 and 3.64), as a lead pipe of unknown date passed from the lower part of the recess through the brickwork of the chimney stack into the interior of the chimney; it is likely that the pipe originally returned to the east and passed through the exterior wall of the stack. Another square-headed and shallower recess in the common wall with the withdrawing room, to the left of the closet entrance, probably housed one end of the privy seat, which would have spanned the closet from east to west on its north side. The floor of the closet is now higher, the present joists having been nailed over the 16th-century ones.

Inner bedchamber (F2)

This room may have functioned as an inner chamber of the withdrawing room or bedchamber (F1), with which it originally communicated across the landing of the east

Figure 3.59
East wing. Internal elevation of the west wall as existing in 1990. The drawing shows the outline of the first-floor doorway between room F1 and the great chamber (F3), which at this time remained blocked.
(Scale 1:100)

Figure 3.60
Room F1. Internal elevation of east wall as existing in 1990 showing the brick relieving arch of the Tudor fireplace. To the left of the fireplace is a blocked door opening to the 16th-century garderobe closet which served the room.
(Scale 1:80)

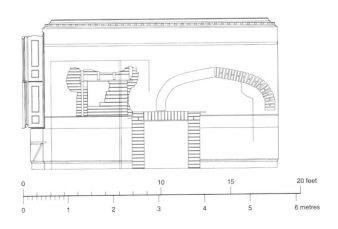

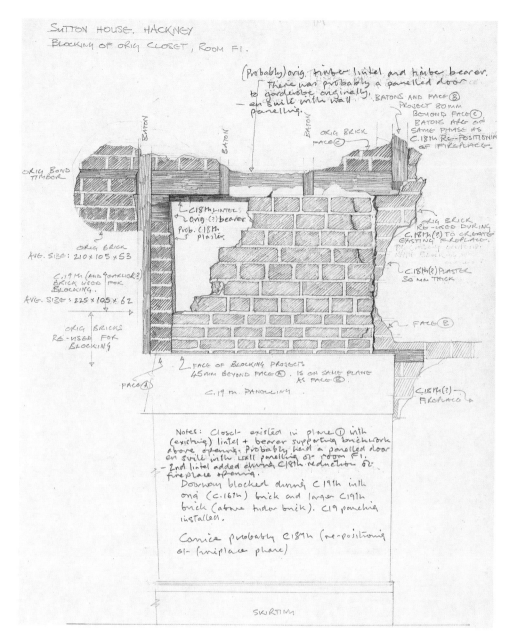

SUTTON HOUSE. HACKNEY
BLOCKING OF ORIG CLOSET, ROOM F1.

(Probably) orig. timber lintel and timber bearer.
There was probably a panelled door
to garderobe originally,
en suite with wall
panelling.

BATONS AND FACE ⓒ
PROJECT 80 MM
BEYOND FACE ⓒ
BATONS ARE OF
SAME PHASE AS
C.18TH RE-POSITIONING
OF FIREPLACE.

BATON

BATON

BATON

ORIG BRICK
FACE ⓒ

ORIG BOND
TIMBER

C18TH LINTEL
ORIG (?) bearer
PROB C18TH
plaster

ORIG BRICK
RE-USED DURING
C.18TH (?) TO CREATE
EXISTING FIREPLACE.

ORIG BRICK
AVG. SIZE: 210 × 105 × 53

C.18TH (?) PLASTER
30 MM THICK

C.19TH (AND EARLIER?)
BRICK USED FOR
BLOCKING.
AVG. SIZE: 225 × 105 × 62

FACE Ⓑ

ORIG BRICKS
RE-USED FOR
BLOCKING

FACE ⒶⒷ FACE OF BLOCKING PROJECTS
45 MM BEYOND FACE Ⓐ. IS ON SAME PLANE
AS FACE Ⓑ.

FACE Ⓐ

C.18TH (?)
FIREPLACE

C.19 M. PANELLING.

Notes: Closet existed in plane ① with
(existing) lintel + bearer supporting brickwork
above opening. Probably had a panelled door
en suite with wall panelling of room F1.
2nd lintel added during C18th reduction of
fireplace opening.

Doorway blocked during C19th with
orig (c.16th) brick and larger C19th
brick (above tudor brick). C19 panelling
installed.

Cornice probably C18th (re-positioning
of fireplace plane)

SKIRTING

Figure 3.61
Room F1. Survey note of entrance to garderobe closet with 19th-century brickwork in situ.

Figure 3.62
Room F1. East wall prior to the unblocking of the garderobe closet.

Figure 3.63 (above, left) Room F1. Arched recess in south wall of garderobe closet.

Figure 3.64 (above, right) Room F1. Interior of the garderobe closet showing the southern edge of the blocked window opening (on the left of the photograph) and the remains of an early wallpaper scheme, probably dating from the 18th century.
[Mike Gray]

staircase via opposing doorways in the north-east and south-east corners of the rooms respectively. The staircase compartment was originally much narrower and the north partition wall of the room was probably aligned with that of the kitchen (G2) below and with the extant roof truss above (Fig 3.65).

It is evident from the bond timbers incorporated in the 16th-century brickwork that the chamber was intended to be furnished with panelling. It was lit by two double-height windows, both probably of eight lights, one situated slightly north of centre along the west wall, overlooking the courtyard (Fig 3.66), and the other south of centre in the east (outer) wall. The window openings had splayed reveals and timber lintels supporting the brickwork above. The presence of two large window openings diagonally opposite each other raises the possibility that the room was originally subdivided by a partition across the centre, but there is no evidence for this. Additionally there

appears to have been only one fireplace, situated in the western half of the south wall (Figs 3.67 and 3.68), and presumably built in this off-centre position to avoid the flue of the large kitchen fireplace beneath. The eastern half of the brick relieving arch has survived and shows the fireplace to have been of modest size. The opening was 430mm deep.

In the double-floor frame of the room, a transverse beam measuring 350mm square runs east–west between the side walls of the wing and supports a north–south run of floor and ceiling joists. The joists themselves were replaced in the 18th century but, as in several other places in the house, there are carpenters' assembly marks inscribed along the top face of the beam and the floor joist mortises are numbered in a complete sequence of Roman numerals from east to west.

The removal of a decayed 18th-century plaster ceiling shortly before the room was surveyed in 1990 revealed that the

▨	1752
▨	19th C
▨	Walls, partitions, ceilings, etc in section

*Figure 3.65 (above)
East wing. Internal
elevation of the east wall
as existing in 1990.
(Scale 1:100)*

*Figure 3.66 (left)
Room F2. View to north-
west showing blocked
window opening at the
north end of the west wall.
[Mike Gray]*

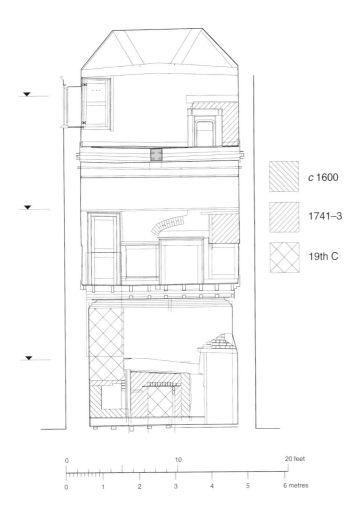

c 1600

1741–3

19th C

| 0 | | | | | 10 | | | | | 20 feet |

| 0 | 1 | 2 | 3 | 4 | 5 | 6 metres |

Figure 3.67
East wing. Internal
elevation of the south wall
as existing in 1990.
(Scale 1:100)

16th-century frame for the second floor over the room is in a remarkably complete condition (Fig 3.69). A primary transverse beam spanning east–west supports secondary axial north–south beams which are jointed to the transverse beam by double tenons. The joint with the south axial beam was strengthened by the addition of a soffit spur below the lower tenon, but such an additional support was not considered necessary for the north

beam (Fig 3.70). The axial beams in turn supported runs of floor and ceiling joists. Carpenters' numerals were recorded on three of the floor joists of the east run only, and it appears to have been common practice in the construction of the house to mark only one side of a floor frame. At the south end the falling away of the south end wall, which must have occurred before a new ceiling was installed in the 18th century, had led to the almost complete withdrawal of the south axial beam from its socket.

Great chamber (F3)

The great chamber of the Tudor house was adaptable for many functions including dining and entertaining. It is readily recognisable as such today, its basic dimensions largely unchanged although new door openings have been made and its fenestration altered. Moreover, it still looks like a Tudor great chamber as its high quality oak panelling has survived the vicissitudes of taste. The present panelling is, however, of various periods and, as none of it is thought to date from Ralph Sadleir's decoration of the room, it is largely discussed in the next chapter (Fig 3.71; *see also* Fig 1.8).

In the original layout, the room had diagonally opposed doors in the northeast and south-west corners (*see* Fig 3.22). The doorway to the withdrawing room/bedchamber (F1) in the east wall was blocked up when the house was divided in the 1750s and only reopened during the 1990s restoration. Its position, and the absence of any other doorway on this side of the room, would appear to indicate that the builder of the house wanted to isolate the chamber from the east 'service' staircase, to which access could only be gained, rather awkwardly, through the withdrawing room/bedchamber. The door in the west wall, however, was immediately opposite the head

Figure 3.68 (near right)
Room F2. View of south
wall as it appeared with
panelling and wall finishes
removed during restoration.
[Mike Gray]

Figure 3.69 (far right)
Room S2. View to south-
east, showing the original
16th-century floor
construction exposed during
restoration.

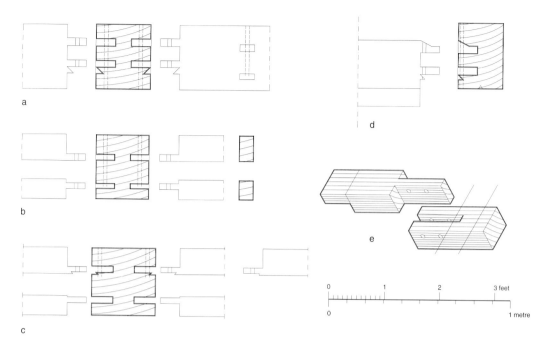

a

d

b

c

e

Figure 3.70 *A selection of examples from the detailed record made of the surviving 16th-century carpentry within the house (Scale 1:20):*
a) *typical arrangement at the junction of the main structural timber floor beams (main beams over rooms F2 and F5 differ);*
b) *typical floor/ceiling joist fixing to the main structural floor beams (rooms G5 and F5);*
c) *typical floor/ceiling joist fixing to the main structural floor beams (rooms F2 and F3), with floor joist tenon variation;*
d) *detail of the joint between the main structural timber beam over the west staircase (second floor) and bridging beam to the north; and*
e) *purlin scarf joint found in the east range roof assembly.*

Figure 3.71 *The great chamber (F3). View to west following restoration. [B000343]*

Figure 3.72
Room F3. View to north-
west in 1990 showing
inserted 18th-century
windows and the 19th-
century opening which
provided access to room F4.

of the west staircase, as at present, and the route to the great chamber was probably through the hall (G3) and the high (linenfold) parlour (G4) and up the west staircase. When meals were served in the room it is likely that the food also travelled in the same direction, although originating, of course, in the kitchen.

The removal of the 18th- and 19th-century doorcases from the western entrance to the room revealed the original 16th-century doorcase to be still in position although much of its decoration was lost during alterations to accommodate later frames. As with the other surviving moulded doorcases in the house, it was apparently constructed off-site, brought in and positioned, and the brickwork built up around it, thus forming a structural unit in much the same way as the window frames. The door was hung on stout hook hinges hammered into the frame. The deep and thick threshold, over which it would have been necessary to step, is extant, but its effect is now somewhat muted by the raising of the floor of the chamber.

The east, south and west walls of the room are constructed of the original 16th-century brickwork laid in English bond with

oak bond timbers approximately every fourteenth course for the fixing of wall decoration (Figs 3.72 and 3.73). The north wall was completely rebuilt in the 18th century, but 16th-century bricks were reused for the inner face and core work, some of which still bear traces of a thin skim of lime plaster. These may have come from the original front wall at second-floor level, which was also rebuilt at the same time in the 18th century, as no evidence of plaster was found on the other walls of the great chamber and it is likely that this important room was panelled from the outset. The mock Tudor fireplace in the south wall dates from the early 20th century (Fig 3.74) but the brick relieving arch and the lintel of the 16th-century fireplace, slightly offset from the present one, remain. During the restoration in the 1990s the panels covering these were hinged to enable these 'hidden' features to be seen.

The rebuilding of the north wall has removed most of the evidence for the original fenestration (*see* Fig 3.38), but traces of window splays in the brickwork behind the panelling at the edges of the room indicate that there were probably three double-height, ten-light windows across this wall. The south wall had one double-height, probably eight-light, window overlooking the courtyard at the eastern corner (*see* Figs 3.40 and 3.41).

The floor was lower than at present, apparently having been raised in the 18th century, perhaps because it had become uneven. In the course of the alteration most of the original joists were removed; what remains of the initial floor construction indicates, however, that its installation was not undertaken with the care that is evident in most of the house. The main structural members were three structural beams spanning north–south over the hall (G3) below (*see* p 52). It appears that all the extant, though now vacant, upper mortises in these beams contained the tenons of the floor joists, randomly and haphazardly pegged. No carpenters' marks have been found, and some mortises were altered to take oversized joists. This lack of attention to detail may have caused sagging which necessitated the subsequent raising of the floor. At the point of entry into the south wall, the central beam has had part of its top face cut away to accommodate the later hearth of the repositioned fireplace, and the remaining original floor joists have also been trimmed back here. A section of the original floor can now be seen under hinged floorboards.

There is no evidence of the appearance of the original ceiling of the room but

it would presumably have been decorated in some way. It appears to have been completely removed and a new ceiling constructed some 75mm lower in the 18th century.

Bedchamber (F4)

This is the third of the fine panelled rooms in the house; in common with the rest, however, the present panelling does not appear to date from the earliest build and is therefore considered in subsequent chapters. The room was almost certainly used as

Figure 3.73
Room F3. View to north-east in 1990 showing inserted sash windows, the blocked door opening leading to F1 and, on the right, a 20th-century door opening to provide access to the east staircase.

Figure 3.74
Room F3. South wall before restoration. The existing fireplace dates from the early 20th century, but the lintel of the 16th-century original remains and can now be viewed by lifting a hinged panel.
[Duncan Murray/The National Trust]

1741–3

c 1800

GROUND
FLOOR

0   10   20 feet

0   1   2   3   4   5   6 metres

Figure 3.75
West wing. Internal
elevation of north wall as
existing in 1990.
(Scale 1:100)

The brickwork of the east and west walls is laid in English bond with random, horizontal, continuous bond timbers. There is a well constructed, four-centred, relieving arch over the fireplace in the west wall with two wood blocks coursed in to provide fixings for panelling or other wall covering; the brickwork has been well laid and coursed and closed around openings and projections on this wall. No bond timbers are present in the wall at high level, however, which may suggest that the original wall covering did not extend to ceiling level. Sockets cut at this level in the brickwork, some still filled with timber blocks with evidence for nail fixings, may be later (Fig 3.76; *see also* Fig 3.47).

The present mullioned-and-transomed window in the west wall, although dating only from the 1990s restoration, was formed in an original opening which had been blocked up at a later date, probably during the 1740s. Despite the substantial degree of rebuilding of the north wall, evidence has also survived of the splayed reveal and cut-back lintel of a large double-height window. This latter feature has been described in the account of the fenestration of the main, north front of the building (*see* p 31).

The extant stone fireplace in the west wall, like other surviving fireplaces in the house, is constructed of four pieces of Reigate stone. Two of these form the jambs, while the other two, set at an angle and bearing on both the jambs and each other, form the head. The upper two pieces are thus intentionally raked, and the four stones together form a strong and rigid structural unit. The arch and jambs are moulded, with vine decoration to the spandrels and carved shields in the corners, the latter painted with coats of arms at a later date (*see* pp 128–9). The fireplace is set centrally in a projecting chimney breast which is pronouncedly north of centre in the room. It was presumably constructed in this way to allow for the vertical passage of the flue from the fireplace of the room below, but it also provides room for the large window opening to the south.

The timber-framed south partition wall, dividing the room from the staircase and inner chamber (F5), has remained in its original position and provides a good example of how such walls were constructed (Fig 3.77). Two beams running east–west and forming a sill and a top-plate were built into the brickwork on each side as the house rose, the sill being designed to take part of the first-floor loading with the ends of the original north–south floor joists resting

a bedchamber, probably by Ralph Sadleir or a member of his family, for, although it was spacious and well lit, it had a solitary and somewhat private entrance in the south-west corner. Access would have been gained from the inner chamber (F5) via a floored-over area at the west end of the single-flight staircase which rose from the ground floor (*see* Fig 3.22).

The removal of much of the panelling for safe-keeping before the room was surveyed enabled the structure of the walls to be examined. The north wall was substantially reconstructed when sash windows were inserted in the 18th century (Fig 3.75), but the east and west walls for the most part retain their 16th-century brickwork. The south wall is an original timber-framed partition.

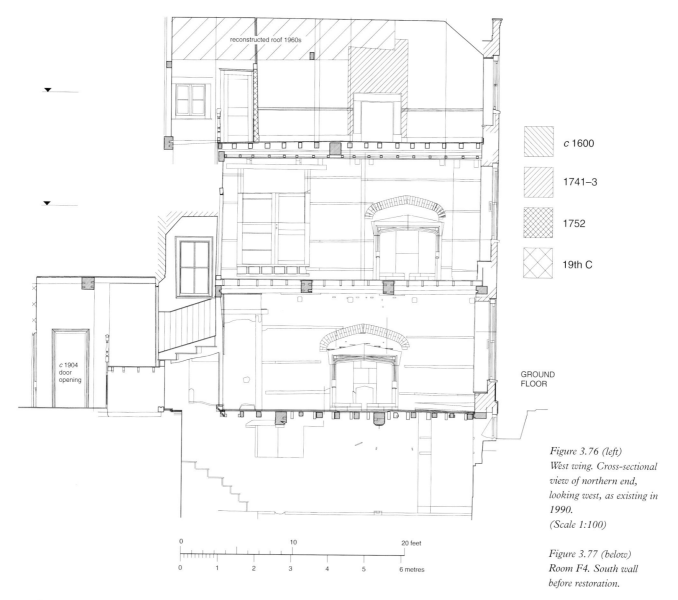

reconstructed roof 1960s

c 1904
door
opening

	c 1600
	1741–3
	1752
	19th C

GROUND
FLOOR

0   10   20 feet

0   1   2   3   4   5   6 metres

Figure 3.76 (left)
West wing. Cross-sectional
view of northern end,
looking west, as existing in
1990.
(Scale 1:100)

Figure 3.77 (below)
Room F4. South wall
before restoration.

on its top surface. A central timber post was attached to the horizontal timbers by mortise-and-tenon joints and double-pegged and, with this basic structure in place, flexible framing could be erected on each side of the central post. Random mortises cut into the underside of the top-plate do not appear to relate to the frame-filling of the wall and may indicate that this was a reused timber (Fig 3.78).

The framing to the west of the central post appears to be largely unaltered. In particular, the door frame for the original entrance into the room is still in place. It consists of four substantial timbers making up the sill, jambs and head. The sill would have sat on the 16th-century floor joists, forming a raised threshold like other doorways throughout the house; it extends from

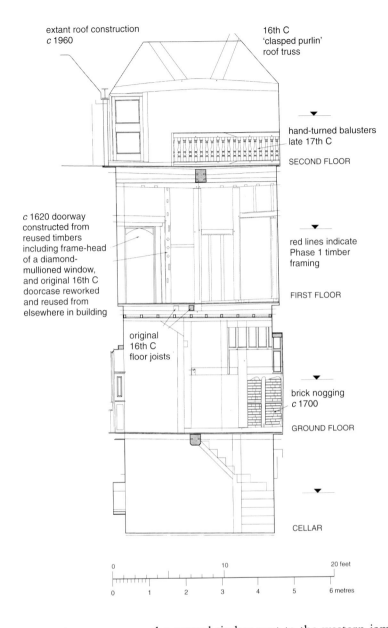

extant roof construction
c 1960

16th C
'clasped purlin'
roof truss

hand-turned balusters
late 17th C

SECOND FLOOR

c 1620 doorway
constructed from
reused timbers
including frame-head
of a diamond-
mullioned window,
and original 16th C
doorcase reworked
and reused from
elsewhere in building

red lines indicate
Phase 1 timber
framing

FIRST FLOOR

original
16th C
floor joists

brick nogging
c 1700

GROUND FLOOR

CELLAR

0   10   20 feet

0   1   2   3   4   5   6 metres

Figure 3.78
West staircase. North
elevation of north partition
wall as existing in 1990.
(Scale 1:100)

the central timber post to the western jamb of the door opening. Mortises in its upper face again suggest that it was a reused timber. The eastern jamb extends from the sill to the underside of the top-plate, to which it is crudely nailed, and it is rebated to receive the door from the underside of the door head to a point 50mm above the sill. The western jamb only extends to the door head and has two groups of broken iron nails and pattern marks where the hinges would have been. The head has been mortised, tenoned and pegged to the west face of the eastern jamb and the top of the western jamb and it continued into the brickwork of the west wall. The whole door frame is tied back to the central post by another horizontal timber rail which is mortised, tenoned and

pegged at each end and attached to the post at its approximate midpoint.

The framing to the east of the central post is similar but has been much altered to accommodate the later opening; it appears that originally no opening existed here. The rebates and other provisions for the door in the now-blocked western opening and the use of finishing plaster between the framing suggest that this wall was deliberately left uncovered for some time after it was constructed.

Neither the present floor nor ceiling are original. The floor level has been maintained, but only two 16th-century joists survive as secondary bridging beams for a new floor which was laid in the 18th century. The ceiling has been lowered by approximately 75mm, probably at the same time.

Inner chamber (F5)
The first floor of the west wing was originally divided into three chambers, reflecting the arrangement of the ground-floor rooms below. The middle chamber was separated from that to the south by the continuation of the 1m-wide brick cross-stack described on page 57 which was demolished in the 18th century (*see* Fig 3.22).

The precise arrangement of the north end of the room is uncertain (Fig 3.79; *see also* Fig 3.86). The staircase from the ground to the first floor rose on the immediate south side of the partition wall forming the south end wall of the bedchamber (F4) to a landing in the north-east corner opposite the door to the great chamber (much as now). The presence of mortises and stave grooves along the soffit of the transverse second-floor beam which would have been immediately above the south side of the staircase opening suggests that a partition was built beneath the beam. Whether this was merely a lightweight screen with an opening at each end or was substantial enough to extend across the room with framed door openings is not known. The latter arrangement is possible as the extant small, high-level window in the west wall would have provided sufficient light for such a narrow compartment (*see* Fig 3.23).

The chamber was heated by the extant stone fireplace towards the north end of the west wall, which has survived in good condition because for much of the subsequent history of the house it was blocked up (Fig 3.80). The fireplace jambs are roll moulded and the spandrels carved with foliate designs and carved shields. (The armorial bearings

Figure 3.79
Room F5. View to north-west before restoration.

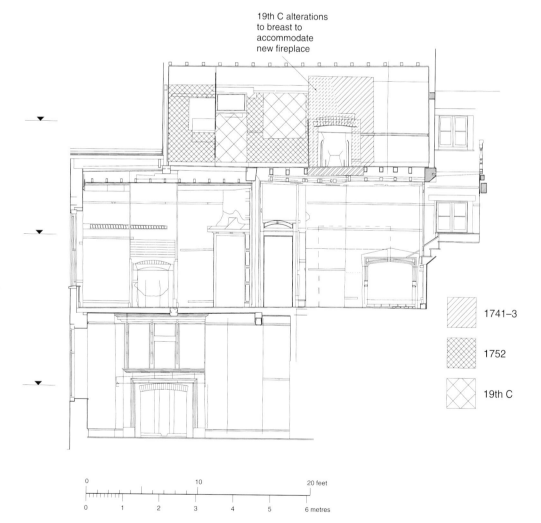

19th C alterations
to breast to
accommodate
new fireplace

1741–3

1752

19th C

Figure 3.80
West wing. Cross-sectional view of southern end looking west, as existing in 1990.
(Scale 1:100)

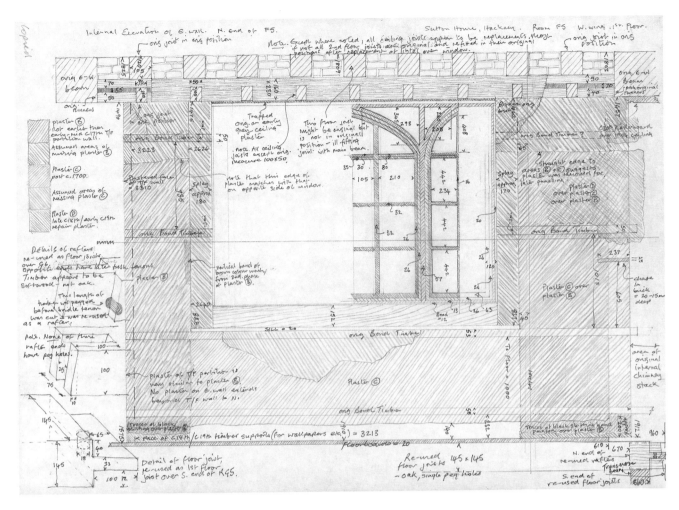

Figure 3.81

Room F5. Survey note of internal elevation of north end of east wall as existing in 1990. This drawing illustrates the different areas of surviving historic plaster wall finishes, mainly dating from the 17th and 18th centuries.

which were painted on these shields at a later date are discussed on pages 128–9.) The room was lit by a large window in the opening in the east wall now occupied by the 18th-century 'Gothick' window (Fig 3.81). The outer part of the 16th-century frame remains embedded in the brickwork surrounding the opening, and empty peg holes in the side members show that it had a central transom. The opening, which was built with splayed reveals using wire-cut bricks, is slightly narrower than that of the room below and may have housed a ten-light rather than a twelve-light window. It is evident from bond timbers within the walls and from the bare brick face of the east wall as it passes behind the later partition wall at the north end of the room that the chamber was originally designed to be furnished with wall panelling.

The ceiling of the room was largely renewed in the 18th century, and most of the ceiling joists are softwood replacements of that date. Nevertheless, fragments of the original lath and plaster ceiling have

survived, trapped along the soffit of the transverse floor beam at the north end and above the present window frame of the east wall. These fragments, consisting of a grey base coat and a thin, white finishing layer, are similar to those found in the high (linenfold) parlour (G4) and the west corridor on the ground floor.

South-west chamber (south end of F5)

Little of the construction of the south-west chamber survived the collapse and consequent rebuilding of the south end of the west wing after the brick cross-stack had been removed in the 18th century. The entire west and south walls, and all of the east wall except a small section at the north end, were rebuilt, largely reusing the 16th-century bricks, together with the floor and ceiling (*see* Fig 3.53).

A vertical splay at the end of the remaining section of original brickwork, formed using wire-cut bricks, indicates that the chamber was lit by a large window in the east wall (Fig 3.82). On the same wall,

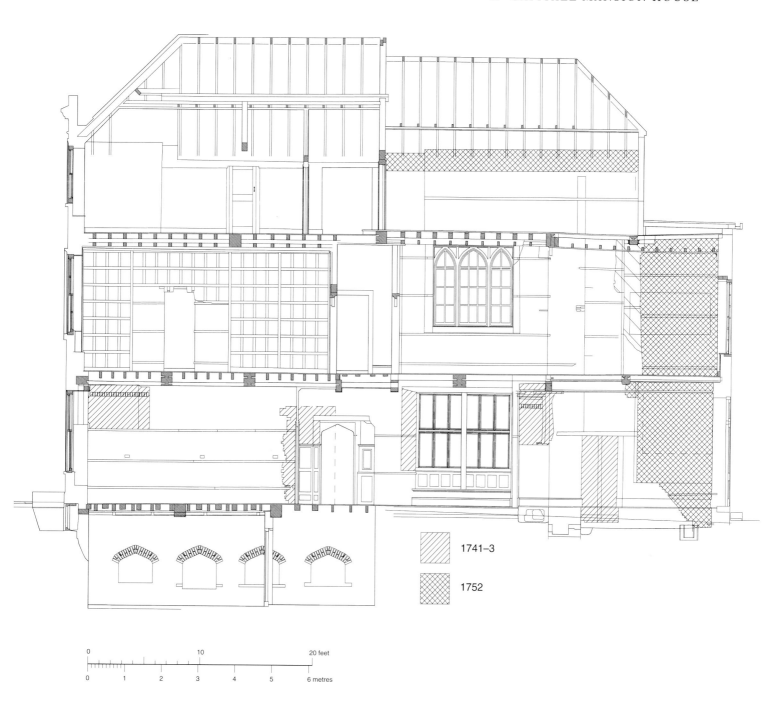

1741–3

1752

0   10   20 feet

0   1   2   3   4   5   6 metres

approximately midway up the south edge of the hacked-back brickwork of the demolished cross-stack is the mortar impression of what may have been the end bricks of a relieving arch (Fig 3.83). This suggests that there was a fireplace near the east end of the cross-stack. A fireplace in such a position would have allowed room for an opening at the west end of the stack for a passage between the inner (F5) and south-west chambers. Archaeological examination of this area revealed no evidence of a staircase between the isolated south-west room (G6) on the ground floor and the south-west chamber above, and so the existence of such an opening in the cross-stack at first-floor level must be presumed. Little else can be said about the original form of this chamber.

Figure 3.82
West wing. Internal elevation of east wall as existing in 1990, showing extent of 18th-century alterations.
(Scale 1:100)

Copied

(and subsequently 1890-1904 ceiling plaster)

Line of orig. ceiling plaster - now missing

1890-1904 cornice

Section through return of post 1890-1904 cornice

1890-1904 panel board

Possible position of original bond timber

Plaster (D)
hard creamy colour plaster (used after removal of top part of C18th partition?) pre-dates C19th wall papers. Varies in thickness between c.2mm - c.1.2mm

Long bond timber under
Impression of edge of (removed) partition along edge of plaster (C)

28-18mm deep chase in brickface. For shelf? It was cut after plaster (B) phase and filled in with plaster (C)

Plaster (C)
Post - c.1700 plaster washes over plaster (B)
plaster wash layers, below.
Sequence of post-c.1700 layers as follows:-
(1) White plaster wash above dado height / light blue plaster wash below dado height.
(2) White plaster wash above dado height / Sap green plaster wash below dado ht.
(3) light yellow ochre plaster wash below dado ht./ white above.
(4) light grey plaster wash - floor to ceiling
Wallpapers over plaster
Sequence:-
(1) lining paper with light grey /blue emulsion over.
(2) lining paper with lighter grey emulsion over.
(3) Wallpaper with floral designs set within rectangular grid (irregular sizes).
(4) Floral patterned wallpaper
(5) 2nd Floral patterned wallpaper

Plaster (B)
2-3mm thick. Long tufts of animal hair used as binder. Original finishing coat was a harsh chalky off-white. This was followed subsequently with this sequence:-
(1) brown colour wash
(2) light grey colour wash
(3) white colour wash

Orig. Bond Timber

Plaster (B) return around N. face of demolished stack still survives.

Traces of pre-c.1700 black skirting band survive on plaster (B)

120 mm

Sutton House, Hackney. Room F5. Internal elevation of E. wall.
Scarred brickwork and adjoining wall plaster in area of demolished Internal chimney stack.

Post-1904 Plaster-board

1890-1904 ceiling plaster

1890-1904 cornice

53 Brick courses between floor + ceiling

Join

gap between rails

1890-1904 panel board

Early rail - double pegged for muntins

No muntins now in place - position shown by pegs + leads in rail

Orig. Bond Timber

Plaster (A)
5mm thick chopped straw used as binder

Orig. Bond Timber

Bricks now missing

Section

wedge shaped brick

Impression of edge visible in plaster

This area of brickwork appears to have been covered over during the application of plaster (A) - possibly with a fireplace surround

pit 3 phases before demolition of chimney stack

Orig. Bond Timber

mortar line of return brick face of demolished stack still visible along this line on face of stretchers

Orig. Bond Timber

this may replace an original bond timber

Floor boards

1010 mm

The second floor (Fig 3.84)

Unusually for a modest-sized house of the 16th century, the accommodation on the second floor was of full storey height. Nevertheless, there is evidence of much partitioning of rooms and it is likely that the floor was used for bedrooms, servants' chambers and storage. Unless there was another staircase at the rebuilt end of the west wing, the floor could only be reached via the staircase in the east wing which functioned as a service stair (Fig 3.85; *see also* Fig 3.21).

In terms of the early layout, the upper floor is the least understood area of the house. The 18th-century alterations to the gables, roof and windows at the front of the house, the remodelling of the staircases, and the addition of a concrete ring beam at the level of the former wall plate in the 1960s, all contributed to the loss of crucial evidence. Other repairs and alterations have included the demolition of the cross-stack and rebuilding of the south end of the west wing, the remodelling and insertion of fireplaces, and changes to the early window openings in both wings (*see* Fig 3.85).

In the first hearth tax return of 1662, Sutton House was assessed at twenty-one hearths: even allowing for outbuildings, it seems likely that several of the second-floor rooms were heated from an early date. However, only the fireplace opening in the south wall of the east wing can be shown with certainty to date from the construction of the house. The blocked opening in the room at the front of this wing may also date from the original build. Elsewhere, there are later fireplaces but no evidence that earlier ones preceded these.

The extant second-floor window openings at the front of the house date from the remodelling of 1741–3. The evidence for early window openings in the other external elevations has been much mutilated.

Figure 3.83 (facing page) Room F5. Survey note of exposed brickwork in east wall showing evidence for former cross chimney stack.

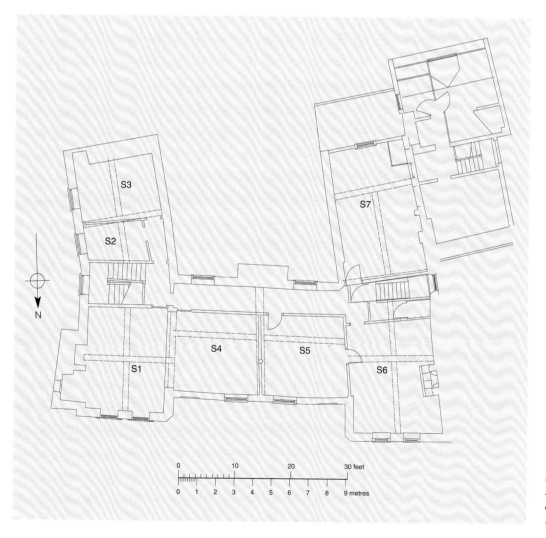

Figure 3.84 Plan of the second floor as existing in 1990. (Scale 1:200)

Figure 3.85
Plan of second floor as it
may have appeared c 1535.
(Scale 1:200)

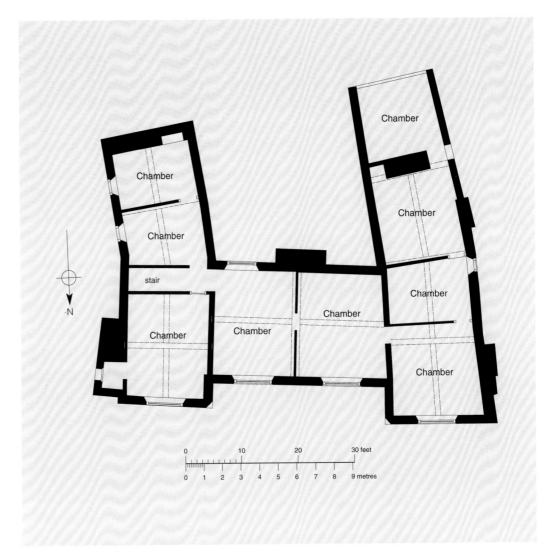

Figure 3.85
Plan of second floor as it may have appeared c 1535.
(Scale 1:200)

The existence of 16th-century closing bricks beneath the concrete beam towards the rear of the east wing suggests that the present opening here has taken the place of a high-level window, possibly of a gabled dormer type, and there is some evidence that the existing window to the north of the latter may also occupy the site of an original opening. In the 16th century, as at present, there appear to have been no windows at second-floor level in the courtyard elevations of the wings. The only window facing on to the courtyard was at the east end of the hall range, in the position of the present opening but wider.

The frames of the surviving 16th-century roof trusses over the staircase partition walls are closed with infill panels composed of a double skin of lath and plaster which extend to the apex of the roof, indicating that the rooms on the upper floor were not ceiled originally but were open to the rafters.

The hall range, where there is some evidence that the rooms were ceiled at roof-collar level, may have been an exception.

Roof structure

The roofline has remained much the same since the 16th century, the roof framing itself having been altered structurally only at the front of the building and rear of the west wing. The house had a pitched roof over each wing and twin pitched roofs over the central hall range. The roof framing was of oak and constructed to the same high standard of carpentry as the floor framing within the house.

All four roof pitches were of clasped purlin type. The intermediate roof trusses comprised a cambered tie beam, a pair of raking queen struts, and principal rafters, the struts serving to trap the purlins and support the principal rafters. The gable roof

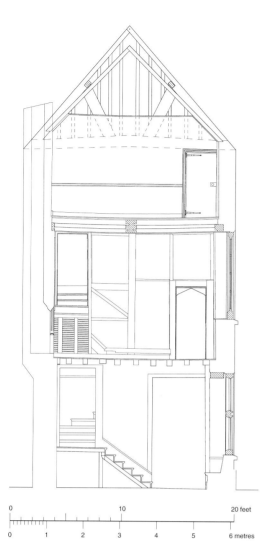

Figure 3.86
West staircase. South
elevation of south partition
wall as existing in 1990.
(Scale 1:100)

to the wall plate forming a valley between the twin pitched roofs (*see* Fig 3.21). As indicated above, the frames of the roof trusses over both the staircase partition walls are infilled with lath and plaster.

The grounds

Very little evidence has survived to show the original disposition of the garden and grounds. Documentary sources show that there were barns, stables and a dovehouse, but where they were situated is not known. The grounds of the house sloped away quite sharply to Hackney Brook to the south (*see* Fig 6.38). Excavations revealed evidence of a terrace on the immediate south side of the house with boundary walls and probably a flight of steps leading to the garden beyond, but this feature has been tentatively dated to the early 17th century.

Otherwise only fragments survive and it is not clear if any of them relate directly to the 1535 construction of the house. The western boundary wall of the property at the front of the house has been much repaired and, although it contains a significant

trusses over the rear wall of the hall range had a straight collar and vertical struts, and were clad externally with a skin of lath and plaster supported on thin timber studs (Fig 3.86; *see also* Fig 3.16). The principal rafters were reduced in depth above the level of the purlins and were joined together at the apex using a bridled tenon joint. The roof had windbraces to provide additional longitudinal stability. The purlins included bridled tenon scarf joints (*see* Fig 3.70e).

Almost all of the 16th-century common rafters and purlins have been replaced. It is likely that there would have been an intermediate truss over each of the twin roofs over the hall range, but any evidence for this was lost during repairs carried out in the 1960s. An early 20th-century photograph appears to show a brace extending across the passageway in this range (Fig 3.87). This probably formed part of a timber-framed partition in the centre of the hall range which would have acted as a support

Figure 3.87
Second floor. Photograph
taken at the turn of the
20th century showing a
brace extending across the
rear passageway of the
central range.
[BB87/9640; © Crown
copyright.NMR]

amount of diaper patterning, it is doubtful if this dates from the first building of the house (Fig 3.88).

A circular, brick-lined well to the south-west of the west wing (Fig 3.89; *see also* Fig 3.20) is almost certainly 16th-century in date. Built mainly in stretcher bond in its lower courses and in header bond in its top eleven surviving courses, its internal diameter is 1.2m and it is 3.5m deep, descending into natural gravel. Whether it is as old as Sutton House and, if so, whether it fell within the curtilage of the house are cast into some doubt by its being on the far (west) side of a wall which probably marked the original boundary of the Sutton House property. The well was capped in the 18th century.

Conclusions of the fabric survey

Nothing in the survey of the fabric of the house, or in the archaeological investigation which was carried out prior to restoration, revealed the whereabouts of earlier buildings on the site which are referred to in documents. The most likely explanation is either that they were demolished before the house was constructed or, if some of them continued to exist, they were elsewhere on the larger site.

Nevertheless, there are one or two puzzling features of the building which cannot be easily explained. One is the large arched recess in the east cellar which would have formed a low-level niche in room G1 above (*see* Fig 3.65). If it was specifically designed for this purpose, the carefully laid brickwork of the arch shows a remarkable degree of elaboration for such a minor feature. There is, however, some doubt that the recess extended to the outside wall to form an opening and, unless it was the result of a change of plan in building, it is difficult to adduce any other reason for its construction.

Even more problematical are the form and function of the isolated south-west room (G6) which, although structurally part of the main house, was apparently accessible only from the courtyard (*see* Figs 3.19, 3.21 and 3.27). Archaeological evidence suggests that the room may have originally been used as a brewhouse or a still room. If so, that might account for its lack of communication with the other rooms on the ground floor of the west wing, but it does not resolve the issues raised by its incorporation into the envelope of the building. The archaeological excavation also revealed that the plinth for the rear wall of this room was of narrow dimensions, more suitable for a timber-framed wall than one of brick. If this room was part of an earlier feature which had been incorporated into the house during building without adequate structural safeguards, it might help to explain the structural collapse which apparently occurred here at a later date. Unfortunately, that collapse and subsequent rebuilding have removed most of the evidence on which an understanding of the room might have been based.

The architectural and social context of Sutton House

Sadleir and Cromwell

In order to better appreciate the architecture and design of Sutton House in the 16th century, the social sphere in which Ralph Sadleir moved must be thoroughly understood. As has been mentioned, Sadleir was born in 1507 and he entered the household of Thomas Cromwell (1485?–1540) probably when only 7 years of age.[44] Cromwell, chiefly remembered for the part he played in the dissolution of the monasteries, was one of the most powerful men in England during the reign of Henry VIII. In the 1510s and 1520s, Cromwell's career was closely linked to that of his own master, Cardinal Wolsey. Remarkably, Cromwell managed to escape the king's displeasure after Wolsey's death in 1530. In fact, Cromwell's subsequent rise was meteoric: an astute organiser and administrator, he was made a Privy Councillor in 1531 and was appointed secretary to the king in 1534, Lord Privy Seal in 1536 and Lord Great Chamberlain in 1539.

Ralph Sadleir's own good fortunes were undoubtedly due to his connection with Cromwell. By the age of 19, he was working as his secretary and held a special place in Cromwell's household.[45] Just as Cromwell dealt with much of Wolsey's business, especially his legal work, so all issues dealt with by Cromwell came through Sadleir. By the mid-1530s, Sadleir was a familiar figure at court and was often with the king, acting as a go-between for Henry and his minister until Cromwell's execution in 1540.[46]

Sadleir, Cromwell and building

In terms of his architectural knowledge, Sadleir's upbringing, connections and experience were of the utmost importance.

Through Cromwell, who was appointed Vicar General in 1535, he would have had some involvement with the dissolution of the monasteries and possibly with subsequent conversions of monastic property to domestic use.[47] More importantly, he would have seen his master's building activities at first hand. Building has been termed Cromwell's 'greatest extravagance' and his projects were chiefly centred on London, where he was most at home.[48] By the mid-1530s, when his building activities reached their peak, Cromwell had houses at Mortlake, Islington, Stepney and Hackney.[49] Of his two houses in the City, the most ambitious and well known was at Austin Friars, acquired *c* 1524 and much extended ten years later. Cromwell's house in Hackney, later known as Brooke House (*see* Fig 2.10), was granted to him by Henry VIII in 1535 and, after extensive alterations had been carried out, was surrendered back to the king in 1536.[50]

Cromwell's interest in architecture was of long standing. His cousin Robert had headed Wolsey's construction office in Battersea in the mid-1510s, dealing with the works at both Hampton Court and York Place, and by the 1520s Cromwell was executing Wolsey's building programme for his two colleges at Oxford and Ipswich.[51] Cromwell would have visited his master at Hampton Court often and would have been very well acquainted with his team of craftsmen, which included the master masons John Lobyns (or Lebons) and Henry Redman (the two men who later designed Cardinal College, Oxford, renamed Christ Church in 1542).[52] They worked on buildings and monuments of the highest quality. Lobyns, for example, was described as one of the king's master masons in 1506 and was one of the three men who had worked on Henry VII's tomb.[53] Howard Colvin suggested that James Nedeham's promotion from Master Carpenter to Surveyor of the Works in 1532 was engineered by Cromwell, who knew him well.[54] Indeed, at the time of this appointment, Nedeham was working for Cromwell in a private capacity.[55]

Cromwell's involvement in large scale building works did not stop with Wolsey's death. He went on to remain closely connected with Henry VIII's work in this area, for example, initiating repairs at the Tower of London in 1532, purchasing land in Westminster in 1536 for redevelopment as part of Whitehall, and overseeing works at Calais in the 1530s.[56]

Figure 3.90
Hampton Court, Surrey,
begun c 1515. View of
Base Court, showing some
of Cardinal Wolsey's
original work with
diapering to the brickwork.
(3 0301004/31; Crown
copyright: Historic Royal
Palaces; Reproduced by
permission of Historic
Royal Palaces under licence
for the Controller of
Her Majesty's Stationary
Office)

It is therefore reasonable to assume that, through Cromwell, Sadleir had acquired an interest in building. He certainly knew the workmen; indeed, one of his two daughters was to marry Sir Richard Lee, Nedeham's successor as Surveyor of the Works, who had been in charge of the building works at Cromwell's house in Hackney (later Brooke House) between 1535 and 1536.[57] Sadleir's biographer, A J Slavin, noted that early in his career, working in Wolsey's entourage, Sadleir had learned how to make surveys, the techniques of land transfer and the craft of seisin (conveyancing).[58] In connection with his legal work, he acted for the Crown in matters of property surrendered to the king's use.[59] It is certain that he knew Hampton Court from an early date, during the residences of both Wolsey and Henry VIII, and by the early 1530s he had regular access to the king's chambers at a number of his palaces. Through Cromwell and Wolsey, he would have had the opportunity of visiting important houses and palaces including Hanworth, Eltham, Bridewell, Guildford and The More, Hertfordshire. In the 1540s Sadleir had living quarters in his own right at Hampton Court, Westminster and Whitehall, each with a stable of good horses attached.[60] In January 1541, Sadleir, now Sir Ralph, was appointed first Keeper of the Chief Messuage of Nonsuch, and of the Park, Wardrobe and Gardens, a further measure of his involvement with the king's buildings.[61]

Brick and the external design of Sutton House

It has already been suggested (*see* p 21) that timber supplied to James Nedeham for the king's house at Hackney in 1535 could have been used at Sutton House. It is also tempting to think that bricks and other materials could have derived from the king's works, with which Sadleir was so familiar. Whatever the case, Sadleir's use of brick for his new residence must surely have owed something to his knowledge of royal buildings. Brick had been strongly favoured by Henry VII, whose Richmond Palace (completed 1501) was built almost wholly of the material. This preference was inherited by his son Henry VIII, who used brick at many of his London palaces, including Greenwich, Bridewell (1515–23), Whitehall (1530–6) and St James's (1532–40). Hampton Court (Fig 3.90), begun by Wolsey *c* 1515 and presented to Henry VIII in 1529, was of brick adorned with exquisite diapering work on a scale unprecedented for domestic building and was to be hugely influential. Other precedents for Sadleir's choice of material, which had been used frequently in East Anglia since the 15th century at, for instance, Rye House, Hertfordshire (*c* 1443) and Buckden, Cambridgeshire (1472–96), were the Bishop of London's palaces at Lambeth (Morton's Tower, 1490–5) and Fulham (1506–22) (Fig 3.91).

Sadleir was by no means unique in being led by royal example. Other courtiers who chose to build in brick included Sir Richard Weston, an intimate of Henry VIII, whose Sutton Place, Surrey (1525–32) was a prominent house of the time (Fig 3.92); Lord Sandys at The Vyne, Hampshire (1518–27); Sir Henry Marney at Layer Marney, Essex (*c* 1520–30); Sir William Compton at Compton Wynyates, Warwickshire (*c* 1520); Sir Thomas Cheyney at Shurland House, Sheppey, Kent (completed 1532); Lord Rich at Leez Priory, Essex (begun 1536–7); Sir William Petre at Ingatestone Hall, Essex (externally complete 1548); and Sir William Gasgoigne, Comptroller of Wolsey's Household, at Cardington, Bedfordshire.[62] On a local level, Sadleir would have known of the Bishop of London's residence at Stepney, which dated from the 14th to the 16th centuries and was built mostly of brick; he would also have been familiar with Cromwell's work at the King's Place (later Brooke House), which was described in 1547 as 'a ffayre house all of bricke'.[63]

Figure 3.91 (above) Fulham Palace, London, built by Richard Fitzjames, Bishop of London, 1506–22. West courtyard, south-west side. Detail showing projecting hall porch with brick diapering work.
[CC73/2714; © Crown copyright. NMR]

Figure 3.92 (left) Sutton Place, Surrey, built 1525–32 for Sir Richard Weston. View from north looking on to courtyard. The original north range was demolished in 1786.
[CC000727; © Crown copyright. NMR]

Sadleir's choice of this material, although practical in many ways, was primarily linked to architectural pretension and showiness. Houses built close to the metropolis, especially by courtiers, were of the most fashionable kind and were often expected to be sophisticated. The unusual design of brick-built Wickham Court at Bromley, Kent (c 1490), for example, can be explained by its proximity to the capital.[64] Several brick houses have been referred to, but these were almost all situated outside London and were intended to be country seats, more comparable to Sadleir's later brick-built Standon Lordship, Hertfordshire (c 1546) than to Sutton House.

Just how many brick houses were built in urban or suburban locations is hard to surmise, largely because of substantial rebuilding and redevelopment. John Summerson argued that stone or brick town houses were uncommon before 1600,[65] but this may not have been the case, especially given the royal influence which has been discussed. The antiquary John Leland, who toured England in the 1530s and 1540s, noted that brick and tile were replacing timber and thatch for houses in the London region,[66] and John Schofield has affirmed that by the early 16th century brick was in general use for London houses.[67] However, physical evidence of these buildings is hard to find. Of the vast residences on the Strand, nothing survives, and there is also very little record of the houses nearer the City.

In addition to Sutton House, the principal 16th-century suburban London houses that are well known or recorded in detail are Beaufort House, Chelsea; Bruce Castle, Tottenham; and Eastbury Manor House, Barking. Of these, Beaufort House, and possibly Bruce Castle, pre-date Sutton House. Beaufort House, demolished in the mid-1700s but known from a series of contemporary plans, dated from the 1520s and was home to Thomas More until 1535. It was a grand house of brick, standing adjacent to the river, and was later acquired and reworked by the Cecils.[68] Bruce Castle (Fig 3.93) was granted to Sir William Compton in 1514 and seems to have been built mainly c 1530–40, although it was considerably altered in the 17th century. The house appears to have been of brick and to have a gabled, symmetrical main façade. Thus, brick was certainly becoming more generally used in and around the capital by the time Sadleir built Sutton House.

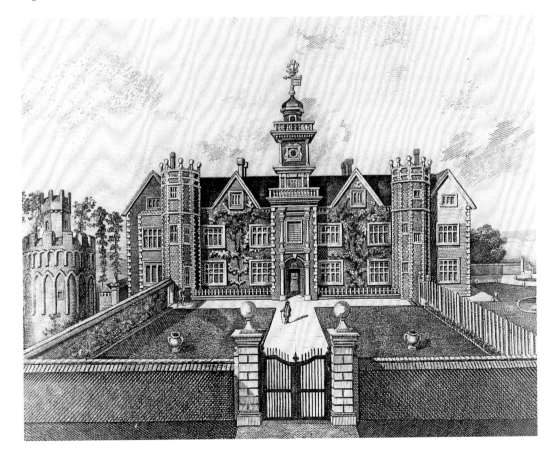

Figure 3.93
Bruce Castle, Tottenham, London, built mainly c 1530–40. Anonymous drawing of c 1685. The turrets on the front of the house probably contained matched stairs. The clock tower was added after 1660.
[AA021508; © Crown copyright.NMR]

Nevertheless, Sadleir made certain concessions in the use of brick at Sutton House, either for aesthetic or for functional reasons. When it came to the construction of the rear (and also perhaps the front) gables (*see* Fig 3.16), he appears to have preferred the more familiar technique of timber-framing. It is not proven that the gables at the front of the house were timber-framed, but the surviving gables at the rear of the central range certainly were. However, evidence from other Tudor houses shows that this was a feature in use in the 16th century. Brick or stone houses with timber-framed gables include Moat Hall, Parham, and Baylham Hall, both in Suffolk. In the latter case, a T-shaped fragment of a large early Tudor house, the use of timber-framing appears to have been restricted to the gable of the rear projecting wing, the main range having shaped gable ends. In some examples, the exterior of the gables may have been colour-washed, or even painted in imitation of brickwork, to match the appearance of the walls. Painted bricks were used in some parts of Hampton Court in place of genuine face patterning and some early 17th-century painted *trompe l'œil* brickwork applied to an area of timber-framing overlooking the rear courtyard was recently discovered at Isaac Lord, a wool merchant's house in Ipswich.[69] At Sutton House, the gables appear to have been set off with decorative bargeboards which were later taken down and reused as hip rafters (*see* Fig 3.17).

Despite comparative examples, there are no surviving houses built in the London area (or even elsewhere) in the early to mid-1500s that can be said to have directly inspired the design of Sutton House. Had the house been built in the later part of the 16th century, the story would have been rather different. Eastbury Manor House at Barking in east London, dated by dendrochronology to 1566 and little altered,[70] has a plan remarkably like that of Sutton House, with a courtyard to the rear (Figs 3.94 and 3.95). Other, more distant, parallels are Plas Mawr in Conwy, a gabled, virtually symmetrical town house built mainly in the 1580s,[71] and Monaughty in Bleddfa, Powys, erected in the mid- to late 16th century. That Sutton House inspired the design of such houses is unlikely. What is more possible is that all derived from a common type, a form of Tudor town house which has all but disappeared and which blended medieval ideas and arrangements with the favoured materials and symmetry of the age.

The plan of Sutton House

The plan of Sadleir's Hackney home is much easier to explain and understand. It is a curious mixture of old and new, and of medieval arrangements blended with fashionable trends of the early 16th century.

The H-plan used by Sadleir had its origin in the 'double-ended hall', the classic house-type of the late-medieval period, comprising a central hall open from ground to roof, flanked at each end by a pair of storeyed cross-wings. In terms of room layout, the house appears to have conformed to the general principle that the most important rooms should be situated at the corners of the building (important, that is, in terms of function as well as social status), a feature later common in Elizabethan small-courtyard houses.[72] At Sutton House, this placed the low parlour (G1) in line with the hall (G3) and cross-passage, while the kitchen (G2) lay diagonally opposite the high parlour (G4).

The main entry into Sutton House was still into one end of the hall (*see* Fig 3.19), placing the entrance off-centre in the north façade. Sadleir followed his medieval predecessors in not building a great staircase, a feature uncommon until after the mid-1500s. Sutton House has two staircases, deliberately planned to regulate the flow of movement around the building of, on the one hand, the owner, his family and his guests and, on the other, the servants and staff. The staircase on the east side rose through all four floors from cellar to attic, allowing servants access to all the principal areas of the house in a way which disrupted the private, family spaces as little as possible. The west, or upper, staircase extended only from ground to first floor, linking the private accommodation in the west wing.

The adoption of upper and lower staircases was by no means unique to Sutton House. The paired staircase arrangement also had its origins in the medieval hall house, with its central, open hall forming the main living area, and provision for services and private rooms in separate storeyed accommodation at each end. Evidence for an almost identical staircase layout, with a pair of narrow stairs leading to the front cross-wing chambers at either end of the house, exists at Old Wilsley, Cranbrook, Kent, a timber-framed 'Wealden' house dating from *c* 1500. The plan of Bacon House, a mid-16th-century courtyard house in the City

Figure 3.94
Eastbury Manor House,
Barking, London, dated by
dendrochronology to 1566.
View from south showing
courtyard and stair turret.
[London Metropolitan
Archives]

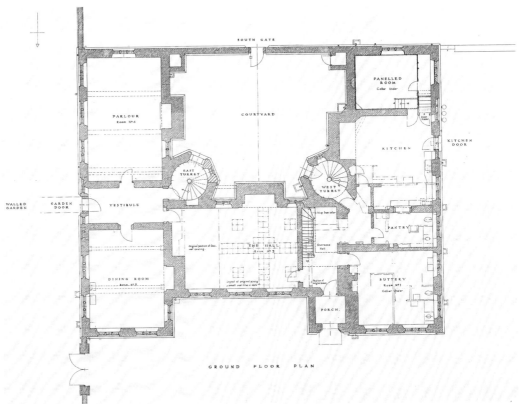

Figure 3.95
Plan of Eastbury Manor
House. [96/05906;
Reproduced by permission
of English Heritage.NMR]

of London, reconstructed from a detailed inventory taken in 1612, shows stairs at both the upper and lower ends of the house, leading to functionally different spaces; a similar scheme is seen in the plan of 'a plaine man's country house' published in 1613 in Gervase Markham's *The English Husbandman*.[73] Eastbury Manor House had a pair of projecting newel staircases in round brick towers set in the angle of the hall and crosswings at the rear of the house, overlooking the courtyard. Whereas at Sutton House the staircases were of unequal height, at Eastbury both the upper and lower staircases rose the full height of the building, the division being maintained by means of a partition wall at attic level. This allowed the staircase at the upper end to open into a small room, perhaps intended as a prospect chamber, which looked out over the walled garden and the surrounding countryside. Certainly, by the mid-16th century the H-plan house with matching upper and lower staircases was common throughout England and Wales.

In other respects, the plan of Sutton House was innovatory. The compact form of the house, with its small courtyard on the south side, meant that it faced largely outwards and that the exterior was uniform. The idea had not developed as far as at Eastbury, which has chimney stacks placed on the inner walls, but this apparent symmetry makes Sutton House an early example of what came to be a Tudor ideal. The courtyard at Sutton House also allowed the service functions to be concentrated in one area of the house and thus the servants did not have to use the hall or high parlour as routes of passage. This segregation of public and private, high and low, is evident from other features of the house, as we have seen with the staircases. The use of a courtyard was well established by the 1530s. Indeed, it has been termed 'the norm for all large-scale domestic building in the early Tudor period'.[74] Sutton Place, Compton Wynyates, Hampton Court and Hengrave Hall, Suffolk (1525–38) are all prominent examples. However, to find a courtyard in a building as modest as Sutton House is more unusual and may reflect Sadleir's indebtedness to royal and courtier's houses.

The other feature of particular interest at Sutton House is its single-storey hall, which was unusual for this date. As Nicholas Cooper has pointed out, the use of this arrangement did not become general practice until late in the 16th century, although

it did enjoy a brief fashion among men of rank around 1530,[75] which may explain its use at Sutton House. Sutton Place, Surrey, also originally had a hall of only a single storey, as did Coldharbour, an early Tudor house in the City of London,[76] and East Barsham Manor, Norfolk, built mainly between 1525 and 1530 for Sir John Fermor. However, conventional, double-height open halls were much more common in the first half of the 16th century and were used by Sir William Compton at Compton Wynyates, Sir Thomas Kytson at Hengrave Hall, and Sir William Fitzwilliam at Cowdray, Sussex (c 1535). In London, the list of 16th-century open halls includes those at Lambeth Palace (probably c 1500, rebuilt 1660–3), Fulham Palace (1506–22), Hampton Court (1532–4) and the Middle Temple (1566).

The trend for single-storey halls appears to have been led by royal example. With the exception of Hampton Court, none of the houses altered or acquired by Henry VIII after 1530 has an open hall and the king even seems to have taken pains to remove open halls where necessary. In 1535 at The More in Hertfordshire, for instance, acquired by Henry on Wolsey's fall, the king started works designed to remove the open hall by dividing it horizontally to create a new room above, which was named the 'new chamber'.[77] Sadleir would, as has been shown, have had a thorough understanding of the arrangements of royal palaces by the mid-1530s, and no doubt tried to emulate these new levels of comfort and convenience, placing a chamber above the hall in his Hackney home.

The working of the household

In terms of the functions of the rooms at Sutton House, much has to be assumed. There is no surviving inventory for the house on which any statements can be based, no building accounts and no contemporary descriptions. However, using what is known about other houses of the period, a likely picture can be built up. This will be done by looking at service rooms, reception and common areas, and finally private rooms.

Service areas

As has been shown, the principal service rooms were concentrated at the east end of the house. The kitchen (G2) would have been a hive of activity, with servants preparing food for a family which eventually numbered eleven. Here, the servants would have eaten on a day-to-day basis. Typical inventories of the period list kitchen items including 'brasse potts greate and smale', 'ketils', 'gret spitts', 'drippinge pannes', 'fryenge pannes', 'platters', 'dishes', 'saw-cers', 'tryvettes', and 'chopping knyves for herbs'.[78] The incorporation of the kitchen within the house was a relatively new idea in the early 16th century and was made possible by the use of brick as the principal building material. In the majority of larger households during this period, the kitchen would have been a detached structure, a necessary precaution since most houses were still of timber and in many cases possessed just one open hearth for heating the hall.

Close to the kitchen, the east cellar probably served as a pantry and larder. The buttery, where drink was put into flagons and pitchers to be taken to the table, was likely to have been housed in the west cellar, entered by an external staircase. Items kept there could have included 'basons and ewars of pewter', 'lether pottes and bottelles', 'bredde bynnes' and 'a joyned frame to sett cuppes upon'. Also commonly listed in inventories are 'greate candlestickes', 'table clothes', 'napkyns' and 'towelles'.[79] In addition, in most houses of the period there existed a bakehouse and brewhouse, often ancillary structures detached from the main building. At Sutton House, however, there is strong evidence that the south-west room on the ground floor (G6) had a service function, perhaps as a brewhouse.

From the kitchen, food would have been carried through to the various rooms of the house used for dining: the hall (G3), high parlour (G4) and great chamber (F3). Linking the kitchen and east cellar, the east staircase led up to the second floor and gave access to the servants' and perhaps also the owner's childrens' bedchambers, as well as any rooms being used for storage. The servants are unlikely to have slept exclusively in the garrets, however. Inventories of the period show that beds were included in many of the principal rooms of the house, including the parlours and great chamber, and were often concentrated around service areas. Although pertaining to a much larger house, the inventory taken in 1517 at the Lovett family's home in Astwell, Northamptonshire, for instance, lists beds in 'the kechyn chamber' and 'the bruhowse chamber'.[80]

Reception and common areas

The hall (G3) was the main reception and common area of Sutton House, in common with nearly all houses of the period. It may have been used as a formal eating room by the household servants and would have been the province of the owner and his family during feasts or public eating. All guests would have passed through the hall which was traditionally decorated with panelling and tapestry wall hangings. The hall in Edmund Dudley's London home included 'an old hangyng of Arys at the hye deace,' and this would not have been atypical.[81] At Sutton House, there is no direct evidence for such decoration, but all the major rooms of the house were certainly designed to be panelled or at least lined, perhaps with stained or painted cloths. Typically, the hall would have contained a long table on trestles, a 'cupbord' (a stepped structure with open shelves on which to store and display plate),[82] side tables and various hangings. At the west end of the hall was the high table and the seat of the head of the household. The table was raised above the level of the hall floor upon a low wooden dais and was lit by windows on opposite sides of the hall.

At the eastern end of the hall, beyond what conventionally would have been the position of the screens passage, was an entrance leading through into what seems to have been a low parlour (G1). Such a space would traditionally have been a service room, but the presence of a rather elaborate Tudor fireplace and some painted wall decoration points to a higher status. Such 'low' parlours were increasingly common by the early 1500s, the additional space becoming available, as in this case, following the removal of the buttery and pantry to the cellars below. The room would have been ideal as a family dining and sitting room for everyday use and had the advantage of warmth, being close to the kitchen. By the end of the 16th century, rooms in this position are often termed the 'winter parlour'.

At Sutton House, it is possible that this room served as private accommodation for the use of Sadleir's steward, Gervase Cawood. Cawood was a senior figure in the household, whose job it was to oversee the work of the servants and to ensure the smooth day-to-day running of the house in Sadleir's absence. The inventory of Compton Wynyates, undertaken in 1522, lists a 'Steward's Chamber', although no position is given for the room,[83] and there was a steward's room next to the hall at Sadleir's later house at Standon (see p 43).

Private areas

At Sutton House the rooms reserved for the owner, his family and guests would have been at the high end and on the first floor. This hierarchy of upstairs and downstairs, high and low ends, had been almost universal since the late Middle Ages and continued in use until the 17th century. The room (G4) off the dais end of the hall was the parlour, one of the key rooms of the house, used as an everyday sitting and eating room and a space for entertaining guests. On the plan in Gervase Markham's *The English Husbandman*, the room in this position is labelled 'The Dining Parlor for entertainment of strangers'.[84] Such a room formed a convenient middle level between the hall: a public, reception area, and the great chamber: a more formal space. In Tudor times, it could also have been used as a bedchamber, although this is unlikely to have been the case at Sutton House, as by the 1530s beds were far less commonly found in parlours. At Sir Thomas Lovell's house at Enfield in 1524, for instance, there was a 'dining parlour' and a 'great parlour', neither of which contained beds.[85] Furnishings and items that the room is likely to have contained include tables, chairs, cupboards, hangings, carpets, 'a fyer forke', a 'fyre pan', and 'a payr of tonges'.[86] In 1522, the parlour at Compton Wynyates included five 'hangings of Tapestry imagery' and six 'cushions feather-stuffed covered with verdure and his [Compton's] Coat of Arms'.[87] Similarly, in 1540, the parlour at Richard Fermor's Easton Neston, Northamptonshire, contained 'six cushions of tapestry with arms in the midst'.[88]

Next door, accessible via an entrance in the south wall, was an inner chamber (G5). Little is known about this room's function, but it appears to have been a secondary or 'little' parlour. Such a room could have been used for relaxation, for informal conversation, or perhaps as a study. On the plan in Gervase Markham's 1613 work the room in this position is marked 'A strangers lodging within the Parlor', which is another possible function, as is that ascribed to a nearby room on the plan, 'An inward closet . . . for the Mistresses use, for necessaries'.[89] In 1517 the Lovett family's home in Northamptonshire had an 'Inner Parlour' containing a 'gret fedd bed with a bolster' and within the room was a 'gentil-wemense chamber'.[90]

From the high end of the house, the family and their guests would have ascended the west staircase and passed into the great chamber (F3), the principal entertaining room of the house. The great chamber, often placed above the hall, increasingly took over the functions of the latter room in the 16th century. It was a formal space, reserved for the entertainment of honoured guests, where great ceremony was attached to the preparation of the table and the serving of meals. One would like to think that Thomas Cromwell dined here when visiting Sadleir. Typically, the great chamber would have contained a large table on trestles, chairs, cupboards, coffers, sometimes a bed for the owner or his guests, and would have been richly adorned. The 'Gret Chambre' at Edmund Dudley's London house, an exceptionally ornate mansion, included 'courteyns of grene say hangyng in the wynddowes', 'a long cussion and ij [two] short cussions of crymeson and blewe velvytt' and 'vij [seven] peces of ymagerie, enbrodrid for the monethes of the yere, to set upon a cloth'.[91] Following the meal, the furniture of the Great Chamber might be pushed back against the wall to provide space for the room's other principal uses: music, dancing and gaming.

Traditionally, a withdrawing room formed a suite with the great chamber and could be used as a place to which guests retired while the main space was being prepared or tidied. At Sutton House, room F1 at the east end of the great chamber could have served such a purpose. There was a door connecting it directly with the great chamber and it was placed at what seems to have been, using the evidence of the windows (see Fig 3.41), the high end of the room. The withdrawing room (F1) could also have been used as a bedchamber but it is unlikely to have been used solely for sleeping. This is implied, as mentioned, by the door connecting it to the great chamber and also by the presence of a garderobe. Garderobes, used since the late Middle Ages, were a private space and were desirable mainly when a chamber had a secondary purpose, perhaps as a living room, as they were not strictly necessary in a principal bedchamber, where only the owner, his immediate family and attendants would have had access.

The room to the south of the withdrawing chamber, F2, would most probably have been an inner bedchamber. Such a room could have been used by guests and, bearing in mind its location adjacent to the east service stair, at other times by the steward.

It is probable that Sadleir's own bedchamber, the place where he would sleep and retire during the day, was that at the west end of the great chamber (F4). This position, above the parlour, was that traditionally occupied by such a room, although by the 17th century the best bedchamber had moved to the low end, which was warmer and more convenient for the overseeing of the household.[92] That F4 was a private bedchamber is suggested by its lack of direct communication with the great chamber; it was accessed only from the west staircase, via the middle chamber at first floor level (the north end of the present room F5). The bedchamber is likely to have been panelled from an early date, as it is now, and would have contained some of the more precious possessions of the house, where the owner could watch over them. In 1539, Sir Adrian Fortescue's 'owen chamber' in his house at Blackfriars in London included 'a cheste at the beddes feete with writings', a 'chest of napery', 'course sheites for servauntes', 'towelles' and 'table clothes'.[93]

The inner chamber (F5) to the south of this room seems to have formed a suite with it and may have been used as a bedchamber by Sadleir's wife or steward, or as a dressing room. At Adrian Fortescue's London home the 'chamber at the stere hedde' appears before his bedchamber and contained a bed, a chest 'with writynges in hit', a cupboard and hangings. Also listed is an 'Inner Chamber' which contained a bed, a press, a chest and various clothes, carpets and cloth.[94]

Beyond the inner chamber was another room, the south-west chamber. This, largely rebuilt in the 18th century, is of uncertain function but could, like the inner chamber, have been used as a bedchamber or dressing room.

Conclusion

As has been seen, Sutton House is a remarkably complete example of a suburban courtier's house of the early 16th century. The house was constructed in brick, a relatively prestigious and expensive material at that time, and was designed and executed in a single build. Although clearly a very modest house compared with the great houses of its time, Sadleir's 'bryk place' was certainly meant to impress. The compact form of the house, with its small courtyard on the south side, resulted in a bold and uniform exterior with an imposing, multi-gabled north façade. In appearance, if not in scale, Sutton House must have vied with some of the best London houses of the day.

As an up-and-coming young courtier, Sadleir was careful not to unsettle or threaten, using certain principles of design and planning that had been common since the Middle Ages. As has been seen, however, Sutton House was built in a most fashionable style, and Sadleir's intimate associations with Thomas Cromwell, Cardinal Wolsey, Henry VIII and the king's works all help to explain unusual features of its plan and external appearance.

As a building type, the 16th-century Sutton House is probably best described as a 'small gentry house'. As a small, early Tudor courtier's house in London, the house has no direct parallels and remains a unique architectural and historical survival.

4
'The Bryk Place'

In the second half of the 16th century Sutton House was owned and occupied by one family, the Machells. Indeed, John Machell the younger, who would have been about 4 years old in 1550 when his father acquired the house, probably lived in it for a longer period than any other resident during its long history. For the most part, this was a period of stability as far as the house was concerned. The Machells were wealthy and, in the person of John Machell the younger, prominent in the local community. Like virtually all the other owners, they left no written record of how they lived in and treated the house, but it can hardly be doubted that they would have used some of their wealth to embellish its still relatively new appearance and to place their own stamp on it. There is a strong probability that the principal surviving 16th-century decorative features, especially the fine panelling, belong to this period.

The stability that characterised most of this period came crashing to a halt as John Machell the younger's occupation of Sutton House ended. A likely date for his departure is 1605 but, as Machell plunged increasingly into debt, there were so many claims and counter-claims about ownership and even tales of physical battles over possession that it is difficult to be certain. In fact, even our relatively certain knowledge of the ownership and occupancy of the house in the 16th century gives way to a period of considerable doubt and confusion for the early 17th century, which is examined in Chapter 5.

John Machell the elder

John Machell purchased 'the bryk place' and most of Ralph Sadleir's other landholdings in Hackney in 1550 (see Fig 3.1). Machell was a highly successful cloth merchant in the City of London, who in his business affairs dealt with the royal household and he may have had dealings with Sadleir in the latter's capacity as Master of the Great Wardrobe before he arranged to buy his house in Hackney.[1]

Machell was born in Kendal in Westmorland but nothing is known of his early life. He was admitted to the freedom of the Clothworkers' Company in London in 1530–1, which suggests that he was born c 1509. He had been apprenticed to a William Corbett, probably a member of the Shearmakers' Company, one of the predecessors of the Clothworkers' Company, not itself formed until 1528. Subsequently he was very active in the affairs of the Clothworkers' Company, being Quarter Warden in 1537–8, Second Warden in 1541 and Master in 1547–8. He was an alderman for Vintry Ward from 1553 to 1556 and for Bassishaw Ward from 1556 to 1558. He was Sheriff of London in 1555–6.[2] He lived in Milk Street, where he died on 12 August 1558. Henry Machyn reported at length on his elaborate funeral at St Mary Magdalene, Milk Street, describing him as a Muscovy merchant who was due to become Lord Mayor had he lived one year longer.[3]

Machell was married first to Ellen Castlelocke of Faversham in Kent; they had three daughters and two sons, both of whom appear to have died young. His second wife was Joan Loddington (or Luddington) and with her he had three sons (John, Mathew and Thomas) and three daughters.

Machell's interest in owning property in Hackney may have sprung from this second marriage. His second wife's mother, also named Joan, had married Sir William Laxton after the death of her first husband, Henry Loddington.[4] Laxton, Lord Mayor in 1544 and founder of Oundle School, was one of the outstanding Londoners of his age. He died in 1556 and Machell was a prominent mourner at his funeral. Lady Joan Laxton outlived him by some twenty years, dying in 1576. Shortly after her death, she was described as having owned land in Hackney a short distance to the east of Sutton House and immediately adjacent to one of the plots purchased from Sadleir by John Machell.[5] Whether she owned this land at the time of the sale, and whether this had some bearing on Machell's decision to buy property in Hackney, is not known. Certainly she appears to have been on good terms with her son-in-law and his family and, in her will, left legacies to the Machell children and made John Machell the younger, whom she described as her godson, one of the overseers of the will.[6] Thus by marriage as well as wealth Machell was drawn into the London aldermanic merchant élite.

John Machell's principal residence appears to have been in Milk Street and he used Sutton House as a 'country' retreat. When he granted a lease of the Tanhouse next door in 1552 to Thomas Knotte, a barber-surgeon, the terms of the lease included a clause that if Machell sold 'his said mansion house at Hackney aforesaid which he now occupiethe' Knotte would be permitted to stop up a door which communicated between the two properties.[7]

Machell's will and the descent of his property

Machell's will, drawn up about two weeks before his death in 1558, was a long and complex document, with each separate property elaborately entailed, but it was defective in many ways and made no specific mention of his property in Hackney.[8] There may be a number of reasons for this. By the time of his death, John Machell the elder had acquired vast estates in Westmorland, Cheshire, Hampshire, Dorset, Hertfordshire and Middlesex besides other property in the City of London. His main concern, after making due provision for his wife, appears to have been to divide his property as equally as possible between his three surviving sons, all of whom were then under age. He was clearly very ill, so he appointed a number of 'supervisors or overseers' to help him draw up the will and to carry out its provisions after his death. There were eleven in all, including his wife, and in allotting specific tasks to them, some matters may have been overlooked.

Mathew Machell, the second son, later claimed that the Tanhouse, which was to be the subject of a lengthy dispute, had been left out of the will by the overseers because they were trying to determine whether it was freehold or copyhold.[9] The manors of both Lordshold and Grumbolds in Hackney were subject to the custom of *gavelkind*, whereby on the death of a copyholder who did not devise his property by will that property was divided between his male heirs. As this was

Machell's overall intention, it may not have seemed crucial to include specific provision for the copyhold property in his will, especially as he appears to have made arrangements for the descent of at least some of it before his death. However, such a will, with its omissions and complications, was a recipe for disputes, and the Machells certainly became a litigious family, frequently taking out suits in the Court of Chancery against each other as well as against third parties.

Exactly how all of John Machell the elder's copyhold property in Hackney was distributed is not known, but each of his three sons received some property there and lived in the parish. Fragmentary surviving records indicate that the small amount of property in Kingshold manor which had been included in the land purchased from Sadleir by Machell was inherited by his second son Mathew, while the cottage or tenement with 3 days' work of land attached in Lordshold manor to the east of Sutton House went to Thomas, the third son. The 18 acres (7.3ha) parcel of pasture called Churchfield (including the field formerly known as Alford's Croft), which was copyhold of the manor of Grumbolds and had been acquired by Sadleir in 1537 together with the Tanhouse, passed to John Machell's widow, Joan, with remainder to John, his eldest son.[10]

The grounds of Sutton House adjoined the southern part of Churchfield, but the whole property was in Lordshold manor, not Grumbolds. Nevertheless, it appears that Machell had made arrangements shortly before his death (subsequently ratified in the manorial court) for the house also to pass to his wife Joan for her lifetime and, after her death, to his eldest son John and his heirs.[11] Joan Machell quickly remarried after her husband's death, her new husband being Sir Thomas Chamberlain, a courtier of some status who had once been Ambassador to the Queen of Hungary. They appear to have continued to live at Sutton House (Chamberlain being assessed for the lay subsidy in Hackney in 1563). After bearing three more children, Joan died in 1565.[12] The house then passed to her eldest son, John, who was still a minor. On 21 October 1567, having attained his majority, he was granted a licence by letters patent to enter into possession of his property and, on 16 December of that year, he was formally admitted into the copyhold ownership of Sutton House in the manorial court.[13]

John Machell the younger

John Machell the younger appears to have inherited little of his father's enterprise. He lived to a ripe old age and was clearly an important person in the context of the history of Sutton House, but what little is known about his life and career has to be pieced together from fragmentary evidence. He was a Justice of the Peace and a Deputy Lieutenant for Middlesex. Although he was described in one pedigree of the Machell family as a Captain of Horse at Tilbury and Master of Horse to Queen Elizabeth, it seems unlikely that he would have occupied such an exalted position as the latter, usually reserved for the upper echelons of the aristocracy. The compiler of the pedigree may have mistaken 'master' for 'muster', as one of the duties occasionally imposed on him as a Justice of the Peace was to muster companies of horse and foot in time of need, as happened in 1595 and 1596.[14] In fact, he seems to have played no significant part in the life of the City and no achievements in any other field are recorded. Were it not for the many legal disputes in which he was embroiled and which cast some light on his character and activities, he would be a very shadowy figure indeed.

The younger John Machell may have gained a taste for litigation at an early age when, in 1563, he was a witness in a suit involving Sir Thomas Lodge, brother-in-law of John Machell the elder and a trustee of his will. The substance of the case was that Katharine, the elder John Machell's sister, had given money to her brother for safe keeping at the beginning of Mary's reign because, as a devout Protestant, she feared that her fortune might be confiscated by the order of the Catholic queen. Her daughter and son-in-law were now claiming that the money had not been repaid, but young John Machell testified that he had been present as a 'servant in house' to Katharine when it had been repaid. Given the elastic use of the term servant in the 16th century, this by no means indicates that he occupied a menial position in his aunt's household. In his deposition he stated that he was 20 years old, but in the inquisition post-mortem taken on his father's death in 1558, he was said to be 12 years and 2 days old when his father died, which would make his age only 16 at the time of his deposition. Thus, even at an early age, he seems to have been prepared to display the cavalier attitude to truth which characterised his later years.[15]

Young Machell may have had good reason to testify on Lodge's behalf, and even perhaps to exaggerate his age to enhance his probity as a witness, for Lodge had been granted the wardship and marriage of the young man on his father's death.[16] He was related to the Machell children through his marriage to their mother's sister, Anne, and was a prominent member of the Grocers' Company. It was probably through his influence that John Machell the younger was apprenticed to a grocer and, in 1568, admitted to the Company, though Machell subsequently played no significant part in the Company's affairs.[17]

John Machell the younger first married Frances Cotton, the daughter of William Cotton of Panfield in Essex, but she died at Sutton House in 1574 giving birth to twins, John and Frances, and was buried at Hackney, where a hatchment to her memory was placed in the old church.[18] However, he soon contracted a highly advantageous second marriage to Ursula Hynde, the daughter of Sir Francis Hynde of Madingley Hall, Cambridgeshire, one of the major landowners in that county. With Ursula he had two sons and a daughter.

Towards the end of his life John Machell the younger said that he had lived in Hackney 'for the greater part of 50 years'[19] and, although he also owned property elsewhere, Sutton House appears to have been his principal residence at least until the first decade of the 17th century. His close attention to his interests there, and his concern to consolidate his position as a landowner in Hackney, are indicated by disputes with his brother, Mathew, particularly over the neighbouring property of the Tanhouse.

Disputes between the Machell brothers

Mathew Machell felt aggrieved because he believed that it had been his father's intention to leave the Tanhouse to him, but that it had been left out of the elder John Machell's will because his 'overseers' were uncertain whether it was freehold or copyhold. Although transactions relating to the Tanhouse continued to be recorded on the court rolls of the manor of Grumbolds, it was categorically declared to be freehold, not copyhold, when Ralph Sadleir bought it in 1537. It was sold on by him as such to Machell in 1550.[20] As freehold, it was not subject to the custom of the manor and descended by right to John Machell the younger as the eldest son and heir.

Initially Mathew Machell received the rents from the property, but this may have been at the insistence of the trustees of the elder John Machell's will who were appointed as guardians of the children while they were minors, even though the younger John Machell later claimed that he had allowed it out of brotherly love.[21] As soon as both children came of age, John Machell appears to have asserted his right to the property, even though at first the brothers combined to seek the forfeiture of a bond entered into by Thomas Knotte, who had assigned his lease of the Tanhouse without seeking the consent in writing of the elder John Machell as was required in the lease.[22]

By 1564 Francis Bowyer, a prominent City merchant, had become the assignee of Knotte's lease and, from about 1570, he was unwittingly caught up in the dispute between the Machell brothers. Mathew Machell claimed that Bowyer had forfeited his lease, presumably by no longer paying rent to him, while John Machell sought to reinforce Bowyer's resistance to these claims. In 1572 John wrote to Bowyer urging him to stand firm and saying that he hoped that Mathew would be content with the mansion house at Shacklewell where he lived.[23] In 1574, after at least one lawsuit and further acrimonious exchanges between Mathew Machell and Bowyer, John Machell sold the Tanhouse to Bowyer.[24] Mathew, however, refused to accept that his brother had the right to sell it and threatened to repossess the house by force. In 1577 John Machell wrote to Bowyer to warn him of his brother's plans:

> I have talked with my brother Mathew Mauchell meeting with him at the church this after noone who stormed rather lyk a myd sumer morn, than of sobrietie, he so fell out with me concernyng yr house as yt was straunge, he meaneth as he sayeth to enter yr house with force & therefore I think yt good that you caused some body to lye the night . . . he sayed yf thear was a great personage wch would be thear on mychellmas day & keap yt by force I belev they be but his mad wordes rather than mater of truth yet to avoyed the worst I thought it good thys much to signefie you having further to empart to you wch I refer to our next meating I hartely byd you faer well, hackney 6 of July 1577
>
> yr assured neyghbor
> John Mauchell [25]

Bowyer continued to enjoy possession of the Tanhouse, even if somewhat uneasily at times, and Mathew Machell continued to fulminate, becoming involved in lawsuits with all and sundry, including his brother John, whom he accused of wrongfully depriving him of his inheritance.[26] It was all to no avail. Mathew Machell died in 1593 and Bowyer retained the ownership of the Tanhouse.

The third Machell brother, Thomas, lived in the house on the south side of Homerton Street with 3 days' work of land attached which lay to the east of Sutton House. He also held other property nearby but his behaviour was sometimes erratic and, taking advantage of the confusions attendant on their father's bequests, John Machell laid claim to this property, ostensibly to protect his brother's interests. In 1577 a commission of lunacy was issued against Thomas Machell, and he died in 1581. His death almost inevitably led to yet another Chancery case between John and Mathew Machell. Mathew was apparently being sued for slander by someone he had called a cheat for trying to rob his brother Thomas. Taking advantage of Thomas's 'simplicitie', Mathew had persuaded him to enter into a bond to indemnify him against the results of this suit. John Machell, who was his brother's administrator, thereupon contested the validity of the bond. At his death Thomas left an infant son, Francis, but he died shortly afterwards and John Machell inherited his brother's property as his next heir.[27]

The origin of the name Sutton House

In 1605 Sir William Bowyer, son of the Francis Bowyer who had purchased the Tanhouse from John Machell the younger in 1574, sold the property to Thomas Sutton, founder of the hospital and school of Charterhouse.[28] Sutton lived at the Tanhouse and on his death in 1611 bequeathed the property to Charterhouse. The perpetuation of his name in Sutton Place, the terrace of houses which was laid out on the site in the early 19th century, later gave rise to the misconception that Sutton had lived in the adjoining mansion, which was accordingly given the name Sutton House in the 1950s. One of John Machell's last recorded acts as the owner of this house took place in June 1605, when he granted to Sutton the ground on which he had built a brick wall bordering on

Machell's property.[29] In fact, as will be explained below, Machell may have undertaken this uncharacteristic act of largesse in the full knowledge that his claim to still be the owner of Sutton House was tenuous in the extreme.

Machell's land dealings

In the 1590s John Machell the younger appears to have been at the height of his power and influence, at least in local affairs. He played a major part in the deliberations of the Hackney vestry, and in an assessment made in 1594 for the fitting out of three soldiers, he was the highest-rated resident in Homerton. In addition, as we have seen, in 1595–6 he was appointed by the Privy Council to take musters of troops in Middlesex.[30] However, at the very time that he was achieving such a prominent position in the community, he was beginning to encounter the serious financial problems that were eventually to undermine him totally.

From the 1570s Machell had begun to accumulate land in Cambridgeshire, the county of his second wife's family. In 1588 he purchased the substantial manor of Hinxton, subsequently said to be worth £300 *per annum*. Three years later he bought an even larger estate centred on the manor of Woodbury or Westhorpe which appears to have consisted of over 1,800 acres (728.5ha) with sundry houses and other buildings attached.[31] These purchases must have severely stretched his financial resources and, to help pay for Woodbury in 1591, he borrowed £600 from Edward Holmeden, a member of the Grocers' Company and fellow Hackney resident, at the high rate of interest of 10 per cent, mortgaging Sutton House and the 18 acres (7.3ha) of Churchfield as security. Three years later he mortgaged the property to James Deane, another City merchant, presumably in order to repay Holmeden, and in 1596 he borrowed a further £1,000 from Deane on the security of the manor of Hinxton, although in the latter case the mortgage was executed in the name of Richard Deane, James Deane's brother.[32]

(Sir) James Deane

James Deane, born in or near Basingstoke in 1545, had been apprenticed to a member of the Drapers' Company, becoming free in 1570. He was Warden of the Company in 1594, 1598 and 1600, and served as Master from 1602 to 1603. Deane was also a founder-director of the East India Company in 1600, a position which may have had some bearing on the history of Sutton House. In 1604 he was elected as an alderman of Farringdon Ward Without. He also received a knighthood in the same year, an honour which probably owed more to his wealth than any other factor, given the propensity of James I to bestow knighthoods on anyone he felt might help him out of his financial difficulties. He was married three times, firstly in 1576 to Susan Bomsted, secondly in 1585 to Elizabeth Offley, daughter of Hugh Offley, Sheriff of London in 1588, and thirdly to Elizabeth Thornhill, but had no surviving children (Fig 4.1).

As well as being a successful merchant, probably in the clothing trade, Deane was also one of those quintessential early 17th-century figures: a money-lender. In 1601 he was upbraided by the Privy Council for hounding another merchant who had fallen into his debt, and the ferocity with which he prosecuted his claim against Machell suggests that he was quite unscrupulous in pursuing anyone who encountered difficulties in repaying his loans.[33]

Deane's principal residence was in Mark Lane in the City, but from at least the late 1590s he also lived in Hackney, where he had a substantial copyhold house with an orchard, garden and other land attached on the south side of Homerton Street. Subsequent transactions involving this property suggest that it was close to Machell's house: it may have been the house to the east of Sutton House with 3 days' work of land attached which had formed part of the estate sold by Sadleir to Machell's father in 1550 and was subsequently occupied by Thomas Machell before passing, on his death and that of his infant son, to John Machell. There is no indication, however, that Deane acquired the house from John Machell, and it may have passed through other hands first. Nor is it known when Deane moved there, but by the time he came to draw up his will in 1607, he was sufficiently well established to have built a barn and two stables in the grounds.[34]

Machell's dispute with Deane

By the mid-1590s Machell was having to sell some parcels of land in Cambridgeshire and grant annuities on others on unfavourable

Figure 4.1
Monument to Sir James
Deane (d 1608) *in the*
Church of St Olave,
Hart Street, City of
London.
[Mike Gray]

terms to cover debts.[35] He was clearly in considerable financial difficulties, although apparently determined to hold on to Woodbury. In 1594 he narrowly avoided arrest in London for a minor debt and his brother-in-law, William Hynde, was sufficiently worried about the situation to take out a Chancery suit against him in 1598 complaining that Machell had agreed to convey property in Woodbury to him in trust for his sister Ursula, Machell's second wife, and their children. He said that a deed had been drawn up but that he had mislaid his copy of it and he thought that there was 'great danger' that Machell would not honour the deed.[36]

By this time Hynde had every reason to be concerned. None of the principal and very little of the interest on the mortgages to James Deane had been repaid and the debts now amounted to over £2,000. Deane had been prepared to accept a remortgage of Hinxton, still in his brother's name, to cover the excess amount, but demanded as recompense that Machell should sell him an orchard in Hackney at a nominal price,

setting a deadline of midsummer 1598 for repayment of the debts. When that time passed and still no repayments were forthcoming, Deane took legal steps to obtain possession of the mortgaged properties.

Exactly what happened next was subsequently disputed between the parties. Certainly, the records of the manor of Grumbolds show that in 1598 Deane was admitted into possession of Churchfield because the small amount of the mortgage (£160) secured on that property had not been repaid, but Machell appears to have resisted Deane's attempts to possess Sutton House, perhaps by force, and to have tried to retain some hold on Hinxton. As a result Deane obtained a writ of extent on Machell's main manor of Woodbury and temporarily seized possession of it.[37]

The dispute was then referred to the courts. In 1600 a thoroughly exasperated Richard Deane instituted a lawsuit in which he accused Machell of 'unconscionable dealinge', describing him as a man 'without respect of truthe or regard of his own conscience' and his prevarication as 'most odious and hatefull'.[38] Richard Deane died in the following year, and James Deane became the actual mortgagee of Hinxton as well as Sutton House. This time it was Machell who sought redress in the Court of Chancery, relying on his equity of redemption and claiming that Hinxton and Sutton House were worth far more than the amount owed and that Deane had already received his money back through taking the profits of Woodbury. The matter was referred to two Masters in Chancery who found that Machell still owed Deane over £2,000, and a decree was made in June 1602 ordering Machell to pay the outstanding amount within three months or lose his case. He failed to make the payment and in October 1602 judgement was made against him.[39]

From this point James Deane could probably be said to have had a clear title to the properties in dispute or, as Machell's grandson was later to put it, to have secured 'the forfeiture of Hinxton and Hackney absolutely'.[40] Machell, however, appears to have retained physical possession of Sutton House and refused to admit defeat. Deane thereupon brought a case against him in the Court of Star Chamber which lasted from at least 1603 to 1605. For a civil suit to be heard in Star Chamber, a degree of riot or assault had usually to be demonstrated, and for this reason the violence which was said to have taken place was frequently exaggerated. By no means all the records of this particular case have survived, but the impression left is of a very bitter conflict between Machell and Deane and their respective supporters.

Deane claimed that he had taken possession of Sutton House in 1598. According to the account of witnesses favourable to the Machells, Ursula Machell accompanied by a companion and a servant then entered the house by stealth through a back door into the kitchen and regained possession. A witness for Deane asserted, however, that a party of Machell's followers headed by his wife and younger son, William, had come to the house armed with swords, halberds and bills and had seized the house back, retaining possession ever since by force. This latter scenario seems inherently unlikely, as it is improbable that Machell could have kept possession of the house for several years under such circumstances.

More credible, largely because it resulted in an appearance before the Quarter Sessions, is the account of a fight in the fields of Woodbury between the headstrong William Machell, with others of his father's party, and some of Deane's supporters, involving the use of pikestaffs and poles; one of the group also had a rapier, but he claimed not to have used it. From the corroboration of witnesses, there is also a ring of truth to Machell's claim that in 1599 Deane, in the company of the Under-Sheriff of Cambridgeshire and armed with a writ of liberate, had seized the manor house of Woodbury and forcibly ejected his wife and servants who had taken refuge in some upper rooms. The precise outcome of the case is not known but the judgement appears to have favoured Deane.[41]

The grant of a small piece of land adjoining Sutton House to Thomas Sutton (see pp 94–5) would suggest that Machell was still in possession of the house in June 1605 and that Sutton recognised him as the owner. His name was not, however, included in a list of contributors to the church rate in Hackney in the latter part of that year, although that of his brother-in-law, Sir William Hynde (knighted in 1603) was, which gives rise to an intriguing possibility. Several years later, Machell's grandson claimed that his 'Grandmother in Lawe', that is his step-grandmother Ursula Machell, had been 'kept from the sight of his said Grandfather and made even as a straunger to him and all his estate' during John Machell's time of trouble. We have seen how Hynde, who was a Member of Parliament, had already been concerned for his sister's interest, and it may be that Ursula Machell and her family remained at Sutton House, perhaps by arrangement with Deane, and that her brother lived with her to protect her when he was in London, while Machell was forced to take up residence elsewhere. Certainly, Deane would have wished to remain on as good terms as possible with such an important landed family, and Edward Hynde, another brother, was the actual lessee of his manor of Hinxton. Additionally, Sir William Hynde was, with Deane, one of the founder-directors of the East India Company.[42]

Machell's imprisonment

When John Machell finally met his nemesis in 1606, it was surprisingly not in the shape of Deane, but of one Walter Halliley, the son of Richard Halliley, a long-time resident of Hackney who had died earlier in that year, bequeathing to his son an outstanding debt from Machell. Halliley had Machell arrested in Hackney, though not apparently at Sutton House but at another house where he was said to be in hiding (which fits in with the suggestion that he was no longer living at Sutton House). Machell claimed that the shock of being so publicly disgraced in a place where he had lived in such good repute for so long caused a long and languishing sickness, during which several judgements were recorded against him in the Court of King's Bench. He was committed to the King's Bench Prison, where he remained for over six years.[43] Ironically, his erstwhile guardian and mentor, Sir Thomas Lodge, had also suffered imprisonment for debt.[44]

Later lawsuits

When Machell was finally released from prison, apparently in 1612, he brought a number of cases in Chancery to try to recover his property. By now he was describing himself as of Woodbury, not of Hackney. One of his first actions, in July 1612, was against Holmeden, accusing him of failing to resurrender his Hackney property in the manorial courts as he should have done when the mortgage was repaid. Holmeden replied that he couldn't remember whether he had actually resurrendered the property, but that in any event he was under the impression that it had been surrendered since then to James Deane, who had died, and that Deane's heirs or assigns had asserted their right and title to the property.[45]

Machell then appears to have turned his ire against his eldest son, John, accusing him of conspiring with his (John's) wife, Katharine, her brother, Jasper Leake, and another relative, Thomas Hughes, to steal his title deeds to the property in question.[46] He also claimed that his son had been the principal author of his misfortunes by his 'undutiful and unthrifty courses' leading to considerable debts which, as his father, he had had to repay by borrowing money. He further asserted that his son had 'unnaturally and most wickedly' conspired with his creditors and connived at his arrest, preventing him from receiving bail. Warming to his theme, he declared in a most unfatherly way that 'Yet such was the will of God that the said John Mauchell the Younger [his son] not long after died . . . And now that yt has pleased God by the death of the said John Mauchell the

Younger to prevent all their purposes'. Halliley, against whom this particular suit had been brought, denied vehemently that Machell's son had conspired against his father and claimed that the debts in question had been entirely those of the older Machell. John Machell thereupon retired to Woodbury, 'worn out with care and grief for his great losses', and died in 1624 or 1625, when his remaining estates descended to his grandson, also named John.[47]

The disposition of Machell's former property

Sir James Deane, who was the author of so much of Machell's misfortune, had himself died on 15 May 1608. In his will he left the manor of Hinxton 'sometime John Mauchell's' to five of his nephews. He also said that, besides his own house in Hackney, he was seized of 'one great capitall messuage or tenement orchard and garden thereunto belonging . . . in homerton streete . . . and eighteen acres of pasture ground . . . knowne by the name of Churchfeilde . . . which I late had and purchased of John Machell'.[48] There seems little doubt that the 'great capitall messuage' to which he was referring was Sutton House and that 'purchased' was a euphemistic way of describing how he had acquired the property. He left the house to his widowed niece, Olive Clarke, for her lifetime and then to her children, share and share alike. He likewise bequeathed his own house in Homerton, after the death of his own wife, to Olive Clarke and her children.

The Machell family, however, continued to seek redress for the wrongs they felt they had suffered. In 1627 John Machell's grandson instituted proceedings in Chancery against Deane's heirs, claiming 'relief' for his grandfather's losses. His argument was that Deane had taken advantage of all his grandfather's difficulties and that Hinxton and Sutton House were worth far more than the actual sum borrowed. The matter was referred to one of the Masters in Chancery who placed a total value of £5,300 on Hinxton and Sutton House with its accompanying land in Hackney, of which a quarter was approximately the value of the latter. The defendants argued that the property was overvalued, that money had been spent in resisting claims to it, and that some shares of the ownership of Hinxton had already changed hands for money. The court nevertheless looked sympathetically on Machell's case and was inclined to accept that his grandfather 'was gott out of the said manor and lands at an undervalue'. It asked the parties to come together to see if some accommodation could be made, but whatever compensation was offered to Machell proved to be unacceptable and finally, in some exasperation, the court threw out his case. The whole proceedings had lasted some seven years.[49]

Machell was still not prepared to admit defeat. In 1641 he submitted a petition to the House of Lords on the grounds that the dismissal of his suit had been contrary to all equity. The Committees for Petitions set a date for the hearing of the cause before the House, but this was a time during the early period of the Long Parliament when private petitions were continually being set aside because of the press of state business, and there is no record of the case ever coming to judgement.[50]

The fabric

The exterior of the house appears to have remained relatively unaltered during the Machells' occupation, apart from some changes to the fenestration which are discussed in the accounts of individual rooms below. The most substantial work consisted of alterations to both staircases and the installation of panelling in several of the principal rooms. As the use of the hall diminished, other rooms would have assumed greater importance. These included the great chamber (F3) above the hall, and the bedchamber (F4) at the front of the west wing, on the first floor, and particularly the ground-floor high (linenfold) parlour (G4) in the same wing, which would probably have been the room in which the family took their main meals and where they received guests during the day. These three rooms retain the oldest and best panelling in the house.

Leaving aside the question of whether Ralph Sadleir himself might have made some changes to the house during his relatively brief occupation, alterations would have certainly been carried out by the wealthy John Machell when he purchased the house in 1550, and by his son, John Machell the younger, during his long period of occupancy. The latter's financial difficulties may have been caused in small part by expenditure on his house, but the main reason was undoubtedly that he had

overextended himself in purchasing land elsewhere.

The survey of the fabric revealed evidence of some later 16th-century alterations, and there may well have been others which have been obscured by later rebuilding. Only those rooms in which significant changes are thought to have taken place during the Machell family's occupation are described below.

The interior

The cellars

The inconvenience of having only an external access to the west cellar was remedied at an early date when two joists were removed at the southern end and an opening was formed to create the present staircase descending from the ground floor (*see* Fig 3.23). The lower flight of the staircase was reconstructed in 1981, but elsewhere those treads which have been formed from solid lengths of squared timber split diagonally may be original. Apparently at the same time as the interior stairs were formed, the floor of the cellar was lowered by some 240mm. The external entrance must have remained in use, however, as notches were made in the brickwork below the door threshold to enable a removable ramp or steps to be used to facilitate access.

Any changes to the east cellar at this time have been obscured by the substantial alterations of later periods (*see* Fig 8.14).

The ground floor (Fig 4.2)

Low parlour (G1)
As discussed in Chapter 3, there are indications that this room was intended to have a relatively high status from the outset or was raised in status at an early date. If it did serve as a buttery or steward's room during Sadleir's occupancy of the house, its function would almost certainly have changed when John Machell moved in. Machell was a merchant, not a politician or courtier, and moreover one whose principal residence was in the City of London, where he would have fulfilled whatever obligations of hospitality his aldermanic status dictated. He would have had little need in Sutton House for elaborate service quarters, and the room may have been converted into a low parlour at this time.

A decorative scheme was applied to the wall plaster (Fig 4.3; *see also* Fig 3.28). This consisted of painted golden-yellow bands,

Figure 4.2
Plan of the ground floor
c 1600.
(Scale 1:200)

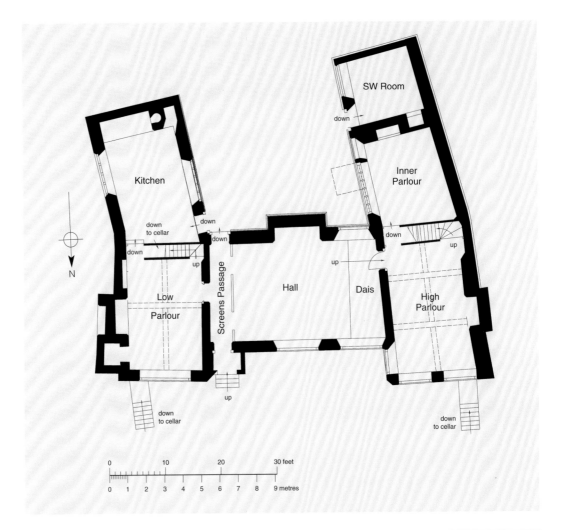

Figure 4.3
Room G1. Decorative late
16th- or 17th-century
painted wall decoration,
discovered behind panelling
removed from the west wall
during restoration.
[Mike Gray]

approximately 200mm in width, both horizontal and vertical, which formed 'frames'. A thin black border emphasised the bands in some areas, and the plaster panels left in between these 'frames' appear to have been lime-washed. Traces of a similar golden-yellow paint were found on a 'filling' applied over the mouldings of the stone fireplace, on its northern jamb.

This scheme was possibly intended to imitate timber-framing but there is evidence that wall-coverings or hangings were stretched and crudely fixed with nails over the plaster. The presence of green wool in the weaving of the few surviving fragments and the coarse quality of the material suggest that they were thick woollen hangings. Thus the painted bands, which are particularly evident at the junctions of walls and ceiling and around the original openings and other features in the walls, but which otherwise form no distinct pattern, may have been intended to 'frame' the wall hangings. At some point these were crudely torn down, leaving strands attached to the fixing nails, possibly when the present panelling was erected in the 18th century, as no other later form of decoration is apparent.

The south partition wall may well have been moved northward to its present position in this period to accommodate changes to the east staircase. This would have occurred at the same time as, or before, the decorative scheme was applied to the walls. The door opening at the west end of this wall would have been blocked in as part of these alterations and was reopened in the 18th century.

East staircase

The insertion of the present staircase in the 18th century has obscured much of the evidence of the earlier form of the staircase here, but it appears that the original steep and uncomfortably narrow stairs from the ground to the first floor were widened during this period. The winders at the bottom were straightened and a new opening was formed in the recess in the west wall to allow direct access to the hall (Fig 4.4). This involved chamfering the timber lintel over the new opening to ease the headroom, still plainly evident today.

Kitchen (G2)

Early changes to the kitchen which can be deduced include the reduction in overall size of the range, the sealing of the original bread

oven and the creation of a new bread oven on the east side of the range. The high-level window near the southern end of the east wall was made double-height by lowering the sill, and the floor of the room was raised, although it would still have been lower than the present level (*see* Figs 6.12 and 6.15).

Hall (G3)

The hall may have declined in importance as the century progressed, but any changes that were made to its appearance during this period have been obscured by the wholesale later alterations.

Figure 4.4
East staircase. View from half landing down to ground-floor level, prior to the exposure of the lintel.

High (linenfold) parlour (G4)

Dendrochronological examination of some of the oak panels carved with a linenfold pattern which cover the walls of the high parlour (Fig 4.5; *see also* Fig 8.15) has indicated that the panelling is probably as early in date as the construction of the house, or may even be older. The test results also suggest that even the uniformly early panels (excluding those that were introduced later as alterations were made to the room) are not particularly homogeneous and may have come from different sources. Such finely carved panelling was valuable and it was quite common for it to be moved from house to house. In this instance variations in the size of the panels, and the way in which they were assembled in various parts of the room, may indicate both that the panelling was adapted to fit the room and that subsequent rearrangement has also taken place.

As discussed in Chapter 3, there is also evidence that the present panelling was not the earliest form of wall covering in this room. Wool fibres found trapped behind nails in the brickwork above the fireplace on the west wall may have come from a hanging.

Additionally, a row of four square sockets to house timber blocks which would have acted as fixing points for the panelling were cut into the brickwork along the top of the west wall after the original construction of the wall (*see* Fig 3.47).

The weight of evidence, therefore, indicates that the very fine linenfold panelling in this room, shown reinstated and restored in Figure 4.6, was introduced soon after the house was built, perhaps by the second owner, John Machell the elder. Subsequently, adjustments were made and some new panels carved to accommodate alterations to the room. The panelling survived the many changes made to the house and the vicissitudes of fortune of its owners over four centuries. While it was in store following its theft and subsequent recovery, it was subjected to a minute examination (Fig 4.7). This close analysis, aided by photographs and drawings, not only enabled the sequence of panelling which existed immediately prior to the theft to be recreated, but has also assisted in the interpretation of earlier arrangements of the panels and subsequent adjustments to these. This in turn has provided a better understanding of the changes which were made to the room.

The panelling of the east wall has been least altered and displays best the pattern of framing which would have been generally adopted when the panelling was introduced. The sections are five panels in height and all framing pieces are joined with single pegs. The panels of the top row are of reduced

height and allowed for a cornice 90mm deep (replaced in the mid-18th century by a deeper cornice). As an aid to assembly, Roman numerals were scribed on the rear face of the top two rails of some sections to indicate the correct sequence of panels.

Even here, however, changes were apparently made soon after the panelling had been installed. In particular, a high opening (Fig 4.8) was cut into the wall at its northern end

Figure 4.8
Room G4. Blocked window opening at north end of east wall.

to form a window in the short stretch of walling of the west wing which projected from the centre of the north front. The only feasible reason for such an opening at a high level appears to have been to let in more light to a rather dark room; awkward as the alteration now appears, in the 16th century it would have seemed appropriate as a continuation of the high-level window or windows in the north front of the wing. The opening may have been closed internally by a pair of shutters, as there is a simple hook hinge driven into the brickwork at the upper south corner of the opening. In making the opening, little consideration was given to supporting the brickwork above, and the absence of a lintel led subsequently to the loss of the lowest brick course and necessitated plaster repair. Eventually the opening was filled in with reused 16th-century bricks and timber props during the 18th-century alterations and only rediscovered during the survey of the fabric.

The uncovering of the opening assisted in an understanding of the wall panelling and its early decoration. Not only was the size and shape of the opening determined by the framing pattern of the panelling, but its plaster reveals were painted in a *trompe l'œil* manner to simulate the carved panels. The colours found here provided startling evidence of the vivid decorative treatment

Figure 4.9
Room G4. One of the painted and plastered reveals of the former window opening surviving behind the 18th-century brickwork blocking.

which had once been applied to the panelling as a whole (Fig 4.9). A similar effect was observed on the remains of the plaster reveals of the high-level window(s) at each end of the much-altered north front.

Some plain wooden panels which were recovered along with the carved linenfold panelling were similarly painted in a *trompe l'œil* fashion to simulate linenfold carving (Fig 4.10). From the analysis of the sequence of panels, these had originally been placed on the lower part of the east wall but were subsequently covered with carved panels, perhaps in the 17th century. The unmoulded panels appear to have been erected in a position where the scraping of chair backs and other furniture would have done most damage to the carved panels themselves. Their use may relate to a decision taken either when the panelling was first introduced or slightly later to extend its use into the middle room of the west wing (G5), in which case there might not have been enough carved panels for both rooms. During the restoration in the 1990s several of the carved panels which cover these uncarved, painted panels have been hinged to facilitate inspection by visitors.

The evidence, of which a surprising amount has survived, shows that in the dominant decorative scheme the framing of the panels was painted a dark Indian red, perhaps with black dry-brushed over to create a marbled appearance. A cross motif was stencilled in gold at each intersection of the framing pieces, and a smaller oval motif stencilled midway between the intersections (Figs 4.11 and 4.12). The panels were initially given a coat of pale yellow paint, and the plain fielded background was then painted olive-copper green, leaving the raised, carved linenfolds in pale yellow. Where a *trompe l'œil* effect was desired, the same colours were used with the addition of vertical stripes of light cream and orange-brown over the pale yellow area to suggest the relief of the carved panels (Fig 4.13). A parallel for this bold decoration of the panelling occurs at Canons Ashby, Northamptonshire.

It is not known when this particular decorative scheme was applied. The panelling appears to have been painted prior to its erection in this room, and more than one phase of decoration can be traced. There is some evidence of earlier colours such as grey or cream on the framing pieces, and of the use of Venetian red immediately after the opening was cut in the east wall.

Figure 4.10 (above left) A trompe l'œil *painted plain wooden panel from room G4, discovered during the detailed study of the* ex-situ *panelling.*

Figure 4.11 (above right) Section of dismantled panelling from room G4 with traces of decorative gold stencilling.

Figure 4.12 (above left) Two abutting sections of linenfold panelling with the later cover strip removed to reveal the early decorative stencilling.

Figure 4.13 (above right) Reconstruction of the linenfold panelling in room G4 as it might have appeared in the late 16th or early 17th centuries.
[Richard Bond]

Figure 4.14
Room G6. High-level window opening in the east wall uncovered during the restoration, which may have lit a small closet area formed within the south end of the former central ground-floor chamber.

The panelling may have been repainted as part of a bold redecoration of the west wing which was undertaken by the Milward family in the 17th century (*see* pp 121–2), and further evidence for this possibility is noted in the account of the inner parlour (G5) below. However, the fashion of painting the panelling in bold colours appears to have continued in this house from its first installation until the major alterations of the mid-18th century.

Subsequent rearrangements of the panelling which occurred in succeeding centuries are described in later chapters, but it should be borne in mind that its present appearance is a 20th-century interpretation of what Tudor linenfold panelling would have looked like. It is largely the result of stripping and varnishing which was first undertaken *c* 1904 and is far removed from reality, at least in the case of Sutton House.

Inner parlour (G5)

The high status formerly accorded to this room has been alluded to in Chapter 3 and, as a result of that status, it seems likely that it was also decorated with carved oak linenfold panelling now found only in the high (linenfold) parlour (G4). No trace of the actual panelling now remains in the much altered room, but its presence at one time appears to be the only satisfactory explanation for two remaining areas of painted decoration.

The first of these is on the plaster surfaces of a small, splayed high-level window opening which, like that in the north-east corner of the high (linenfold) parlour, was cut into the brickwork shortly after the house was built (Fig 4.14). This opening, which was also subsequently filled in, is now in the north-east corner of room G6 but was originally in the south-east corner of the inner parlour before the rearrangement of these rooms after the demolition of the cross-stack which formerly divided them (*see* Figs 3.82 and 4.2).

The reasons for the insertion of such an opening here are even more mysterious than those for the similar opening in the high (linenfold) parlour (G4). It would have been immediately next to the surviving large, double-height, twelve-light window which should have provided ample light to the chamber already. If part of this window had been blocked off, perhaps by the construction of an external structure in the courtyard, there might have been a need for an extra window. Similarly, if such a large

window did not offer enough privacy to the occupants of the room, the lower lights might have been blocked and the window extended at high level. The sill of the opening appears to follow the line of the transom of the main window, and such an alteration would have produced an arrangement similar to that which prevailed in most of the rooms on the ground floor. One other possibility, that the window may have been cut to light a closet which was formed in this corner of the room, might just have worked on plan, but takes no account of the decoration of the interior of the opening which is far too elaborate merely to serve a small closet.

All of the internal surfaces of the opening, including the splayed sill, were coated with a thin skim of lime plaster, bound and reinforced with hair and then decorated. The decoration is in the same style as that of the similar opening in the high (linenfold) parlour (G4) and also simulates linenfold panelling in a *trompe l'œil* manner.

Here, however, the colours are not as rich and the panels are smaller. The background is formed by yellow ochre with light brown stencilling for the framing and bands of dark green paint for the raised, carved parts of the panels. Several later coverings of lime wash were applied to the decoration and the scheme may be an earlier version of that in the high (linenfold) parlour.

The other area of painted plaster imitating linenfold panelling is to the left of the doorway into the cellar (Fig 4.15). Here the technique and colours more closely resemble the decoration of the window reveals and wooden panels in the high (linenfold) parlour (G4). Close analysis of this painting in conjunction with the strapwork decoration of the staircase, which is thought to date from the 1630s, has revealed areas of overlap which suggest that the two schemes were contemporary. This may indicate that the particularly bold painting of the linenfold panelling and adjacent areas of *trompe l'œil* decoration in the high (linenfold) parlour dates from the 17th rather than the 16th century, when perhaps more muted colours were used, or at least that an earlier scheme was retained and presumably embellished when the west wing was modernised by the introduction of a new staircase in the 17th century.

The area in front of the door to the west cellar would have formed a small passageway between the high (linenfold) parlour (G4) and the inner parlour. This makes the use of such elaborate decoration to produce the appearance of linenfold panelling by the side of the cellar door all the more remarkable. When considered in conjunction with the survival of a similar, but perhaps earlier, decorative scheme in the previously blocked window opening described above, it strongly suggests that in the later 16th century the entire sequence of domestic rooms and linking passageway on the ground floor of the west wing was either lined with multi-coloured linenfold panelling or, in some areas, painted to give the appearance of being panelled in such a manner. (It will be recalled that the south-west room (G6) was cut off from the other rooms on the ground floor of the wing and was only accessible from the outside at this time.)

The first floor

Great chamber (F3)

The rise in importance of the great chamber during the course of the 16th century as the use of the hall beneath declined is reflected

Figure 4.15
Traces of the early trompe l'œil *decorative scheme in the area adjacent to the entrance of the west cellar (room G5) undergoing conservation.*
[Ken Jacobs]

in the high quality of the oak panelling with which its walls were lined. Most of the present panelling, although much adapted and rearranged as changes have been made to the room, dates from the late 16th or early 17th century (*see* Fig 3.71).

There are three main types of panelling. The predominant type is to be found on the east, west and north walls. It has been determined by dendrochronological analysis that the timber which was used to make this panelling came from trees which were felled between 1598 and 1618. Formed of regular panels, measuring approximately 325 × 365mm, it is assembled in vertical sections, six panels in height. The identical mouldings on the muntins and the bottom of the rails were worked out of the solid and mitred at their junctions, the top edge of the rails having a plain chamfer. Four round oak pegs were used to join the muntins and rails. Planted beads used during construction in difficult areas, such as over doors, have identical profiles to the other muntins and rails. On the east wall, where a doorway led into room F1, a new door was constructed out of a section of panelling, moulded on both sides, and positioned in the opening. When this wall was made into a party wall during the alterations of the mid-18th century the doorway was bricked up and the

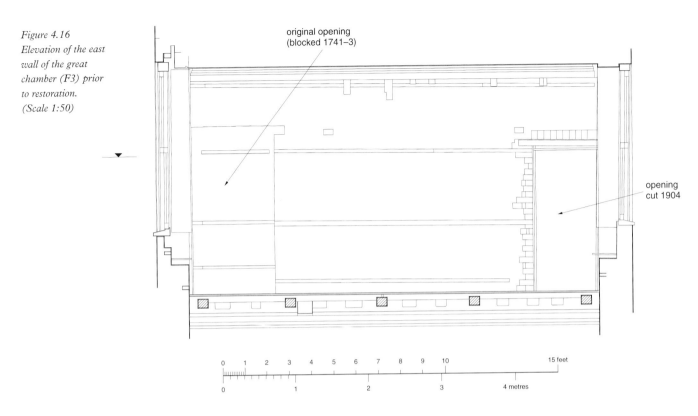

original opening
(blocked 1741–3)

opening
cut 1904

```
0   1   2   3   4   5   6   7   8   9   10        15 feet

0           1           2           3        4 metres
```

panelled door simply nailed shut over the new brickwork (Fig 4.16).

The main sections of panelling on the south wall are formed of rectangular panels with plain chamfers to the top rails, moulded muntins and scratch beads over the panels on the bottom rails (Fig 4.17). The sections are basically six panels in height but the dimensions of the panels themselves vary and the rails do not always form a continuous horizontal line. The results of the dendrochronological investigation indicate that this far less homogeneous panelling is earlier than the remainder in date and has been reset. Apart from the panels above the fireplace, which are described below, the areas of different panelling on this wall, such as that in the recess at the west end formed to facilitate the opening of the door into the room from the head of the west staircase, are probably the result of later changes.

The third type of panelling in the room consisted of ten elaborately carved panels above the fireplace in the centre of the south wall (Fig 4.18; *see also* Fig 6.24). These panels were stolen when the house was untenanted in the 1980s and have not been recovered. Nevertheless, they were well recorded in drawings and photographs, and these were used to recreate the panels during the restoration of the house in the 1990s (*see* Fig 3.71). Several of the reproduction panels have been hinged to allow sight of the Tudor brickwork behind them.

The original panels are difficult to interpret. They were raised and carved with a central rose and a *fleur-de-lis* in each corner. The rails had continuous scratch beads and stopped chamfers on the top and bottom edges respectively, and the slender muntins had similar scratch beads with a raised centre.

At first sight they would appear to have been early-Tudor in date, but the central design was not the usual representation of a Tudor rose and the panels appear to fit the present reduced fireplace opening, not the original larger fireplace. Additionally, the rails did not line up with those of the plain panelling on each side. They may date from the 17th century when elaborate wooden overmantels were created in the panelled rooms at the front of the west wing, but there is no evidence that the fireplace in this room was altered before the 18th century.

The panelling would seem to have been painted shortly after its first fixing, as several layers of mainly cream-coloured paint were found on it, but less is known about its original appearance than of that in the high (linenfold) parlour (G4). As is the case in that room, when looking at the fine and mostly old panelling in the great chamber today, the caveat has to be made that it has been substantially rearranged, particularly as a result of the major alterations made to the room in the mid-18th century. Insofar as it was possible to determine where changes had been made to the panelling, these are described in later chapters.

Figure 4.18
The fireplace of room F3 in 1920 showing the former decorative carved panels above the fireplace. These panels were stolen in the 1980s and were replaced by reproductions during the restoration.
[London Metropolitan Archives]

Bedchamber (F4)

The mid- to late-16th-century oak panelling on the east, south and west walls of the bed-chamber at the front of the west wing is approximately contemporary in date with that on the south wall of the great chamber (F3). The panelling on the north wall, where the fenestration was radically altered in the 18th century, dates mainly from the 18th and 19th centuries (Fig 4.19).

The older panelling, which would once have also extended across the north wall, may have been designed specifically for the room; at least there is no clear evidence that it was adapted from elsewhere. Chalked Roman numerals and other identification marks on the rear of most of the sections indicate that it has been re-erected at least once, possibly in the 17th century, and some repair and alteration has taken place, especially on the south, partition wall, where changes to the doorways have had to be accommodated.

The panels themselves measure 375 × 265mm, unassembled; they are plain with no decoration, although they are fielded on the back face to allow fitting into the grooves of the muntins and rails. The panels are approximately 12mm thick and the muntins and rails are 70mm wide and

15mm thick. The rails have a running plain chamfer cut into their top edge, and scratch beads, cut over each panel, on their bottom edge. The muntins have identical running mouldings on both sides. They are joined to the rails with mortise and tenon joints held with four round oak pegs 6mm in diameter. The sections of panelling are basically seven panels in height and eight in width. How they were finished at the top

Figure 4.19
Room F4. View to north-west prior to restoration.
[87/2011; © Crown copyright. NMR]

is now unclear. The present plaster ceiling, probably dating from the mid-18th century, is approximately 75mm lower than the 16th-century ceiling and was constructed with the panelling still in position. Underneath the later small cornice several layers of paint were discovered and a painting sequence for the framing of the panelling was established. The earliest layer was red, followed by a grey-green wash, a grey-blue wash and several layers of cream wash as in the great chamber. The present finish dates from the early 20th century and was renewed in the 1950s.

Apart from the alterations to the north front in the 18th century, the main changes to the panelling occurred when an over-mantel (Fig 4.20) was installed above the fireplace in the 17th century (*see* p 127).

West staircase

There is surviving structural evidence that a number of alterations were made in the area of the west wing staircase between first- and second-floor level during the 16th century, only for those changes to be superseded in turn by later ones in the complex evolution of the staircase (*see* Fig 3.23).

Originally, as described in Chapter 3, the staircase rose only to first-floor level to a landing outside the door to the great chamber (F3) (*see* Fig 3.21), as at present. A partition appears to have been erected on the south side of the staircase opening to divide it from the inner chamber (F5). The first alteration, shortly after the house was built, seems to have been the removal of this partition. Why this was done is difficult to understand. Certainly the space between the partition and the end wall of the bed-chamber (F4) would have been cramped and ill-lit, and by taking away the partition the inner chamber would have been enlarged, but only at the expense of having an awkward stair opening at its north end. Moreover, its removal involved structural changes at second-floor level. Because the ceiling above the staircase opening was at the same level as that of the bedchamber and lower than that of the inner chamber it had to be rebuilt at a higher level. This involved cutting back the main north–south second-floor beam at this point, so that instead of being joined to the east–west tie-beam of the roof truss which spanned the wing immediately above the partition, as in the original construction, its truncated end rested subsequently on the timber-framed south wall of the bed-chamber. The effect was to produce a sagging and general weakening in the latter, and in the long term the alteration may have contributed to the structural problems which beset this wing.

The removal of the end of the beam, however, allowed an opening to be made in the second floor for a staircase to be built between the first and second floors. Logic would suggest that the stairs were installed at the same time as the structural alterations described above were carried out, but the evidence indicates that there were two phases of work and that the construction of the staircase belongs to the second phase. The stairs, which rose eastwards immediately above the staircase from the ground to the first floor, were steep and the opening was small. The position of the opening is marked by an area of white plaster wash across the north face of the east–west floor beam. Two or more pairs of ceiling and floor joists were removed to make room for the opening, and the empty mortises which were left in the face of the beam were filled with broken brick and plaster prior to the application of the plaster wash.

The installation of the staircase from the first to the second floor would have provided a good reason for the reinstatement of the partition on its south side, but there is no evidence that this occurred.

Inner chamber (F5)

The changes described above would have affected the inner chamber and its function may have changed in consequence. It would certainly have been much less of an enclosed room. The presence of bond timbers in the brickwork of the walls indicates that it was intended to be panelled, but insufficient evidence has survived to be certain how this room and the one to its south were decorated, or indeed used, in this period.

The second floor

The construction of the staircase from the first to the second floor in the west wing would have greatly improved the access to the second-floor rooms in this wing, which otherwise appear to have been little altered in this period.

5

The House in the 17th Century

The loss of most of the records of the manor of Lordshold before the later 17th century is not an insuperable obstacle to an understanding of the pattern of ownership and occupation of Sutton House in the 16th century. To a large extent other records compensate for the loss. For the 17th century, however, this is no longer true and the absence of documents becomes more of a handicap. The problem is compounded by the divorce of the ownership of the house from its occupancy. This occurred when Sir James Deane foreclosed on John Machell the younger's mortgage at the beginning of the century and probably lasted, apart from a brief period in the second quarter of the 17th century when there was a remarriage of the two, until the end of the 19th century.

The owners in the early 17th century

We have seen in the previous chapter how the process whereby James Deane came to acquire Sutton House from John Machell the younger was a complex one, involving a number of court cases between the two men. As a result it is difficult to give a precise date to the transfer of ownership, but it occurred at the beginning of the 17th century, probably by 1605.

By this time, Deane had followed the path of several of the other founder-members of the East India Company in taking a residence in Hackney. His house was also on the south side of Homerton or Humberston Street, as it was then called (now Homerton High Street), a short distance to the east of Sutton House. In 18th-century maps it is possible to make out the shape of a house in this locality, by then subdivided, and an archaeological evaluation undertaken in 1995 on a site to the west of Link Street revealed the remains of a Tudor cellar where that house would have been. It seems most likely that this was Deane's residence (Fig 5.1, *see also* Fig 2.2).

When he drew up his will in 1607, Deane referred to the two houses on the south side of Homerton High Street, both copyhold of the manor of Lordshold, which he then owned. He distinguished between them by referring to one of them as 'one coppiehoulde or customarye messuage . . . now in the occupacion of me the said Sir James Deane' and the other as 'one greate capitall messuage'.[1] The implication may be that the latter, Sutton House, was the more substantial of the two, as it was built of brick, whereas Deane's own house may have been timber-framed. Nevertheless, as one of the homes of a leading member of London's merchant community, Deane's house would undoubtedly have been well-appointed. Both houses were grand enough to attract rich and well-connected occupants, and although it is frequently possible to identify persons who lived in one or other of the houses it is sometimes impossible to be certain which of the two houses they inhabited.

Sir James Deane died on 15 May 1608 and was buried on 2 June in St Olave's Church, Hart Street, near to his house in Mark Lane.[2] Following directions given in his will, a magnificent marble monument was erected in the church displaying effigies of Deane, his three wives and his three children who had died in infancy (*see* Fig 4.1). He bequeathed all his property in Hackney to his niece, Olive Clarke, for her lifetime, and then to her children, making provision for his widow, Lady Deane, to live in the house he had occupied in Hackney until her death. From there, on 29 September 1608, she married John Brewster of the Middle Temple, a secondary in the Fine Office. She was then only 38 years old but died on 23 October in the following year. Her funeral, on 2 November 1609 in St Sepulchre's Church in the City of London, was a particularly lavish affair, attended by over a hundred mourners.[3]

On Lady Deane's death, Olive Clarke entered into possession of all of Sir James Deane's former property in Hackney. By his will, she had already acquired the copyhold ownership of Sutton House, its grounds and

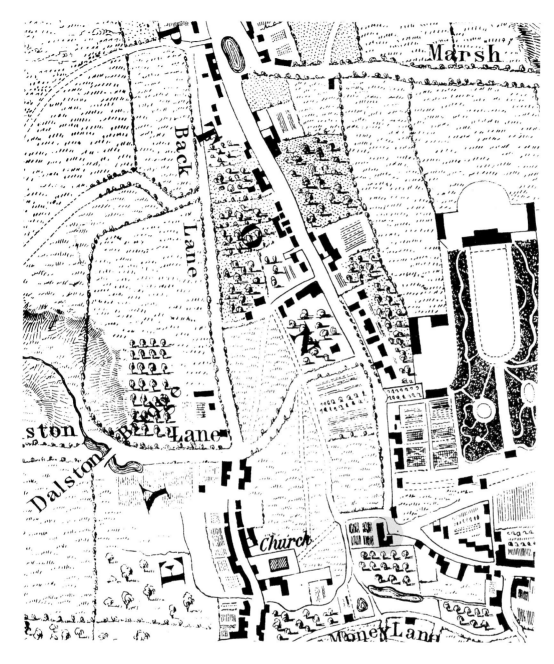

Figure 5.1
Detail of John Rocque's
map of 1745 showing
Sutton House (with the
Tanhouse adjoining) in its
18th-century setting at the
corner of Homerton Street,
to the east of the church.
[A copy of this map can be
found in the Sutton House
archive]

the 18-acre (7.3-ha) Churchfield in the neighbouring manor of Grumbolds. Olive Clarke was the daughter of Deane's sister, Margery, and her husband John Chamberlain, a clothier of Kingsclere in Hampshire. On 8 July 1594 Olive had married Richard Clarke at St Katharine Coleman's Church.[4] Whether he was the Richard Clarke who was one of the original shareholders of the East India Company in 1600 is not known but, given the connection with Sir James Deane, it seems likely. He had died by 1608, leaving Olive Clarke a widow with three young children, which doubtless accounts for Deane's wish to see that she and her

children were well provided for by leaving them a landed estate. After receiving his bequests, she was said to have money and goods worth £400 and land to the value of £100 per annum.[5] The latter figure would be a close approximation to the value of her land and property in Hackney.

Like Lady Deane, Olive Clarke soon remarried. She chose as her second husband another James Deane, a kinsman of her uncle. There are at least three James Deanes mentioned in Sir James Deane's prodigiously lengthy will, but the one who married Olive Clarke appears to be the son of his cousin Richard Deane, who is also referred to in the will as his 'godson' and his 'servant'. It was this James Deane who was one of the group of men who was involved in the fracas in the fields of Woodbury mentioned in the case brought by Deane against John Machell in the Court of Star Chamber (*see* p 97) and he seems to have occupied a prominent place in Deane's household. He was also most probably the James Deane who was made free of the Drapers' Company by the elder Deane in 1604, when his address was given as 'with Sir James Deane'.[6]

Olive Clarke married James Deane early in 1609. Their marriage may well be that entered in the register of St Benet Fink on 12 January 1609 as between James Deane and Ellen [sic] Clarke, a presumption reinforced by the fact that on 9 January 1609 Deane had entered into an agreement with Olive Clarke designed to protect the interests of her children by her first marriage.[7] James Deane had landholdings in Hampshire, where he had been bequeathed the manor of Deane by Sir James Deane, and the couple appear to have made their home in that county. By 1618 Deane was described as a gentleman of Whitchurch.[8]

Thus, as far as Hackney was concerned, James and Olive Deane were almost certainly absentee landowners. James Deane was, however, assiduous in looking after his wife's inheritance, even though she (and therefore he) only had a life interest in the property. He later claimed to have spent over £300 in defending the property against claims (presumably by John Machell). When Machell's grandson brought a suit in Chancery in 1627 to seek redress for his grandfather's losses he cited Deane as a defendant because he was under the impression that the land had been surrendered to him. Additionally, when in 1617–18 an agreement was concluded between the lord of the manor and most of his copyhold tenants concerning some rights and privileges, a James Deane was numbered among the copyholders. Later, Olive's children by her first marriage said that their stepfather had 'enjoyed' the land and property.[9]

James Deane also claimed that he had spent a considerable amount of money in bringing up the children of his wife's first marriage. The eldest son, Andrew, went to Oxford, where he received a BA from Magdalen Hall in 1617 and an MA in 1620; he subsequently became a clergyman. The younger son, James, was apprenticed to a member of the Grocers' Company, of which

he later became free. The daughter, Margaret, had married Anthony Mason of Whitchurch by 1624. James and Olive also had a daughter of their own, Susan, who had married John Horwood, apparently also a Hampshire man, by 1627.[10]

Olive Deane died in 1623 or 1624 and James Deane in 1628, when the manor of Deane descended to his son-in-law, John Horwood.[11] On Olive's death her four children, including Susan Deane, inherited the Hackney property under the will of their great-uncle. A summary of transactions for the manor of Grumbolds shows that they were admitted in manorial court to the copyhold tenancy of Churchfield in 1624, and a similar ceremony would probably have taken place in the manor of Lordshold for the property there. Subsequently, the Grumbolds records indicate that a number of complex family settlements were made until Churchfield was finally sold in 1668 by a son of James Clarke, citizen and Grocer (Olive Clarke's younger son) and his wife, Elizabeth.[12] The property in the manor of Lordshold also appears to have come into the sole possession of James and Elizabeth Clarke but was alienated at a much earlier date.

Possible occupants in the early 17th century

What happened to Sutton House during these years of absentee ownership by James and Olive Deane and their children is obscure, a problem compounded by the failure of the records to distinguish between the two large houses on the south side of Homerton High Street which were in common ownership during this period.

In April 1610 a licence was given in the manorial court for James Deane and his wife Olive to grant a 7-year lease to Thomas Havers, citizen of London, of a customary messuage with garden, orchard and other appurtenances in Humberston Street 'quondam Jacobi Deane militis'.[13] The wording suggests that this was Deane's former residence, although it could just mean that it was in his former possession. The former interpretation is reinforced by the inclusion in the lease of Slow Meadow, which had been coupled with his house in Deane's will, and by the date of the lease a short time after Lady Deane's death. Little is known of Havers. He may have been the Thomas Havers, citizen and goldsmith of London, who died c 1620 but, if so, he made no mention of Hackney in his will.[14]

Havers' name is included in lists of ratepayers compiled in 1613 and 1614 in connection with assessments for provisions for the king's household. Another name that appears close to Havers' in the list, and also to that of the occupant of the Tanhouse, Sir John Peyton, is Henry Thoresby, a bencher of Lincoln's Inn and one of the Masters of the Court of Chancery; he was a prominent resident of Hackney and after his death in 1615 a substantial monument was erected to him in the parish church. Thoresby may be a possible candidate for the occupancy of Sutton House but several factors suggest that he was living elsewhere: he paid a rate towards the repair of the parish church as early as December 1605; in his will he referred to his house in Hackney as being worth about £20 per annum (probably somewhat low for Sutton House even without adjoining land); and he made no reference to its being leasehold or copyhold when bequeathing it to his wife and grand-child in succession.[15]

A notable resident of Hackney who certainly lived in one of the two houses was Frances, Dowager Countess of Warwick. She was the widow of Robert Rich, who was created Earl of Warwick in 1618 and died in 1619. The Rich family had long been connected with Hackney. Lord Rich, as he was then styled, was one of the residents of Homerton assessed for the repair of the church in 1605 (although he does not appear to have paid anything, perhaps because he was only occasionally present in the parish).

Earlier in 1605 his 17-year-old son (by his first wife) also named Robert, later the second Earl of Warwick (d 1658), had married a 14-year-old heiress in Hackney. Three of the children of the young couple including Robert, the future third Earl (d 1659), were subsequently baptised in Hackney parish church between 1609 and 1614. The second Robert, who succeeded his father in 1619, became famous as a privateer and later as Commander of the Fleet in the parliamentary cause during the Civil War. He was also a pioneer in the early colonisation of America, and must rank as one of the most notable of the overseas merchants and adventurers who gravitated to Hackney at the end of the 16th and the beginning of the 17th centuries. The Hackney home of the Rich family, although clearly favoured for lying-in, was, however, only one of several houses they owned and its exact location is unknown.[16]

Lord Rich had married his second wife, Frances, in 1616. Wherever the earlier residence of the family may have been, Frances was living in either Sutton House or the nearby house by November 1627, when James Clarke surrendered to the use of himself and his wife Elizabeth a messuage in Humberston Street in the occupation of the Countess of Warwick. She continued to live there until her death in Hackney on 15 August 1634, but she was buried elsewhere. In her will she left the lease of the house with its furnishings, plate and linen and her coach at Hackney lined with purple velvet, together with four of her coachman's best mares, to her nephew, Edward Wray.[17]

The Milward family

The transaction of 1627 referred to above may have been one of a series designed to settle the inheritance of the copyhold estate in Lordshold among the beneficiaries of Sir James Deane's will prior to its sale. If so, the purchaser was a prosperous City merchant, John Milward, who was certainly the owner by the mid-1630s. Milward first appears in the records of Hackney parish in October 1627 when he was elected as a vestry man.[18] Although he is likely to have been living in the parish for some time before this, it may not have been for long as the vestry would have been eager to invite such a major City magnate to join its ranks. In the lay subsidy for 1628, he was among the highest rated residents of Homerton, but for 'goods' not 'land', perhaps because his main residence was elsewhere, in the City.[19]

John Milward was the tenth and last child of Henry Milward of Sinfin (Derby-shire) and his wife Elizabeth. The date of his birth is not known, but as he was apprenticed to his older brother, Humphrey Milward, a member of the Vintners' Com-pany, in 1597 and made free of the Company in 1605, he is likely to have been born c 1583. By 1608 he had married Anne Lawrence of Sinfin, of whose background nothing further is known. After the death of one child in infancy, their eldest surviving son, Thomas, was born on 9 November 1609.[20]

Milward probably set up in business as a vintner, as he himself took three apprentices between 1609 and 1613.[21] By then, how-ever, he had already branched out into a potentially more lucrative form of mercan-tile activity. His older brother and mentor, Humphrey Milward, was one of the 216 founder-members of the East India Company in 1600, and John Milward was an 'adventurer', that is a shareholder, in the Company's third voyage which was embarked upon in 1607.[22] Thereafter, the Company and its affairs came to play an increasingly important role in his business career. Whether the Milwards knew Sir James Deane and the other merchants with Hackney connections (like Sir Edward Holmeden, one of John Machell's early mortgagees) who had been instrumental in establishing the East India Company, can only be conjectured, but it would not be entirely surprising given the close-knit world of City merchants who engaged in overseas trade.

Humphrey Milward died in 1609 (his widow afterwards marrying Paul Ambrose Croke who had a house on the north side of Homerton High Street),[23] but John Milward continued to prosper. By 1613 he was living in the parish of St Bartholomew by the Exchange in the City, where he had a large house (one of the highest rated in the parish) at the corner of Bartholomew Lane and Capel Court, next door to the parish church. He was an active member of the parish vestry, serving in several local offices and from 1627 to 1636 he served as a common councilman on the City Corporation.[24] He was a leading member of the Vintners' Company. As Warden in 1623 he lent the Company £50 interest free to enable the hall of Vintners' Hall to be painted with biblical scenes by Richard Greenebury, and he was Master from 1633 to 1634.[25] He was also a captain of one of the trained bands of the City, a commission he had held since at least 1616 and one which frequently led to his designation as 'Captain Milward' even in non-military matters.[26]

In 1612 Milward was among a large body of the nobility, gentry and merchants who formed a company to exploit what was thought to be the discovery of the north-west passage by Henry Hudson.[27] Despite his diverse mercantile interests, his rising prosperity was based firmly on the trade of the East India Company. He does not feature largely in the Company's records until the 1620s, although he did acquire additional stock from a widow in 1618, but thereafter he played an increasingly important part in the Company's affairs.[28]

In 1621 he petitioned the Company to be allowed to take a shipment of raw silk, perhaps in lieu of a dividend due to him. Although he occasionally dealt in other commodities such as tobacco, the silk trade, especially with Persia, became his major concern. From 1626 to 1627 he was inadvertently caught up in a triangular dispute between the Company, the Persian merchant who had brought over the silk and the volatile Persian ambassador. A sheriff had to be present to keep the peace when the cargo of ninety-four bales which Milward had indented for was weighed out. He, in turn, insisted on an allowance being made for wet or rotten silk, which led to more ill feeling. The Company backed Milward but subsequently ordered him to pay £200 towards the household expenses of the Persian ambassador, who was apparently being entertained in London by the Company.[29]

By this time Milward was a member of the influential Court of Committees (in effect the board of directors), which guided the Company's affairs. He was first elected in 1625 and remained a committee until 1636, apart from a brief interval in 1630–1 when he stood down.[30] He was not averse to using the position to his personal advantage, as in 1628 when he was allowed as a favour to ship out a valuable bejewelled salt-cellar and use the proceeds of its sale to purchase some oriental carpets for his house.[31] It is tempting to speculate that they were intended for the house he had just acquired in Hackney but they could, of course, have been for his house in Bartholomew Lane. On a later occasion he was allowed to ship out a box of silk waistcoats and receive the money for them, an occurrence which was unusual enough to warrant recording in the Company's minutes.[32]

The silk trade was a highly unstable one, however, as Milward was later to find out to his cost. Not only did prices often fluctuate quite wildly, but the trade was also ill-regulated and open to abuses. In order to try to eliminate some of the worst malpractices in the dyeing of silk, a short-lived Company of Silkmen of London was established by letters patent in May 1631. Milward was its Governor but in 1635 he found himself hauled before the Court of Star Chamber, together with his assistants in the Company, indicted with practising the very abuses which the setting up of the Company had been designed to control. He vigorously defended himself against the charges.[33]

By the end of the 1620s Milward was associating with some of the most powerful merchants in London. In 1627 he joined a syndicate of merchants to take a lease of the petty farm of the customs on wine and currants. Customs farming was one of the means by which the early Stuart monarchs sought to raise ready money and although the profits were potentially great, the sums demanded by the king in return were very large indeed. In order to obtain a 1-year lease of the customs, Milward and the eight fellow members of the syndicate were required to pay a premium of £12,000 and an advance rent of £20,000. The other members of the syndicate included Sir Morris Abbot, Governor of the East India Company 1624–38, Sir John Wolstenholme, Henry and William Garway and Abraham Jacob (all subsequently knighted), who were central figures in London's mercantile elite. Milward may have been small fry among such giants, but the episode is indicative of the company he kept and the aspirations he harboured.[34]

At the same time he was also building up his investment in the East India Company. When he was made a committee in 1625 it was a requirement that anyone so elected should have at least £2,000 invested in the Company. The total extent of his stock-holding is not possible to determine but some indication is given by the amount of stock transferred to him (in other words bought by him from other investors). In 1628 £1,000 was transferred; in 1629 £3,200; in 1630 a staggering £9,150; in 1631 £6,600 and an unspecified portion of £4,000; and in 1633 over £5,900. Thereafter the amounts transferred tailed off but Milward's overall stock in the Company by that date must have been very substantial.[35]

Thus, by the early 1630s John Milward's standing in the mercantile community was high and his prosperity seemed assured. His family, too, seemed set on an upward progression. On 7 July 1631 his eldest son, Thomas, married Audrey, the daughter of Ralph Carter of Derbyshire, of whose background nothing is known, in Hackney parish church.[36] Of more dynastic significance, however, was the marriage on 7 February in the following year at the church of St Bartholomew by the Exchange of his daughter, Elizabeth, to Edward Abbot, the third son of Sir Morris Abbot. Morris Abbot was then Governor of the East India Company and subsequently became Lord Mayor of London; he has been described as 'the nearest equivalent to the merchant princes of other lands and other periods'.[37] Moreover, he was by no means the only distinguished member of his family: one brother, George, was Archbishop of Canterbury and another,

Robert, by then deceased, had been Bishop of Salisbury.[38] A union with such a remarkable family must have seemed to John Milward the very height of social achievement.

The Milwards and Hackney

The marriage of his son, Thomas, in 1631 seems to have led to some rearrangement of John Milward's domestic arrangements in Hackney, but whether this was more nominal than actual is uncertain. In a document which appears to be a much abbreviated account of transactions in the manorial courts, perhaps prior to entry in the court books, under the date 1636, a conditional surrender (probably a mortgage) of John Milward's holding is recorded in which the property is said to consist of two houses, one in the possession of 'Tho: Milward' and the other in the possession of 'Comitis Warwick'.[39] Even if the latter is taken to mean the Countess of Warwick it is out of date, for she had died in 1634, and the note may have been repeating an old formula of words. From 1631 to 1638 Thomas Milward also had a house, separate from his father's, in the parish of St Bartholomew by the Exchange and his eldest children were christened there in 1632 and 1633.[40]

Whether or not John Milward actually vacated his house in Hackney in favour of his son in 1631, he was back by 1634. On 17 August 1634, within two days of the death of the Countess of Warwick, he asked if he could sit in her former pew in the parish church and the vestry acceded to his request for as long as he lived in the parish.[41] In fact, it was not merely the countess's pew that Milward took over, but her house as well; either the countess's lease had already run out and she had remained there by agreement or he purchased what was left of her leasehold term from her nephew. Thus by the mid-1630s John Milward and his family were occupying one of the large houses in his copyhold ownership and Thomas Milward and his family the other. Which of them lived in Sutton House and which in Sir James Deane's former house is impossible to say with certainty.[42]

This arrangement, called the unit system, whereby two branches of an extended family lived in close proximity to each other has been noted elsewhere in the 17th century. Usually the houses were closer together and sometimes physically linked, but as an adaptation of two formerly quite separate houses, the example of the Milwards' use of Sutton House and Deane's former house could probably be regarded as a parallel instance.[43]

Both John and Thomas Milward also kept up their separate households in St Bartholomew by the Exchange – an indication of their wealth and social standing – but thereafter Hackney seems to have been their principal place of residence. Two further children of Thomas and Audrey Milward were christened in Hackney in 1635 and 1636. Although John Milward remained active on the Hackney vestry, after March 1635 he does not appear to have attended that of St Bartholomew and was replaced as a common councilman in 1636.[44]

John Milward's financial difficulties

John Milward was still acquiring additional stock in the East India Company as late as 1635 but the depression in commerce generally during that decade, which was felt particularly acutely in the silk trade,[45] was beginning to have an adverse effect on him. In April 1636 he reported that he was unable to pay for nineteen bales of silk and the Company sold them to someone else. Later in the same month one of his creditors requested an account of his stockholding in the Company and was told it amounted to £12,093 but that this sum was charged with 'interest, brokes, and debts' of £5,644.[46] One of his problems may have been that he had so much capital tied up in the Company which, because of its own straitened financial position at this time, paid little in the way of dividends. He appears in that same year to have mortgaged his property in Hackney to John Eldred, a fellow member of the East India Company, to help him out of his difficulties.[47]

By the end of the decade matters had come to a head. In February 1640 he was still seeking a 'division' (dividend) in silk, but by April of that year he petitioned for the interest and charges on his debts to the Company to be remitted, 'he having failed and most of his creditors having agreed to accept 10s in the pound'. The Company was sympathetic 'in regard of the great losses he has sustained' and reduced the amount due. In May 1641 he transferred what remained of his holding in the Company's third joint stock, amounting to £3,023, to a consortium of four individuals including his son, Thomas, on behalf of

his creditors.[48] It was virtually his last act, for he died later in that year and was buried at Hackney on 7 August 1641.[49]

Two years earlier, in October 1639, Milward had surrendered his copyhold property in Hackney to Edward and Elizabeth Abbot, his son-in-law and daughter. The details of the transaction are not known but it may have been designed to protect his family by preventing his property from being seized by his creditors. The holding was described as consisting of two houses with their gardens, orchards, barns, stables and other appurtenances in the respective occupations of John and Thomas Milward and 5 acres (2ha) of land.[50]

Edward Abbot

To John Milward, it must have seemed that he could hardly entrust his property to safer hands. Edward Abbot was born in 1605, the fifth, but third surviving, son of (Sir) Morris Abbot, one of the greatest merchants in London, and his wife Margaret, the daughter of Bartholomew Barnes, an alderman of London. Edward Abbot was granted the freedom of the Drapers' Company by patrimony in 1631 and, like his father, was an overseas merchant, a member of the Levant and East India Companies, trading in currants and cloth and, at times, other commodities. In 1630, when his mother died, he was living in Leghorn in Italy.[51]

Shortly afterwards he returned to London, settling in Coleman Street, where his father then lived. He was called to the livery of the Drapers' Company in 1632 and took on several apprentices over the next eight years, including three members of the extended Milward family.[52] In 1636 he was elected to the Court of Committees of the East India Company, of which his father was then Governor. Ironically he replaced John Milward as a committee and retained the position until stepping down himself in 1640.[53]

Abbot's bankruptcy

By then Edward Abbot was running into pecuniary difficulties himself. Whether he had taken on some of his father-in-law's debts in 1639 is not known, but it is certainly possible. When another John Milward, a kinsman of the Milwards, who was an agent of the East India Company, died in Bantam in 1638, the administration of his estate and effects was granted to

THE HOUSE IN THE 17TH CENTURY

Abbot as his principal creditor.[54] Whatever the circumstances, the deterioration in Abbot's position was rapid for, in May 1641, a number of clothiers and clothworkers who were his creditors petitioned the House of Lords, claiming that he was seeking to avoid payment by secretly conveying his estate to his father and brother. The Lords were immediately concerned because Abbot apparently owed £12,000 to the king, perhaps a debt arising out of customs farming, and they recommended that a commission of bankruptcy should be issued speedily. Following a petition from Abbot himself, he was granted protection from arrest, but by the following year the quarterage books of the Drapers' Company record that he had 'run away' from his house in Coleman Street. In 1643 he wrote a letter to the Levant Company from Chios, 'as a member of their Society in a dejected condition', asking to be appointed as consul in Smyrna and offering in return to repay the money he owed the Company. Not surprisingly, his request was rejected.[55]

It took a long time to sort out Abbot's affairs and, as late as 1657, his account with the East India Company was still unsettled.[56] The property in Hackney, acquired when his father-in-law found himself in similar difficulties, was taken over by his assignees in bankruptcy in 1644. Thomas Milward and his mother, Anne, continued to live there, presumably by arrangement with the assignees, although whether in both houses or just in Sutton House is not clear.[57]

Thomas Milward

Thomas Milward's first wife, Audrey, died in 1640 and was buried in Hackney on 9 June. Before the end of the year he was married again to Jane Littleton, niece of Sir Thomas Littleton. They had three children who were christened in Hackney between 1642 and 1644.[58] Thomas Milward also invested in the East India Company, although not to the same extent as his father. He was a stockholder by 1632 and in the same year stood as joint security with his father for an unpaid bill on two lots of silk. Also following in his father's footsteps, he played a part in local affairs and was appointed headborough for Upper Homerton in 1642.[59] John Milward had died intestate and it was not until 1645 that the administration of his estate and effects was granted to Thomas as his son, his widow

Anne renouncing her right.[60] One reason why it may have taken so long is the disruption caused to the Prerogative Court of Canterbury by the Civil War. In 1643 the presiding judge of the court had fled to Oxford to join Charles I and Parliament did not appoint another judge to sit in London until November 1644.

How far Thomas Milward was affected by his father's failure can only be conjectured. As late as 1648 the East India Company was assisting him in making arrangements with his father's creditors and the final instalment of money the company had retained was not released to him until 1650.[61] There is no record of his own activities during these difficult years when civil war raged in England; he merely fades from view. Circumstances suggest that he was the Thomas Milward of the City of London, merchant, whose will was proved in November 1655. It was a very short will, simply bequeathing his worldly estate to his mother, Mistress Anne Milward, asking her to dispose of it for the benefit of his children. Earlier in that year a re-grant of the administration of the goods and chattels of John Milward had been made to Anne as John's widow.[62] In 1658 the records of the East India Company record that a Mrs Milward was allowed to assign her late husband's adventure in the third joint stock to whomsoever she pleased.[63] If this was Thomas Milward's widow, Jane, it is surprising that she is not mentioned in his will; it is more likely to be the resilient Anne Milward.

The ownership of Henry Whittingham

In June 1656 the remaining assignee in bankruptcy of Edward Abbot surrendered his copyhold estate in Hackney to the lord of the manor and Henry Whittingham, merchant, was admitted as tenant. In the following year, perhaps because Whittingham was concerned about the security of his title to the land, Edward Abbot, then living in Pisa, by letter of attorney, and Elizabeth Abbot, who attended in person, also surrendered the property to Whittingham in the manorial court. In these transactions the small estate was sometimes said to consist of two messuages and sometimes three, and 5 acres (2ha) of land. The messuages were described as being now or late in the respective occupation of Anne Milward, Dorothy Clempson and Mrs Scott, widows. The discrepancy in the number of houses may be accounted for by the subdivision of the house to the east of Sutton House into two residences, perhaps on an informal basis: a possibility given added likelihood by a brief entry in the manorial records stating that in 1657 Whittingham granted a short lease of the west end of a tenement and garden plot in Homerton.[64] The timing of the sale of the property to Whittingham supports the conjecture that the Thomas Milward whose will was proved in November 1655 was the Thomas Milward of Sutton House.

Henry Whittingham, who was born in Islington, the son of Nicholas Whittingham, lived in the parish of St Helen's, Bishopsgate, in the City of London. When he drew up his will in 1673, he said that he had lived there for a long time; by then he had a large house in Great St Helens but he also owned houses in Bishopsgate and other parts of the City.[65] He appears to have been a royalist sympathiser during the Civil War, writing at one point to Endymion Porter, a Groom of the Bedchamber, to recommend his nephew 'who is tall enough to do you service [and] hath a spanish blade by his side, and a welsh heart in his body'.[66] His house in Bishopsgate was briefly sequestered but was restored to him on payment to the commissioners of a sum of money for compounding.

By 1656, however, such loyalties were of less importance and Whittingham had clearly prospered. He appears to have purchased Abbot's former holding as an investment and he also acquired other copyhold plots in Homerton at the same time.[67] Whether Anne Milward was still in residence when Sutton House was sold is not known, but by November 1657 Whittingham had granted a 13½-year lease of the house to Sarah Freeman, widow, at the high annual rent of £55. The lease was subsequently extended for a further twenty-three years in 1670.[68]

Sarah Freeman's school

Sarah Freeman's purpose in leasing Sutton House was to establish a girls' school there. Little is known of her besides the fact that she must have been a young widow, for she ran the school, latterly with the help of her daughter, for more than 30 years, perhaps over 40. She may have been the widow of Robert Freeman, who was buried 'from Humerton' in February 1657.[69] That she was by no means impecunious is suggested

by the high rent of the house from the outset and from her willingness to erect a new gallery in the parish church for her scholars in 1672.[70] In the assessment for the hearth tax of 1662, she paid one of the highest sums in Hackney for twenty-one hearths and by 1674 the number had risen to twenty-four.[71] Such a large number of fireplaces indicates that by this time there must have been a number of heated outbuildings either attached to Sutton House or within its curtilage.

Hackney was noted for its girls' schools in the 17th century and was described as 'the ladies' university of female arts'. John Aubrey thought it a matter of regret that girls were sent to Hackney schools 'to learn pride and wantonness', but Samuel Pepys predictably adopted a different perspective. In 1667, on one of his occasional visits to the district where he had been boarded as a child, he went to the parish church, 'chiefly', as he confessed, 'to see . . . the young ladies of the schools, whereof there is great store, very pretty'. A guidebook to London, written in French and published in 1693, praised the 'bonnes écoles' of Hackney. There is little specific record of Sarah Freeman's establishment, although as late as 1694 it was included in a list of well known ladies' boarding schools in London.[72] Sarah Freeman herself died in 1700 and probably continued to run the school right up to that date.[73]

Successful as Sarah Freeman's school may have been, for Sutton House it represented a distinct change of status. Despite the embellishments to its interior in the first half of the 17th century, its early-Tudor appearance was by now unfashionable and its long-term use as a girls' school probably represented as good a utilisation of the premises as its absentee owners could expect. That ownership in the meantime had passed through several members of the Whittingham family.

The ownership after Henry Whittingham's death

Henry Whittingham died in 1674 and by his will left his property in Hackney to his grandson, Robert Whittingham, the son of his eldest son, also named Robert, and his wife Hester.[74] The younger Robert Whittingham could have been no more than 22 years old when he inherited the property, but he himself had died by 1680, apparently without heirs, and the copyhold ownership

Figure 5.2
Fragments of worked stone discovered during archaeological excavations in the Wenlock Barn, used in the foundations of an 18th-century dividing wall. [Mike Gray]

passed to his father and mother. They in turn surrendered it to the use of the elder Robert Whittingham's will. When he died in 1694 his daughter Sarah inherited the property. She had married William Wagstaffe of the Middle Temple in 1672 but he had died by 1690, leaving her a widow with four young daughters.[75]

According to his widow, William Wagstaffe, who had at one time been Town Clerk of the City of London, had suffered 'great losses', but at the time of his death he was still able to honour a commitment made at the time of his marriage to leave £2,000 to her and a further £1,600 to be divided between his daughters. By the time of her own death in 1709 or 1710, Sarah Wagstaffe, who was then resident in Holborn, owned two houses on London Bridge besides her copyhold estate in Hackney and had investments in government stock and the East India Company.[76]

Thus, as the 17th century drew to a close, Sutton House accommodated a flourishing girls' school and was owned by a widow who, if not vastly wealthy, had a comfortable endowment and was concerned to provide a decent inheritance for her young daughters.

The fabric

The chequered history of the house in the 17th century – from a period of absentee ownership to one in which it was owned and occupied by a very wealthy merchant family and, through the precipitate decline in that family's fortunes, to its conversion into a girls' school – has left its mark on the fabric. Despite later alterations, ample evidence remains of a dramatic transformation which occurred at some point in the first half of the century. The main physical change was the insertion of a new, grand, painted staircase in the west wing, but other rooms were embellished and seemingly decorated in glowing and vibrant colours.

It is difficult to be certain how far this work extended within the house as some rooms have been subjected to greater degrees of subsequent change than others. During excavations in the area of Wenlock Barn in 1990 remains of fireplaces and a stone doorcase were found (Figs 5.2 and 5.3; *see also* Fig 3.50). These included substantial fragments of a painted stone fireplace, or more probably two fireplaces. The colours used (gold, red, light brown, dark pink and yellow ochre) are similar to those

Figure 5.3
Drawing showing part of a
former stone doorcase
(below), based on an
analysis of stone fragments
(above) uncovered during
archaeological excavations.
(Scale 1:20)

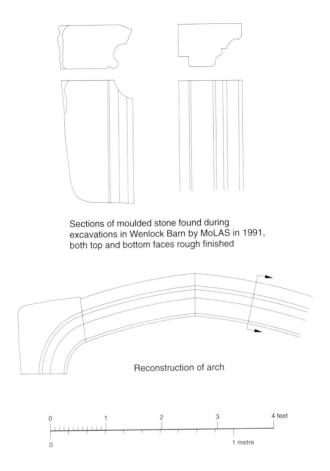

Sections of moulded stone found during
excavations in Wenlock Barn by MoLAS in 1991,
both top and bottom faces rough finished

Reconstruction of arch

0   1   2   3   4 feet

0   1 metre

found elsewhere in the house and it seems likely that the remains are those of fireplaces from rooms where the original fireplaces have been removed or replaced. The broken head of what was probably a door opening rather than a fireplace, with the Milward coat of arms painted in the centre, was discovered lying beneath the hearth of room F4 during the restoration of the house. It is unlikely to have come from that room, where the original Tudor fireplace, similarly decorated, was discovered intact behind a Georgian chimneypiece (*see* Fig 6.27) during the works carried out in 1904, but it probably came from elsewhere in the house or from an outside gateway.

The surviving evidence, which is chiefly to be found in the rooms of the west wing, probably does not indicate the full extent of the decorative scheme. Nevertheless, the work seems to have been largely confined to the centre and west of the house, where it would have reinforced the hierarchical division between the lower, service wing on the east side and the remaining rooms for the use of the owner and the entertainment of his guests.

It is reasonable to assume that the work was carried out in the late 1620s or, more probably, the 1630s, when the house was occupied by the Milward family. This was a period when the family's fortunes were rising rapidly and when they were cementing dynastic ties with another, even wealthier and more powerful merchant family, the Abbots. Fortunately, confirmation appears to be at hand in the ubiquitous presence of the Milward coat of arms, painted on fireplaces and probably incorporated in the decorations of the staircase although, in the latter case, painted over at a later date so as to be heraldically incorrect (*see* Fig 5.5). The house at this time would also have been opulently furnished with carpets and silk fabrics imported from the orient in the course of the Milwards' business and, with its brilliant colours and extravagant furnishings, must have presented an ostentatious display of mercantile wealth.

As in previous chapters, the following account of individual rooms only covers those in which significant evidence survives of changes that were made during this period.

The interior

The ground floor

Hall (G3)

The extensive alteration of this part of the house in the 18th century removed most of the traces of any earlier changes, but archaeological excavation in the area of the present eastern corridor (*see* Fig 7.12) has revealed evidence that a wooden floor was laid here in the 17th century. Timber joists running north–south were bedded into slots cut in the mortar bedding of the original tile floor and floorboards were laid over these. When the floor was replaced at a later date, these joists remained *in situ*. The work may well have been carried out in the second half of the 17th century during the adaptation of the house for use as a school.

Linenfold parlour (G4)

The main feature from the 17th century which survives in the linenfold parlour is the wooden fireplace surround and overmantel (*see* Figs 3.44 and 9.1). This consists of three pilasters, fluted in the upper part and reeded in the lower, the outer ones wider and extending down to floor level with plain pedestals decorated with lozenge-shaped motifs. Between the pilasters are panels carved with a more elaborate linenfold design than those in the rest of the room, the whole forming a handsome ensemble in a Jacobean style. The discovery of a coin dating from the reign of Charles I (1625–49) in one of two square sockets cut into the brickwork at the top of the wall above the fireplace, apparently to house timber blocks for use as fixing points for the panelling, is compelling evidence that the overmantel was erected after that king's accession to the throne.

The original Tudor fireplace may have been covered up by a later chimneypiece at this time. It retains no traces of any painted decoration on its surface, unlike the similar fireplaces on the first floor, and it can be assumed that the fireplace in this otherwise highly decorated chamber would have been painted. Conversely, however, the fireplaces on the first floor are known to have been covered from at least the mid-18th to the early 20th century and this may account for the survival of their decoration, whereas if that in the high (linenfold) parlour had been left exposed all traces of paint might have been removed over time. The overmantel itself was certainly obscured by later

decorations in the 19th century. When the house was restored in 1904 the outer pilasters were discovered lying in one of the cellars. They were found to 'fit exactly into the positions they now occupy; the bases only needed to be restored'.[77]

An account has been given in the preceding chapter of the painted decoration which was evidently applied to the linenfold panelling from an early date. There evidence was adduced to show that the brightest of the colour schemes – with red framing pieces, green background and yellow relief – may have been contemporary with embellishments undertaken elsewhere in the west wing in the early 17th century (*see* Fig 4.13). At the very least this vivid colour scheme would still have existed when the Milwards sought to turn this part of the house into a decorative showpiece.

The doorway at the west end of the south wall of the room, which originally led on to the staircase to the first floor, was blocked up when the staircase was remodelled and the panelling was rearranged over the blocked opening (*see* Fig 3.26).

West staircase

When, approximately a century after the house was built, a decision was taken to bring it up to date and make it a more suitable venue for lavish entertainment and the display of wealth, the existing staircase arrangement must have seemed woefully inadequate. The staircase in the east wing continued to function principally as a service stair and may even have been reinforced in that usage. Thus in order to reach the great chamber on the first floor, which would have been the principal room used for entertaining at this date, guests would have been compelled to use the steep staircase in the west wing, to which access could only be gained through the doorway in the south-west corner of the linenfold parlour (G4) at the front of the wing. This was hardly an imposing approach in keeping with the lavishness of the decoration of the main rooms.

The solution was to build an entirely new staircase in the west wing from the ground floor upwards and remove both the existing steep stairs from the ground to the first and those from the first to the second floors. To moderate the steepness of the ascent a dog-leg stair was installed between the ground and the first floors but, in order to provide sufficient width for what was intended to be a grand staircase, the lower flight was built to the south of the previous staircase compartment, thus impinging on space formerly occupied by the inner parlour (G5). The south walls of the linen-fold parlour (G4) and the bedchamber (F4) were retained as the north wall of the staircase compartment rising to second-floor level, but the former south partition wall of the staircase was rebuilt marginally to the south of its former position (thus providing more width to the upper flight of stairs), becoming the spine wall between the two flights of the new staircase. An opening was made in this wall where the lower flight turned into the upper and the upper flight was lit by the previously existing window high up in the west wall. A further partition wall was built on the south side of, and enclosing, the lower flight. This wall was removed in 1904 when the lower flight was replaced by the present balustraded stairs but it shows up clearly on earlier plans and drawings (see Figs 3.23 and 7.16).

Thus the new staircase was formed in two basically rectangular compartments, the southern one enclosing the lower flight and ceiled at first-floor level, and the northern extending upwards and ceiled at second-floor level. The upper part of the latter compartment consisted of a void space as no replacement was provided for the staircase from the first to the second floor which had been removed. The opening in the second floor was closed, and two pairs of ceiling and floor joists were fixed into the mortise joints which had been previously filled with brick and plaster fragments (see p 111). Once again the second floor of the house would not have been accessible from the staircase in the west wing, reinforcing the segregation of functions in different parts of the house.

The staircase was constructed in such a way as not only to provide a gentler and more direct approach to the principal rooms on the first floor, but also as the setting for a series of wall paintings of strapwork cartouches and *trompe l'œil* architecture which was designed to delight and impress guests as they ascended. Even the double enclosure may have been specifically designed to produce a sense of surprise and awe as the brilliantly decorated upper flight rising to the first-floor landing, with its soaring space above, was dramatically revealed. This space and the decorative scheme were drastically cut into when the present staircase was constructed from the first to the second floor. In later centuries the wall paintings were covered over by layers of paint and wallpaper until, by 1904 when the lower flight and its enclosing wall were removed, little if any of the scheme would have remained visible.

Some restoration took place in the 20th century, and from 1992 to 1993 a programme of conservation and consolidation involving the careful removal of covering layers revealed that more had survived than had been anticipated. As a result it proved possible to obtain a much clearer understanding of the original scheme.

The style of the scheme, with its strapwork and paintings of balustrading, pendants, newel posts and supporters imitating the great wooden staircases of Hatfield House, Aston Hall, Audley End and Knole, is indubitably Jacobean (Fig 5.4). But that style, introduced so successfully in the reign of James I, extended well into that of his successor and there is nothing inherently inconsistent in attributing the

Figure 5.4
West staircase. First floor. The staircase was reconstructed on a lavish scale in the early 17th century. The scheme of wall paintings, although subject to later alteration, is contemporary with this remodelling.
[87/2011; © Crown copyright.NMR]

work to the later 1620s or 1630s when the Milward family occupied the house. There is, indeed, confirmation of a kind. One of the cartouches, appropriately over the doorway to the great chamber, contains a coat of arms (Fig 5.5). In outline this is similar to the Milward coat of arms in that both have a fess containing three roundels but the colours appear reversed. For instance, the roundels here are dark on a lighter background rather than gold on a red background as in the family arms. The cartouche, however, is in monochrome and has been heavily overpainted. A drawing of *c* 1906 shows that it was exposed then (and possibly earlier) and it has been restored on a number of occasions, including in the 1970s when it was damaged by salt penetration after a water leak. It is certainly feasible that the arms are those of the Milward family, altered by overpainting.

The decoration extended into the area at the foot of the staircase which was turned into a small lobby. Here, on the underside of the stairs immediately below the first-floor landing the painting of a female classical figure has been revealed and above this an entablature similar to those elsewhere on the staircase (*see* Fig 4.15). Much of the plaster in this area has had to be renewed but above the cellar door a fragment of early plaster revealed traces of a strapwork design surmounting a horizontal band of red with black marbling. These colours are also present on the lintel and posts of the cellar

doorway and on the background framework of the painted *trompe l'œil* linenfold panelling to the left of the doorway, indicating that both schemes were probably undertaken at the same time. Reference is made in the previous chapter to the similarity of the linenfold design here to the painting of the linenfold panelling in the linenfold parlour (G4). This suggests that it was either done to harmonise with the latter or that both painting schemes date from the second quarter of the 17th century. How the remainder of the lobby area was treated is uncertain, but it was probably decorated with a combination of brightly painted linenfold panelling and wall paintings.

Sufficient evidence remains to be certain that the lower flight of stairs was included in the overall decorative scheme. Although the south wall of this flight was unfortunately demolished in 1904 (by which time it had been replastered), fragments of strapwork were discovered on the earliest coating of plaster on the west wall above the half landing, hidden under several layers of paint and wallpaper and a final covering of lath and plaster on new timber battens. The 16th-century brickwork had been hacked back to a depth of about 100mm at this point before the plaster was applied to take the wall painting. Some paint traces have also been found on the north wall of the lower flight but it has not been possible to analyse these.

The *pièce de résistance* of the whole scheme was the first-floor landing, where the three doorways to the great chamber (F3), the bedchamber (F4) and the inner chamber (F5) were surmounted by elaborate cartouches nestling under overhanging pendants. The fine moulded oak doorcases themselves formed part of the whole ensemble: that to the great chamber was in its original position, but those facing each other to the north and south had been moved from elsewhere in the house and, after some alteration and adaptation, incorporated into the partially rebuilt south wall of the bedchamber and the wholly rebuilt north wall of the inner chamber (Fig 5.6). The latter wall was a continuation of the spine wall of the staircase on the ground floor and was erected on a slightly different and more southerly alignment than the partition wall which had preceded it in order to accommodate the wider and more regular staircase (*see* Figs 6.29 and 8.16).

The extensive area of plaster repair around the opening to the great chamber,

Figure 5.5
West staircase. Detail of the wall paintings above the doorway leading into the great chamber (room F3). At the centre of the design can be seen a coat of arms, thought to be that of the Milward family.

Figure 5.6
West staircase. View from
first-floor landing into
room F5.
[87/2011; © Crown
copyright.NMR]

been inconvenient for the second floor to have been accessible only via the one staircase in the east wing. The utilitarian way in which the upper staircase was planned, with a short flight at the south end of the middle chamber (room F5) leading to a half landing from which access was gained to the upper flight through an opening which had to be cut in the decorated wall of the staircase compartment, is also perhaps indicative of a somewhat makeshift arrangement, even though it has survived to the present day (Fig 5.7; *see also* Fig 6.29). At the same time, the wall paintings were unlikely to have been valued as highly as when the house was in private hands, and they must have been vulnerable to damage. The design of the remaining hand-turned balusters of the upper flights is compatible with a late-17th-century date (Fig 5.8), while the earliest layer of dark green paint which was found covering the lower part of the painted decorations has a hint of the institutional about it.

Inner parlour (G5)

The construction of the lower flight of stairs had a dramatic impact on this room, reducing its size considerably. The south partition wall of the staircase formed the new north wall of the room and was extended to the east wall where it abutted the large mullioned-and-transomed window so that the two northernmost pairs of lights of the window thenceforth illuminated the lobby and the lower flight of the staircase (*see* Figs 6.21 and 7.4). The function of the room is likely to have changed and it may have served as little more than a cloakroom in the new arrangement. The linenfold panelling may have been removed at this time and used elsewhere. There is evidence, however, in the form of the remains of two timber floor joists partially buried in the ground, that a timber floor was laid in this period. It would still have been some 120mm below the present floor level, so that it would have been necessary to step down into the room.

South-west room (G6)

The archaeological investigation has revealed that a similar timber floor was laid in this room, on six joists running north–south which were bedded in grooves cut through the previous mortar floor into the soil beneath. This construction pre-dated the demolition of the large cross-stack which divided the room from the inner parlour (G5) to the north (*see* Fig 3.51) and,

especially to the right of the door frame, has unfortunately led to the loss of a crucial part of the decoration at the head of the stairs. What remains is not symmetrically disposed. The theory has been advanced that the cartouche and pendants above the door to the great chamber were pushed over to the left-hand side as part of a deliberate attempt by the artist to create an exaggerated sense of perspective when seen from below, but repairs to the plasterwork at later dates may mean that the explanation is altogether more mundane.

This splendid painted staircase may only have survived in its full glory for a few decades. There are indications that the construction of the extant upper staircase from the first to the second floor, which had such a damaging effect on the painted decorations, took place in the second half of the 17th century when the house was used as a school. At that time it would certainly have

in common with that of the latter room, is a relatively early example of a ground-bedded wooden floor.

The first floor

Great chamber (F3)

Much of the evidence for how the great chamber would have looked in the 17th century was removed during the substantial alterations of the 18th century, including the rebuilding of the north wall and the construction of a new ceiling at a lower level than the original. There can be little doubt that the room would have been lavishly decorated, particularly as such an imposing approach was created to it up the west staircase, but the form of the decoration can only be conjectured. Both main types of panelling which presently line the room have been shown to be older than the wall paintings of the staircase and, although the panelling appears to have been painted a cream colour from an early date (perhaps to imitate the pale biscuit colour it would have been when new), there is no evidence that it was decorated in the same intricate manner as the linenfold panelling on the ground floor. Of course, the panelling may have been covered by wall hangings or the decorative focus might have been fixed on the broad expanse of ceiling which could have been moulded or painted, or both. No fragments of such a ceiling have, however, been found.

Bedchamber (F4)

The principal new feature introduced into this room in the 17th century, as in the ground-floor chamber beneath, was an elaborate wooden overmantel and fire surround in a Jacobean style which was added to the existing panelling (*see* Fig 6.27). The overmantel consists of three fluted and cabled pilasters stopped off at mantel shelf level. Beneath the outer pilasters two more pilasters, of a similar design but with pedestals, frame the stone fireplace. The whole composition thus forms a subtle contrast with that in the linenfold parlour (G4) where the outer pilasters are continuous from floor to ceiling. The pedestals are ornamented with lozenges and the frieze rail with pyramidal forms on rectangular bases and fluted panels cut to represent triglyphs. Between the central and outer pilasters of the overmantel are two sections of panelling, each consisting of eight panels similar in type to the panelling on the remainder of the fireplace wall but arranged so that the panels

Figure 5.7
Room F5, showing flight of stairs to second floor and outline of early 16th-century fireplace.

Figure 5.8
View of the west stairwell at second-floor level in 1920.
[London Metropolitan Archives]

Figure 5.9 (above, left)
Room F5. 16th-century
fireplace at north end of
west wall, uncovered
during restoration and
following the removal of
the lower flight of stairs
rising from first- to
second-floor level.
[© James Morris/Axiom.
London]

Figure 5.10 (above, top
right)
Room F5. Detail of the
original 16th-century
fireplace, showing later
applied decoration and
marbling from the 17th
century.

appear to be on their side, with the longer side horizontal. On close examination, however, it can be seen that these sections have been made up by fixing the framing pieces on to larger panels in a somewhat crude manner. The present arrangement may, therefore, differ from the appearance of the original overmantel but it is, nevertheless, the arrangement shown on a water-colour of the late 19th century (*see* Fig 6.27), before the panelling was restored in 1904.

In fact, the whole feature shows much sign of repair and alteration. The pilasters on the north side of the fireplace have only ten flutes and cables instead of the twelve in those on the south side and have been butt jointed together at the centre throughout their length. The lower part of the central pilaster has also been repaired where it appears to have been cut away to house the mantelshelf of a wooden mid-Georgian fire surround which once completely covered the stone fireplace and was still in place

when the watercolour drawing referred to above was done.

When the stone fireplace was uncovered in 1904, it still retained traces of a scheme of decorative painting which had been applied to it at the same time as the overmantel was fixed in place or slightly later, a 'painting line' marking the join between them. The decoration is virtually identical to that of the smaller stone fireplace in the inner chamber (F5) which, because the fireplace there remained blocked until restoration work began on the house, has retained its painted surface better and provides a clearer impression of what was originally intended (Figs 5.9, 5.10, and 5.11; *see also* Figs 5.13 and 5.14). The main stonework of the fireplaces was delicately painted to simulate the appearance of red marble, while the spandrels with their intri-cate foliate carving were gilded. The shields in the corners of the spandrels were painted with coats of arms which have been blazoned as follows: that on the left-hand side of each fireplace, ermine on a fess gules three bezants; and that on the right, sable a chevron between three human legs (or boots) argent. The former coat of arms was clearly that of the Milward family, and the latter has been identified, more tentatively, with that of the Shrigley family.[78] The Shrigleys were predominantly a Cheshire family, apparently originating from the vicinity of Pott Shrigley near the border with Derbyshire, but they also had branches in Derbyshire, the home county of the Milwards. No connection between the two families has been found, however, and the presence of the Shrigley coat of arms (if it is that) on the fireplaces remains a mystery.

That the panelling was also painted at this time is suggested not only by the evidence of the decorative treatment of other rooms in the west wing but also by the discovery of traces of paint on the framing pieces, as described in the previous chapter. The colour of the earliest paint layer – red – would be compatible with the decoration of the fireplace and the apparent propensity of the Milwards for bold colours, and it seems to have been a colour much favoured at Sutton House, as in the painting of external features such as bargeboards and window frames.

The main structural alteration to the room was at the south end and was connected with the construction of the west staircase. Here the eastern half of the timber-framed south wall appears to have been rebuilt, partly to accommodate the repositioned doorway opening on to the landing at the head of the stairs but also perhaps because the wall had been weakened as a result of having to take the weight of the main north–south beam at second-floor level after the erection of the short-lived ladder staircase from the first to the second floor (see p 111) (Fig 5.12, see also Figs 3.77 and 3.78).

A vertical post was inserted between the timber sill and top-plate of the wall, the lower part forming the western side of the new door opening. It is a substantial timber but clearly reused from elsewhere, and appears to have been the head or sill of a four-light, diamond-mullioned window, weathered on one face. It has been mortised at door head height and the tenon of the horizontal timber rail forming the door head has been pegged into the mortise. A thin timber rail also connects it to the central post approximately at midpoint. The moulded oak doorcase which has been fitted into the opening has also come from elsewhere and has been adapted for its new position. Its base has been cut away by approximately 150mm on both jambs; the head is not pegged to the jambs as in similar

Figure 5.12 Room F4. View looking southwards towards the timber-framed staircase partition wall. [87/2011; © Crown copyright.NMR]

doorcases, and the plain, sunk spandrels do not appear to be original but have been worked into the altered frame. The panels between the timber-framing of the wall appear to have been renewed throughout the partition. They were infilled with a double skin of lath and plaster, after which each side was given a layer of finishing plaster. A smooth finish was necessary on the staircase side of the wall to provide a flat surface for the wall paintings but why it was considered necessary to apply finishing plaster to the room side is unclear as the panelling would have been reinstated over it. During the restoration in the 1990s some of the panels in this part of the room have been hinged to allow the timber-framed construction underneath to be seen.

Inner chamber (F5)

The wall on the other side of the staircase, which also forms the north end wall of this room, was rebuilt as a timber-framed partition wall on a new alignment when the staircase was constructed. The moulded oak doorcase at the east end is similar to that of the bedchamber opposite in having been brought from elsewhere and adjusted to fit its new position (*see* Fig 5.6).

Once this major alteration had taken place the walls of the room appear to have been plastered and colour washed, or were perhaps partially plastered and partially panelled. Areas of extant decorated plaster remaining on the east wall at the time of the survey had a similar composition to the base layer and finishing plaster of the lath and plaster infill panels of the partition wall. The absence of any trace of such plaster across the 16th-century brickwork between the sill of the window in the east wall and the floor suggests that this lower area may have been panelled. During the renovations of 1904 some older panelling was found in this room, to which new panelling was then added (*see* Fig 3.81).

At least four stages of colouring applied to the plaster can be discerned. The first was an off-white or light yellow ochre thin finishing coat of a hard lime wash, followed by two coats of a light grey plaster wash (with randomly occurring traces of extremely thin and friable dark brown and dark grey washes between them suggesting an intermediate stage of applied decoration), and a white plaster wash with a 200mm-deep black plaster-washed skirting band. Traces of the skirting band survive across the east, west and north walls, and a slight west return at the south end of the area of plaster on the east wall reveals that the band continued across the north face of the cross chimney stack before the demolition of that cross-wall in the 18th century.

The white plaster wash and black skirting band were also carried across the blocking of the fireplace in the north-west corner of the room. Once the partition wall between the room and the staircase compartment had been built on its more southerly alignment, this fireplace must have been uncomfortably, even dangerously, close to the wall and may have gone out of use soon after the new staircase was constructed. When precisely it was blocked is uncertain, but the bricks used were not common before 1670. The plaster finish described above was applied to the brickwork and carried across the jambs and head of the fireplace concealing its earlier painted decoration. At a later date, the short, lower flight of the staircase to the second floor was constructed in front of the blocked-up fireplace. Before this occurred a single skin of reused 16th-century bricks was added on top of the plaster and itself plastered over to level up the wall surface (Figs 5.13 and 5.14).

The removal of these various stages of blocking during works to the house revealed the stone Tudor fireplace and its 17th-century decoration substantially intact. The decoration is essentially the same as that of the fireplace in the bedchamber (F4) which has been described more fully above but, because it had been covered up for some three hundred years, it is in much better condition. The discovery of the existence of this previously unsuspected fireplace with its painted decoration was an unexpected bonus of the fabric analysis undertaken in the 1980s (*see* Figs 5.9, 5.10 and 5.11).

The short flight of stairs referred to above in the discussion of the west staircase was constructed against the southern timber-framed partition wall. The flight ended at a half landing in front of the blocked-in fireplace and a doorway was made in the wall at this height for access to the upper flight of stairs up to the second floor. The west end of the partition wall was cut away to make the doorway, causing damage to the adjoining lath-and-plaster infill panels. The panel below the doorway was, in fact, completely replaced. On the staircase side of the wall the damage to the painted decorations must have been very considerable, if they had not already been covered over.

Figure 5.13
Room F5. North end of
west wall prior to the
restoration. Traces of the
earlier decorative scheme
and shadows left after the
removal of the later
framing battening can be
clearly seen.
[Engineering Surveys
Ltd/The National Trust]

The second floor

Most of the changes on the second floor which can be attributed to the 17th century centred around the alterations to the staircase in the west wing. When the great, painted staircase was installed below, probably in the 1620s or 1630s, the steep staircase to the second floor, which had itself been built after the original construction of the house (*see* p 111), was removed and the small opening which had been made in the second floor was once again closed and ceiled over.

When the staircase from the first to the second floor was reinstated, in the arrangement which exists today, a much larger opening was made and a balustrade was erected on its north side (*see* Fig 5.8). The shape of the hand-turned balusters is more typical of the late 17th century than the mid-18th century and is further evidence that the installation of this staircase is likely to have taken place before the major alterations of 1741–3 and 1751–2 described in Chapter 6.

Because of the length of the opening, the doorway into the southern room on the second floor of the west wing was moved from the west end of the partition wall to the east, as in the present arrangement. A new

Figure 5.14
Room F5 during the
dismantling of the lower
flight of stairs at the north-
west corner to reveal the
blocked 16th-century
fireplace. The work was
undertaken by National
Trust specialists.
[Ken Jacobs]

stud-and-plaster partition wall was built to the north of the balustrade to close off the landing from the front room in this wing. This wall was built with a central doorway rather than one at the east end as at present (*see* Fig 6.17).

The grounds and outbuildings

The twenty-one fireplaces recorded in the first hearth tax return of 1662 would appear to be too many for the house alone, and the existence of a number of outbuildings can be presumed. Archaeological excavation has revealed evidence of a sequence of buildings to the south-west of the west wing, and this area, completely reconstructed in the Edwardian period, may have been built up from an early date. The boundary with the neighbouring property of the Tanhouse to the west at this time is unclear. Some adjustments are known to have been made in the 17th century, and the earliest plans of the Tanhouse suggest that there may

have been a 'flying freehold' at one point.[79] Whether there was any direct communication between the outbuildings and the south end of the west wing, as at a later date, is virtually impossible to determine because of the degree of rebuilding that has taken place in this area.

The excavation also disclosed evidence of a terrace, composed of a layer of compact orange sandy gravel which had been rammed down to form an even surface, at the rear of the two wings and the courtyard. The terrace was fronted by low brick walls (possibly balustraded) and had a projection to the south opposite the east door of the hall range, perhaps leading to a flight of steps down to the remainder of the garden as it sloped down to Hackney Brook. The site of the terrace, which must have been a dominating feature of the garden while it remained, is now largely occupied by Wenlock Barn. From the sequence of later finds it is thought to have been formed in the early 17th century (*see* Fig 3.20).

6

The House Transformed

Sutton House was subjected to a greater degree of alteration in the mid-18th century than at any time since it had been built, and indeed than at any time subsequently. The documentary evidence suggests that most of this work was carried out between 1741 and 1743, with further changes from 1751 to 1752 when the house was subdivided. The events leading up to that transformation and the extent of the alterations are the subjects of this chapter.

The ownership of the house

The copyhold ownership of the house remained separate from its use and occupation throughout the 18th century, and the impetus for 'modernisation' in the middle of the century appears to have come from a leaseholder rather than one of the copyhold owners.

By the end of the 17th century, the ownership had passed to Sarah Wagstaffe, a widow, who was a granddaughter of the Henry Whittingham who had purchased the property in 1656. She died in 1709 or 1710 and thereafter the copyhold ownership changed hands a number of times in a complex manner. In her will, proved in July 1710, Sarah Wagstaffe left her copyhold property in Hackney to her daughters Rebecca and Lydia Wagstaffe.[1] They were young women, barely in their twenties, and in 1718 they sold the property to Thomas Foster of the Artillery Ground, Tower Hamlets, a dyer, who promptly surrendered it to the use of his will.[2] Foster had been assiduously buying up copyholds in Homerton for some time and in 1714 acquired some land with two houses on it which appears to have been situated a short distance to the east of Sutton House, thus initiating a process of consolidating a number of interspersed holdings into a compact copyhold estate.[3]

Foster, who lived in one of the newly acquired houses himself, died in 1723, leaving some of his copyhold property to his daughter Elizabeth and some to his son William who gave his share to his sister, thus reuniting the holding.[4] Elizabeth Foster continued to live in the house formerly occupied by her father but barely had time to enjoy her estate before she too died in 1727. In her will, after expressing a wish to be buried in Hackney churchyard where her father and brother were buried, she divided her property into two moieties, one to be inherited by her uncle, John Foster, of Penitent Street, Ratcliffe Highway, and the other by her cousin, Mary Foster, the daughter of another uncle, Richard Foster.[5]

Shortly afterwards Mary Foster married Robert Aldwinckle, a tallow chandler of Hackney, and in 1728 they reconveyed the moiety she had inherited to their joint ownership. By the following year John Foster had died, leaving his only daughter, Jane Cooke, the wife of John Cooke of Stepney, a shipwright, as his heir, and in April 1729 she was admitted to the ownership of the other moiety in the manorial court.[6] Robert Aldwinckle and Jane Cooke died at approximately the same time, both of their wills being proved in March 1740. Aldwinckle fittingly left his share of the moiety he had acquired through marriage to his wife for her own property. Jane Cooke, who was widowed and had run up a considerable mortgage debt and arrears of interest, made an agreement with Thomas Wilson of Glasshouse Street, Westminster, that he should inherit her moiety on condition that he paid her debts and funeral expenses. Wilson was described as a tinman, which was a term used at the time for either a tinsmith or a retailer of tinware.[7]

Mary Aldwinckle quickly remarried, becoming Mary Davison, and in 1743 she and her husband, Thomas Davison, surrendered her moiety to Mary Garthwaite of Eltham, spinster, who was admitted as the new owner in the manorial court. Within two years, however, she had surrendered the property to Thomas Wilson, who thus in 1745 reunited the moieties and became the owner of the extended copyhold estate which included Sutton House, its grounds, and other land and houses to the east on the south side of Homerton High Street. At this date his property comprised all of the land on the south side of the street from Sutton House to Bridge Street (now Ponsford Street) with the exception of a broad corridor, some 100 to 120ft (30.5 to 36.5m) wide, a short distance to the west of Bridge Street and extending the whole distance between the High Street and Hackney Brook. This approximately rectangular piece of land was never part of the estate of Thomas Wilson or his successors in title and was a reminder both of the typical division of the land into long strips under the open field system and of how fragmented ownership here may once have been.[8]

The continuation of the girls' school

Sutton House continued to be used as a girls' school until the 1740s. Sarah Freeman died in 1700 and the administration of her estate and effects was granted to her daughter Priscilla Story.[9] There is then a gap in the records until the first extant rate books for Hackney in 1716 show the occupant at that time to have been Amy Hutton, later joined by Ann Webb.

In 1718 the owner, Thomas Foster, insured the house with the Hand-in-Hand Company, when it was described as 'a Brick House together with a Schooll House & Brew House and other offices thereunto adjoyning . . . known by the name of the Ivey Schooll, now in the Possession of Amy Hutton & Ann Webb.'[10] The diary of the young Dudley Ryder, later Attorney General and Chief Justice, which he kept from 1715 to 1716, refers to Mrs Hutton's school. The Ryder family lived nearby and in August 1715 he sought to assuage the loneliness of a friend in a manner familiar to young men down the centuries:

> After prayers saw Mr. Hudson at the door. He was telling me how lonely he lived without any of his family with him. I told him he must find out a way to get some of the ladies at the school to visit him now and then, and I promised him to assist him in that if I might receive some of the benefit of it by coming to see them at his house. So we went together to the back gate and there they were. He after a little time of silence spoke to them. They took him at first for a servant of the house but afterwards they discovered he was not so they seemed very much inclined to have a correspondence with him, but they

told him Mrs. Hutton was coming and desired he would go and come again half an hour afterwards. I came home and stayed longer at supper than half an hour, that when I came they were gone. However, Mr. Hudson called to them at their window and asked them to come down. They told him they could not but seemed very much inclined to it. I did not discover myself to them.

Two days later he returned to the theme:

> As I came home went to the back door of the schoolhouse in the field and there found Mr. Hudson, Milbourn and Gould at the door. The girls were at first very merry at dancing but presently comes the schoolmistress and reproved them very severely for their having held discourse with a man and entertaining them upon the wall.[11]

The tight discipline that Mrs Hutton maintained must have recommended itself to parents, for the school appears to have been well attended. In 1720 the Vestry debated whether to accommodate Mrs Hutton and her scholars 'out of the Gallery now used by the said Mrs Hutton'. The gallery was presumably the one built by Sarah Freeman and the implication is that it could not cater for all of the girls.[12]

In 1723 the ratebooks show that Amy Hutton and Ann Webb had left and that the house was now occupied by Mary Joseph, initially with Sarah Baldwin as a co-ratepayer.[13] Mary Joseph appears to have taken over Amy Hutton's school. In 1732 she was allocated a pew in the parish church for her own use as long as she remained in the parish and kept a school there, which she apparently continued to do until her death in 1741.[14] In her will she gave £100 and all her wearing apparel, silk, linen and wool, and a set of cherry-coloured bed curtains lined with green to Susanna Baldwin of Hackney, spinster. A Sarah Baldwin, spinster, had been buried in the parish church in September 1723 and Susanna, who may have been her sister, was probably an assistant schoolmistress or companion to Mary Joseph who, from the evidence of her will, also had a number of servants.[15]

The early land tax returns for Hackney show that Mary Joseph's school had substantial grounds, for which it was assessed at a far higher rate than nearby properties. For a brief period some land 'behind Mrs Joseph's house' was rated separately, suggesting that there might have been a field or fields which could be let independently, but by 1741 this was once again included in Mary Joseph's property. Dudley Ryder refers to 'the schoolhouse in the field,' and it is likely that at this time the grounds of the house certainly extended as far as Hackney Brook and perhaps beyond to Morning Lane on the south, and to the modern Churchwell Path on the west, with additional open land to the east. This is the impression conveyed by John Rocque's map of 1745 (see Fig 5.1) and reinforced by the tithe apportionment survey of a century later (see Fig 6.39) which shows some 5 acres (2ha) of land, including over 2 acres (0.8ha) of 'meadow', attached to the property (see p 171).[16]

Despite its idyllic setting, the school closed on Mary Joseph's death. By 1742 individual parishioners were being given permission to erect pews in her former gallery (presumably originally Sarah Freeman's) in the parish church, and the house itself appears to have remained empty for two or three years.[17]

John Cox and the alterations to the house

The manorial records are relatively informative about changes in copyhold ownership, at least for those periods when they are available for consultation,[18] but they are less forthcoming about the disposition of the property in the way of leases. From other evidence, however, it is clear that various parcels of the copyhold had been let to John Cox, a local bricklayer. Shortly after Mary Joseph's death, he also appears to have been granted a long lease of Sutton House.[19] From 1741 to 1743 the land tax returns show Cox in possession of the house but apparently paying no rate because it was listed as empty. At the time of his death in 1760 he still retained a sufficient leasehold interest in the by then much transformed property for it to constitute the principal bequest in his will.[20]

Cox was living in Hackney by 1713 when his son, also named John, was born. The boy died in 1723, and his wife Sarah two years later in her thirty-fifth year. In November 1725, when described as a widower, he remarried, his second wife being Mary Cratchfield or Crutchfield, and between 1727 and 1731 they had three children, Elizabeth, Sarah and John. Mary, John Cox's second wife, died in 1751. Cox was a quite prominent local figure, serving at various times as a churchwarden, constable and overseer of the poor, and he was one of the parishioners who was allowed to erect a pew in the gallery which had formerly been Mary Joseph's.[21]

It is possible that John Cox had been building in Spitalfields in the first decade of the 18th century. A John Cox was granted building leases for houses in the vicinity of Wentworth Street and Bell Lane, where Cox's Square (now demolished) was named after him and Cox's Court survives as a place name.[22] The name Cox is common enough but the pattern of occupancy of Sutton House after its conversion by Cox suggests a Spitalfields connection.

What is certain is that Cox was active as a builder in Homerton for some years before he took a lease of Sutton House. In 1721 the rate collector noted that he was building a house there, and his name frequently appears subsequently as the ratepayer for land that belonged to someone else.[23] Cox appears indeed to have been responsible for several of the houses that were erected on both sides of Homerton High Street as the area became increasingly built up in the 18th century. His purpose in acquiring Sutton House in 1741 seems to have been to add it to his sphere of building operations, not by demolishing it but by modernising and eventually subdividing the house.

Commentators have generally ascribed an earlier date of c 1700, mainly on stylistic grounds, to the major alterations to the house. However, if as appears likely, the house was occupied by a girls' school from 1657 to 1741, it is unlikely that such extensive and expensive alterations would have been undertaken during that period. (At one time it was thought that a lease of the house had been granted in 1701 to Daniel Stacey, a brewer, but evidence has come to light that the property so leased was in another part of the copyhold, near the bridge over Hackney Brook known as Blue Bridge, where Stacey established a brewery on the site of the present public house at the corner of Ponsford Street and Morning Lane.)[24]

The visual evidence may also be misleading. Cox was a local builder and doubtless somewhat conservative in his building methods. The presence of such features as segmental-headed openings and window frames mounted nearly flush with the wall surface on the side and rear elevations is not compelling evidence of an early date.

It is on the main, north front, however, that the present appearance is most misleading. A partial view of this front, photographed in the late 19th century (Fig 6.1), shows the sash windows at ground- and first-floor level in the centre to have had thin glazing bars, rectangular panes, six over six, and slightly recessed frames without horns, entirely consistent with a building date of the 1740s. The outer windows on the first floor (the left one of which is visible in the photograph) are later insertions in previously blocked openings, but were designed to match those already existing from the 1740s. Apparently during the major alterations for St John's Institute carried out in 1904, these sash windows were replaced by ones of a new design, in a style which can perhaps best be described as an Arts and Crafts version of early Georgian, with thick glazing bars and small panes (*see* Fig 7.8), thus misleading later commentators.

Mary Tooke and the beginning of the Huguenot connection

If the weight of evidence makes it increasingly likely that the main Georgianisation of Sutton House was undertaken by John Cox between 1741 and 1743 when the house was empty, there is still considerable uncertainty about the precise sequence of work. In 1743 the name of a new occupant, Mrs Mary Tooke, was entered in the rate book; she was paying a sufficiently high rate to suggest that she may have been occupying the whole house and, as a wealthy widow, there is no doubt that she could afford to do so. She had been born Mary Lethieullier in 1676, the daughter of William Lethieullier, a merchant. The Lethieulliers were a prominent Huguenot family in London, William's grandmother having emigrated from Brabant in 1605. Mary's uncle, Sir John Lethieullier, was an alderman and sheriff of London, and a cousin, Smart Lethieullier, was a noted antiquary, collector and Fellow of the Royal Society.[25]

Mary Lethieullier had been married to Edmund Tooke, another eminent merchant who was also clerk of the Salters' Company and had died at Salters' Hall in 1729.[26] Thus when she came to live at Sutton House, as the first of several occupants of Huguenot descent over the next hundred or so years, she had been a widow for fourteen years and her four children were all grown up. She lived there until her death in 1751. In her will, which made no mention of her late husband, she expressed a wish to be buried in her father's vault at Clapham, and gave directions that at her funeral there should be a hearse and coach, each pulled by six horses. She left legacies totalling over £10,000 to her children, and although not citing Sutton House itself, presumably because she merely held the house under a tenancy agreement with John Cox, her bequests of furniture, china and furnishings attest to an opulent lifestyle. Among specific items mentioned were a 'silk damask bed' with crimson damask and green silk, and a 'red China bed', presumably one decorated in the newly fashionable Chinese taste.[27]

The subdivision of the house

In 1748 the name of another ratepayer, Timothy Ravenhill, was interlined in the rate book next to that of Mary Tooke, suggesting that he was occupying new premises which had not been previously rated. Ravenhill's assessment for the poor rate was half that of Mary Tooke's (and was further reduced for that year because he had only been in residence for six months), but Mary Tooke's rate stayed proportionately the same in relationship to that of other nearby householders and remained so until her death. She was succeeded as ratepayer by George Garrett. In 1752 Garrett's rate was

reduced and Ravenhill's increased so that they both ended up paying the same. In 1753, when the fire insurance was renewed, the house was described as formerly the Ivy School, now in the possession of Ravenhill and Garrett.[28]

The continuing sequence of ratepayers after Garrett and Ravenhill makes it clear that Sutton House had been divided into two residences by 1752. It is possible that the division had taken place at the same time as the main series of alterations and that Mary Tooke lived in the western half of the house, while the eastern part, where more Georgian features were introduced internally, was still undergoing renovation. However, the high rate she paid and the long time-span involved militate against such an explanation. Moreover, the physical evidence, which is described in more detail later in this chapter, suggests that the work was done in two stages.

At some time in the mid-18th century another building was erected across the rear of the east wing, partially utilising the end wall of the wing as a party wall. It was demolished for the building of Wenlock Barn in 1904, but shows up on earlier maps. A drawing made by F C Varley at the end of the 19th century (Fig 6.2), by which time it had been altered, depicts it as a substantial

Figure 6.2
Sutton House, viewed from the south, as it appeared at the end of the 19th century. Watercolour by F C Varley.

HACKNEY, London.   Milford House, Hackney

two-storeyed structure with a double roof. It would certainly have been large enough to have constituted a small house in its own right and may have been built as such by John Cox and occupied initially by Timothy Ravenhill. When Mary Tooke died in 1751 Cox may have taken the opportunity to divide the larger house and add the east wing to Ravenhill's, thus making two roughly equal-sized houses, as the changes in rateable value in 1752 would imply.

George Garrett and Timothy Ravenhill, who appear to have been the first occupants of the subdivided Sutton House, had much in common. Garrett, who was of Huguenot descent, was in business with his brother Alexander as a weaver and warehouseman in Paternoster Row (now Brushfield Street), Spitalfields, in the late 1730s and early 1740s. Alexander Garrett died in 1748 owning some land in Hackney, and George Garrett, who succeeded his brother as a local Justice of the Peace, was recognised by the manorial court as guardian to his infant son. In the late 1740s and early 1750s Garrett was living in a house in Fournier Street, Spitalfields, where he was listed as a merchant in directories.[29] He may have moved from there to Hackney, or may have decided to acquire a second home in somewhat leafier surroundings than Spitalfields, which was by then becoming overcrowded. Whatever the circumstances, his stay in the western half of Sutton House appears to have been brief, for he had left by 1754.

Timothy Ravenhill had a house in Milk Street in the City, where he carried on business as a mercer. He, too, may have been following the time-honoured practice of City merchants of seeking out an additional 'country' residence in Hackney. Two of his children were christened in St John's, Hackney, in 1751 and 1753, but a subsequent child was baptised at St Mary Magdalene, Milk Street, in 1755. By the 1760s he had moved his business, and seemingly his residence, to Spitalfields. In 1765 Timothy Ravenhill and Son carried on business as merchants in Paternoster Row, and a few years previously Ravenhill and Auber had been listed as silk weavers in the same street. By 1771 Timothy and William Ravenhill, merchants, occupied the largest house in Spital Square, a square whose residents were for the most part silk merchants and master weavers. Timothy Ravenhill appears briefly to have returned to live in the eastern part of Sutton House c 1778, perhaps on retirement, but he had moved to Cheshunt

in Hertfordshire by the time of his death in 1780.[30]

Garrett was succeeded in the western house in 1754 by Thomas Hyam, and when he left in 1758 John Cox took up residency himself. The eastern house passed from Ravenhill to Mary Norton in 1753. In 1757 she was succeeded as ratepayer by William Norton, who may also have been a merchant as a William Norton of Hackney was listed as a merchant in a directory of 1758.[31] In 1758 John Cox and William Norton were jointly arraigned before the manorial court for stopping up Hackney Brook to the great annoyance of other tenants of the manor and they were ordered to reopen the watercourse.[32]

John Cox's will

John Cox died in May 1760. In his will he divided up the leasehold property in which he still had an interest between his three children. The western house in which he himself lived passed to his daughter Sarah (who succeeded him as ratepayer), and the eastern house in Norton's occupation to his other daughter Elizabeth. There was a third leasehold house (presumably subdivided) that he bequeathed to his son John and which is described as being in the occupation of his son and of Mary Seedon, a widow. From the evidence of ratebooks this house stood some distance to the east of Sutton House, with other properties intervening, but in his will Cox referred to a yard 'belonging and adjoining to' the three houses containing stables and sheds. Later maps show a complex of non-residential buildings on the east side of the eastern of the two houses into which Sutton House had been divided (see Fig 6.38); their site is presently occupied by the northern end of Isabella Road and the houses on its north-east corner. Exactly how this complex, which had presumably been built by John Cox, could have adjoined all three houses is difficult to interpret, but Cox may have been using the term in an elastic manner. He also left to Elizabeth Cox some garden ground and closes of land which had been sublet to other tenants. By the 19th century the eastern of the two houses which had been formed out of Sutton House had very much more extensive grounds than the western, and this may have been the result of the incorporation of the additional land bequeathed to Elizabeth Cox.[33]

Thus by 1760 the Georgianised and subdivided Sutton House would have fitted appropriately into a much changed, and changing, local scene. There were some old houses remaining, including the Tanhouse, itself subdivided into three houses, but there were also many new houses in the Georgian style as ribbon development spread along Upper Homerton (now Urswick Road) and Homerton High Street.

The fabric

The evidence that the house was substantially altered in two phases, in 1741–3 and 1751–2, is generally borne out by an examination of the fabric (Figs 6.3 and 6.4). Nevertheless, it is impossible to be precise about dates and some alterations (for instance the replacement of older windows with the newly fashionable sashes on the side and rear elevations) may have taken place earlier. All parts of the house were affected, but the main thrust of decorative change was directed towards the east wing which, as the service wing, had perhaps been more neglected in earlier periods of change. As a result, while the east wing was heavily Georgianised, the west wing was left internally with its Tudor and Stuart character largely intact in the principal rooms.

The exterior

The transformation of the exterior of the house was indeed dramatic, and affected all the elevations to a greater or lesser degree. The main object appears to have been the replacement of most of the mullioned-and-transomed casement windows with sash windows. To effect such a change it was also necessary to rebuild much of the brickwork around the openings, and it seems likely that the principal disruptions to the diaper patterning occurred at this time. Not all the windows were affected. The large twelve-light window on the ground floor of the west wing overlooking the courtyard was left intact and the first-floor window above it may also have been preserved at this time, the present 'Gothick' window appearing to have been inserted into the Tudor opening at a later date (see Figs 8.3 and 8.9).

The principal, north elevation was the most altered (Fig 6.5). The front of the east wing was apparently rebuilt, but using the original Tudor bricks (a degree of change that became apparent when much of the render that subsequently covered this part of the façade was removed in the course of the restoration). Although a substantial degree of rebuilding had to take place at the front of the west wing, some of the brickwork was left intact, which may account for the degree of survival of the diaper patterning.

The centre of the north front, between the wings, was completely rebuilt from the ground-floor plinth to the roof level. When the old wall was taken down, however, many of the 16th-century bricks were carefully salvaged and reused to form the core work and inner face of the new wall. On the outside a 100mm skin of new 65mm bricks of a purplish-reddish hue was laid in Flemish bond and randomly bonded in. The colour of the new brickwork may have been chosen to blend in as far as was possible with the orange-red Tudor brickwork of the wings.

Although the width of the wall dictated that there should be a four-bay pattern to the fenestration, only the two central bays were provided with box sashes, the outer 'openings' on the upper floors being blind and, at first-floor level, shorter than their present length. It is presumed that the western of the present two doorways was inserted in the second phase of alterations, but whether the 'window' that would have briefly existed here on the ground floor was blind is not known. The evident desire for symmetry in the composition of the new elevation would suggest that it was.

Such an extreme degree of reconstruction was probably necessitated by the size and secondary structural function of the original large mullioned-and-transomed windows. As the surviving window in the courtyard elevation of the west range shows, the frames supported the facing brickwork, the inner brickwork or core-work being supported by separate and independent timber lintels. Once these frames were removed, with the intention of replacing them with narrower sashes, the extent of reconstruction involved probably rendered demolition and rebuilding as the best option.

The Georgianisation of the façade was completed by the removal of the four gables, the hipping back of the roofs and the raising of the front walls to form parapets. During this work lengths of carved bargeboards (see Fig 3.17), presumably taken from the demolished gables, were used as hip rafters in the reconstructed twin roofs over the central range. These were removed when the roof was restored in the 1970s and subsequently put on display on the ground floor of the west range, from where they were stolen in the 1980s.

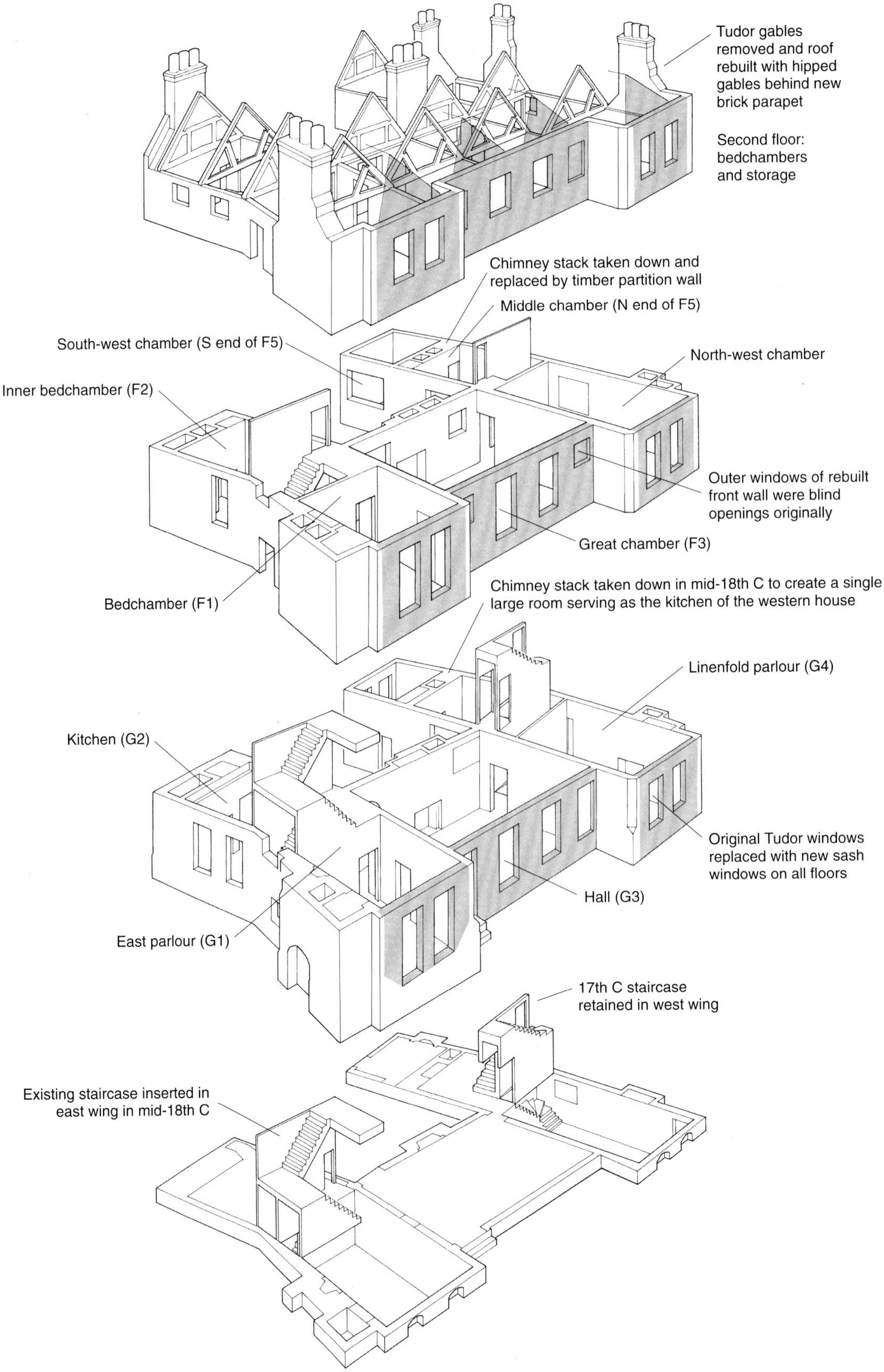

Figure 6.3
Exploded perspective
drawing showing how
Sutton House functioned in
the period 1741–52.
Changes included the
removal of the front gables,
construction of the extant
hipped roof, remodelling of
the main façade and the
insertion of sash windows.
[Richard Bond]

Tudor gables removed and roof rebuilt with hipped gables behind new brick parapet

Second floor: bedchambers and storage

Chimney stack taken down and replaced by timber partition wall

Middle chamber (N end of F5)

South-west chamber (S end of F5)

North-west chamber

Inner bedchamber (F2)

Outer windows of rebuilt front wall were blind openings originally

Great chamber (F3)

Bedchamber (F1)

Chimney stack taken down in mid-18th C to create a single large room serving as the kitchen of the western house

Linenfold parlour (G4)

Kitchen (G2)

Original Tudor windows replaced with new sash windows on all floors

Hall (G3)

East parlour (G1)

17th C staircase retained in west wing

Existing staircase inserted in east wing in mid-18th C

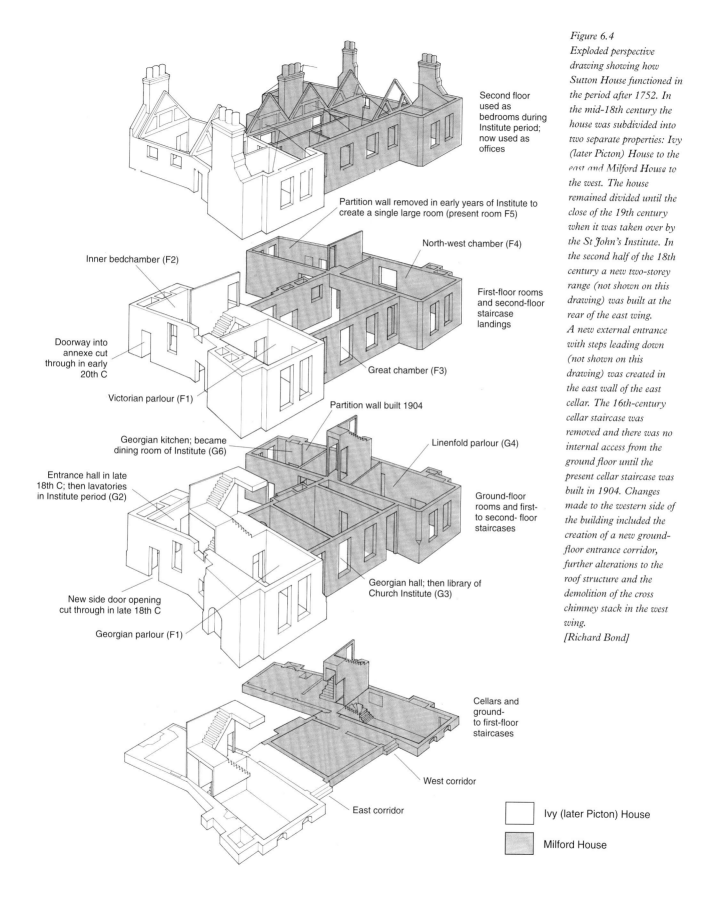

Second floor used as bedrooms during Institute period; now used as offices

Partition wall removed in early years of Institute to create a single large room (present room F5)

North-west chamber (F4)

Inner bedchamber (F2)

First-floor rooms and second-floor staircase landings

Doorway into annexe cut through in early 20th C

Victorian parlour (F1)

Great chamber (F3)

Georgian kitchen; became dining room of Institute (G6)

Partition wall built 1904

Linenfold parlour (G4)

Entrance hall in late 18th C; then lavatories in Institute period (G2)

Ground-floor rooms and first- to second- floor staircases

New side door opening cut through in late 18th C

Georgian hall; then library of Church Institute (G3)

Georgian parlour (F1)

Cellars and ground- to first-floor staircases

West corridor

East corridor

Ivy (later Picton) House

Milford House

Figure 6.4
Exploded perspective drawing showing how Sutton House functioned in the period after 1752. In the mid-18th century the house was subdivided into two separate properties: Ivy (later Picton) House to the east and Milford House to the west. The house remained divided until the close of the 19th century when it was taken over by the St John's Institute. In the second half of the 18th century a new two-storey range (not shown on this drawing) was built at the rear of the east wing. A new external entrance with steps leading down (not shown on this drawing) was created in the east wall of the east cellar. The 16th-century cellar staircase was removed and there was no internal access from the ground floor until the present cellar staircase was built in 1904. Changes made to the western side of the building included the creation of a new ground-floor entrance corridor, further alterations to the roof structure and the demolition of the cross chimney stack in the west wing.
[Richard Bond]

Figure 6.5
Reconstruction drawing of
the main (north) elevation
c 1741. Major structural
alterations were undertaken
during this period,
including the replacement
of the former gables with
hips and the complete
rebuilding of the front wall
of the hall range. Although
the main entrance appears
to have remained, it has
not been included as no
positive fabric evidence was
found as to its form.
(Scale 1:200)

Although the present north front essentially retains the appearance given to the house by the reconstruction of the mid-18th century, there are some important later changes which must be removed in the mind's eye before an accurate picture of how the house would have looked then can be formed. Obvious later features include the Victorian sash windows and stucco rendering of the east wing. Less obvious, but equally important changes, are the insertion of full-length windows in the formerly blind outer openings of the first floor (but not the second floor) of the central range (*see* Fig 6.23), and, most pertinently, the replacement of the Georgian sash windows by ones with thicker glazing bars and smaller panes (*see* p 136).

On the courtyard elevations it was apparently not considered desirable or necessary to make such drastic changes; nevertheless, the present appearance of the brickwork indicates a considerable degree of reworking to incorporate new fenestration, with old window openings blocked up or changed and new ones opened up. In addition, once the house had been subdivided, a new doorway into the courtyard was provided at the end of the newly formed passageway at the west end of the former hall (*see* Fig 6.4).

More substantial alterations were made at the rear of the west wing, where an almost complete rebuilding had to be undertaken as a consequence of what appears to have been a structural failure. The precise timing of this work is uncertain, but the collapse may have followed quite soon after the removal of the internal brick cross-stack (*see* Fig 3.51), which appears to have been the immediate cause of the failure, and the subsequent complication in the conversion of the house may account for the length of time it remained untenanted. The reconstruction was carefully executed, using the original bricks, and because the seat of the problem was in the south-west corner of the wing, the courtyard elevation did not have to be entirely rebuilt. Nevertheless the work resulted not only in the removal of the Tudor windows, which might have been anticipated, but also in the blocking up of the doorway from the courtyard into room G6 (*see* Fig 3.82).

The southern wall of the wing was completely demolished down to part of the original footings and rebuilt on widened footings, using 16th-century bricks laid in header bond. The openings on the ground floor still retain the remains of mid-18th-century casement windows, despite much later alteration and the conversion of the eastern opening into a doorway. Although fragmentary, these are rare survivals, and indicate a utilitarian function for the room behind, in contrast to the first floor, where the more fashionable sash windows were used (*see* Fig 3.53).

The southern end of the west wall was also rebuilt incorporating a chimney stack for new fireplaces on the ground and first floors and, on the ground floor, a new door-way in the south-west corner. Excavation has shown that at the time this was an external doorway which communicated with a gravelled yard and doubtless outbuildings beyond, and that the infilling of the yard which made it an internal doorway, as shown on later plans, was a subsequent development (*see* Fig 8.11). At second-floor level not only the end gable but also part of the roof structure appears to have collapsed. The south end of the wing and roof frame were not reconstructed at this level; instead the south wall was set back by some 2.5m and the roof hipped back on a shallow pitch at its apex, thus producing a sharp contrast in appearance to the original high gabled wing (*see* Figs 3.80 and 3.82).

The south end of the east wing with its massive end stack was largely unchanged at the upper level, but at the lower level the building of what seems originally to have been a separate house *c* 1748 across the end of the wing also had a dramatic effect on the view of the house from the south. An impression of the result can be gained from the watercolour painting of the 1890s by F C Varley (*see* Fig 6.2), with the caveat that the appearance of the additions, even ignoring the growth of ivy, was altered by a remodelling in the late 18th century.

The plan *c* 1741–3

How far the basic plan of the house was affected by the first stage of the mid-18th-century alterations, before the house was subdivided, is uncertain. The introduction of high quality softwood panelling and other Georgian features into the east (service) wing certainly betokened a change in both form and function. Likewise, the removal of the massive cross-stack in the west wing, apparently to create a larger room on the ground floor (at first-floor level the brick stack was replaced by a partition wall), may

have signalled an intention to place the kitchen in that wing. There is then, a hint that a reorientation of the house might have been planned, but so soon were the further changes in plan carried out, consequent on the division into two houses, that this must remain a matter of conjecture.

The plan *c* 1751–2

The division of the house into two separate dwellings was not a simple matter. On the ground floor it entailed the building of a brick party wall to separate the former screens passage at the east end of the hall, which now became the entrance passage of the eastern house, from the hall itself, and the formation of another corridor at the west end of the hall to serve as an entrance passageway for the western house. In the process the hall itself disappeared as a unit and what was left of it was turned into a smaller room (on later plans designated as a library) for the western house (*see* Fig 8.11). On the first floor the great chamber was left intact and allocated to the western house, thus at its eastern end 'flying' over the entranceway to the other house. What happened at second-floor level is unclear. The new party wall formed by the eastern wall of the great chamber may have been continued upwards, in a fairly insubstantial manner, but, if so, no trace of it remains. On the other hand there is evidence that a timber-framed partition wall existed beneath the valley between the twin pitched roofs of the central range, and this may have been adapted as a party wall to provide a more equal division on this floor, at the expense of a further complication to the vertical arrangement of the two houses (*see* Fig 3.87).

After the division the western house emerged as the larger of the two, at least in terms of the number of rooms from the original structure, but the eastern house had the benefit of the substantial two-storeyed addition at the rear of the east wing.

There is only limited evidence for precisely how each house functioned. It is clear that in the western house the large room (G5 and G6) at the rear of the west wing became a kitchen. By the date of the first extant large-scale plan of the house, made in the 1890s after the two halves of the house had been reunited (*see* Fig 7.16), the linenfold-panelled room at the front of the wing (G4) was used as a dining room, while the room to the east of the entrance passage

(G3) was a library. Certainly, one or other of these two rooms would logically have served as a dining room when subdivision first took place.

In the eastern house the picture is complicated by the demolition of the rear addition for the building of Wenlock Barn in 1904. We know from excavations that the structure contained a number of rooms and was subject to several changes over the century and a half of its existence (*see* Figs 6.34 and 6.35). It seems likely that the kitchen and other service rooms were moved into this block at an early date, thus freeing up the older part of the wing for a complete change in function, but the handsomely panelled room at the front of the wing (G1) may have been intended as a dining room from the start. Further speculation on the use of some of the surviving rooms is included in the descriptions below.

The interior

There is a paucity of information about any alterations during the long period between the 1750s and the reasonably well documented conversion of 1904. Thus, the room descriptions below, while seeking in the main to confine themselves to the changes of the mid-18th century, may, because of the difficulties of dating, include accounts of some work carried out later.

The cellars

East cellar

The mid-18th-century alterations to the east cellar have been largely obliterated by later changes. As part of the reconstruction of the front wall, the original external entrance appears to have been converted into a window, and another new window was inserted into the 16th-century opening at the west end of the north wall. A new external entrance was made either at this time or later in the east wall immediately south of the projecting brick chimney stack (where it is shown on the first large-scale Ordnance Survey map of 1870; *see* Fig 7.1). To accommodate this, the central and southern recesses on this wall were cut away to the south and north respectively and the

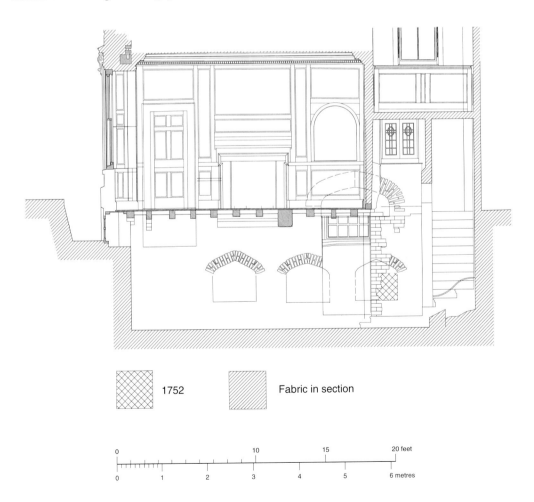

Figure 6.6
Room G1. Internal elevation of the east wall of room G1 and the east cellar as existing in 1990. (Scale 1:80)

1752   Fabric in section

0   10   15   20 feet
0   1   2   3   4   5   6 metres

remains of the openings supported with brick infilling (Fig 6.6). Evidence also survives of a lath-and-plaster ceiling which was applied to the underside of the floor joists, leaving the underside of the main beams exposed. The cellar was divided into two by a north–south partition, possibly when the house was subdivided.

West cellar

Not only has more evidence survived in the west cellar of the major alterations of this period, but there are also indications of two distinct phases of work. As in the east cellar, the external doorway (which appears to have remained in use until this date) was blocked up and converted into a window, and a new window inserted into the other 16th-century opening. The walls appear to have been plastered and a ceiling was constructed in a similar manner to that of the east cellar. Remnants of this ceiling remain trapped above the brick walls of a slightly later enclosure in the south-east corner of the cellar. The plaster remains consist of lime and sand bound together with ox hair, as a base coat, with a thin skim of lime and fine sand as a finish coat.

The brick enclosure, of uncertain usage, was created as part of the second phase of alterations. The north and east walls forming the enclosure are constructed in 60mm bricks in a mixture of English and Flemish bond. Both walls are one brick thick and the north wall is built into, and partly seals, the second from the south of the four original recesses in the east wall. At the north-east external junction of the 18th-century walls the brickwork has been rubbed away to form a rounded corner, which is stopped about 1.7m above the extant floor level. Access is gained to the enclosure through a doorway in the north wall, of which the substantial mortised-and-tenoned frame survived until the restoration in the 1990s. It had to be replaced because of decay but the 18th-century threshold survives. The door itself was replaced earlier, in the 19th century.

Inside the enclosure the southernmost recess was sealed with a skin of brickwork to make the east wall flush at this point. At least two timber shelves were incorporated along the whole length of both east and west walls. Small channels were made in the north wall and hacked out of the south wall to accommodate the ends of these shelves. Brick storage bins were constructed around the east, south and west walls, of which only those against the west wall remain.

They appear to have had sloping wooden covers, now lost but replaced in the 1990s.

The building of the enclosure appears to have taken place at the same time as remedial works were undertaken to the ceiling of the cellar and the floor construction of the linenfold parlour (G4) above. Whether this work was related to the major reconstruction of the south end of the west wing is not known, but it is possible that a collapse there made the remedying of other perceived structural defects in the wing seem more urgent. Whatever the reason, the earlier ceiling was removed and the structure above strengthened. Both the northern and southern main transverse beams were provided with independent supports at their junctions with the west wall in the form of substantial posts, probably of timber, positioned flush against the wall. A chase was cut under each beam to house the posts and sockets were cut in stone pads inserted at floor level to support them. Both posts were removed during later repairs, but one of the pads remains in position under the northern beam and was used as the base for a new post during the 1990s restoration work.

In addition, the survival of clamp nails in the brickwork of the east and west walls suggests that wallplates were introduced to support the ends of the joists. More drastically, some original joists were replaced and additional ones inserted. One of these joists was a reused sill from one of the original Tudor windows, but for the most part they were new joists, measuring 180mm deep by 75mm thick, housed in new sockets cut into the 16th-century brickwork on each side. Some of the sockets from which the original joists had been removed were filled with brick. The other ends of the later joists were dropped into 30mm sockets cut into new chamfered timber plates which were nailed to the north–south bridging beams. A new ceiling was then constructed, at a lower level because of the greater depth of the new joists, up to, but not inside, the brick enclosure.

The ground floor (*see* Fig 7.4)

Georgian parlour (G1)

The present name given to this room, the 'Georgian parlour', is an indication of the degree to which its present appearance reflects the substantial changes made in the mid-18th century. As in the case of the west cellar, two distinct phases of work can be identified, probably separated by only a short time span.

The dominant features are the fine soft-wood panelling and the wooden dentilled box cornice which were installed around the room (Fig 6.7). The panelling is in the standard classical proportions with smaller panels below and large panels above separated by a moulded dado rail. On the west wall, however, where the panelling is now uninterrupted by an opening, the presence of one bay of panelling distinctly wider than the other bays is a clue to the complex sequence of alterations. When the panelling was first erected the doorway from this room directly into the hall remained in use, although examination of the brickwork of the wall shows that the opening was reduced by about 450mm at its southern end and widened by about 100mm at its northern end to accommodate the panelling. Within a short time, however, presumably when the house was subdivided and the east end of the former hall was made into an entrance passage for the eastern house, the reduced doorway was blocked up and the panelling simply adjusted over the former opening (*see* Fig 3.28).

When the doorway into the hall was blocked up, the former opening at the western end of the south wall, which had probably been blocked since the later 16th century, was reopened to form the present doorway into the room. As on the west wall, there is evidence that the panelling was altered to accommodate this change (*see* Fig 3.29). Before the doorway could have been reopened, alterations would have had to have been made to the staircase. A logical conclusion is that the change was made when the present staircase was installed, but there is structural evidence of an intermediate phase of alteration to the staircase which may have complicated the sequence of events.

Most of the panelling on the north wall has been altered to fit the new windows which were inserted in the 19th century (*see* Fig 3.31). The 18th-century shutters survive but were cut in half and rehung with new boxes and casings that extended the depth of the openings. The 18th-century form of panelling may have included window seats, as now, but any evidence for their existence is lost.

Figure 6.7
Room G1 as it appeared in the early 20th century.
[London Metropolitan Archives]

On the east wall, the Tudor fireplace was bricked up at its southern end, reduced in size and made more central to the room at this time, but the exact form of the fireplace that was installed over the earlier opening is unknown. The fireplace surround shown in photographs of this room, although harmonising stylistically with the panelling, is of the late 18th or 19th century. Marks found on the panelling when the mantel-shelf, brackets and sections of dado rail were removed show it to be a later replacement.

The former garderobe closet to the north of the fireplace was converted into a cupboard (see Fig 6.6). The door opening was widened by cutting back the 16th-century brickwork on its northern side, and a new frame and door inserted to fit the dimensions of the new panelling. The jambs and head of the door opening and the east wall of the closet were lined with vertical sections of timber planking, and shelving was installed. The arched display cupboard to the south of the fireplace was formed in a recess which had already been created by hacking back the Tudor brickwork. Its architrave has the same profile as that of the doorway in the south wall. The glazed doors to the cupboard with interlacing tracery are later.

Analysis of paint samples taken from the framing pieces and dado rail of the panelling reveal that they were initially painted pale cream, and that there were at least six further applications of this colour before a duck-egg blue was introduced. The present ceiling, which appears to have been relaid on new joists and lathings, and most of the floorboards also date from the mid-18th century. The ceiling and cornice (Fig 6.8) were originally treated with a lime wash.

East staircase

The fine open-string Georgian staircase (Fig 6.9) with its twisted balusters on high pedestals, carved step ends and wide, moulded handrail (Figs 6.10 and 6.11) was almost certainly installed as part of the major alterations of the mid-18th century. However, the history of both the staircase itself and its adaptation to the house is complex and raises a number of problems of interpretation.

The robust construction of the staircase and, in particular, its wide handrail are suggestive of a date earlier than the mid-18th century and there are several indications that it was not made for the house but was brought from elsewhere. The most obvious

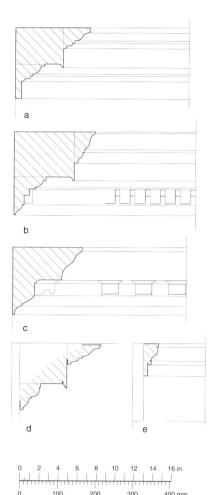

Figure 6.8
Cornice profiles recorded during the investigation of the house (Scale 1:10):
a) 18th-century 'box' cornice from room G2;
b) 18th-century dentilled 'box' cornice from room G1;
c) late 18th-century dentilled fibrous-plaster cornice from the ground-floor east corridor;
d) 18th-century 'box' cornice surviving over the fireplace in room G6; and
e) struck plaster cornice above the panelling of room G3 and room F3.

Figure 6.9
First flight of the staircase in the east wing. This staircase was brought to the house c 1740 and inserted into an irregular, existing opening.
[London Metropolitan Archives]

147

scrapes show that there were many more applications of paint to the staircase than to the wainscoting, which was constructed when the staircase was installed.

The staircase clearly appears to have been adapted to fit an existing space and yet that space itself seems already to have been much altered before the staircase was installed. In particular, the compartment was considerably broadened by rebuilding the southern partition wall, which is of 18th-century braced construction, about a metre southwards of its original position on all three main storeys, thus reducing the size of the rear rooms in the wing on each floor. If the partition wall had been rebuilt specifically to accommodate the present staircase, it makes no sense for it to have been constructed in such a position and at such an angle that the staircase had to be radically altered to fit. Moreover, the staircase is not framed into the wall but butts up against it. The only logical conclusion appears to be that there was another, short-lived phase of alteration to the east staircase before the present stairs were installed.

As part of the alterations to the staircase compartment new openings for sash windows were made on the east wall to light the staircase. There is also evidence that an opening was formed in the west wall, at first-floor level, to provide light from the courtyard, but that this was later sealed as failing structurally.

of these is the difference in width between the alternating northern and southern flights of the staircase. The former have a constant width with little sign of alteration, but the latter are significantly narrower and vary in width from the bottom to the top of the flights. The top steps of some of the flights have also been reduced in height, and other adjustments made. Additionally,

Kitchen/breakfast parlour (G2)

This room underwent a succession of very considerable changes in the 18th century and it is not always possible to be certain of the precise sequence of events (Fig 6.12). The first alterations would have occurred before the small house was built to the south. The building of that structure, and in particular its subsequent incorporation into the divided house, led to further changes, and there is evidence for yet another stage of significant alterations when the small house was remodelled later in the century. The first two stages of alteration are discussed here.

The repositioning of the north wall of the room as part of the alterations to the staircase compartment described above reduced the floor area considerably. The new wall cut across the former opening into

Figure 6.12

Room G2. Reconstruction drawings showing the evolution of the south wall. (Scale 1:80)

c 1535: Original build, showing kitchen range incorporated into the south-east corner of the room.

c 1600: The floor level was raised and alterations were made to the 16th-century window arrangements to provide better lighting to the area. Facilities for the range were also improved with the introduction of additional cooking ovens.

1741–3: The status of this room changed with the conversion of the house to separate properties. The window arrangements were again altered, wall panelling was installed and the kitchen was moved into the additional accommodation provided at the rear of the east wing.

c 1800: During the late 18th century this room became an entrance hall, with access from the east wall. Circulation to the rear addition was improved by cutting through the former range and inserting a staircase direct to the upper level. The fireplace was reduced in width and a smaller range added to provide heat to the room.

Figure 6.13
Room G2. Earth-bedded joists running north–south, prior to their removal during repairs to the floor carried out in 1981. [Caroe & Partners]

introduced into the room and the extant ceiling and cornice were constructed. The east wall was substantially altered to accommodate large windows with low sills (Fig 6.15). All of these works are indicative of a change in the function of the room, perhaps to a breakfast parlour, with the large windows designed to admit the morning sun.

East corridor

This corridor was created as the entrance hallway into the eastern house when the building was subdivided *c* 1752. Its position probably occupies that of the screens passage of the Tudor house. A new brick cross-wall, 230mm thick, was built to form the west wall of the corridor. It was built mainly of reused 16th-century bricks and was only minimally bonded into the main north and south walls. This general lack of bonding, also the case for the wall which was built to form the west corridor, is an indication that these cross-walls were erected after the main alterations of the mid-18th century had already taken place. Some of the bricks which were reused in this wall have signs of sooting and may have come from the demolished cross chimney stack in the west wing.

The east wall of the 16th-century hall formed the east wall of the corridor. The former central opening in this wall, which had already been reduced in size to accommodate the new panelling in the Georgian parlour (G1) in the first phase of mid-18th-century alterations, was apparently blocked up in the second phase when the corridor was formed (*see* Fig 3.42). The extant southern doorway in this wall, leading on to the staircase, is of mid-18th-century construction but may have replaced an earlier opening when alterations were made to the previous east staircase. Sixteenth-century floor tiles, probably from the hall, were used as packing above the lintel of the new opening.

The extant entrance door to this corridor is almost certainly that installed when the house was subdivided. It retains its 18th-century hinges, although it has been rehung, and the coach-house style bolt on the bottom of the door may also be original. It would probably have had a decorative fanlight above instead of the present plain glazing. The door casing has been altered but is basically Georgian in style. Photographs (*see* Fig 6.1) show that externally a small decorative canopy, supported by console brackets, existed until the beginning of the 20th century.

the courtyard, which was filled in, and there may no longer have been any direct access to the courtyard from the room. The floor level was raised and a new wooden floor was laid on a series of earth-bedded joists which ran north–south (Fig 6.13). The range was reduced in size, but at this time the room may still have functioned as a kitchen.

With the division of the house, however, the range appears to have gone out of use as a cooking area (Fig 6.14), the kitchen presumably having been moved into the small house and access gained to it by knocking through the rear wall of the recess to the west of the range. Panelling appears to have been

Figure 6.14
Room G2. 18th-century ash pit revealed during the archaeological excavations.

c 1535

c 1600

c 1741–3

c 1850

```
0            10              20 feet
├┬┬┬┬┬┬┬┼───┼───┼───┼───┤
0    1    2    3    4    5    6 metres
```

Figure 6.15
Room G2. Reconstruction drawings showing the evolution of the east wall. (Scale 1:100)
c 1535: Original build, showing the high level window in this elevation, with the kitchen range on the southern wall at the right of the drawing.
c 1600: The floor level was raised and the former window arrangement was altered to improve lighting to the area.
c 1741–3: With the conversion of the house to separate properties, the kitchen was moved into additional accommodation provided to the rear of the east wing. The room had become reduced in length due to the insertion of the new east staircase, and large sash windows were introduced.
c 1850: At the turn of the 19th century, the room became an entrance hall and reception room with access provided, via a short stair, to the upper level accommodation to the rear.

The southern doorway, but not the door itself, which is later, also dates from the mid-18th century and represents a widening of the original Tudor doorway at the southern end of the screens passage. The new doorway, however, was constructed at right angles to the east wall of the courtyard and projects, on its western side, in front of the south face of the central range. This peculiar construction may have been the result of the building of a large conservatory on to the eastern courtyard wall. This conservatory, from the evidence of marks on the wall, was probably of lean-to construction and was replaced by the conservatory which is shown on later ground plans and in the watercolour drawing of c 1895 (*see* Fig 6.2).

The majority of the plaster presently visible in the corridor is probably of the 19th century, including the cornice and ceiling, but during works in the 1990s some of the plaster applied in the 1750s was revealed beneath later applications on the west wall, accounting for the unusual thickness of the plaster here.

Georgian hall (G3)

This room, which at the time of writing is in use as the National Trust shop (Fig 6.16), is all that remains of the hall of the Tudor house, its origins virtually unrecognisable once the east and west corridors had been taken out of it, presumably during the second phase of mid-18th-century reconstruction. Interestingly, as a result of its wholesale transformation, it was probably the only out-and-out Georgian room in the western house once subdivision had taken place.

The present softwood panelling in the room is of mid-18th-century appearance, but it has been much repaired and altered, and several of the sections from which it is made up appear to have had other uses. The framing pieces have a variety of forms, some with 'stuck' and some with 'planted' beads, and profiles which vary from section to section. The panels are made up of thin planks and have been fixed in either a vertical or horizontal position, their joints being glued together. Most of the panels have been

151

fielded on the rear to allow them to be fitted into the framing grooves but some are plain and of a thin and more uniform section. Much alteration has taken place at the base of the panelling as a result of the later raising of the floor level but the original bottom rail is still in position buried beneath the extant floorboards. The panelling beneath the windows has likewise been reworked or reset following the change in floor level. The window shutters are 18th-century in style but also bear marks of alteration. The dado rail is later, as is the struck plaster moulded cornice, although the flat plaster band which forms the lower part of the present cornice is contemporary with the panelling. Paint samples indicate that the first colour applied to the panelling and the flat plaster cornice was a greyish brown.

On the south wall, the large Tudor fireplace, which appears to have survived until the subdivision of the house, was now substantially blocked in (see Fig 3.39). Only a much smaller opening remained, centrally located in the room but to the left of centre of the former opening. A simple brick arch was constructed to support the blocking brickwork and some of the original 16th-century floor tiles were used as packing in the reduced opening. The mid-18th-century fireplace no longer survives, but evidence from the brickwork suggests that it consisted of a substantial chimneypiece, possibly with a large overmantel, and that the fireplace opening has since been further reduced. The cupboard to the west of the fireplace appears to have been built into the wall when the first blocking of the fireplace took place. It is constructed under, and damages part of, the wide 16th-century relieving arch. Inside the cupboard are several different sections of reused 16th- and 17th-century panelling. An architrave, now removed, once surrounded the door framing.

The entrance to the room, in the newly-built west cross-wall, appears always to have been in the centre of the wall, as now. However, there is some evidence in the brickwork to suggest that the opening may have been slightly wider when first constructed. The door casing on both sides of the opening has had another use and there is evidence on the corridor side for a slender door which opened outwards into the corridor. Such a door may have been required because of the need to step down into the room from the corridor before the floor was raised to its present level. Certainly the extant door bears evidence of having been reworked and reused from another location.

When the present ceiling to the room was constructed is uncertain, but it is likely to have been during one of the phases of major mid-18th-century alterations. Although it is at the same level as the 16th-century ceiling, it has clearly been completely reconstructed. In the process some 60mm were shaved off the underside of the central north–south beam, new mortises were cut, and new joists assembled with a different arrangement of tenons to fit the new mortises; packing was inserted under the beam to maintain the old ceiling level. Such a complex repair may have been necessary because the bottom edge of the beam had decayed, perhaps weakened by the slip mortises which had been cut near to its edge to take the original ceiling joists (see p 53 and Fig 6.26).

West corridor

Like its counterpart, the east corridor, this was formed c 1752 to serve as an entrance hallway to the western half of the subdivided house. It took the place of the dais of the Tudor hall, the change in floor level being maintained at that time, with a step down into the Georgian hall (G3). The 230mm brick cross-wall which was erected as the eastern wall of the corridor is in this instance constructed of mainly 18th-century 60mm bricks. The only bonding with the north and south walls appears to have taken place around the top of the opening on the south wall which was altered from a window to a doorway, the lack of bonding with the north wall providing one of the clearest pieces of evidence that the cross-wall was built after the house had been re-fronted.

Apart from the insertion of a new screen and doorway during the restoration of the 1990s, the corridor has largely retained its mid-18th-century appearance. The lower parts of the walls are covered with timber wainscoting, made up of plain planking, 25mm thick, laid horizontally. To this timber mouldings have been applied to form a skirting and dado rail. Above, the walls have been plastered. Initially the dado appears to have been painted brown and the plastered walls above duck-egg blue. The ceiling plaster, which is the only surviving complete section of ceiling plaster remaining from the original build, seems always to have been white.

The entrance door to the corridor appears to be the original entrance door of

Figure 6.16
Room G3, now in use as
the National Trust shop.
[B000350]

the Tudor house (*see* p 31), adjusted to fit a square-headed opening (*see* Fig 3.14). It was moved here either from its original position or from another short-term reuse when the house was subdivided, perhaps because the western of the two newly created houses retained more historic features than the eastern, heavily Georgianised house. The semi-circular glazed fanlight with spider's web tracery over the door is typically mid-18th century (*see* Figs. 7.15 and 8.8). Any window or 'blind' opening that existed before this entrance was created must have been widened considerably to accommodate such a large door. A porch, presumably added when this entry was created, was removed in 1904 (*see* Figs 6.1 and 8.8).

The large, heavy, solid-framed doorcase at the south end of the corridor was constructed in a cut-down window opening to provide access to the courtyard when the corridor was formed. The 60mm thick door is more or less in its original form, but has later glazing and evidence for many locks and applied ironmongery. The glazed fanlight above is a copy of that above the entrance door but the pattern is more complicated and may have been installed later.

The four-centred, 16th-century, moulded doorcase in the south-west corner of the corridor (*see* p 52) was moved slightly southwards to its present position and turned through 180 degrees as part of the alterations of this period. Its door would have originally opened on to the Tudor hall but was henceforth reversed to open on to the enlarged lobby area at the foot of the west staircase.

Linenfold parlour (G4)

Although a number of alterations were made to this room in the mid-18th century, its basic appearance changed less than might have been expected because earlier fittings and panelling were retained and rearranged to fit the new door and window openings.

The existing sash window openings were formed at this time as part of the re-fronting of the north elevation of the house. To make these openings, the whole of the central section of the north wall was removed and rebuilt with reused 16th-century bricks. Timber props were embedded in the brickwork at the ends of the wall to support the original timber lintel beam that runs above the window openings. It is possible that another prop remains buried within the central brick pier between the present window openings. After the completion of these major construction works, the linenfold panelling was carefully rearranged and reframed around the new window openings.

On the east wall, the high-level window opening was blocked and refaced with panelling and, as described in the account of the west corridor, the doorway between the room and the former hall was moved further south along the wall so that from thenceforth it no longer communicated directly with this room.

This followed the foreshortening of the room by the erection of a new partition wall about a metre to the north of the former south end wall and the creation of an area between them which was divided into two closets. The linenfold panelling was removed from the former south wall of the room and the opening at its west end which had given access to the first staircase of the west wing was finally bricked up. The closets were lined with reused late 17th-century panelling and the linenfold panelling was rearranged over the north face of the new partition wall. Two door openings were made at either end of this wall, the eastern leading onto the enlarged lobby area at the foot of the staircase from which another door at right angles provided access to the eastern of the two closets, and the western directly into the other newly formed closet. This mid-18th-century arrangement essentially exists today, although the two closets have been made into one.

A new skirting and a deeper cornice were placed over the linenfold panelling, itself much rearranged in places, resulting in the survival of narrow areas of painted decoration along the edges of some sections of panelling (*see* p 104). The ceiling was left intact over the closets at the south end of the room but elsewhere it was taken down and the original timber joists were stripped out, probably for use as props in works throughout the house. The earliest colour that has been traced on the cornice is grey-green. The same colour also appears to have been applied uniformly to the panelling and framing pieces at this date.

West staircase

Whether any major changes were made to the west staircase during the structural alterations of the 18th century cannot be stated with certainty. There is some internal evidence, particularly the shape of the surviving balusters, that the installation of the upper staircase from the first to the second floor occurred in the later 17th century, and the use of the premises as a school at that time, when easy access to and from the second floor would have been highly desirable, tends to reinforce this hypothesis about the dating of the work. For this reason the work is described in the previous chapter, but it could have taken place later. What is abundantly clear is that it must have been completed by the time the house was subdivided into two separate residences, to provide access to the second floor of the western house. Whether any of the scheme of painted decoration (*see* pp 124–6), which would have been severely damaged by the insertion of the upper flight of stairs, remained visible at this time must also be doubtful. Most of it would almost certainly have been painted over.

At the foot of the stairs, as indicated above, the small lobby area was broadened

so that direct access to it could be gained from the west corridor (Fig 6.17). It took on essentially its present plan form although it would have been enclosed on the south side of the staircase by the partition wall erected in the early 17th century (*see* Fig 7.4) and demolished in 1904. Several other alterations have taken place but the ceiling plaster appears to have survived from the mid-18th-century reconstruction of the area.

Georgian kitchen (G5 and G6)

A single, large room was created by the demolition of the brick cross chimney stack which formerly divided rooms G5 and G6. The structural effect of the removal of the cross-stack, and the subsequent rebuilding of much of the south end of the room is described above (*see* p 142). If there were

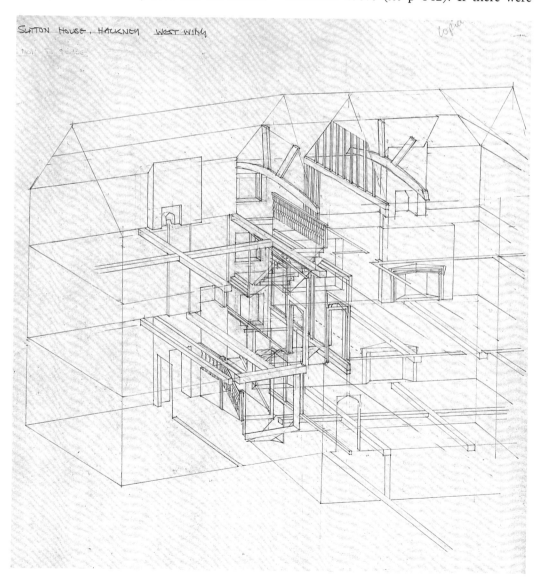

Figure 6.17
Unmeasured 3-D sketch taken from survey notes showing the layout of the west wing staircase and the adjacent floor construction in 1990.

155

Figure 6.18
Room G6. View to south-west prior to restoration, showing the Georgian fireplace surround and wooden spit-rack above.

and chimney breast with its wooden spit-rack on the west wall, although the brick-tiled, splayed-back insert in the fireplace is Edwardian (Figs 6.18, 6.19 and 6.20). The flat timber surround, measuring approximately 300mm wide × 25mm thick and probably of oak, was decorated with a painted brecciated marble (Jaspa) design in red and cream, similar to the designs on the stone fireplaces in the north-west chamber and the middle chamber (F4 and F5). Traces of a similar design were also found on the broad wooden window frames which survive inside the openings in the south wall. There was an applied relief, now lost, in the form of a raised tablet above the centre of the fireplace. The surround has been truncated by the raising of the floor level and the construction of a plinth. The timber bressumer above the fireplace is more slender than that used in the kitchen/breakfast parlour (G2), measuring 240 × 180mm; it bears evidence, in the form of faint traces of gold and black paint and a peg hole, of having been reused from elsewhere.

The breast over the fireplace was completely covered with plaster after its construction and most of this plaster still exists under the wooden framework. The elaborate rack for hanging rails or 'spits' and its associated framing was added shortly after the construction of the fireplace and is doubtless contemporary with the conversion of this room into a kitchen when the house was subdivided. This remained its function

two phases of reconstruction here, they were probably very close together in terms of time, and little evidence has remained of the first phase apart from the hacked-back areas of brickwork, approximately 1.04m wide, on both the east and west walls which mark the original position of the cross-stack (see Fig 3.51). Even the final mid-Georgian form and appearance of the room, after all the rebuilding work had taken place, has to a large extent been obscured by the further changes which took place in 1904, when the room was once again subdivided.

The most prominent survival from the Georgian period is the fireplace surround

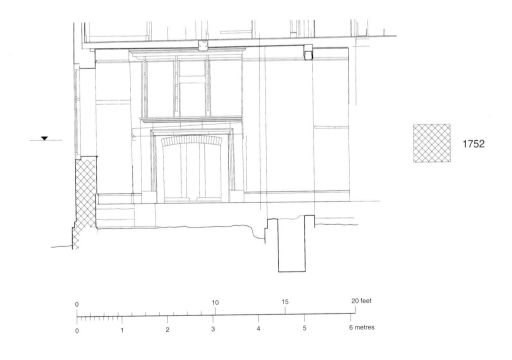

1752

Figure 6.19
Room G6. Internal elevation of west wall as existing in 1990, showing the excavated ground line and the brick-lined cesspit from the former cross-stack. (Scale 1:80)

Figure 6.20 Room G6. View to south, towards the modern café extension. [B000348]

HACKNEY, London.

Wilford House, Hornerton.

Figure 6.21
Room G6. View to
north-east. Watercolour of
1898 by F C Varley.
[AA009976; Reproduced
by permission of English
Heritage. NMR]

shoring and was left *in situ*, with its associated framing pieces and a bearer at its base, while the brick filling was built up. At the same time the doorway into the courtyard was removed and the opening filled in, a piece of reused oak being used in a similar manner as a prop to support the brickwork formerly supported by the 16th-century door frame and left in place when the opening was bricked up. Further along the wall, another high-level window opening was blocked with reused 16th-century bricks when this part of the wall was substantially rebuilt. The only opening which was retained in this wall of the room was the four double-lights of the original Tudor window to the south of the partition wall dividing the room from the staircase at the north end.

A drawing of 1898 by F C Varley of part of this room (Fig 6.21) shows the walls covered with plain wainscoting in large panels, similar to that existing in the inner bedchamber (F2). This may have dated from the mid-Georgian period and may have been the predominant finish applied to the room. Most of the extant plaster dates from 1904 and the only surviving area of 18th-century plaster is above the fireplace beneath the spit-rack.

The ceiling would presumably have been plastered but evidence for this has been obliterated by later boarding. Both of the exposed beams which support the floor construction above are reused and reworked timber wall plates. The beam over the fireplace was probably positioned here during the reconstruction of the south end of the west range and the other beam during the demolition of the cross-stack. This beam originates from a timber-framed building. It has been positioned on its side and the mortises to take wall-framing, from its former use, have been covered over on its southern side. Under the covering to its northern face can be seen a series of V-shaped housings which were used to seat the feet of the former rafters. It is unclear what it supported prior to the extant ceiling and floor of the 1750s, as a secondary timber beam of similar section is now placed above it for that purpose.

The hacking-back of the brickwork of the cross-stack continues below the underside of the present skirting line for four brick courses, suggesting that the mid-18th-century floor was at this lower level. Excavations indicate that a mortar floor was laid, perhaps as a base for tiles or paving.

until the building passed out of domestic use at the end of the 19th century. The rack was unfortunately altered at its north end when shelving or a dresser was introduced at a later date, which accounts for the odd, plain panel at this end (*see* Fig 6.18).

The insertion, during the mid-18th-century alterations, of a doorway in the west wall to the south of the fireplace, which originally led out into a rear courtyard, is discussed above (*see* p 143), as is the form at that time of the window openings in the south wall.

On the east wall, the high-level opening immediately to the south of the large Tudor window, which had been made after the house was built (*see* Fig 4.14), was blocked up. The method of filling was similar to that of other openings which were blocked at this time. A timber strut was used as a form of

The first floor

Bedchamber (F1)

The appearance of this room is now pre-dominantly Victorian but the structural alterations which gave it its present form date principally from the mid-18th century (Fig 6.22). The window openings were constructed then as part of the general refenestration of the house, although the sash windows were subsequently replaced in the 19th century, and the fireplace opening was reduced in size and moved to the centre of the east wall. The doorway in the west wall which communicated with the great chamber (F3) was blocked up when the house was subdivided and this became a party wall. The doorway at the east end of the south wall which formerly led across the stairwell into the inner bedchamber (F2) was also blocked up and the present doorway into the room in the south-west corner was formed. These changes were a necessary consequence of the introduction of the grand Georgian staircase into the east wing. The present plaster ceiling and finely detailed modillion cornice probably also date from this period of major change.

The garderobe closet in the northeast corner of the room was retained during the 18th-century alterations but whether for its original function is unknown. The ceiling was lowered and plastered and new floorboards laid over 55mm deep joists which were nailed over the 16th-century floor joists. Three 25mm thick shelves were at one time set into the north wall of the closet, the chases for them being cut into the 16th-century brickwork. These perhaps suggest a change of use for the closet but whether they date from this period is uncertain. Following the lowering of the ceiling, the walls and ceiling were given one or more white plaster washes, but the discovery of a sequence of three wallpapers over these washes indicates that the closet remained in use for some time before its opening was bricked up in the 19th century.

Inner bedchamber (F2)

In common with most of the east wing, this room was substantially altered in the mid-18th century. The insertion of a wider staircase meant that the partition wall separating the staircase from the room had to be rebuilt further to the south, thus making the room smaller. The large window opening in the east wall was completely bricked in and a new opening for a sash window made further to the north. The present window, however, is a 19th-century replacement. On the west wall the similar large window opening was reduced in size and a sash window inserted.

The fireplace opening to the west end of the south wall was reduced in size and given a smaller fireplace surround. The brickwork above the west half of the original fireplace was rebuilt with a horizontal coursing of reused 16th-century bricks, replacing the

Figure 6.22
Room F1. View to north-east showing site of fireplace and blocking of opening to the 16th-century garderobe closet in 1990.

western half of the original relieving arch. This area of brickwork was closed at the west end to form the straight reveal of an opening 850mm wide at the extreme west end of the south wall, which was finished with a layer of plaster. The opening may have been built as a cupboard or, as the evidence of closing bricks built into the exterior face of this gable-end wall would suggest, was cut through to make a new window opening. If it was a window opening, it had a short life, as it appears to have been blocked up again either when the small house to the south was first built *c* 1748, or when it was remodelled later in the century (*see* Figs 3.67 and 3.68).

The floor of the room was reconstructed and in the process all the floor joists, and the ceiling joists of the kitchen/breakfast parlour (G2) below, were replaced. The floor joists are deeper and narrower, and the ceiling joists more square, than the typical 16th-century joists used in the house. The plaster ceiling of this room was also renewed this time but had to be replaced once more during the restoration in the 1990s. Simple panelling was fitted around the room to dado height and the upper parts of the walls were plastered.

Great chamber (F3)

Although a considerable degree of reconstruction took place in the great chamber during the alterations of the mid-18th century, its basic dimensions were left intact and the late 16th-century or early 17th-century panelling was rearranged around the walls. The whole of the north wall was rebuilt but the remains of the 16th-century construction is evident in both corners of the wall; salvaged 16th-century bricks were used for its inner face. Initially, the rebuilt wall had only two box-sash windows in the openings occupied by the present two central windows, but with lower sills. The present outer windows were blind externally, with no internal openings, and were covered with panelling (*compare* Fig 6.23 with Fig 6.5). Bond timbers were incorporated into the rebuilt brickwork for the re-erection of the panelling. There was no definable bond used in the reconstruction but there are distinct construction lines where brick-on-edge is often used, a characteristic feature of several other areas reconstructed at this time.

A new window opening was made in the south wall towards the west end, while a matching window at the east end was inserted in the pre-existing splayed 16th-century opening. The large stone fireplace was removed and the opening reduced in size and moved slightly westwards to make it more central to the room. A baroque chimneypiece, probably made of marble, with incised patterning and a raised keystone, was placed around the reduced opening (Fig 6.24) but was removed in 1904.

When the east wall was made into a party wall on the subdivision of the house, the doorway in the north corner was bricked up and the door itself, which had been constructed out of a section of panelling, was simply nailed shut over the new brickwork. The principal entrance into the room from the west staircase was retained but the opening was fitted with an 18th-century doorcase, later removed.

The floor of the room is presently some 75mm higher than its original level and this raising of the floor level probably took place at the time of the major reconstructions of the mid-18th century. In the process approximately three out of every four of the 16th-century joists were removed and new joists made out of reused timber were laid across those that remained. To level the new floor, packing was inserted under some of these secondary joists and others were cut to

Figure 6.24
Room F3. View of fireplace on south wall c 1890. The fireplace was removed from the house in 1904. The panelling appears to have been painted in a light coloured wash at this time. [BB87/8096; © Crown copyright. NMR]

Figure 6.25
Room F3. View to south-west showing first-floor frame during restoration. [Mike Gray]

Figure 6.26
Room F3. Various details of the floor construction. Among the alterations carried out to the floor frame in the mid-1700s was the removal of many of the 16th-century floor joists and replacement of the ceiling joists over G3 below. Additional timbers were nailed to the sides of the principal floor beams as a means of attaching the ends of the replacement ceiling joists.

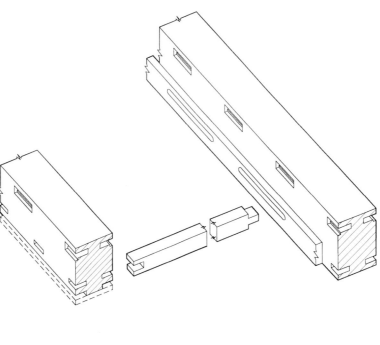

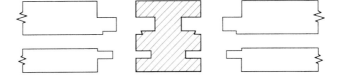

fit over the original joists. So much remedial work has since been carried out to the floor that much of the 18th-century work and the reasons for it have been obscured, but defects in the original floor construction may have led to sagging (Figs 6.25 and 6.26, *see also* Fig 10.6).

A new plaster ceiling was constructed following removal of all traces of an earlier, possibly decorated, ceiling; apart from areas of repair, this has survived to the present day. During its construction new softwood joists were used and the whole ceiling was lowered by approximately 75mm, apparently because of a weakening of the main, central second-floor cross-beam. The beam was repaired by cramping together its main fracture with iron bolts and strong timber clamps; the load of the new ceiling was then taken on the new independent ceiling joists at the lower level.

Once all the structural work had been carried out to the room, the panelling was refitted to the walls. A considerable amount of adaptation had to take place, particularly on the north wall where the fenestration had been so completely altered. There may not have been enough panelling to go round, as the amount of wall space had been substantially increased because the outer 'windows' were left blind when the room was first reconstructed. This may account for the different (and earlier) panelling on the south wall (*see* p 108), which may have been reused from elsewhere in the house. There are several infelicities in the arrangement of the panelling, especially in the south-east corner where one section is laid on its side, but these could be the result of later, partial rearrangements. The carved panels above the fireplace (*see* Fig 6.24) fit too neatly into the reduced opening to have any relationship to the earlier, Tudor fireplace and may have been introduced at this time.

North-west chamber (F4)

The principal alterations to this room occurred on the north wall, where sash windows were introduced. No attempt appears to have been made to refit the 16th-century panelling once the reconstruction had taken place. The present, plain panelling appears to date from the early 19th century and only the shutter boxes survive from the mid-18th-century panelling which would presumably once have existed here.

Elsewhere, on the west wall the window opening to the south of the fireplace was blocked up with the same facing bricks as

those used on the centre of the north front. The timber sill and brickwork below the window were cut back and a recess formed and plastered. Whether this was always used as a cupboard, as it certainly became later, is unclear. Alterations were also made to the fireplace, including the exterior face of the chimney breast. Splayed sides were constructed within the opening and the flue was substantially rebuilt and reduced in width, apparently to produce better combustion. The stonework of the fireplace was fortunately retained but covered over by a plain surround with an elaborate decorative mantelshelf (Fig 6.27) covering the join between the top of the surround and the lower rail of the Jacobean overmantel. The mantelshelf appears to have had a previous use elsewhere and was in the form of a projecting, broken cornice with a *fret-dentil*, an unusual motif. Its frieze was decorated with festoons with ribbons and *paterae* and it had a central tablet and plain supporting brackets with

Figure 6.27
Fireplace in room F4 in a late 19th-century watercolour by F C Varley. [AA009978; Reproduced by permission of English Heritage.NMR]

guttae and volutes at each end. This striking piece of classical ornament was removed during the works of 1904 and is now lost.

The floor of the room was reconstructed although the original level was maintained. Apart from the central joist of each run, all the 16th-century joists were removed. New softwood joists, mostly of reused timber, were laid at right angles, using the surviving original joists as secondary bridging beams. Most of the floorboards laid during this reconstruction have survived. They are of pine, measuring on average 215mm wide, and some have rebated edges. A new ceiling was also constructed, some 75mm lower than the original as in the great chamber (F3), on new ceiling joists, once again consisting mostly of reused timbers. The thickness of the plaster, however, suggests that there were several later applications. The ceiling was apparently lowered while the panelling remained in position. Parts of the upper rails of the panelling sections were trapped behind the ceiling plaster and the oak band which forms the topmost member of the overmantel was notched to enable the new joists to be placed in position.

Middle chamber (F5)

The southern end of the west wing at first-floor level is one of the least understood areas of the house in terms of the form, function and appearance of its rooms

between the changes of the mid-18th century and the further substantial alterations of 1904 (Fig 6.28). The demolition of the massive brick cross-stack appears to have been followed by the erection of a partition wall, probably of timber and plaster, in line with the former north face of the stack, thus preserving the division into two chambers on this floor. The blocking of the fireplace in the north-west corner and the construction of a flight of stairs in front of it, probably before the major works of the mid-18th century but certainly no later than that period, would have left this middle chamber unheated. It may have served as little more than a broad landing, or upper hall, for the west wing staircase once it had been extended to reach the second floor (Fig 6.29).

The room was probably not affected by the rebuilding of the south end of the wing which appears to have been a consequence of the removal of the cross-stack. As in the Georgian kitchen (G5) below, the original mullioned-and-transomed window in the east wall may have been retained, as the present 'Gothick' window inserted into the 16th-century opening appears to be of a later date. The ceiling was renewed on new softwood joists but other alterations may have been minimal. The room was largely, or wholly, plastered, and traces of a white plaster wash above a light-blue dado-height

Figure 6.28
Room F5. View to south-east.

wash which were revealed at the time the room was surveyed may date from this time.

South-west chamber (south end of F5)

In contrast to the relatively limited amount of work done in the middle chamber, the southernmost room in the west wing was almost completely rebuilt as a result of the structural collapse which appears to have occurred shortly after the removal of the cross-stack. The entire west and south walls, and all but a small section at the north end of the east wall, were rebuilt, together with the floor and ceiling. Sixteenth-century bricks were reused to rebuild the walls and to construct the fireplace and lateral chimney stack against the west wall and the floor was reconstructed using timbers which probably came from the fallen south end of the roof frame.

The large window opening that had formerly existed in the east wall was apparently reduced, or completely blocked, during the first phase of mid-18th-century work, before rebuilding took place. The upper part of the splayed window reveal was broken back, together with the top of the window sill, and rebuilt with 16th-century brick. Internally, the face of the brick blocking was set back approximately 100mm behind the face of the original brickwork and left the outer part of the window reveal exposed, resulting in a splayed return to the wall where the blocking meets the main wall surface. The splayed return was then extended from floor to ceiling. It was incorporated into the brick blocking at the head of the former window using crudely shaped bricks overlaid with mortar and, below the sill, the 16th-century brickwork was hacked back flush with the blocking above (Fig 6.30).

Henceforth the room was lit by new sash window openings in the south wall,

Figure 6.29
Room F5. View to north following restoration.
[© James Morris/Axiom. London]

165

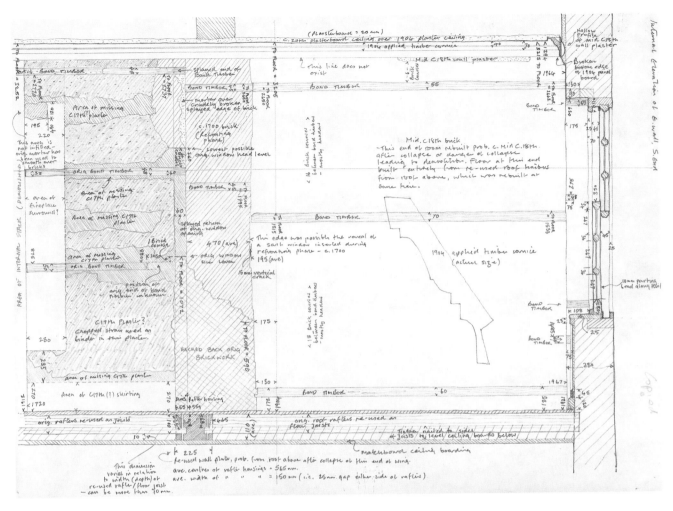

Figure 6.30 (above) Room F5. Survey note showing blocking of original early 16th-century first-floor window opening at the south end of the east wall of the west wing.

Figure 6.31 (right) Room F5. Fireplace at south end of west wall, before loss of the 19th-century fireplace surround and cast-iron firegrate. (Caroe & Partners)

Figure 6.32 (facing page) Room S6. Survey note of exposed brickwork in the east wall, showing evidence for former cross chimney stack at second-floor level.

although the windows themselves are later replacements. It was heated by the fireplace in the newly formed chimney stack erected when the west wall was rebuilt. How the room was decorated is uncertain but a description of the work that was undertaken in 1904 states that oak panelling was discovered under wallpaper here. It may be that panelling which had existed before rebuilding took place was refixed after the walls had been reconstructed (Fig 6.31).

The second floor

The second floor was just as significantly affected as any other part of the house by the alterations of the mid-18th century. At this level these included the rebuilding of the north front; the hipping back of the gables and the reconstruction of the roof in this area (see Fig 3.15); the insertion of the east staircase; the demolition of the cross chimney stack in the west wing; and the demolition of the rear wall of the west wing and its rebuilding on this storey some 2.5m to the north (Fig 6.32).

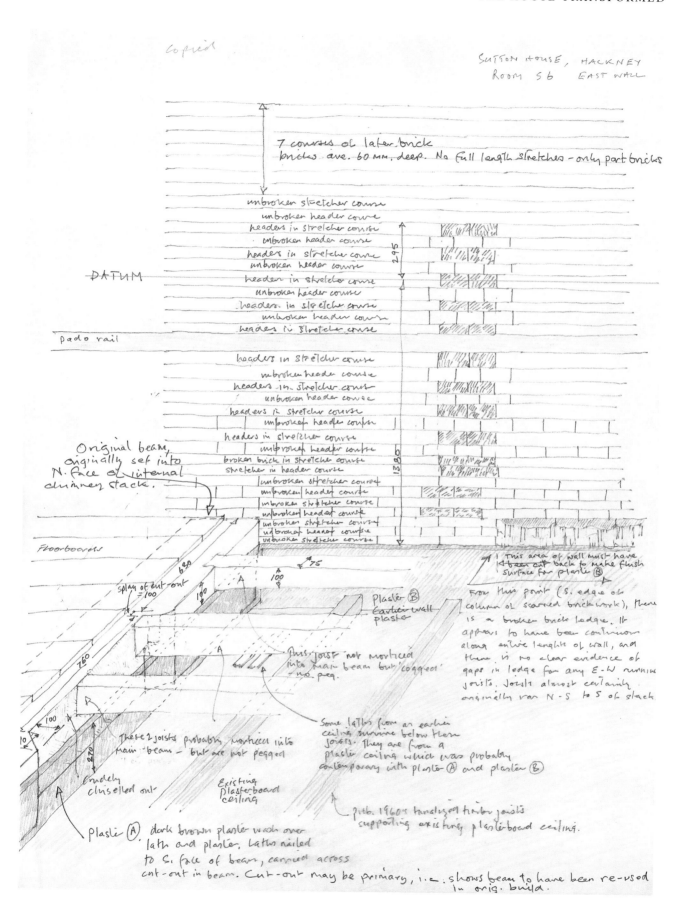

Copied

SUTTON HOUSE, HACKNEY
ROOM 5b   EAST WALL

7 courses of later brick
bricks ave. 60 mm. deep. No full length stretches - only part bricks

unbroken stretcher course
unbroken header course
headers in stretcher course
unbroken header course
headers in stretcher course
unbroken header course
DATUM   header in stretcher course
unbroken header course
headers in stretcher course
unbroken header course
headers in stretcher course

pado rail

headers in stretcher course
unbroken header course
headers in stretcher course
unbroken header course
headers in stretcher course
unbroken header course
headers in stretcher course
unbroken header course
broken brick in stretcher course
stretcher in header course
unbroken stretcher course
unbroken header course
unbroken stretcher course
unbroken header course
unbroken stretcher course
unbroken header course
unbroken stretcher course

Original beam,
originally set into
N. face of internal
chimney stack.

Floorboards

splay of cut-out
= 100

This area of wall must have
been cut back to make flush
surface for plaster B

From this point (S. edge of
column of scarred brickwork), there
is a broken brick ledge. It
appears to have been continuous
along entire length of wall, and
there is no clear evidence of
gaps in ledge for any E-W running
joists. Joists almost certainly
originally ran N-S to S of stack

Plaster B
Earlier wall
plaster

This joist not morticed
into main beam but 'cogged'
no peg.

These 2 joists probably morticed into
main beam - but are not pegged

crudely
chiselled out

Existing
plasterboard
ceiling

Some laths from an earlier
ceiling survive below these
joists. They are from a
plaster ceiling which was probably
contemporary with plaster A and plaster B

prob. 1960's handised timber joists
supporting existing plasterboard ceiling.

Plaster A dark brown plaster wash over
lath and plaster. Laths nailed
to S. face of beam, carried across
cut-out in beam. Cut-out may be primary, i.e. shows beam to have been re-used
in orig. build.

In addition the fenestration was generally changed throughout, including new openings in the east elevation to light the upper flights of the east staircase, in the south wall of the central range to the west of the chimney stack, and in the rebuilt south wall of the west wing. The fireplace openings in the west wing also appear to date from this period, although the fireplace in the southernmost room of the wing was further remodelled in the 19th century.

The overall effect was to give the second floor essentially the form it has today, although remedial works to the roof in the 1970s produced further changes and have led to the loss of any ceilings which might have been installed in the 18th century. There is residual evidence of one of these in the form of a series of empty mortises along the north face of the tie beam of the east staircase partition, indicating that the staircase compartment was formerly ceiled at this point. As indicated above, it is still unclear exactly how this floor was apportioned when the house itself was subdivided into two residences.

Figure 6.33
Plan of Sutton House site showing the location of the archaeological excavations carried out by MoLAS in 1990.
[Museum of London Archaeology Service]

The grounds and additional buildings

The comprehensive rebuildings of the Edwardian period have removed all aboveground traces of the 'small house' built across the end of the east wing in the 1740s and of the complex of outbuildings that lay to the south-west of the west wing in the same period. Archaeological excavations have, however, revealed much about the ground plan of the former, and rather less about the latter because of an intervening stage of building activity in the 19th century (Fig 6.33; *see also* Fig 3.20). The excavations also revealed the foundations of the walls built to separate the gardens of the eastern and western houses when subdivision took place in the 1750s.

The west wall of the small house was built to align with the west wall of the east wing and extended southwards from it. Its foundation was composed of layers of broken bricks, chalk, sand, and a series of large medieval stone architectural fragments from a moulded doorcase of unknown provenance (Figs 6.34 and 6.35; *see also* Figs 3.50 and 5.3). Above the foundations the wall was built in a variation of English bond with reused 16th-century bricks (possibly from the demolished cross-stack in the west wing) and was rendered with plaster on its east, interior, face. At the south end of the wall was a doorway leading from the house to a yard to the west which used the gravel of the former garden terrace here as its surface. Bonded to its north end was the north wall of the house which was added to the rear wall of the east wing as an extra skin. Only a fragment of the east wall was uncovered, again built mostly of reused 16th-century bricks in an English bond. The south wall was not discovered but, from later maps and the configuration of the ground, the small house was about 8m wide from east to west and 6m or more deep from north to south.

Inside the newly built house, dumps were deposited over the former garden terrace and beyond it to the south to level up the ground for mortar and brick floors. The former wall of the garden terrace appears to have been used as the base for an internal east–west partition and another wooden partition ran north–south parallel with the west wall. This formed a corridor at the west end of the house which communicated with the east wing of the main house when an opening was formed between the two buildings to the west of the large chimney stack in

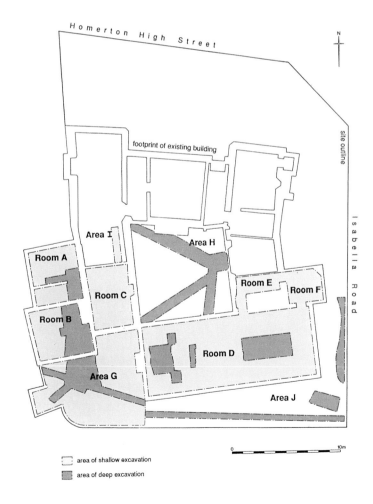

Homerton High Street

footprint of existing building

N

site outline

Isabella Road

Area I
Area H
Room A
Room C
Room E
Room F
Room B
Room D
Area G
Area J

☐ area of shallow excavation
▨ area of deep excavation

0   10m

the south wall of the wing. In the area within the angle of the two partitions a brick floor was laid with the bricks forming a herring-bone pattern; elsewhere they were aligned north–south and east–west. All of these floors were later robbed of their bricks and heavily disturbed.

To the west of the small house, the remains of a substantial north–south wall which divided the western from the eastern property were uncovered. It ran southwards from the south-east corner of the chimney breast on the south wall of the central range, and was built in a construction cut. Its base was composed of reused blocks of 16th-century masonry. Remains were discovered over a length of 16m although it almost certainly extended further to the south. A similar trench-built garden wall was erected at the front of the house running north–south from the west side of the entrance to the eastern house to the street frontage.

To the west of the wall which ran south-wards through the courtyard, on the prop-erty of the western house, a yard was formed sloping down from north to south. In the extreme north-west corner of the yard the construction cut for a step to the new doorway at the south end of the entrance passageway was excavated.

At the rear of the west wing, an east–west wall was trench-built in a construction cut, extending westwards from the wing and aligned with its south face (*see* Fig 8.22). It was initially built from large reused frag-ments of 16th-century masonry, and shortly afterwards rebuilt as a brick wall in random bond. This was apparently a garden wall with a yard on its north side, a conclusion borne out by the evidence that the doorway in the west wing that formerly existed on the south side of the fireplace in room G6 was originally an external doorway which led into this yard. On the north side of the yard, and probably abutting the west wing, was a small structure with brick footings and a brick and mortar floor. This has been inter-preted as a coalhouse from the layer of loose dark-grey silty clay full of ash and charcoal which was subsequently deposited over the site (Figs 6.36 and 6.37).

At the east end of the wall, adjacent to the west wing, there appears to have been a gateway based on a wooden sill leading to the garden to the south. In this area the level was raised by a series of dumps contain-ing building materials. The well to the south-west of the west wing was rebuilt at the top and capped over in a large, shallow

construction cut, although a lead pipe was inserted to enable water to continue to be drawn from the well. The capping consisted of an arch made up of a double skin of bricks with small walls added at each end. The cut was then backfilled over and around the capping arch with a mixture of mortar and gravel (*see* Fig 3.89). More dumps of gravel and garden soil were deposited over the western end of the former terrace and the well-capping to create a sloping surface, presumably preparatory to the establish-ment of a garden for the western house, which is shown on later maps extending south-westwards as far as the churchyard (Fig 6.38).

When Sutton House was subdivided in the 1750s, the manner of distribution of the wider lands which had formed part of its curtilage in the early 18th century and were attached to the eastern house by the 19th century, is unclear. John Rocque's map of 1745 (*see* Fig 5.1), which is not entirely

Figure 6.34 (top) Wenlock Barn. Brick and stone foundations of the demolished 18th-century southern extension range, uncovered during the MoLAS excavation in 1990.

Figure 6.35 (bottom) 18th-century foundations uncovered beneath the floor of the Wenlock Barn during the MoLAS excavation. The foundations incorporated layers of broken bricks, chalk, sand, and a series of stone architectural fragments, possibly from a moulded doorcase. [Museum of London Archaeology Service]

Figure 6.36 (above, left) Brick footings, possibly of a former coalhouse which abutted the west wing, uncovered during the MoLAS excavations of the Edwardian extension. [Museum of London Archaeology Service]

Figure 6.37 (above, right) Edwardian extension. South room. View to east during excavation, showing the below-ground remains of a former structure which occupied the site. [Museum of London Archaeology Service]

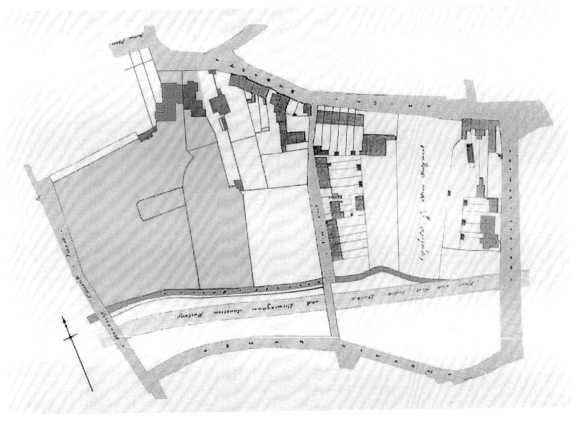

Figure 6.38 Composite drawing of plans in manorial court books c 1850, showing Sutton House as it was when still divided in two, with property boundaries and associated gardens. [After original held in London Metropolitan Archives]

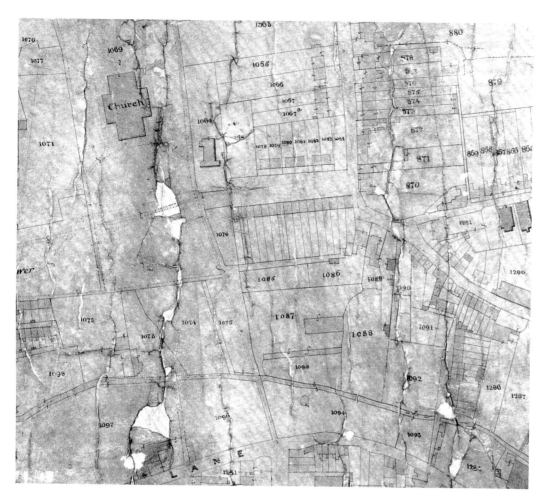

Figure 6.39
Detail of the Tithe Award map of 1843. Sutton House is shown to the right of the newly laid out Sutton Place, in the centre of the map. There is some indication that in the 18th century the land surrounding Sutton House was divided into fields, the layout of which was still evident at the time this map was drawn.
[Public Record Office, Kew IR 30/21/19 (2)]

reliable, shows what appears to be a large, single holding to the south of Sutton House which is roughly coterminous with the holding shown on the much more precise tithe apportionment survey of 1843 (Fig 6.39). On Rocque's map most of the land is depicted as occupied by what appears to be a large orchard (for which there is no other evidence), while south of the orchard, Hackney Brook has been widened to form an elongated pond, but no buildings are shown.

There is some indication, however, in the wording of John Cox's will of 1760 and in the poor rate books and land tax returns of the period that, at that time, the land was divided into fields which were mainly sublet to tenant farmers, rather than forming the extended grounds of either of the houses into which Sutton House had been subdivided. The division into fields, several of which are described as meadows, is still evident in the tithe apportionment survey of 1843, although by then they are all shown to be in the single occupation of the lessee of the eastern house. It may be, therefore, that the consolidation of the land as part of the property holding attached to this house was a gradual development of the later 18th century.

Where the schoolhouse, brewhouse and other offices described in the insurance policy of 1718 were located within the extensive curtilage of the house can only be a matter of conjecture.

7

A House Divided

Sutton House remained divided as two houses until the 1890s. During this long period the copyhold, and later the freehold, ownership of the property remained divorced from the occupancy of either house.

The ownership to the 1890s

As we have seen in the previous chapter, in 1745 Thomas Wilson reunited the moieties into which the copyhold had been divided and became the outright owner of a sizeable estate on the south side of Homerton High Street. In 1762 he sold part of his land at the corner of Morning Lane and Bridge (now Ponsford) Street to Daniel Stacey, the brewer, who already held a lease of the brewery there. (Three years later Stacey also acquired the ownership of the plot of land to the west of Bridge Street which split Wilson's holding into two parts.) Wilson retained the remainder of the land, letting some of it for speculative development.[1]

In April 1780 it was reported in the manorial court that Wilson had died, bequeathing his copyhold estate to Robert Hopkins of Warwick Street, Westminster, gentleman. Wilson's will has not been found and there is no indication that the two men were related, but, as Warwick Street was adjacent to Glasshouse Street which was Wilson's address, the two men may have had a business association. At that time there were seventeen houses standing on the estate, an indication of the flurry of building activity which had already taken place. Hopkins died on 1 December 1782, leaving a 19-year-old daughter, Isabella, as his only child and heir to the copyhold.[2]

In December 1783, while still under age, Isabella married John Ball, a stationer with premises in Holborn and a house at Coleshill, near Amersham, Buckinghamshire. Shortly after she achieved her majority in the following year, they drew up a deed establishing an entailed line of descent for the property. By this John Ball was to be

the owner for his lifetime, and after his death it was to pass to Isabella for her lifetime and thereafter to their sons in order of birth. One of John Ball's first acts after he came into possession of the estate was to let part of the ground to the east of Sutton House for speculative building. The property leased included Sir James Deane's former house, by now also subdivided, which was thereupon demolished. A new street, originally New Cut, later Ball's Buildings, and now Link Street, was laid out in 1792–3 between Hackney Brook and Homerton High Street, and a number of small houses were built alongside it and on the High Street frontage.[3] All of the houses built at that time have since been demolished, as indeed have all the houses built on the estate in the 18th century.

John and Isabella Ball had at least eight children, six daughters and two sons.[4] The eldest son and prospective heir, also named John, was born on 24 February 1786. John Ball the elder died in 1823 but Isabella Ball lived to the age of 88. Shortly before her death in 1851, part of the ground at the southern edge of the estate was sold in 1848 to the East and West India Docks and Birmingham Junction Railway Company for the construction of a railway line (now the North London Line) a short distance to the south of Hackney Brook.

John Ball the younger was 65 years old when he came into his inheritance in 1851. There were a number of legacies in his mother's will which had to be paid and he took out a substantial mortgage to satisfy these obligations. He also sought to remove the entail on the estate, a move which was made easier by the absence of a male heir of his own. In 1857 he took the final step to enable him to obtain complete control over his property by purchasing the enfranchisement of the copyhold from the lord of the manor for £755.[5] By this time Ball had married, his wife Mehetabel being some 37 years his junior. (Whether he had been married before is not known, but if so there were no surviving children of that marriage.)

They had three children, a son who died young and two daughters, Mehetabel and Isabella.[6]

John Ball died in 1861, leaving his estate in trust for the benefit of his children with his widow as the principal trustee. Shortly afterwards she decided to increase the value of the estate by developing the land immediately to the east and south of Sutton House. Isabella and Mehetabel Roads, presumably so named after her young daughters, were laid out and terraced houses erected along the new street frontages. The first building leases of the new houses were granted in 1865.[7] Most of the land for the new development was taken from the very extensive grounds attached to the eastern of the two houses into which Sutton House had been divided.

Mehetabel Ball remarried, becoming Mehetabel Ramsay, but had no further children before her death in 1874. By her will she appointed new trustees to administer the estate. Her daughter Mehetabel married later in 1874, having four children, and Isabella married in 1881 but died in 1887. Whether she had children is not known. By this time the ownership of the estate had become so complicated by the various trusts under which the land was held under wills and marriage settlements, compounded by a number of mortgages, that the Court of Chancery was called on to sort out matters. The Court ordered that the estate should be partitioned, the line of division running approximately north–south. The western half, including Sutton House, fell to the lot of the trustees of Isabella Young, as she had become following her marriage. Despite this simplification, when the rector of Hackney, the Reverend Frederic Evelyn Gardiner, completed the purchase of the freehold of Sutton House in 1895 under circumstances which will be explained in the next chapter, there were still six parties to the deed of sale.[8]

The transformation of the area

The semi-detached houses into which Sutton House had been converted were largely untouched by the building activities around them until the 1860s. Thereafter they became increasingly hemmed in as this part of Homerton declined rapidly in social standing. The change in the district over a relatively short period was the subject of an article in *The Builder* in 1873:

The Homerton of to-day is very unlike the hamlet it was fifty years since, or even twenty-five years ago. The whilom hamlet contained a number of well-built red brick mansions, with large gardens, and these were occupied by wealthy merchants of the City. Several of these old residences still remain, but are sadly altered, and others have completely disappeared, and their site and that of their gardens are built upon. Numerous streets of houses have cropped up, and many more at this moment are growing, centrally and at either end of the ancient hamlet which has now swelled into a very populous neighbourhood. The great majority of dwellings now in course of erection, are of the cheap and speculative kind. They are built by a class of small employers, to suit the wants of mechanics, clerks, or those with small annuities, and their owners do not care to let them on any other condition than that of receiving the rent in weekly or monthly payments.[9]

This relatively rapid change in the character of their immediate environment had much to do with the sale of the two houses in the 1890s and their reamalgamation for use as a young men's institute. Their separate occupancy up to that time is described below.

The east house

The name Ivy House was given to the east house in continuation of the name of the former school. Some time after 1815 it was renamed Picton House, presumably after General Sir Thomas Picton, who was said to have lodged at the house. Picton was one of the heroes of the Battle of Waterloo in which he lost his life. In 1867 the number 4 was assigned to the house when High Street Homerton (renamed as Homerton High Street in 1935) was officially numbered. For ease of reference, in the account below the house will be referred to as Ivy House until 1815 and Picton House thereafter.

At John Cox's death in 1760, the occupant of Ivy House was William Norton. Cox left the leasehold interest in the house and land to its south and east to his daughter Elizabeth, but Norton continued to live there until, in 1763, the rate collector noted that he had 'gone away'.[10] He was followed by Thomas Young until 1767. In the meantime, Elizabeth Cox had died in 1764 leaving all her possessions including the leaseholds to her sister Sarah who lived in the western of the two houses into which

Sutton House had been divided, having been bequeathed the leasehold interest in this half of the converted house by her father. Sarah Cox thereupon became the leasehold owner of both houses.[11]

The Coussmakers and Sarah Gay: the re-establishment of the Huguenot connection

The next occupants of Ivy House after Thomas Young's departure were the family of John Newman Coussmaker, thereby re-establishing a Huguenot connection which had begun with Mary Tooke in 1743 and was to last in this particular house for almost another century. The Coussmakers who settled in England had come from west Flanders in the early 17th century. By the 1730s the branch of the family that was later to live in Hackney was established in Wandsworth, where John Coussmaker was a scarlet dyer and where three children were born to John de Coussmaker and his wife Elizabeth between 1735 and 1740. (A John de Coussmaker was a brewer in Westminster in the 1750s but whether he was the same John Coussmaker is not known.)[12]

The family had moved to Hackney by 1762, when two of the children, John Newman and Lannoy (or Launay) Richard Coussmaker married their cousins Ann and Jean Coussmaker respectively on the same day in St John's Church in what was probably a double wedding. Where they were then living is not known, but John Newman and Ann Coussmaker moved soon afterwards to Shoreditch, where their eldest children were born, and apparently moved back to Hackney to live in Ivy House in 1767. Two more children were born while they were living there, but they moved elsewhere in 1774, only to return to Hackney later. Ann Coussmaker died in 1784 and John Newman Coussmaker in 1800, when he was described as of Hatton Garden, Holborn, formerly of Hackney.[13]

As well as their own children, while they were living at Ivy House the Coussmakers brought up a young orphan girl, Sarah Gay, who was to play a conspicuous role in the later history of the house. Sarah, who left some record of her early life, called her guardians her 'dear friends', but it is likely that they were related, however distantly, as a genealogy of the Coussmaker family in French records that several members of a family called 'le Gay' were linked to them by marriage.[14]

Sarah Gay was the daughter of Thomas and Mary Gay and was christened in Hackney on 23 April 1761. Her father died in 1765 and her mother shortly afterwards, leaving five young children including Sarah. In his will, Thomas Gay had enjoined his wife to consult Sarah Cox and be advised by her on all matters relating to the welfare of the children. In attesting to the will's authenticity Sarah Cox, who was present when it was written, said that she had known Thomas Gay for over twenty years.[15] Sarah Gay may have been named after Sarah Cox (perhaps as a godchild) and two other of Thomas and Mary Gay's children were called John and Martha, perhaps after John and Martha Cox, Sarah Cox's brother and his wife.

The obviously close association between the Cox family and the Gay family on the one hand, and the Gays and the Coussmakers on the other, gives rise to a number of intriguing possibilities. The speculation that John Cox the elder was in some way connected with Spitalfields was raised in the previous chapter; it may also be possible that the Cox family itself was of Huguenot descent (perhaps as an Anglicisation of le Coq). Whatever the family connections, by 1780, when the land tax returns for Hackney first name 'proprietors' as well as occupants, the young Sarah Gay had become the leaseholder of John Cox's former property, including the two houses into which Sutton House had been divided and other land and houses further to the east. Exactly how this state of affairs had come about is unknown, but it may be that all of John Cox's heirs had died and had left the property to Sarah Gay.[16]

In the meantime, the occupancy of Ivy House had changed hands a number of times but always with families of Huguenot descent. In 1775 the ratepaying occupant was a James Fruchard, followed in 1776–7 by Susannah Fruchard. Susannah was the widow of another James Fruchard, a silk merchant with premises in Spitalfields who had died in 1768, and the daughter of Peter Nouaille, Fruchard's business partner. The elder James Fruchard was a prominent member of the Huguenot community; he was one of the purchasers of the site on which the French Protestant chapel was built at the corner of Brick Lane and Fournier Street, Spitalfields, and a director of the French Protestant Hospital. The James Fruchard who lived at Ivy House in 1775 was probably the eldest son of James and Susannah. He later emigrated to India, perhaps shortly after taking up residence in the house, leaving his mother as the ratepayer. She subsequently moved to a smaller house a short distance to the east of Ivy House, apparently preferring to live in Hackney although she owned property in Spitalfields.[17]

After a brief period in 1777 or 1778 when the elderly Timothy Ravenhill apparently returned to the house (*see* p 138), it was taken in the latter year by another Huguenot silk merchant, John Perigal. His forbears had been among the wave of Huguenot settlers who fled to England after Louis XIV had signalled the end of the policy of toleration towards French Protestants by revoking the Edict of Nantes in 1685. He was a junior partner in the firm of Batchelor, Ham & Perigal, some of whose pattern books are kept at the Victoria and Albert Museum. Perigal lived at the house until 1793, carrying out 'improvements' in the mid-1780s which raised its rateable value.[18]

Nicholas de Ste Croix

In the meantime, in 1783 the young Sarah Gay had married yet another French émigré, Nicholas de Ste Croix. He was also an orphan and *c* 1760 at the age of 8 had been sent to England from the island of Jersey following the death of his parents, Charles and Françoise Neele de Ste Croix. In the marriage licence he was described as a bachelor of Hackney and Sarah as a spinster of Chigwell in Essex, but the marriage took place at St John's, Hackney.[19]

In a later family memoir Sarah Gay was described as having had money of her own at the time of her marriage, but this may have been little more than the leasehold interests she had acquired from the Cox family which would have made a handsome dowry. Within a short time of their marriage Nicholas and Sarah de Ste Croix took up residence in a substantial detached house some 100m to the east of Ivy House, which was also part of Sarah's small leasehold estate (and had perhaps been built by John Cox). After the departure of John Perigal in 1793, however, they moved to Ivy House, which although only marginally larger, if at all, had the benefit of spacious grounds to the south and east.[20]

Here Nicholas and Sarah de Ste Croix brought up a very large family: they had sixteen children who lived long enough to be christened although some died in infancy.

In an account written by one of their grandchildren (Sarah, who married a son of the noted writer on agriculture, Arthur Young), the household was described as 'a merry and clever one' and the children were said to have melodious voices and an interest in music and poetry. Their parents were described as 'very small in person, and the wife had an abundance of red hair.' Something of the character of the household is indicated by the following account by the writer. She describes how the eldest son, William, arrived at the house by coach to find his sisters dancing in the hall, whereupon they 'wouldn't let him go and dress, but stop and dance then and there, and he danced in top boots!' The hall in question could hardly have been the narrow passageway from the front of the house and is likely to have been the former Tudor kitchen converted into an entrance hall, with the principal entrance already moved to the side of the house where it is shown on the large-scale Ordnance Survey map of 1870 (Fig 7.1).[21]

In various accounts of the family nothing is said of Nicholas de Ste Croix's occupation, but in a letter to the Earl of Liverpool in 1800 he said that he had been 'for thirty years a very efficient servant of the public as Deputy Comptroller of the Cash at the Excise Office'. (He also said that he had

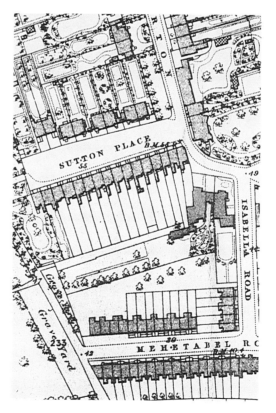

Figure 7.1
Detail showing the extent of the property boundaries of the east and west halves of Sutton House in 1870. [Reproduced from the 1870 Ordnance Survey map; Licence Number GD03085G]

lived in Hackney for thirty years.) If his account of the time he had been employed in the Excise Office is accurate, he must have started working there while still a teenager. He thus occupied a similar position in that office as his neighbour in the other half of the divided house, Thomas Davies, did in the Navy Office. That the two men were on more than just neighbourly terms is indicated by Davies' will in which he left £10 to de Ste Croix for mourning.[22]

The letter of 1800 was not the first time that Nicholas de Ste Croix had been in contact with Lord Liverpool. In 1798 and 1799 he had apparently acted as an intermediary in the shipment of some Chaumontel pears from Jersey to the earl. His purpose in writing in 1800, however, was to solicit the support of the earl, who was President of the Board of Trade, for a proposal to establish a mill near London (probably on the River Lea) 'for the sole Purpose of grinding good Wheat'. In what was essentially a begging letter he referred to his need 'to adopt measures for the support of myself and numerous family (12 children the oldest not 16 years old)' and added that 'with such a moderate income and a small private fortune, now by circumstances of the time reduced, I find myself in a situation to seek support'. In a postscript he said that he had been a captain of the Hackney Volunteers (formed in response to the threat of invasion by the French) until the demands of his family had forced him to resign, doubtless in order to emphasise his patriotic credentials despite his French name. If the earl responded, his reply has not been preserved.[23]

In his letter Nicholas de Ste Croix stated that his salary was £170 per annum, not a large but certainly a reasonable income, especially as it was probably supplemented by other emoluments of office and by the rental income which his wife had brought to their marriage, although the times were highly inflationary. At about this time, however, something appears to have happened in the Excise Office which severely compromised his position. Brief accounts of the family's later years refer to money becoming very scarce. When Nicholas de Ste Croix died in 1816 at the age of 64 there was a long obituary in the *Gentleman's Magazine* which was for the most part respectful but which contained a sting in its tail:

> More would have been said, had not the writer of this paragraph feared to injure the memory of a friend he highly esteemed,

and for the loss of whom he feels, in common with his surviving relatives, the deepest regret. The affliction in which this event has involved a family, consisting of a widow, five sons, and as many daughters, will, it is hoped, be soothed by cherishing those principles which the subject of this memoir ever inculcated, and which he left behind him as the richest legacy he could bequeath.[24]

By this time the de Ste Croixs were no longer the leasehold owners of the house. Whether the lease had expired and had not been renewed to them, or whether they had sold the lease (which, of course, included other properties) to relieve their monetary difficulties, is not known. Whatever the circumstances, although Sarah de Ste Croix survived her husband for nearly five years, she had to leave Ivy House on his death. She was described as a very methodical person and kept several items of clothing which were passed on to her descendants. A waistcoat which formed part of her wedding trousseau and the christening bonnet she used for all of her children are at the time of writing displayed in Sutton House.

The new leaseholder of both Ivy House and Milford House from at least 1809 was Andrew Issanchon, probably a member of a family which appears in Hackney records from the 1760s. In the land tax returns from 1816 the name is changed from Andrew Issanchon to Andrew Johnstone (or, in one year, Johnson), but this may have been yet another Anglicisation of a Huguenot name. Whether he was a new leaseholder or had merely changed his name, Johnstone moved into Ivy House shortly after the death of Nicholas de Ste Croix and remained there until 1821. He was probably responsible for changing the name of the house to Picton House.[25]

Charles Horton Pulley

The next occupant was Charles Horton Pulley, who had taken up residence by 1822 and was to remain there for over forty years. Pulley was a noted, if somewhat controversial, local figure. A solicitor with offices in Great Winchester Street in the City, he was clerk to the Hackney vestry and much else besides. He had been born in 1792 in St Mary Newington, but came from a prominent Huguenot family which had been established in Spitalfields for most of the 18th century. His father, Joseph Pulley, who was a member of the Stock Exchange, later settled in Hackney. Among later generations of the family, a nephew, Sir Joseph Pulley, baronet, was Liberal MP for Hereford. He was educated at Hackney Grammar School in Sutton Place, very near his uncle's house. Two members of the Pulley family, Frances (Charles Horton's mother) and William Mills Pulley were among the last persons to be buried in the vaults below Christchurch, Spitalfields.[26]

Besides being Hackney vestry clerk, Pulley was also clerk to the South Hackney and West Hackney vestries, the Poor Board, the Church Trust, the Lamp Board and the Highway Surveyors, at a total salary of £214. This figure, however, was small compared with the fees he received for legal services, which from the Poor Board alone amounted on average to about £700 per annum. This pluralism and the high income he obtained from his parochial appointments inevitably attracted some criticism and Pulley's detractors saw their opportunity when the old select vestry of Hackney was replaced by an open one under the auspices of the Reform Act of 1832. At a particularly well attended meeting in 1834, however, Pulley was re-elected as vestry clerk by an overwhelming majority, although he later agreed to limit his legal fees to a maximum of £400 a year.[27]

The opposition to Pulley was orchestrated through a new journal, *The Hackney Magazine and Parish Reformer*, edited and published by a local printer, Charles Green. Pulley took exception to several comments in the magazine and stormed into Green's office, at one stage threatening to horsewhip him. He returned the following day with a horsewhip which he laid on the table, where it apparently remained untouched, Pulley contenting himself by declaiming 'you are a sneaking, scurrilous fellow, and may consider yourself as horsewhipped, without my going through the disagreeable ordeal'. Green published a pamphlet on the altercation, with a typically cumbersome 19th-century title, *Ideal "Horsewhipping!" Facts relating to Mr. Charles Horton Pulley (Vestry Clerk of Hackney), Mr. Charles Green (late editor of the Hackney Magazine), and The Almshouse Case*, and Pulley gained a reputation for horsewhipping stubborn vestrymen into shape.[28]

Pulley appears to have lived at Picton House (surprisingly renamed Ivy House in the 1861 census but not in later censuses) until his death in 1864. During his long

residence there he adapted part of the house as an office to conduct at least some of the business of vestry clerk and local registrar.

In 1863 significant changes appear to have occurred at and around Picton House. It was at about that time that the freehold owner, the recently widowed Mehetabel Ball, decided to let most of the extensive grounds which Pulley had enjoyed (amounting to over three acres (1.2ha)) for speculative building, and Isabella and Mehetabel Roads were laid out on the site. The building agreement under which this development was carried out has not survived but, as the term of the building leases of the new houses began on 25 March 1863, it is likely to have been drawn up in that year.[29] Whether Pulley, who had by then turned 70, agreed to give up the land, or whether there was a clause in his lease requiring the land to be surrendered in the event of development is not known.

There may have been a *quid pro quo* involved, for in May 1863 a tender was published in *The Builder* for 'rebuilding premises, High Street, Homerton, for Mr C H Pulley'. This may refer to Picton House, but as Pulley also owned property elsewhere in Hackney including in Homerton High Street the identification is not certain. The architects named in the tender were Wales and Sparks and the successful tenderers at £830 were Skinner Brothers.[30] The 'rebuilding' referred to in the tender may, therefore, have been the Victorianisation of Picton House, which certainly took place at some point in the mid- to late 19th century. The alterations consisted *inter alia* of the addition of stucco render to the front and parts of the side of the house and the insertion of new large-paned sash windows in place of Georgian ones. Some of the Victorian features of the interior may also have been added at the same time.

Despite being over 70 years old, Pulley continued to serve as vestry clerk until his death on 26 December 1864. The place of death given on the death certificate was merely 'Upper Homerton', but there seems little reason to doubt that he died at Picton House.[31]

Pulley left a long will which shows that he was a very wealthy man at the time of his death. Besides the premises of his practice in Great Winchester Street and his 'leasehold house at Homerton', as he described it, he had a house (probably a farmhouse) and extensive land and buildings at Latchingdon in Essex. He also owned a large house near

London Fields, which had been the property of his father, some houses in Charles Street, Hackney Road, chambers in the Albany and some land in Kent. His personal estate alone was sworn at probate at 'under £30,000', a sum equivalent to at least £1,500,000 in the year 2000.[32]

The bequests made in the will reveal details of his family. His first wife, who is not named, had died (probably before 1841 as she is not listed among the occupants of the house in the census of that year). His second wife, who survived him, was named Rebecca, and in his will he expressed his gratitude for 'the very excellent and truly affectionate wife' with whom he had been blessed for several years in the latter part of his life. He had two sons alive at the time of his death, the Reverend Harry Pulley, who had a living in Shropshire, and Charles Oldaker Pulley, who lived at and farmed his father's property at Latchingdon. He had two daughters, Hannah Maria and Julia, while two other daughters, Mary Anne Frances and Caroline, had died. He also had one grandson, Edmund Wood, the son of his late daughter Mary Anne Frances.

He left Picton House and most of its contents to his widow but he recognised that the house might prove too large for her and that she might wish to exchange it for a smaller one. Some idea of the furnishings and contents of the house can be gleaned from the wording of the will. There was a dining room with a 'sarcophagus', a drawing room with 'handsome' books which had been his father's and bibles and other religious books which he and his wife read together, a 'green room' and a dressing room for his wife. Numerous portraits of his father, himself and his wife and other members of the family are mentioned. Other pictures included paintings and drawings by his late wife. Pulley apparently had a large collection of clocks and several sets of silverware marked with his crest. Among other items mentioned was a pianoforte, a chiffonier, a new garden frame and garden utensils and plants.

Later 19th-century occupants

The next occupant of Picton House, with its much reduced but still fair-sized garden, was Henry Grant Baker, but by 1870 Baker had been succeeded by John Henry Heeps, a house decorator with premises in London Wall. At the time of the 1871 census, Heeps, aged 60, lived there with his wife, four

daughters, an unmarried sister and one servant. He was succeeded by John Crowhurst c 1875, a manufacturer of collars and bone, who in 1881, aged 41, lived in the house with his wife, six children of their own and two nephews. Crowhurst continued to occupy the house until 1890, but when the census of 1891 was taken, a 25-year-old police constable, James Blundell, his wife and two young children were listed as the residents. At that time it was common practice for young policemen to live in houses that were temporarily unoccupied in a caretaking arrangement and it may be that Blundell was occupying the house on such a basis while negotiations were in progress for its acquisition as St John's Church Institute.[33]

The west house

The name Milford House was applied to the west house from at least the early 19th century. The origin of the name is unknown. In 1867, when High Street Homerton (the name was changed to Homerton High Street in 1935) was officially numbered, the number 2 was allocated to the house. For ease of reference it is cited as Milford House in the account below.

From the evidence of the parish ratebooks, after the death of John Cox in 1760 his daughter Sarah continued to occupy the house, in which she had been left the leasehold interest by his will, until 1769.[34] A succession of short-term residents followed – Eleanor Rowlands from 1770 to 1774, followed by Thomas Butts until his death in 1778, and then briefly Harriet Butts, presumably his widow – until the house was taken in 1779 by Thomas Davies, the chief clerk in the office for bills and accounts of the Navy Board.

Thomas Davies

Davies was an official of the Navy Board for over fifty years. He started out as a clerk in the office of bills and accounts in 1744, when he must have been about 21 years old, and was promoted to the post of chief clerk in 1756. He kept the position until his resignation in 1795, when he would have been in his seventies. The post was one of considerable responsibility and involved 'examining, assigning, passing and entering all bills and accounts' which passed through the hands of the Comptroller. His salary was a nominal £100 per annum but this was supplemented by a variety of personal fees, gratuities and allowances, which in 1784 alone amounted to £1,737. This sum was cited in a report which advocated the reform of the Navy Office, including the introduction of fixed higher salaries for such officials. Under the old arrangement, however, Davies was able to amass a considerable fortune.

He had apparently lived elsewhere in Hackney for some time as his first wife, Mary, who died in 1770, was buried in the churchyard of the parish church. He remarried, his second wife's name being Henrietta, and had six surviving children at the time of his death, aged 77, on 11 May 1800. In his will he left over £20,000 in stocks, bonds and annuities to be divided between his wife and children. His widow, Henrietta, continued to live at Milford House until her own death on 11 October 1816 at the age of 78. One of their sons, Richard, was a lieutenant in the navy and died at sea aboard HMS *Superb* in 1813.[35]

The Reverend Thomas Burnet and his boys' school

Shortly after Henrietta Davies' death the house was acquired by the Reverend Thomas Burnet, then a curate at St James Garlickhythe, for the establishment of a boys' school. One of his pupils in 1818 was the 15-year-old Edward Bulwer, later Edward Bulwer-Lytton, first Lord Lytton (Fig 7.2), the noted Victorian novelist and author of *The Last Days of Pompeii*. The young Bulwer's stay at what he called 'a receptacle for young men, near London' was brief as a result of an incident which he later vividly recalled:

I had a quarrel with the usher about making a noise; the usher fetched the master; the master was choleric; he became more so at finding that his choler did not influence me; he gave me a box on the ear. I threw myself back in a pugilistic attitude, and the master, retreating, for no glory was to be gained by the contest, requested me to walk into his study. There immured, with a swelling and indignant heart (it was the first blow I had received unavenged from man or boy since the age of ten) I spent two tedious days. No companion visited me, save the servant with my meals, or coal-scuttle; no book cheered me save a volume of Beloe's *Sexagenarian*, which was lying on the sofa, but which, being soon remembered, was, with the usual didascalic malice, summoned away before I had got through fifty pages.

Figure 7.2
Edward Bulwer-Lytton
(1803–73), by H W
Pickersgill, c 1831.
[By courtesy of the
National Portrait Gallery,
London]

My master wrote to my mother, and so did I. …On the third morning the well-known carriage and its stately long-tailed horses, stopped at the gate. I hailed it from the window. The door was unbolted, my mother entered. Scarcely time for a word, before in marched the pedagogue, grim and tall, sullen and majestic. All attempts at reconciliation were in vain. I demanded the first apology. The master, very properly, refused to give it, and, very improperly, put himself into a violent rage. The scene was admirable. It ended by a proof of that spirit of quiet decision with which I have often in later life got out of difficulties. I opened the door, walked through the garden, reached the gate and ensconced myself in the carriage. What more could be said or done? The affair was settled.[36]

According to a fellow pupil of Bulwer-Lytton, the schoolroom was about 40 yards (36.5m) away from the house, and appears to have been specially built for the school. It was almost certainly the long building to the south-west of the house, at the back of the gardens of houses in Sutton Place, depicted on 19th-century maps (*see* Figs 6.38 and 6.39). In the poor rate book for 1819 Burnet was rated separately for 'school rooms', an entry which probably denoted this detached structure.

Thomas Burnet, who was a brother of the noted painters John and James Burnet,

Figure 7.3
East wing of Sutton House
with Victorian stucco
rendering.
[Mike Gray]

ran the school for some twenty years with the help of his wife Maria, neé Faulconbridge, until in 1837 he became rector of St James Garlickhythe, a living he retained until 1875. Another pupil who was later, as a very old man, to revisit the house when it was St John's Church Institute, was Sir Frederick Young, a writer on colonial affairs.[37]

William and Eliza Temple and their girls' school

The boys' school closed on Burnet's departure and was succeeded by a girls' boarding school under the management of a couple barely in their twenties, William and Eliza Temple. Known as the Milford House School, or at one time rather grandiosely as the Milford House Academy, the school catered for girls of all ages. At the time of the census of 1841, besides the Temples and their infant daughter, four teachers, three servants and twenty-four pupils were in residence. William Temple died shortly afterwards, but Eliza continued to run the school for another thirty years. In 1851 there were twenty-six living-in pupils, but in 1861 only twelve, and in 1871 a mere three, but whether these numbers were supplemented by day pupils is not known. In *c* 1875, when she would have been about 60 years old, Eliza Temple gave up the school.[38]

Later 19th-century occupants

The next occupant of the house was William Papineau, a surgeon. He died shortly before the census of 1881, when Harriet Papineau, who described herself as a widow with an income from dividends, lived in part of the house with her two daughters. George Butterfield, an unemployed commercial clerk, his wife, an infant son and a young female servant, also lived there as a separate household. Harriet Papineau, at least, continued in residence for some years, but by the end of the 1880s the whole house was occupied by Llewellyn Nicholas, a retired assistant superintendent in the docks. At the time of the census of 1891 he was living there with his wife, seven sons and five daughters, but no servants.[39]

The fabric

Sutton House was subdivided into two separate units of occupation for nearly a century and a half, and inevitably during that long period a number of alterations were made to the fabric of both parts of the house. On the whole these have not had a major impact on the appearance of the house today, especially as many of the more cosmetic changes, such as the introduction of wallpapers, were undone in 1904 when a concerted attempt was made to return the house to what was thought to be its ancient character. There are exceptions, however, especially in the east wing which still externally exhibits much, though not all, of the Victorian look given to it by the addition of a stucco render (Fig 7.3) and the insertion of new windows. On the first floor of this wing, the room at the front has also retained the dominant characteristics imparted by 19th-century alterations. Elsewhere, however, the changes to fireplaces, windows, floors, ceilings and other features tended to be more piecemeal.

Just as pertinently, the main thrust of structural alterations during these years appears to have been directed to those parts of the building which were completely rebuilt in 1904, namely the additions to the south of the east wing and the south-west of the west wing. No trace of this late 18th- and 19th-century work here is still extant, yet these alterations led to other changes in the main house, and so this work, or rather what little is known of it, will be described before the changes within the main envelope of the building are considered in more detail.

The east wing addition

The archaeological excavations carried out between 1990 and 1992 revealed that the 'small house' at the end of the east wing was extensively remodelled at some time after it was first built and further altered at later dates. The most important of these changes appears to have occurred in the later 18th century when the whole eastern half of the building was virtually rebuilt and extended by some 2m further to the east. A new wall, in a variation of English bond, was built on an alignment with the east wall of the east wing of the main house as a spine wall of the restructured house (*see* Fig 3.20). The backfill of its construction cut included diamond-shaped window panes, probably from the original fittings of the house. At the north end of this wall, a return to the east formed a new north wall of the small house to the east of the east wing. At the north-east corner this was bonded in turn to the

east wall which ran southwards along what is now the Isabella Road frontage (Fig 7.4).

Inside the rebuilt eastern half, a thin partition wall extended eastwards from the spine wall about a third of the way along its length from the north. To the north of this wall the ground was levelled up and a suspended wooden floor was probably laid, while to the south there is evidence of a substantial tiled hearth edged with brick being laid against the spine wall to serve a large room to the east of the new wall.

In the western half of the small house, the east–west partition wall on the line of the former wall of the garden terrace was dismantled. At floor level the gap formed by the removal of its sleeper wall was filled with mortar in which bricks were embedded, thus suggesting that a brick floor continued in use in this area. The doorway into the yard to the west at the south-west corner of the small house appears to have been bricked up at this time.

Figure 7.4
Reconstructed ground plan of Sutton House, as it appeared c 1800 and while in separate ownership. To the rear of the east wing can be seen the outline of the rear addition or 'small house' dating from the 18th century. (Scale 1:200)

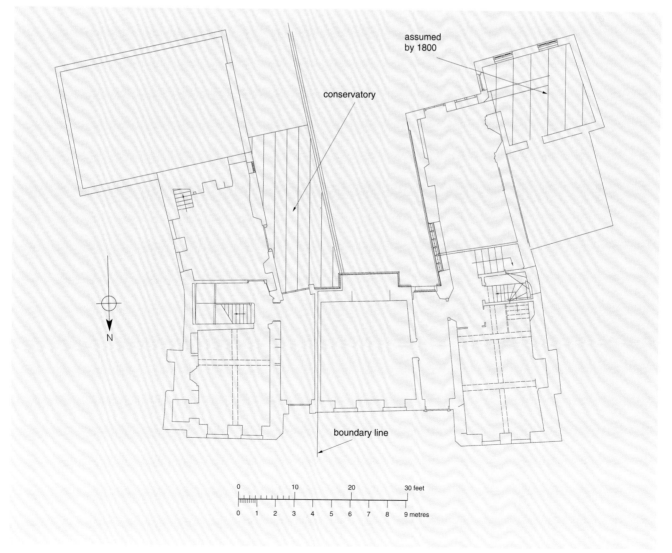

These changes substantially increased the size and utility of the east wing addition, which, after they had been completed, measured some 10m from east to west and 6m from north to south. The form which it took was probably essentially that shown in the watercolour by Varley in the 1890s (*see* Fig 6.2), in which the position of the spine wall between the two roofs can be clearly discerned. It seems that the kitchen had already been moved out of the east wing of the main house into the addition, but it may have been at this time that the former kitchen (G2) was transformed into a large entrance hall. The changes to this room are described more fully below.

Exactly when this rebuilding occurred can only be conjectured, but a likely date is *c* 1783, for in the following year John Perigal had to pay an additional rate of £5, specifically for 'improvements', on top of the normal rate of £45 for the house. Such increases were usually the consequence of alterations which were readily visible to the rate collector, and the rebuilding and enlargement of the rear extension would have fallen into this category. The improvement in accommodation which resulted from the changes doubtless also helps to explain how Nicholas and Sarah de Ste Croix were able to bring up at least twelve children in the eastern half of Sutton House.

Later alterations to the small house which have been revealed by excavation included improvements to the drainage, the construction of a rectangular brick soak-away, and the laying of a floor of York stone flags to form a north–south corridor through the house. All these are strongly suggestive of the use of the ground floor for a kitchen and allied functions.

The west wing additions

A complex sequence of building and rebuilding took place in the area to the immediate south-west of the western house during this period. The archaeological investigations of the 1990s have thrown some light on this activity and for the 19th century there is a series of reasonably detailed maps (*see* Figs 6.38, 6.39, and 7.1), but, even with the benefit of such evidence, very little is, in fact, known about the buildings here as they were comprehensively replaced by the west wing additions of 1904.

The results of the archaeological investigations suggest that much of this building activity took place later rather than earlier, but this is not entirely borne out by the evidence provided by maps and illustrations. So far as can be determined, the sequence of events revealed by archaeology is that in the late 18th century the coalhouse towards the northern end of the yard to the west of the west wing was either demolished or burned down; the presence on its site of a layer of loose, dark grey, silty clay full of ash and charcoal perhaps suggests the latter fate. A system of drains and a large circular soak-away was then constructed, but to what purpose cannot now be determined. At the south end the garden wall was rebuilt in brick in random bond, and a compact gravel surface was laid in the yard, while further north a small east–west wall was erected. Thus the yard was divided into two, but both north and south areas remained external yards.

The earliest large-scale map of the area, Starling's map of Hackney of 1831, however, shows that by that date a substantial sequence of buildings had been erected to the west of the west wing. This is borne out by the tithe map of 1843 that shows the same buildings on a larger scale (*see* Fig 6.39). At least one of these is relatively easy to date. It was detached from the main house and a little to its south-west, behind the houses in Sutton Place; it consisted of a long, rectangular building orientated east–west which, from archaeological evidence, had brick walls. This was almost certainly the detached schoolroom of the Reverend Thomas Burnet's school, about 40 yards (36.5m) from the house (*see* p 179). As such, it was probably built when the school was established *c* 1818.

Besides this building, Starling's map shows that a large addition had been built on the west side of the west wing by 1831. Archaeological evidence suggests that this occupied the precise area of the present west wing addition but was completely demolished in 1904 for the erection of the building which now occupies the site. It may also have been built to provide additional accommodation for Burnet's school, but could have pre-dated it.

The elucidation of the building history of this addition is further complicated by the fact that its northern part appears to have occupied a site which may once have been part of the curtilage of the Tanhouse. It has been suggested above (*see* p 132) that there may have been an earlier sequence of buildings here and that there was some suggestion of a flying freehold. No documentary evidence has been found to indicate that any

part of the Tanhouse property was acquired but the possibility cannot be ruled out.

The addition, which extended slightly beyond the south end of the west wing, was of two storeys perhaps with additional garrets in the roof. It was connected to the main house by a doorway to the south of the fireplace in the kitchen (G6) on the ground

floor and on the first floor by a doorway in the same position as the present doorway in the middle chamber (F5) (Fig 7.5). The southern part of the ground floor was latterly described as a 'stone kitchen', presumably meaning it had a floor of stone flags, but in a late 19th-century survey it is described, probably more accurately, as a scullery (*see* Fig 7.16).

The addition had an M-shaped roof, and the southern face of this and the south wall are shown in Varley's drawing of the rear of the house *c* 1895, shortly after it had been adapted for use as St John's Church Institute (*see* Fig 6.2). The upper part of the north end of the addition is also shown in a faint pencil sketch which has been tentatively dated to the early 19th century (Fig 7.6). The impression given by these drawings is that the structure had a pantiled roof and was quite old, an impression of age reinforced by a report that its west wall apparently fell down when it was being demolished in 1904 and by the discovery of an 18th-century cesspit (Fig 7.7) during the archaeological excavations.

A manuscript map of 1852 in the manorial court books[40] shows a small addition at the east end of the schoolroom (*see* Fig 6.38). From archaeological evidence this was an outside lavatory, presumably for the pupils' use. By 1870, when the survey was undertaken for the first large-scale Ordnance Survey map of the area, however, a further building or buildings had been

Figure 7.5
Room F5. Doorway in west wall, prior to restoration. This doorway served as a first-floor connection between the west wing and the building which formerly stood on the site of the Edwardian extension. [Mike Gray]

Figure 7.6
Undated pencil sketch of Sutton House (probably early 19th-century). Adjoining the west wing, on the right-hand side of the drawing, can be seen the upper part of a smaller building which stood on the site of the present Edwardian extension. [London Borough of Hackney Archives Department P12016.2]

Figure 7.7
Edwardian extension.
Excavated remains of an
18th-century brick-lined
paired cesspit.

erected to link the schoolroom to the main house (*see* Fig 7.1). This completed the sequence of buildings to the west and south-west of the house, all of which were demolished between 1894 and 1904.

The exterior

After the extensive Georgianisation of the exterior of the main house in the mid-18th century, few changes were made to the principal elevations for the next 150 years with one major exception. This was the 'modernisation' of the eastern house (Picton House) by the addition of a stucco façade to the north front and the northernmost part of the east front, and the substitution of large-paned Victorian sash windows for the previous Georgian ones (Figs 7.8 and 7.9; *see also* Fig 7.3). The new facing was

designed to give the house a more 'up-to-date' appearance and may have been added in 1863, as described on p 177.

The work was carried out with some care and involved the use of a render which in the colour of its finish may have been designed to resemble Bath stone. The ground floor was channelled to give the impression of rustication, quoins were simulated at the corners, and the upper storeys were scored to produce the effect of ashlar stonework. The bracketed cornices above the windows and the crowning cornice at parapet level were the kind of Italianate stylistic features to be found on many houses built in the mid-Victorian period. Originally the render was extended around the corner to cover all of the prominent projecting chimney stack and the niche at its base, but this render has since been removed.

Beyond the projecting chimney stack, the remainder of the east elevation was not rendered but new sash windows were generally substituted for the Georgian ones and the window openings were embellished with broad stucco architraves, since removed.

The interior

In this account of the changes which were made to the interior between the 1750s and the 1890s, the same room sequence is followed as in earlier chapters, and no attempt has been made to distinguish between the two houses into which the main house was divided during this period. As in previous chapters, only those rooms which were altered significantly are singled out.

Figure 7.8 (below, left)
Sutton House. North
façade in 1920.
[London Metropolitan
Archives]

Figure 7.9 (below, right)
East elevation of Sutton
House in 1920.
[London Metropolitan
Archives]

The cellars

East cellar

Some of the changes which were made to this cellar either at the time of the main alterations of the mid-18th century or later, including its subdivision into two, have been described in Chapter Six.

One unusual feature which predated the alterations of 1904, because it is shown as already existing in the drawings for those works, and which survived the conversion of the cellar into a chapel, is the small, high-level window in the south-east corner of the room (see Fig 3.65). The window was inserted to light a small area under the half landing of the east staircase, described on the plans of 1904 as a 'dark-room'. The reorientation of the staircase into the cellar during the works of 1904 meant that this area was incorporated within the cellar and that the window, which is at ground level externally, ceased to have an obvious purpose.

The opening consists of a double-hung casement window which originally opened outwards but is now sealed shut; the northern light was accommodated in a bottom-hung, pivoting iron frame. The plain, inward-opening shutters consist of solid timber boards, 18mm thick with a form of 'lipping' at top and bottom to give them additional strength. Security bar hooks were fixed to the frame on each side and another hook on the rear of the shutters accommodated a sprung 'security bell'. The shutters are covered with several layers of paint but a faint foliage decoration can be made out in the centre of each shutter. When the cellar was subsequently converted into a chapel, the glazing in the windows was replaced with leaded lights of an appropriately ecclesiastical cast.

West cellar

The main alteration to the west cellar in the period covered in this chapter was the relaying of the main floor of the cellar, outside the brick enclosure created in the mid-18th century. For this floor, which has survived with some reconstruction, particularly along its eastern edge, to the present day, stock bricks 60mm deep were used, mostly yellow stocks but including some reds. They were building bricks rather than paviours and were laid in a herringbone pattern, frequently with the frog side uppermost, and pointed with sand. The type of bricks used suggests that the work was carried out in the late 18th century.

At some point in the 19th century, the wooden door to the enclosure was replaced, only to be replaced again with a new door during the restoration of the house in the 1990s.

The ground floor

Georgian parlour (G1)

The present form and appearance of this room were largely determined by alterations made in the mid-18th century which are described in Chapter Six. Later alterations were chiefly confined to the north wall and to the east, fireplace, wall.

On the north wall, the Victorianisation of the north front of the east wing included the insertion of new sash windows. The 18th-century panelling was altered to accommodate the new windows and the shutters were cut in half and rehung with new boxes and casings that extended the depth of the openings. The extant cyma-recta moulding was applied to the panelling around both window openings. The dado rails were cut back and crudely mitred and most of the skirting on this wall was installed at this time.

On the east wall, the shouldered, ovolo-moulded fireplace surround with white marble slips which is shown in a number of early photographs (Fig 7.10; see also Fig 6.7) has a superficially 18th-century appearance but probably dates from the early 19th century. At the time of the survey of the house in 1988–90, the mantelshelf and supporting

Figure 7.10
Room G1 in the early 20th century. The interior of the room dates mainly from the 18th century, but was altered in the 1800s. [BB87/9641; © Crown copyright.NMR]

Figure 7.11
Room G1 prior to
restoration, after the
removal of the panelling.
The mantelshelf and
supporting console brackets
at either end of the fireplace
were missing, revealing the
original 16th-century
carved stone fireplace.

East staircase

Few major alterations appear to have been made to the east staircase compartment during this long period, apart from some changes in the cellar area described above and the insertion of Victorian sashes as part of the changes to the exterior of the house.

Entrance hall (G2)

This room, which underwent a transformation in the mid-18th century as described in Chapter Six, was subjected to further alterations in form and function during this period. Many of these changes may have been associated with the enlargement of the addition to the south which has been tentatively dated to c 1783.

After a brief period when the room may have functioned as a breakfast parlour, it appears to have been turned into an entrance hall. The large-scale Ordnance Survey map of 1870 (see Fig 7.1) shows a pathway leading to an entrance, possibly with steps, in the middle of the east front. No corresponding entrance way is shown on the north front, and the doorway on this front may have gone out of use as the main entrance to the eastern half of the divided house at this period. It seems likely that this room was used as an entrance hall as early as the beginning of the 19th century, for the cramped and narrow passageway leading from the door in the north front (Figs 7.12 and 7.13), would hardly have been large enough to allow William de Ste Croix and his sisters to dance (see p 175).

console brackets were missing, but they have been replaced by modern copies. Their removal left a painted outline on the panelling which confirmed that they were not original fittings erected with the panelling (Fig 7.11). Small sections of dado rail on either side of the fireplace were inserted as part of the alterations of the fireplace and are not quite exact copies of the dado rail on the south wall. The removal of one of these sections at the time of the survey revealed the outline of the original rail, chamfered and 'stopped' before it reached the former, 18th-century, fireplace.

The handsome, cast-iron fireplace of c 1860, which is also clearly visible in early photographs, was moved to room F2 during the restoration in the 1990s as more befitting the predominantly Victorian character of that room.

Figure 7.12 (near right)
East corridor. View to
north prior to restoration,
showing wall graffiti
applied by squatters during
their occupation of the
building.
[87/2011; © Crown
copyright. NMR]

Figure 7.13 (far right)
East corridor. View to
south prior to restoration.
[87/2011; © Crown
copyright. NMR]

The access path shown on the map leads to Isabella Road, but before that road was formed *c* 1863, there was a stable yard on the east side of the house from which access could have been gained to the house as easily as from Homerton High Street, perhaps more conveniently and privately.

One of the window openings in the east wall, probably the northern one from the evidence of the Ordnance Survey, was converted into a doorway but there is structural evidence of substantial changes to both openings (*see* Figs 3.34 and 6.15).

At the end of the 18th century, or the beginning of the 19th, a steep staircase was built on the east side of the much-reduced fireplace opening in the south wall to provide access to the upper floor of the enlarged addition to the south of the wing. A new, small fireplace was built in the remainder of the former kitchen range which was otherwise infilled (*see* Figs 3.35, 3.36, 3.37 and 6.12).

Library (G3)

A ground-floor plan of the western of the two houses into which Sutton House had been divided (*see* Fig 7.16), probably dating from the 1890s when the two houses were about to be reunited, shows that this room had been in use as a library. Whether that had also been its use during the long period when the house was first a boys' and then a girls' school is not known.

The appearance of the room chiefly reflects the changes made in the mid-18th century, when the dominant panelling was installed (*see* Figs 1.2, 3.39 and 6.16). The most important later alteration was the raising of the floor by 150mm to the same level as the floor of the west corridor, which had been formed where the raised dais of the Tudor hall formerly stood. The new floor, which was probably constructed in the 19th century, consists of floorboards measuring 25 × 160mm laid on timber floor joists spanning east–west. The joists are notched over wallplates resting on 230mm brick sleeper walls.

Alterations made to the panelling after the floor was raised included the application of a new bottom rail with a crude skirting nailed to it, and the resetting of the panelling under the windows. The struck plaster cornice is also of a later date than the main panelling, and the timber dado rail is yet another later addition. The latter, however, is of a form which was common in good work of the early 18th century, such as at

Hampton Court Palace, and may have been introduced from elsewhere.

Although the entrance to the room appears to have been in the centre of the west wall from the formation of the west corridor, the present door and doorcase are later replacements. Both appear to have been reworked and to have originally been used in another location. When the floor was raised it is possible that the door was changed from an outward-opening to an inward-opening one.

A new, reduced fireplace opening also replaced the one installed in the mid-18th century. The fireplace and grate have been lost but from photographic evidence (Fig 7.14) the former consisted of a plain boxed surround with a mantelshelf supported by wide, decorated console brackets. A late 18th-century Bath pattern hob grate, embellished with neoclassical motifs, stood in the hearth. A report on the house published by the Royal Commission on Historical Monuments in 1935 referred to some late 17th-century Delft tiles in this fireplace.[41] Some loose Delftware tiles were found on the site but these appear to be English and date from the 18th century.

From the analysis of paint samples taken from various locations, it has been possible to determine the decorative sequence in this room. The greyish-brown colour applied when the panelling was first erected was renewed a number of times. After the struck plaster cornice was erected, the whole room was painted a rusty brown colour. Then the dado rails were added and the whole painted

Figure 7.14
Early Victorian fireplace in room G3. Both the plain surround and hob grate were lost shortly after this photograph was taken in the 1970s.
[Caroe & Partners]

HACKNEY, London   Wilford House, Homerton

corridor through the open doorway (Fig 7.15), gives the impression that there was no more than a normal, deep threshold between the corridor and the stone-flagged path outside.

Clarke also referred to the doorcase between the corridor and the staircase lobby (*see* Fig 3.43) as being of stone, 'covered with paint, after the late church-warden pattern'. What this indicates is how thoroughly the overpainting by this date had disguised the true nature of the timber doorcase. It also bears out the evidence of paint samples from elsewhere that, by the last decade of the 19th century, the fairly ubiquitous use of light paint colours would have given this part of the house a very different decorative appearance from that of today.

Linenfold parlour (G4)
There may have been some rearrangement of the panelling which now cannot be readily documented for the long period of divided occupancy, but the dominant feature of the appearance of the room must have been the cream-coloured paint which was applied to the panelling. Seven layers of this colour were found on the panels, framing pieces and cornice. Prior to this, there was light blue paint on the cornice and framing pieces and light brownish-red on the panels and framing pieces.

Kitchen (G5 and G6)
Throughout this period the large room which had been created by the demolition of the former brick cross-stack during the alterations of the mid-18th century appears to have remained in use as a kitchen for the western house.

The survey of the ground floor of this half of the house, undertaken in the 1890s (Fig 7.16), is evidence for the plan of the room at the end of the period. It shows that there was a large larder in the north-west corner of the room against the wall dividing it from the staircase compartment, and that the doorway in the west wall to the south of the fireplace led into a scullery which was part of the additions described above (*see* p 183). The end of the larder, with an unusual ventilating panel in its upper part, can be seen in the watercolour drawing of the north-east corner of the room by F C Varley (*see* Fig 6.21), which also indicates the variety of wainscoting applied to the walls.

Part of the extant boarded ceiling, which was probably erected in the early 19th

Figure 7.15
West entrance passage, looking north, from a late 19th-century watercolour by F C Varley. [AA009977; Reproduced by permission of English Heritage.NMR]

brown. After the present door and doorcase were positioned, the room was painted a deep green; then a more ambitious scheme of decoration was introduced, in which the panelling and cornice were painted cream, while the dado rail and door and frame were rusty brown. The ceiling always appears to have been white.

West corridor
Few changes appear to have been made to this entrance hall during this period, but some comments made by the local historian, Benjamin Clarke, who visited the house *c* 1894, are of interest.[42] He spoke of having to step down from ground level into the hallway, which is a puzzling comment. A watercolour drawing by F C Varley of about the same date, looking outwards from the

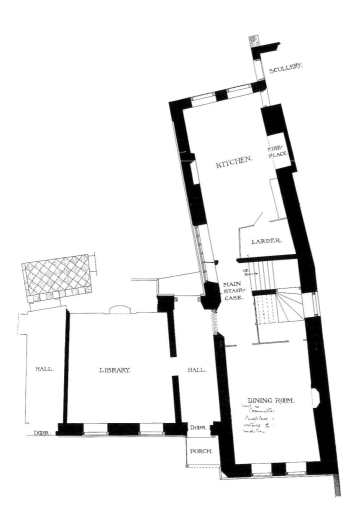

Figure 7.16
Ground plan of the western
part of Sutton House,
based on a survey
undertaken in the 1890s.
The plan shows the layout
of the rear of the west wing
prior to the alterations
carried out in 1904.
[49/00163; Reproduced by
permission of English
Heritage.NMR]

century, is also shown in the drawing. This appears not to have covered the whole room, but only the southern part, as far as the beam which marks the position of the north end of the former cross-stack. The box cornice above the spit-rack was either added or reassembled after the ceiling was installed. At its north end the cornice and the rack beneath it were later cut back to accommodate what was probably a large dresser placed against the west wall. This is shown on the late 19th-century plan. The mantelshelf above the fireplace also dates from this period.

The first floor

Victorian parlour (F1)

The name which was given to this room following the restoration of the house in the 1990s – the Victorian parlour – reflects the alterations to its appearance which were made in the 19th century. With one major exception, however, these changes were cosmetic rather than structural. They consisted of the introduction of dado-height panelling around the room with plaster above, the reduction of the fireplace opening to accommodate a cast-iron fireplace (since replaced) and a Victorian marble surround, and the replacement of the 18th-century sash windows with Victorian ones. The ceiling and fine cornice, however, almost certainly survive from the alterations of the mid-18th century.

The major exception consisted of the blocking of the opening to the garderobe closet in the north-west corner of the room. Both the opening into the closet and the arched recess inside the closet to the right of the doorway were comprehensively bricked-in. On the room side, the dado-height panelling and wall plaster placed over the former opening so completely hid the closet that its existence could only be surmised from plans and the presence of cupboards or recesses on the ground and second floors;

Figure 7.17
Room F1. Unblocking of
garderobe closet.

its reopening during the survey of the house in 1988–90 was a revelation (Fig 7.17; *see also* Figs 3.60, 3.61, 3.62, 3.63 and 3.64).

Inner bedchamber (F2)

The rebuilding of the two-storey range at the end of the east wing, which is likely to have taken place *c* 1783 (*see* p 182), led to some changes at the south end of this room. The recess (now occupied by a cupboard) at the east end of the south wall was probably made during the construction of the staircase from the entrance hall (G2) into the upper floor of the extension. The blocking of the short-lived opening, perhaps a window, at the west end of the same wall is also likely to date from this time. Timber props and a lintel were framed around the opening before it was infilled with horizontal coursings of 18th-century bricks (*see* Fig 3.67).

As was common throughout the eastern house, a new cast-iron fireplace was built into the fireplace opening, which was reduced in width by the insertion of marble slips. The fireplace in this room is one of the few from this period that has survived later alterations and thefts.

The window and frame in the east wall were also altered as part of the 19th-century refenestration of the east front of the house.

Great chamber (F3)

The principal structural alterations made to this room during this long period were the insertion of sash windows in the outer, formerly blind, openings of the north wall and the formation of the present doorway into the north-west chamber (F4), probably to improve circulation when the western house was used as a school. The former change, in particular, would have necessitated yet further substantial rearrangement of the panelling on the north wall. The struck plaster cornice around the room also appears to date from the 19th century and a new doorcase (removed shortly before the restoration in the 1990s) was added to the main entrance into the room from the west staircase.

The general appearance of this room as a panelled room probably changed little over the period. An article on the extensive restoration of the house in 1904, which appeared in *The Builders' Journal and Architectural Record*,[43] described the panelling in the room as having been 'discovered underneath the wallpaper', but there must be some doubt whether this was an accurate description.

A photograph which probably dates from the 1890s, apparently taken after the building had been adapted for use as the St John at Hackney Church Institute but before the major restoration of the house, shows part of the south wall with its panelling exposed (*see* Fig 6.24). The mid-18th-century fireplace is still in place, and the eastern window in the south wall is covered by shutter doors formed out of the type of panelling found on the other walls of the room. The photograph also appears to show that the panelling had been covered with a colour wash. Of course, wallpaper could have been removed prior to the taking of the photograph but, if so, this would have taken place some time before the article referred to above was written. There is no evidence on the panelling in the form of nail holes that it was covered with battens or canvas as a backing for wallpaper. Perhaps the author of the article confused this room with others on this floor at the south end of the west wing where panelling appears to have been covered with wallpaper.

North-west chamber (F4)

The principal changes made to this room during this period were decorative rather than structural, but their effect on the appearance of the room would have been quite considerable.

The watercolour drawing by Varley of the fireplace and overmantel of the room in the 1890s (*see* Fig 6.27) shows the effect of the light-coloured wash which was applied to the panelling. Analysis of sections of the panelling showed that at least four layers of a light yellow-cream wash were applied, and that underneath these is evidence of earlier grey-blue and grey-green washes.

The plain panelling on the north wall appears to be early 19th century in date rather than mid-18th century, when the major alterations for the construction of the new sash windows would have taken place. The cast-iron register grate with side hobs shown in Varley's drawing of the fireplace is also of 19th-century date.

Middle chamber (F5)

It is likely that the partition wall which replaced the brick cross-stack on this floor remained in place throughout this period, thus separating the middle from the southern chamber in the west wing. However, the partition is not shown at all on the plans by Crane and Jeffree for alterations in 1904 (*see* Fig 8.12) and may have been removed at an early stage in the conversion of the building for the Church Institute.

The extant fragments of wallpaper remaining on the walls show that this middle chamber was decorated with a series of wallpapers in the late 18th and 19th centuries. The earliest of these appears to have been applied directly to the plastered wall surface but later papers were backed with canvas stretched over a timber framework. Many of these timber pieces were left in place for the panelling which was assembled as part of the major alterations of 1904.

South-west chamber (south end of F5)

The article on the restoration of the house referred to on page 190 also implies that this room had been decorated with wallpaper but that this had been applied over plain oak panelling.

The second floor

Few readily recognisable changes on the second floor can be attributed to this period, apart from the introduction of new fireplaces in the 19th century, of which the best example is in the southernmost room of the west wing. In the east wing the windows in the staircase compartment and southern room were probably given their present form when new sashes and frames were inserted as part of the 'modernisation' of the east front in the 19th century.

The grounds

The extensive grounds that belonged to Sutton House were first considerably curtailed *c* 1863 when land was taken for house-building in Isabella and Mehetabel Roads. This mainly affected the eastern house (Picton House) to which most of the grounds belonged, the western house (Milford House) having been allocated a more compact garden stretching westwards almost as far as Churchwell Footpath.

The Ordnance Survey map of 1870 (*see* Fig 7.1) shows the resulting gardens of both houses at that date laid out with what appear to be formal paths, lawns and areas of planting. There must, however, always be some doubt as to how far that otherwise meticulous edition of the Ordnance Survey was precisely accurate in depicting gardens and other open spaces.

8

St John at Hackney Church Institute

In 1891 the two halves of Sutton House, then known as Picton House and Milford House, were reunited and adapted as the home of a newly formed men's institute attached to St John at Hackney Church. Initially only a tenancy or lease of the building was acquired. A fund was set up to purchase the freehold but its formal purchase did not take place until 1 August 1895.

According to one document, the price was £2,100 and an additional £215 was paid for the reversion of the lease of some garden ground to the south which had been granted to Edmund Evans, the developer of Isabella and Mehetabel Roads, but not used by him in the development.[1] This additional ground, and the former gardens of Milford and Picton Houses, were earmarked by the church for a purpose unconnected with the Institute.

In 1893 parts of the premises of the parochial church school, Hackney Free and Parochial School in Chatham Place, had been declared unfit by Her Majesty's Inspectorate and a decision was taken to build a new school in the former grounds of Sutton House. Most of the gardens of the two houses and all of the additional land were utilised for the new school, which was built facing Isabella Road in 1895–6.[2] Thereafter, the buildings of Sutton House were used for the Institute but the house was finally divorced from the extensive grounds which had once stretched away to the south. Instead, the north wall of the school playground formed a new boundary with only a small paved area between it and the south side of the house (Fig 8.1).

Thus the decision to found an institute for young men and to acquire Sutton House for its home preceded the need to build a new parochial school but the conjunction of the two purposes was undoubtedly serendipitous and may have aided fundraising.

Figure 8.1
Sutton House from the south, before restoration. The north wall of the school playground, shown here, became the southern boundary of the property in the late 19th century.
[© James Morris/Axiom. London]

192

The founding of the Institute

The initiative for the founding of a new club and institute designed to appeal to young men who were clerks or otherwise engaged in business occupations came from the rector of St John's, the Reverend Frederic Evelyn Gardiner (Fig 8.2). The choice of Sutton House would have been partly dictated by its nearness to the church, its convenient size and its evident availability. The census of 1891 (*see* pp 178 and 180) shows that Milford House, the western of the two dwellings into which the house had been divided, was occupied by a retired assistant superintendent of one of the dockyards and his large family, who may have been content to move, and Picton House by a young police constable and his family, who may have been occupying that house on a caretaking basis.

The St John at Hackney Club and Institute, as it was first named, was officially opened on 26 November 1891 by Sir W Guyer Hunter, MP for Central Hackney. The incumbent rector of the parish was to be the president, and the assistant clergy, the churchwardens and any other persons who might be invited were to be vice-presidents. A committee was appointed to run the Institute, whose objects were said to be 'to provide for its members the means of a healthy recreation and the social advantages of a club, and to promote among the members both spiritual and intellectual improvement'.[3]

Initially, at least, little appears to have been done to the house to adapt it for its new purpose, apart from the reuniting of its two parts into one whole again. Even this was done on a rather *ad hoc* basis, as no internal link was established on the ground floor, a situation which persists to the present day. On the first floor, a doorway was made in the south-east corner of the former great chamber (F3) to communicate with the east wing staircase. What happened on the second floor is obscured by our lack of knowledge of how precisely this floor was divided between the two houses which were formed in the 18th century. Plans made for the alterations carried out in 1904 (*see* Fig 8.13) show an opening at the south end of the braced partition wall in the middle of the central range, which is not designated as new work on the plan, and this may have been where the linkage was made.

Most of the major changes to the building had to await the extensive works which

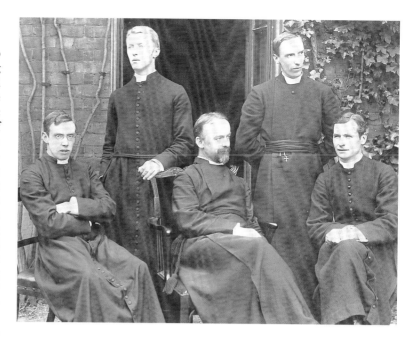

were undertaken in 1904, but it is likely that the boundary walls in the front and back courtyards were demolished and the partition wall dividing the former middle and south-west chambers of F5 may have been removed at this time to make one large 'social room'.

Figure 8.2
The Reverend Frederic Evelyn Gardiner, rector of St John at Hackney (centre).
[From the National Trust collection at Sutton House]

The restoration of 1904

In 1897 Evelyn Gardiner moved from Hackney but he retained his interest in the Institute, becoming a vice-president and remaining as a trustee. He was succeeded as rector of St John at Hackney by the Reverend Algernon Lawley, third son of the second Baron Wenlock and himself later fifth Baron Wenlock. Lawley took a keen interest in the work of the Institute and may have been responsible for changing its name to the St John at Hackney Church Institute, as he was later to be an adamant defender of the retention of the word 'Church' in the title. When, early in the new century, the London County Council declared the building unsafe, Lawley took the initiative in raising funds said to total £3,000 for a major restoration which took place in 1904.[4]

From the start the restoration was imbued with the spirit of the Arts and Crafts movement. There had already been considerable interest in Sutton House as a historic building, much of it stimulated by the presumed association with Thomas Sutton but also aided by the interest of antiquarians like Benjamin Clarke. It seems likely that the house had come to the attention of the

193

watch committee which had been formed by the architect C R Ashbee in 1894 to record and protect the historic architecture of London, starting in the East End. Initially given the cumbersome title of the Committee for the Survey of the Memorials of Greater London, this was subsequently shortened to the London Survey Committee and was the forerunner of the Survey of London.

Among the artists Ashbee enlisted in his cause was the topographical draughtsman, Fleetwood C Varley, great-grandson of the landscape painter John Varley. Several sepia-tinted drawings of the rear of the house and parts of the interior by F C Varley (see Figs 3.43, 6.2, 6.21, 6.27, and 7.15) are now held by the English Heritage National Monuments Record (NMR). They appear to date from the late 1890s, after the building of the Isabella Road schools but before any major changes had been made to the house by the Institute. Their provenance is not known but it is likely that they were among the drawings of the London Survey Committee which were given to the NMR in 1965 when the Committee was wound up. Some of the early photographs of the house in the NMR may also have come from the same source.[5]

One of the earliest subscribers to Ashbee's watch committee was the noted Arts and Crafts designer, Walter Crane.[6] When it came to selecting an architect for the restoration work, the choice fell on Lionel Crane (1876–1943), Walter Crane's son, who had only been in practice since 1900. Walter Crane was clearly involved, for a letter dated 29 July 1903 from Lionel Crane to Thackeray Turner, the secretary of the Society for the Protection of Ancient Buildings (SPAB) and himself a fine Arts and Crafts architect, reads:

> My father tells me that you have been expecting to hear from me about the Hackney Church Institute. Mr Lawley the Vicar is now away in South Africa and nothing will be decided until the autumn. I believe you saw the plans of suggested alterations. I assume that we shall do nothing that will spoil the picturesque character of this interesting old building – and I will see that the plans are shown to you when something is definitely decided, and shall be most happy to fall in with anything that you should suggest should it be feasable [sic].[7]

Thackeray Turner took a keen interest in the building on behalf of SPAB and visited it in the company of Nigel Bond, Secretary to the National Trust. Bond wrote to him to say that the Trust's committee was of the opinion that the matter was more one for SPAB than the Trust, 'at the present stage at any rate', a somewhat prophetic comment in the light of future developments.[8]

The restoration of Sutton House was probably Lionel Crane's first major commission; it certainly came first in the list of works he provided for directories. To carry out the commission he entered into a partnership, seemingly for this job alone, with Sydney Jeffree, who was a surveyor by profession, although both Crane and Jeffree were described as architects on the plans for the work. It is likely that Crane's was the guiding philosophy and design inspiration, while Jeffree provided the practical expertise. Crane's name came first on the drawings; nevertheless, when the completed project was reviewed in an article in *The Builders' Journal and Architectural Record* in 1905, which was probably based on information provided by the architects, Jeffree was given the lion's share of the credit and Crane was said to have been 'associated' with him.[9]

A detailed account of the alterations and new work of 1904 can be found in the second part of this chapter. The builders were Patman & Fotheringham of Theobalds Road, Islington, who were said in *The Builders' Journal* to 'deserve praise for the great care and interest they have taken in the alterations'. The panelling was restored by Keble Brothers of Carlisle House, Soho Square.

The restored and revitalised Institute was reopened on 15 October 1904. The principal guests were Lord Amherst of Hackney and Sir Arthur Lawley, brother of the rector and then Governor of the Transvaal, who planted a tree in the courtyard (Fig 8.3). An anonymous donation of £1,000 from a member of the Lawley family had enabled a large hall to be built at the rear of the courtyard in place of the 'small house' at the end of the east wing. This was named Wenlock Barn in memory of the rector's (and Sir Arthur Lawley's) mother, Lady Wenlock.[10]

The reopening of the Institute led to the appearance of a number of accounts of the house in local newspapers and journals, many highly fanciful in their interpretation of its history. In 1906 a no less fanciful but more seriously intentioned account appeared in the form of a beautifully printed booklet

entitled *The Old House at the Corner*. This was well illustrated and included a number of drawings signed Alfred E Taylor (Fig 8.4). As a portrait of the house at a moment in time it is a valuable record. Most of the information about the work of the Institute derives from such accounts and surviving prospectuses which date from after the restoration of 1904.

The work of the Institute

The object of the Institute was 'to promote the Spiritual, Mental, Social and Physical welfare of Young Men'. To this end Bible classes were held, there was a literary and debating society, lectures were given, a library and reading room was provided, and various games, sports and social gatherings were encouraged. This last category was indeed a focus of the Institute's activities. Billiard tables were provided in the great chamber (F3) and north-west chamber (F4) and the rules required members to pay half the cost if they damaged the cloth of the tables; there was a table tennis table and tables were provided for whist and other card games. There was even a bar but the refreshments were non-alcoholic. Typical entertainments included musical evenings,

Figure 8.3
North-west corner of the courtyard in the early 20th century, following removal of lean-to from north wall but before the addition of the pentice. [BB87/9630; Reproduced by permission of English Heritage.NMR]

Figure 8.4
Detail of the frontispiece of the 1906 booklet The Old House at the Corner *by Florence Warden.*

195

Figure 8.5
Typical entertainments
organised by the St John's
Institute included musical
evenings and charabanc
outings.
[In the collection of
Jim Holland]

The work, which is described in more detail on page 202, was an early commission of the young (Sir) Edward B Maufe (1883–1974), who was later architect of Guildford Cathedral. The chapel was dedicated by the Bishop of Stepney on 30 May 1914.[13]

With the advent of the Great War, Vaisey and a number of the members of the Institute went to serve overseas, and it was closed down. Following its reopening in 1919 the names of 23 members who had died in service during the war were engraved in the panelling of the west wall of the former great chamber (F3), then the Institute's main billiard room, where they remain to the present day.

The Institute in the 1920s and 1930s

The Institute continued to flourish in the 1920s and early 1930s. A red letter day was a visit by the Prince of Wales, later Edward VIII, on 30 April 1926 (Fig 8.6).[14] Several years later a former member, John Dyter, provided a recollection of life at the Institute at this time. He recalled that it was affectionately known as 'the Tute', was popular, and was very selective in its choice of members. He continued:

On entering the building through the porch and the wide oak door, the first room on the left was called the Bar although only soft drinks were sold. It was a plain uninteresting room with cream coloured plastered walls [*sic*] and a large fireplace, round which in winter evenings we sat with hot drinks, talking and laughing mostly. The room on the right was called the Committee Room. This was a panelled room of great interest. Beyond that and past the staircase was a door on the right which led into the caretaker's private quarters and where he did tailoring work. The caretaker's name was Bob Niblett, a kind man of good humour who did his work well. He lived there with his mother, and his sister who was a deaconess of St John's Church. … To the left of the hallway was a door leading to the Courtyard and Chapel.

Up the lovely staircase to the left was a large panelled room which was used for table tennis. To the right was a fine panelled room – the Library. It had a splendid set of book cases, polished tables and armchairs. The Tudor fireplace was another place for sitting and talking and sometimes singing to Albert 'Ike' Groves playing the piano. By the side of

'sing songs' and 'fireside chats'. Outdoor activities included a cricket club and charabanc outings were organised (Fig 8.5).[11]

The membership of the Institute naturally fluctuated over time. In 1906 it was said there was room for 250 members but whether that figure was actually achieved is not known. The figure given at the time of the reopening in 1904 was 150. The Institute was partly residential, with room for between 12 and 20 residents depending on which account is believed. All of the second floor and part of the first floor of the east wing appear to have been given over to bedrooms, or bedsitting rooms as they might now be described. A number of young men with jobs in the City, probably poorly paid clerks, were said to have been among its early residents, but in the later years, the principal residents seem to have been the curates attached to the parish church, to whom most of the responsibility for running the Institute was delegated.

The formation of the chapel

Algernon Lawley left Hackney in 1911, and for a while the Institute fell on hard times, its closure being mooted. In January 1914, however, a new curate arrived at Hackney in the person of the Reverend Francis Dent Vaisey. He became chairman of the Institute, lived there and revitalised its work. He married in 1917 and spent his early married life at the Institute; his eldest daughter was born there.[12]

Vaisey's enduring monument was the conversion of the east cellar into a chapel.

Figure 8.6
Visit by the Prince of
Wales, later Edward VIII
(centre), on 30 April
1926.
[Parish Magazine of
St John at Hackney]

the fireplace was a door into the caretaker's room again. Just inside the door from the staircase and on the right was a small stairway which led to a private flatlet occupied by an old lady. I never did know who she was or how she could live up there with what must have been considerable noise at times from us. Ahead as you reached the top of the stairs was the enormous billiards room which had some fine panelling and a very large Tudor fireplace.

This was always a busy room and much fun was enjoyed on Friday nights when knock-out competitions were held. At the far end of this room was a door which led into the private quarters of the three assistant clergy ...

Despite the club being linked with St John at Hackney there was absolutely no pressure upon any member to attend church, in fact religion was seldom discussed. Quite a number did however regularly go to church and some were in the choir, some sidesmen etc.

Sutton House had for me some extraordinary moods and though I am not in any way interested in ghosts etc., it would, I feel, be very easy for someone who knew about such matters to conjure up some spirits there. I have on many occasions been the only person in the club, often after dark, and I must confess to having had some eerie feelings from time to time. The building was full of odd creaks and whispers, but the life of the club seemed to suppress them most of

the time. The chapel was not used often, certainly not for religious purposes. I only really remember it being used when we opened the club for the day for charity fund-raising efforts. It was then used as a 'ghost-chamber' with hanging cottons, skeletons painted with luminous paint on black sheets etc.

The club was open from 6 p.m. to 11 p.m. Monday to Friday and all day on Saturday. We had our regular cricket and football teams and we played in the London League, table tennis, billiards and snooker.

The membership was mixed. Predominating were the chaps with City jobs in banks, stock exchange etc., tradespeople, local government staff. There were a number of members, however, who were manual workers from factories, building trade etc. Class distinction just did not exist – no barriers of any sort were put up, and everyone was on equal terms. Real friendships were established between the City men and bricklayers, bank officials and factory hands. The ages ranged from 18 to 60 plus.[15]

John Dyter's vivid account of the Institute in the late 1920s and the 1930s shows that at that time at least the aspirations of Gardiner, Lawley and Vaisey were being well fulfilled, though perhaps at the expense of the dilution of some of their religious principles.

It had long been the practice to provide office accommodation in the east wing for a charitable body. Initially this was the Charity Organisation Society and for many years, from *c* 1900, Dr Spurstowe's Charity Convalescent Committee had an office there. In 1930 two rooms were let to the Mission of Help to the Suffering Poor, whose objects were 'to help in emergencies of sickness or temporary lack of employment, and to provide pensions to the aged and infirm, chiefly in the London districts'. Founded in the 1890s, the Mission was under particular pressure at this time of national economic crisis. It continued to operate from Sutton House until the 1950s.[16]

In 1936, however, the St John at Hackney authorities decided that the building, with its relatively high cost of maintenance, was no longer suitable for the Institute. They announced that they were seeking new premises elsewhere, and the whole future of Sutton House was suddenly plunged into uncertainty.

The fabric

Apart from some relatively minor works to reunite the two erstwhile separate parts of the house in the 1890s, and the conversion of the east cellar into a chapel in 1914, most of the alterations which were undertaken while the house was the premises of the Institute took place in one major scheme of restoration in 1904.

The exterior

Relatively few changes were made to the exterior of the older parts of the building but those that were had a significant impact on its appearance. In particular, the replacement of many of the mid-18th-century sash windows by new sash windows with small panes and thick glazing bars led later commentators to ascribe an earlier date than was actually the case to the 18th-century alterations. The effect is most noticeable in the centre of the main, northern front of the house on the first and second floors (Fig 8.7) but several of the windows facing the courtyard also appear to have been replaced at this time.

At ground-floor level on the main front, the canopy over the eastern door (*see* p 150 and Fig 6.1) and the 18th-century porch over the western door (Fig 8.8) were replaced by wooden porches with hipped,

Figure 8.7
Sutton House from the north-west in 2000.
[B000341]

It was, however, in the more sizeable new additions, Wenlock Barn and its ante-room or 'green room', which replaced the former east wing addition, and the caretaker's house which replaced the west wing additions, that Crane and Jeffree were able to make their most distinctive contributions. Although designed to harmonise with the main structure, through the use of a purplish Luton brick laid in English bond, the additions are unmistakably of their own time and are handsome embellishments to the building in their own right. The small-paned wooden casement windows, finely rubbed and gauged red brick arches to the window and door openings, wide overhanging eaves, and carefully laid roof tiles are examples of the superbly crafted, historicist elements that marked the Arts and Crafts movement.

The plan

The survival of Crane and Jeffree's drawings for the alterations of 1904 provides us with evidence not only of their plans for the building but also of how the Institute functioned (Figs 8.11, 8.12 and 8.13).

It is clear from the plans that relatively little had been done in 1891, or was indeed to be done in 1904, to reunite the two parts into which the building had been divided. Both entrances on the north front were retained, although the access from Isabella Road shown on the Ordnance Survey map of 1870 (*see* Fig 7.1) had been closed off before 1904, and on the ground floor the

Figure 8.8
Front door and entrance porch on western side of the house c 1890, showing the 18th-century porch prior to its removal in 1904.
[CC77/48; © Crown copyright.NMR]

tiled roofs in a bold Arts and Crafts idiom that reflected the architects' decision to add features in a contemporary style. A similar effect was achieved in the courtyard by the addition of a wooden pentice, also with a tiled roof, to the north and east walls to provide a covered walkway between parts of the building where there was no communication internally at ground level (Figs 8.9 and 8.10).

Figure 8.9 (far left)
North-west corner of courtyard in 1920, with tiled pentice added in 1904.
[London Metropolitan Archives]

Figure 8.10 (near left)
North-east corner of the courtyard in 1920.
[London Metropolitan Archives]

Figure 8.11
Ground plan of 1904,
showing Crane and
Jeffree's alterations.
[The Rector and
Churchwardens of the
parish of St John at
Hackney]

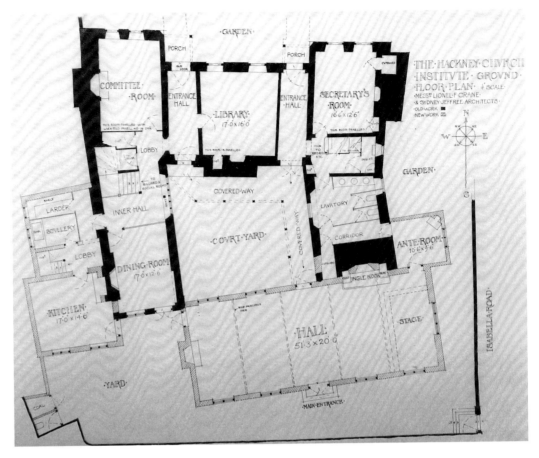

Figure 8.12
First-floor plan of 1904,
showing Crane and
Jeffree's alterations.
[The Rector and
Churchwardens of the
parish of St John at
Hackney]

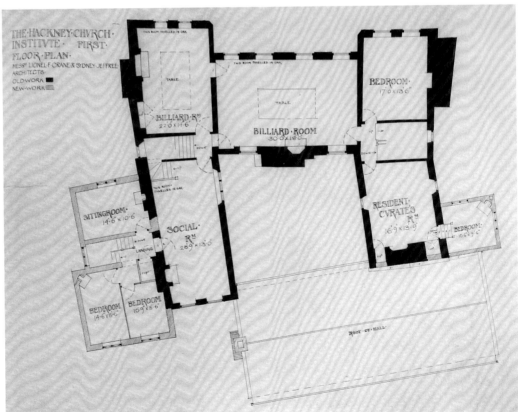

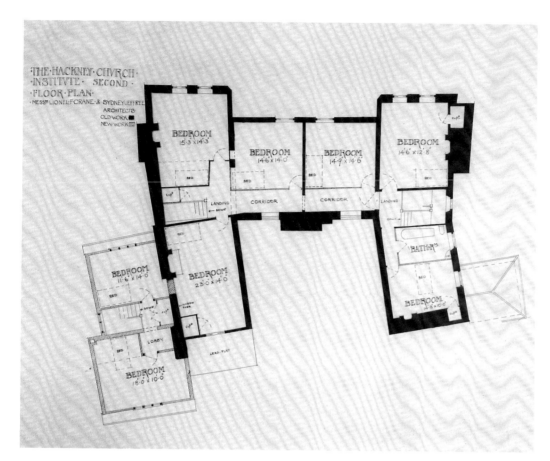

Figure 8.13
Second-floor plan of 1904,
showing Crane and
Jeffree's alterations.
[The Rector and
Churchwardens of the
parish of St John at
Hackney]

only communication between the erstwhile halves was, and is, via the courtyard. An account of the works of 1904 describes the courtyard as having been 'formerly roofed-in with a collection of tumbledown sheds',[17] although some of the 'sheds' appear to have been glass conservatories. This was cleared and opened up and the pentice or covered way added to facilitate communication.

On the first floor, a new doorway was let into the southern end of the east wall of the billiard room (F3, the former great chamber) for access to and from the east staircase, and on the second floor a corridor was formed on the south side of the central range to link the two wings. The retention, however, of many of the features that had marked the division into two houses influenced the way the building was used by the Institute. The 'public' parts of the Institute were largely confined to the ground floor and the parts of the first floor that had formerly belonged to the western house. Even on the ground floor, the east wing was more private, room G1 being the secretary's room and G2 being adapted to house the

Institute's lavatories. The first floor of the east wing and the whole of the second floor were given over to residential accommodation. The use of each room is marked on the plans, although this inevitably changed slightly over time.

The planning of the new additions is also clear from the drawings. The caretaker's house had two main storeys and an attic storey with dormer windows. It was compact and self-contained, with four bedrooms if needed, and was accessible from the Institute on both the ground and first floors. Wenlock Barn was a large hall for concerts and other functions with a stage at its eastern end. It could be accessed separately from the Institute by an entrance in the middle of its south side and thence by a gateway into Isabella Road. This facilitated the letting of the hall for events unconnected with the Institute. The ante-room to the hall was two-storeyed, the upper floor intended as a small bedroom which was linked with the resident curate's sitting room on the first floor of the east wing (F2), a change in level having to be negotiated by steps down into the addition.

The interior

In this account, as in previous chapters, only those rooms in which significant alterations are known to have taken place are described.

The cellars

East cellar

Few alterations were made to this cellar before it was converted into a chapel in 1914. Even the north–south partition which divided the cellar into two apparently remained in place, as a description of the conversion in the St John at Hackney parish magazine for July 1914 refers to its removal.[18]

The same source refers to 'excavating for a staircase', a choice of phrase which indicates the degree of alteration necessary to create the present staircase arrangement from the ground floor. Previously the stairs into the cellar had been similar to those in the west cellar, running in the opposite direction to the present staircase (*see* p 42). The access to the former stairs under the lower flight of the extant staircase to the first floor is shown, although not with complete clarity, on Crane and Jeffree's ground-floor plan in 1904 (*see* Fig 8.11). This also shows the space incorporated into the cellar in 1914, and lit by a high window (at ground level) which was given leaded lights decorated with the design of a Latin cross, in its previous usage as a small 'dark-room'.

To accommodate the new staircase, much of the original south wall of the cellar had to be demolished (doubtless the 'excavating' described above) and the remainder was hidden behind a stud-and-plaster partition. The southern north–south bridging beam in the centre of the room was also truncated and is now supported by a timber column in the centre of the fretwork screen which divides the raised platform at the south end from the body of the chapel (cellar). It is likely that this section of the beam was removed in 1914 to allow for the new staircase, but if the Crane and Jeffree drawings are accurate in showing the access to the former staircase it may already have been cut back to provide head room when ascending and descending those stairs.

In front of the platform, in the main body of the cellar, the floor level was lowered and wooden blocks were laid in a herring-bone pattern on top of a new concrete floor slab. The brickwork of the walls was whitewashed and the exposed beams at the north end were decorated with a leaf pattern.

This end of the cellar was fitted out as a raised 'sanctuary' with steps up in the centre bounded by simple wooden balustrading in a pattern of squares and curtains at the sides separating it from the body of the chapel. New windows were inserted high in the north wall, for the most part utilising existing openings but also involving some reconstruction.

Figure 8.14
East cellar. Interior of the chapel in 1920. The conversion of the chapel was undertaken by architect Edward Maufe. [London Metropolitan Archives]

The effect of the conversion into a chapel, an early work of (Sir) Edward Maufe (*see* p 196), can be seen in early photographs (Fig 8.14) and was described in the article in the parish magazine:

Plain whitewashed walls give simplicity to the whole, while the Sanctuary is set apart by hangings of grey silk and black velvet arranged in deep folds. The Reredos is of blue, purple and gold brocade, parted from the side hangings by grey and black. The frontal is of the same material. There is a beautiful black and silver cross on which hangs a silver figure of Christ, behind Who's head a nimbus of green mother-of-pearl gives the effect of ever present light. The cross is also set with moonstones to typify the water of baptism and amethysts for the vine. Two black and silver candlesticks stand on either side of the cross, these are ornamented in the same way. The vine has also been employed in the decorations of the beams over the Sanctuary. Two low silver bowls stand on either side of the middle posts, holding sweet smelling flowers.[19]

Apart from the raised platform, the whole of the sanctuary and its fittings have been removed, the cross and candlesticks having been given to Benenden School in Kent, which Frances Vaisey's children attended, in memory of their father.[20] Otherwise, the room as a whole has changed little in appearance since the alterations of 1914.

West cellar

In contrast to the east cellar, very little alteration appears to have been made to the west cellar during the Institute years, apart from the replacement of the windows in the front wall in 1904.

The ground floor

Georgian parlour (Secretary's room) (G1)
The only significant alteration to this room was the raising of the floor beneath the windows in the north wall in 1914 as a result of the formation of the chapel in the cellar beneath.

East staircase

The principal alteration to the east staircase compartment also occurred in 1914 when the present staircase arrangement from the ground floor to the east cellar was installed to provide easier access to the chapel which had been created there.

The previous arrangement is shown on the Crane and Jeffree drawings of 1904 (*see* Fig 8.11). Then a hallway at ground-floor level beside the first flight of the staircase up to first-floor level led to a small, low room tucked beneath the half landing of the staircase used as a dark-room by members of the Institute.

Lavatories (G2)
This room, which was adapted to house the lavatories for the Institute, was once more substantially altered, as it has been at virtually every phase of the history of the house. The demolition of the east wing addition and the building of Wenlock Barn in its place meant that the staircase through the south wall was removed and its opening sealed. Likewise the opening into the addition at the south end of the recess to the west of the fireplace was also closed up and a small window to the courtyard in the recess was also bricked in.

On the east wall, the building of the ante-room to Wenlock Barn led to the blocking of the southern window and the making of a new doorway into the ante-room. The northern of the two openings was converted back into a window when the entrance door which had apparently been opened up here in the late 18th century was deemed to be surplus to requirements. This change appears to have already been made before the major works were undertaken in 1904 and may have been one of the early alterations made when the building was adapted for the Institute in 1891.

On the west wall, the Crane and Jeffree drawings of 1904 (*see* Fig 8.11) do not show any doorway into the courtyard and it is likely that the cutting down of the wide opening which originally housed a Tudor window into a doorway post-dates the use of the house by the Institute.

The panelling which had been introduced to the room in the 18th century was removed, the walls were plastered, and new partitions were erected to serve its utilitarian function of providing lavatory accommodation and a passageway to the ante-room. The partition walls were constructed of prefabricated reed and plaster blocks.

East corridor
The present glazed doors and frame at the south end of the corridor probably date from 1904; the doors appear always to have been glazed (*see* Fig 7.13).

West corridor

The heavy oak entrance door appears to have been carefully restored in 1904, when several of the external mouldings were replaced (*see* Fig 3.14). The internal Tudor doorcase in the south-west corner of the corridor (*see* Fig 3.43) was stripped of the innumerable layers of paint that had made the antiquarian Benjamin Clarke think that it was made of stone. When the paint had been stripped away, numerous channels were revealed in the woodwork. These had been formed by wood-boring beetles tunnelling under the paintwork, creating a not-unpleasing decorative pattern that was certainly never intended.

Linenfold parlour (Committee room) (G4)

The most visible change which was carried out to this room was the stripping and varnishing of the linenfold panelling as part of the restoration of the panelling throughout the house by Keble Brothers of Soho Square.

It is also likely that the stone Tudor fireplace was uncovered, having remained hidden under a later chimneypiece, possibly since the 17th century. This speculation is reinforced by a photograph, probably dating from the 1890s, which shows what appears to be the console bracket of an elaborate wooden chimneypiece fixed against the linenfold panelling (Fig 8.15), and a comment in a description of the works carried out in 1904 that the side pilasters were 'discovered in the cellar, and fit exactly into the positions they now occupy; the bases only need to be restored'.[21] The damaged

condition of the stonework of the fireplace, clearly visible in photographs taken of this room shortly after the restoration of 1904 (*see* Fig 3.44), suggests that it was covered up from a relatively early date. The damage may have been caused during the fixing of the later chimneypiece.

West staircase

In 1904 the lower flight of stairs from the ground-floor lobby was reconstructed with an extra tread and the present balustrading was added. The balustrade is made up of machine-turned balusters which imitate those on the second floor dating from the late 17th century. The moulded timber handrail is in one piece and has been set into the brickwork of the west wall. The underside of the staircase is enclosed with vertical tongue-and-grooved, beaded timber boarding similar to the ceiling boards at the northern end of the dining room (G6). These alterations were made necessary by the removal of the south partition wall of the staircase and the creation of the inner hall (G5) described below, to which the lower flight of the staircase is now open.

Inner hall (G5)

The re-creation of this area, which corresponds very approximately to the space occupied by the original middle chamber of the west wing (if the lower flight of the staircase described above is included), occurred in 1904 when a new partition wall was built across the wing, separating room G5 from G6 once more. This wall was constructed a short distance to the north of the line of the brick cross-stack which had been removed in the 18th century, making the room slightly smaller than the former middle chamber. Dominated by the staircase, however, the room functioned merely as an inner hall for the Institute and it still basically serves that function. Nevertheless it was subjected to considerable decorative change.

The new southern wall is a lath-and-plastered, timber-framed partition. A 16th-century oak doorcase, apparently salvaged from elsewhere in the house, was incorporated into the wall to provide access to the Institute's dining room (G6), although in 1904 it was placed at the west end, not at the east end as at present. The dado rail to the wall imitates that of the west corridor and the torus-moulded skirting is similar to that in the dining room.

The removal of the partition wall on the south side of the staircase opened up the

Figure 8.15
Photograph, probably dating from the 1890s, of what appears to be the carved bracket and fluted column of an elaborate wooden overmantel placed over the fireplace of room G4 and apparently removed in 1904. [BB87/8098; © Crown copyright.NMR]

six-light Tudor window in the east wall after its earlier crude division into four and two lights. During the works of 1904, wainscoting beneath the window was removed, the sill was cut down and a window seat was installed (*see* Fig 3.49). Opposite the window, the existing door and frame to the west cellar also appear to date from the 1904 works and were inserted within an earlier door frame.

A new doorway was made in the west wall to communicate with the caretaker's house. That doorway remains and following the 1990s restoration now provides access to the modern lavatories. Elsewhere on this wall, much of the plasterwork was renewed, some of it lath-and-plaster work applied on new timber battens. Beneath the hearth of the blocked fireplace in the social room (F5) above, the brickwork was covered with a hard render to form a mock 'beam'.

Throughout the room the simple wainscoting which had been introduced in the 18th century was replaced with new plasterwork. To complete the transformation the ceiling was removed, along with the ceiling joists, to expose the structure of the floor above.

Dining room (G6)

The shape of this room was redefined by the new partition constructed in 1904 which henceforth formed the northern wall of the room, and other substantial alterations were also made at this time. A new floor was laid, consisting of floorboards laid directly on, and masonry-nailed to, a lightweight concrete floor slab consisting of ash, clinker and cement, averaging 100mm in thickness. This in turn was laid over a rough and very strong concrete mix consisting of broken brick, flint, sand and cement, varying in depth between 80 and 150mm. A similar floor construction is found in Wenlock Barn and the caretaker's house (*see* Fig 3.54).

Most of the plasterwork on the walls also dates from the alterations of 1904, apart from an area of earlier plaster behind the spit-rack above the fireplace and some recent repair work on the west wall. A struck plaster skirting with a torus moulding was applied to the east wall and this was returned to the doorway in the south wall. Apart from the repaired area of the west wall, which has a struck plaster skirting, the remainder of the west wall and the north wall, formed in 1904, have a timber skirting of similar section.

A new wooden casement window, similar to those in the caretaker's house, and a doorway into the rear courtyard were also inserted into the south wall, but into existing window frames, the eastern one cut down to form the doorway (*see* Fig 3.53). Probably at the same time, the interior of the fireplace was given its present brick-tiled, splayed-back form.

The first floor

Curate's room (F2)

In 1904 alterations were made to the south end of this room in connection with the building of Wenlock Barn. A doorway was made through an original 16th-century window opening at the south end of the east wall to provide access to the upper floor of the ante-room of the Barn. The plans of 1904 (*see* Fig 8.12) also show 'new work' in the south wall at the ends of the recesses on each side of the fireplace. That at the east corner was probably associated with the removal of the staircase from the lavatories (G2) to the upper floor of the addition at the end of the east wing which was demolished in 1904. That at the west corner is, however, puzzling. The blocking-in of the opening which had at one time existed here, appears from the type of construction to have occurred much earlier and no opening is shown on the Varley drawing of the south end of the house (*see* Fig 6.2) which certainly predates the alterations of 1904.

At some time the north end of the room was partitioned off to create two small lavatories adjoining the stairwell. Small window openings were made in the east wall and the courtyard wall to light them and the 18th-century wall panelling was refitted around the partition walls. Exactly when this work, which involved damaging alterations to the fabric, was undertaken is unclear. It may have been in the later stages of the house's use by the Institute, but must have been after the room no longer served as the resident curate's living-room. There appears to be no record of the work having been carried out while the house was subsequently in the ownership of the National Trust. The lavatories were removed and the window openings filled in during the restoration of the house in the 1990s.

Great chamber (Large billiard room) (F3)

The present appearance of this room, and in particular of the panelling which is its dominating feature, owes much to the restoration work carried out in 1904. An account of that work states that 'in the course of renovating the larger billiard-room on the first floor some fine old oak panelling was discovered under the wallpaper'.[22] This must be inaccurate. A photograph of the room which was taken before 1904 (*see* Fig. 6.24) shows the panelling clearly visible, but covered with what appears to be a colour wash. In 1904 the panelling was stripped and varnished and possibly stained (*see* Fig 4.17). How much it was also rearranged at that time is not known.

Other changes include the making of a new doorway at the south end of the east wall by cutting an opening through the brickwork, Fletton bricks being used around the edges of the opening. As in the doorway at the north end of this wall, which remained bricked-up, the inside of the door was formed out of panelling. This alteration was probably carried out in 1891 when the building was adapted for use by the Institute.

A mock-Tudor fireplace was installed in 1904 in place of the fireplace shown in Figure 6.24. The new fireplace, which was modelled on others in the house, was made to fit the existing opening, although its size was also dictated by the need to match the width of the section of ornately carved panelling above it (*see* Fig 4.18).

Another feature of the room which dates from the Institute period is the carving on the west wall of the names of those members who had been killed in World War I.

North-west chamber (Small billiard room) (F4)

The principal alterations to this room were the stripping and varnishing of the panelling, and the removal of the later baroque fire surround and mantelshelf to reveal the original Tudor fireplace behind (*see* Fig 4.20). The decorative painting on the stonework of the fireplace, including the coats of arms in the corners of the spandrels, was 'restored' at this time.

Social room (F5/F6)

The partition wall on the line of the former brick cross-stack which had divided these rooms was removed, possibly at an early stage in the adaptation of the house for the Institute. The resulting large room was used as the 'social room' of the Institute, although when the former library (G3) was turned into a 'bar' the bookcases were moved here and at one time the room was known as the 'president's room' (Fig 8.16).

The southern part of this room (F6) had been panelled, although for much of the previous century and perhaps earlier the panelling had been covered with wallpaper. While at least some of the early panelling was restored in 1904, new reproduction panelling was made to fit around the remainder of the room. In installing the new

Figure 8.16
Room F5. View to north
c 1905.
[London Borough of
Hackney Archives
Department P10267.2]

opening was restored to its pre-1904 position.) The sash windows in the south wall were also replaced, probably in 1904 when many of the windows throughout the house appear to have been renewed.

The second floor

A plan of the second floor was drawn by Crane and Jeffree before their alterations of 1904 (*see* Fig 8.13). The floor was to be turned into bedrooms, but relatively little new work was shown apart from some partitioning – to form the corridor across the middle range and a bathroom in the southernmost room of the east wing – and the blocking of an opening in the west wall made necessary by the construction of the new caretaker's residence.

Otherwise, apart from the replacement of sash windows, little appears to have been changed, although substantial later changes may have obscured some alterations. There is evidence that the roof truss over the southern room in the east wing was repaired by the splicing of new timber ends on to the tie beam and principal rafters and the slight realignment of the truss. Where the structural timbers of the roof were exposed with lath-and-plaster infilling, this effect, which fitted in with the Arts and Crafts aesthetic, was retained (Fig 8.18). Whether any lower ceilings were removed at this time is not clear.

Figure 8.17
Room F5. Pencilled inscription found behind the panelling on the north wall, which notes: 'This panelling fixed by Geo. Barnett in the month of September 1904'.
[Mike Gray]

panelling, use was made of the timber stretcher pieces which had been fixed to the walls to take the canvas backing for wallpaper. Following the removal of the panelling, a pencilled inscription was found on the south wall which conveniently notes: 'This panelling fixed by Geo. Barnett in the month of September 1904' (Fig 8.17).

The jib doorway which had been cut through the west wall to provide access to the first floor of the west-wing addition was blocked up, and a new doorway was made slightly to its south to communicate with the first-floor landing of the new caretaker's house. (In the restoration of the 1990s this

Figure 8.18
Following the restoration of 1904, the second floor was converted into bedrooms, one of which (S5) is shown in this photograph of 1920.
[London Metropolitan Archives]

Wenlock Barn

The primary addition of 1904 was Wenlock Barn, which replaced the east wing addition and extended westwards to enclose the courtyard. It is a large, open hall, measuring approximately 16 × 6m, divided structurally into five bays by the dominant trusses of the open, king-post roof (Fig 8.19; *see also* Fig 8.11). There were two fireplaces in the hall: one at the west end and the other towards the east end of the north side, utilising the large chimney breast at the end of the east wing of the main house. A raised stage was built at the east end and a doorway at the east end of the north side led into the small ante-room which was built at the north-east corner of the hall.

The caretaker's residence

The small house for the Institute's caretaker, which appears to have been built on the exact footprint of the previous addition to the west wing, was a more utilitarian addition (Figs 8.20, 8.21, 8.22 and 8.23). Extensive attacks of dry-rot required a more radical rebuilding of this area during the restoration of the house in the 1990s.

Figure 8.19 (facing page) Wenlock Barn, soon after its construction in 1904. [Taken from Warden, F 1906, The Old House at the Corner]

Figure 8.20 (left) Edwardian extension. South elevation in the early 20th century. [BB90/3136; Reproduced by permission of English Heritage.NMR]

Figure 8.21 Sutton House viewed from the west. The twin gables of the Edwardian extension, added in 1904, can be seen to the right.

Figure 8.22
Edwardian extension.
Ground plan prepared in
1990 prior to restoration,
showing phasing.
(Scale 1:100)

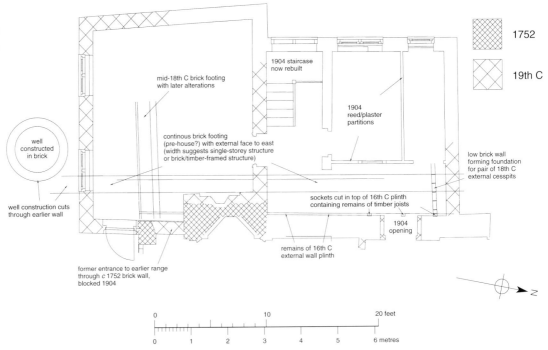

mid-18th C brick footing
with later alterations

1904 staircase
now rebuilt

1904
reed/plaster
partitions

continous brick footing
(pre-house?) with external face to east
(width suggests single-storey structure
or brick/timber-framed structure)

well
constructed
in brick

low brick wall
forming foundation
for pair of 18th C
external cesspits

well construction cuts
through earlier wall

sockets cut in top of 16th C plinth
containing remains of timber joists

1904
opening

former entrance to earlier range
through c 1752 brick wall,
blocked 1904

remains of 16th C
external wall plinth

1752

19th C

0		10		20 feet

0	1	2	3	4	5	6 metres

Figure 8.23
Edwardian extension, as
seen from the yard to the
west of Sutton House in
1987.
[87/2011; © Crown
copyright.NMR]

An undated leaflet about the Institute, which was probably written several years after the works of 1904 took place, links an enduring myth about Sutton House to the rebuilding of the west wing addition:

> Possibly, the oldest portion is the west wing where the excessive thickness of the wall has been tunnelled to make an underground passage from the house to the Marshes and, according to tradition, to the great house of the Knights Templar... . The house-entrance to this tunnel was from an old dry well under the floor of the flagged kitchen demolished to make way for the housekeeper's quarters. Here was a flagstone with a ring attached to it. The stone being lifted, a descent could be made by the iron staves of a ladder set into the side of the well and so into the tunnel – a passage arched with brick.[23]

Although the description seems convincingly full, no evidence for such a tunnel was found during the 1990s archaeological investigation. Instead, a brick-lined drain or soakaway was uncovered in the approximate area referred to. Perhaps the discovery of this in 1904 had fuelled a flight of fancy!

9

In Trust for the Nation

When the rector and parochial authorities of St John at Hackney decided in 1936 to sell Sutton House and use the money to provide new premises for the Institute closer to the heart of Hackney, they were prepared to accept a price of £2,500 for the building. Initially they offered it to Hackney Council, which commissioned a survey by the Office of Works. This took place in August 1936 and cautiously concluded that 'the structure is not in dangerous condition'. The surveyors, however, noticed instances of the ravages of death-watch beetle in the roof timbers and thought that some repairs were required to the brickwork, which had fractured in many places.[1]

Their recommendations reveal an attitude towards the conservation of a historic building which even at that date could hardly have pleased SPAB:

> If the building is purchased by the
> Hackney Council, it is recommended that
> all modern additions should be removed.
> The brickwork should be repaired. The
> modern stucco should be carefully taken
> off. Any new bricks or new pointing should
> harmonise in colour and texture with the
> original work. The roof above the Hall
> should be reconstructed to its original
> design with twin gables. The remains of
> the colour decorations from the wall should
> be carefully preserved by special treatment.
> Stone fireplaces should be repaired.
> Panelling should be carefully cleaned and
> be coated with beeswax and turpentine.
> Deal floor boards should be removed
> and be replaced with oak in the panelled
> rooms.

Whether such recommendations or the unknown cost of repairs deterred the Council is not known, but it soon lost interest in acquiring the building. The future of the house was once more plunged into uncertainty, and there was the distinct possibility that it would be demolished for its site value and the resale value of its panelling and other historic features.

The campaign to save the house

A saviour appeared in the person of Percy Lovell, who was secretary to both the London Survey Committee and the London Society. Lovell was an architect in private practice, having been articled to (Sir) Aston Webb. He had been appointed as secretary to the London Survey Committee in 1907, and in 1913 became also the first secretary to the London Society, of which his mentor, Aston Webb, was the first chairman.[2]

The London Society took the initiative in engaging the interest of the National Trust in the house. A 'very successful visit' to the house on 7 November 1936 was reported in the Society's journal, and on the following day Lovell wrote to the Secretary of the Trust, Donald Matheson, suggesting the formation of an appeal committee to raise the purchase price. The appeal to raise £3,000 (£2,500 for the purchase of the building and £500 for repairs) was launched by a letter to *The Times* on 10 December 1936, followed by a drawing of the house in the *Sunday Times* (Fig 9.1), under the signatures of the Earl of Crawford and Balcarres, President of the London Society and the London Survey Committee; Lord Esher, Chairman of SPAB; and George Lansbury, Vice-president of the National Trust.[3]

The addition of his name to the appeal letter might seem at first sight to be an odd action by George Lansbury, the fiery socialist leader of Poplar Council after the Great War, who was prepared to defy the government and go to prison over the issue of rates equalisation and who was later to be leader of the Labour Party in opposition from 1931 to 1935. However, Lansbury was a keen conservationist, a committed supporter of the work of the National Trust and, when First Commissioner of Works in 1929–31, enthusiastic in his role of preserving ancient monuments. Sutton House particularly appealed to him as a building in community use and as an object of beauty which could

be enjoyed by the people of his heartland, the East End of London. He saw conservation and social reform as entirely compatible aspirations; his views in this respect were similar to those of Octavia Hill, one of the National Trust's founders, and they anticipated the views of a number of influential persons within the Trust who persuaded the organisation to adopt the community scheme for the restoration of the house in the late 1980s.[4]

The time was not propitious for such an appeal, however. The country was only slowly recovering from the financial crisis of 1931; the abdication crisis diverted attention and produced uncertainty, a factor which Lovell took into account but decided to ignore 'for there really is nothing like this house in the East End of London or, for the matter of that, in the rest of the County';[5] and the international situation was threatening. By April 1937 Lovell wrote somewhat despairingly to Matheson that he was 'the only person who is really trying to find money', and the Trust's ardour began to cool.[6]

Early in July, however, both Sir William Power, a former mayor of Hackney who was a keen supporter of the appeal, and Percy Lovell spotted a notice in the *Sunday Times*

that the 'Robertson bequest' was looking for a suitable object in the Home Counties on which to spend money which had been left by William Alexander Robertson (who had died on 5 May 1937) so that the National Trust could purchase land or buildings worthy of preservation. The bequest was to form a memorial to two of Robertson's brothers, Norman Cairns Robertson and Laurance Grant Robertson, who had been killed in World War I, and if a building were to be purchased the nature of the bequest was to be made clear by the erection on it of a large tablet with a prominent inscription.[7]

Lovell urged Matheson to suggest Sutton House as an appropriate object for the bequest and the latter's proposal was accepted. On hearing this, Lovell wrote to Matheson remarking that he had already written to a friend that, 'if the Institute is to be saved, a miracle will have to happen and pretty quickly too!' Now he was witnessing that miracle.[8]

The whole of the purchase money of £2,500 was paid for out of the Robertson bequest and therefore the money collected by the London Society, amounting to £1,079, could be used for repairs. The biggest donation of £250 came from the Pilgrim Trust, there was an anonymous gift of £200 and another of £100. Hackney Council gave £100, as did Lord Wakefield. Smaller donations included £1 7s from the Balham and District Antiquarian Society and a guinea from Mrs Bram-Stoker.[9]

The formal conveyance of the house from the rector and churchwardens of St John at Hackney to the National Trust is dated 17 March 1938. By that time repairs were already in hand under the direction of William Weir, who had been recommended by SPAB. Little actually changed in the use of the house. The Institute remained in possession, but its members were dwindling in number and in August 1939 it announced that it would be giving up the great chamber in September. The possibility of letting the room as a museum was mooted. The Charity Organisation Society and the Mission of Help to the Suffering Poor continued to rent rooms, although in June 1939 the latter gave notice that it would have to relinquish two of them because of a fall in income.[10]

Already there were ominous developments. In 1938 the builders undertaking the repairs had converted the chapel into 'a gas-proof air-raid shelter'. This had been 'during the crisis' (that is, before the Munich Agreement) and they were required to restore the room. In May 1939, however, the Trust agreed to obtain estimates to turn the inner room in the west cellar into a shelter but nothing appears to have been done at the time.

The stone tablet recording the Robertson bequest was erected in the centre of the north front in the early summer of 1939 (Fig 9.2) and it was planned to hold an unveiling ceremony in October which would also serve to mark the acquisition of the house by the National Trust. Events interposed themselves, however, when war was declared on 3 September 1939.

The wartime years

The house continued to be well looked after during the war. Two notable Hackney residents, Sir William Power and Alderman Fisher-Yates, acted as watchdogs or 'wardens', although, perhaps not surprisingly in the confusion of wartime, they had to produce the letter of December 1938 which had appointed them as 'local representatives' to convince the Trust's office staff of their credentials. Power's house on Clapton Common was severely damaged by bombing in November 1940, however, and

Figure 9.2
Detail of the stone tablet erected in 1939 on the north front of Sutton House to commemorate the Robertson bequest.
[The National Trust]

he moved out of London. The lettings of the house were managed by local agents: H J Bliss & Sons of Bethnal Green.

The caretakers of the house throughout the war were Mr and Mrs Willows, who lived in the Edwardian house which had been added to the west wing. They had also catered for various functions which had been held in Wenlock Barn before the war but these activities were now understandably curtailed. Nevertheless, as late as April 1940, a wedding reception was held at the house (an event which was commemorated sixty years later when the couple's diamond wedding celebration was held there).[11] Willows was appointed as a senior air-raid warden and the chapel in the east cellar was converted into an air-raid warden sector post. This was considered sufficient to provide shelter for the tenants of the house during air raids.

The tenant of the flat on the top floor, a Mr Holloway, moved with his family to the country in September 1939, but by the end of October he was asking to return as the threat of air raids had not materialised during this period of the 'phoney war'. He left again in March 1940, however, as he had secured employment outside London and the flat was let to the caretakers of a local school.

The great chamber (F3) had been vacated by the Institute but the billiard table was allowed to remain. The room was subsequently let to an Air-Raid Precautions (ARP) club, of which Willows was a member. Power reported that 'the ARP club folk are making quite reasonable use of the place, and no damage is caused in any way. Their amusements are simple, darts, a small bagatelle table and ping-pong. The darts service is so arranged that protection of the panelled walls is assured.'

The Charity Organisation Society (COS) was probably the principal tenant and in the latter stages of the war appears to have taken over the role of guardian of the interests of the house. The Mission of Help to the Suffering Poor also remained and the Soldiers', Sailors' and Airmen's Family Association opened an office in the house. Children's care officers of the London County Council occupied one room and were admonished for holding whist drives in aid of children who had been evacuated from Hackney because this contravened their tenancy agreement.

The threat of requisitioning was never far away. A captain of the Home Guard requested the occasional use of Wenlock Barn for exercises, pointing out that in an emergency the Barn would be requisitioned in any case. In 1943 the COS warned the Trust that the Quartering Commandant for London District North East was considering the possible use of the building in the event of a special emergency. It was pointed out, however, that while the great chamber and Wenlock Barn might be made available in the event of 'a really serious crisis', the house was 'quite inappropriate for quartering troops' and that 'a good deal of relatively important social work is transacted in many of the rooms here'. In fact, throughout the war the house served the social-service function which had been envisaged for it by the Trust when they purchased it in 1938.

A request in 1944, however, to use Wenlock Barn as an extra classroom for the Hackney Free and Parochial School next door, with possible use by the British Legion in the evenings, was turned down on the curious grounds that such a letting might upset the caretakers. The Trust was not yet ready to consider an educational use for Sutton House.

The house was fortunate in suffering relatively little damage from enemy action. In September 1940 a bomb fell about 20m away causing some damage to the glass and sashes of windows. In 1942 tenants were complaining about the loss of light through the use of felt as a temporary repair for windows which had been blown out and in 1944 the COS renewed their complaint that the Trust seemed unwilling to replace the glass. In the same year, it was reported that some plasterwork in the ceilings had fallen because of the vibration from bombs. Further damage was caused by a V2 rocket which fell in Chatham Place on 19 November 1944. Roof tiles were displaced, some plastering on the ceilings on the upper floor was brought down, and some sash frames and doors were blown out.

In an attempt to ensure that some sort of normality prevailed, even during the dislocation of wartime, the memorial tablet on the front of the building was inspected annually by the National Provincial Bank, as trustees of the Robertson bequest. In 1944 the bank reported that the tablet was 'in need of cleaning and the general appearance was disappointing' and the Trust was asked to take steps to see that it 'was maintained in a proper state of repair and cleanliness'.

The early post-war years

The beginning of the National Trust's disillusionment with its acquisition in the East End of London can be traced to the immediate post-war period. Although the house had survived the war with only minor damage, it was undoubtedly in a shabby state. As late as November 1945 even minor repairs had not been put in hand, but this was perhaps as much due to the shortage of labour and materials and the need to obtain licences for virtually any building work as it was to apathy on the part of the Trust.

Nevertheless, the house could hardly have ranked highly in the order of the Trust's priorities. These were years in which the Country Houses Scheme, pursued with single-minded dedication by James Lees-Milne, dominated the Trust's thinking. The scheme had been started in the 1930s to rescue, in the words of Lord Lothian, 'country houses and their owners in distress' and had gained a new urgency through the ravages of war and post-war taxation.[12] There was little inclination to devote time and resources to smaller houses like Sutton House, especially one in a deprived city area.

Lees-Milne visited the house on 11 April 1946 and found the experience a disagreeable one. He wrote in his diary:

Today went with one of our new agents to St John's Institute at Hackney, the first time I have ever visited this property. And what a wretched one! It is no more important than hundreds of other Georgian houses still left in slum areas. Very derelict after the bombing all around it. Tenanted by a number of charitable bodies. It does have one downstairs room of linenfold panelling. I found it terribly depressing and longed to hurry away.[13]

Lees-Milne had an ally in Jack Rathbone, who became the Trust's Secretary in 1949. An enthusiastic supporter of the Country Houses Scheme, he commented of Sutton House, 'The house is not, I think, one that we should be proud of, and I cannot imagine why we ever bought it'.[14]

In the meantime, life in the house continued much as before (and during) the war. In June 1945 a wedding reception was held in Wenlock Barn, signalling a return to some kind of normality. In April 1946, besides the caretaker's house in the west wing addition and the flat on the top floor, five rooms were occupied by the Charity Organisation Society, three by the Mission of Help to the Suffering Poor, and one each by the Hackney & Stoke Newington Deanery Moral Welfare Association and the London Probation Service. Another room was let for one evening a week to the Civil Defence Club.

In 1946, however, the decision was made to accede to the request of the headmistress of Hackney Free and Parochial Infants' School in Isabella Road to allow Wenlock Barn to be used as a temporary classroom for the school. School days in the Barn were vividly recalled by a former pupil, Geraldine North, fifty years later when she wrote:

Walking through the rooms [of Sutton House], I could still hear in my mind the keys of a typewriter being hit, the smell I remember of warm sunshine on wood, the grooves in the panels on the walls, little odd flashes of memories of my childhood, the stairs, being shouted at due to the noise I made. The Barn where I spent happy hours as a tiny 4 or 5 year old being taught lessons. The old smelly stove in the middle of the room with a cage around it to stop us children getting a burn. The stage, where

I performed a small part as an Indian girl, as I stepped out of a huge book. My first Punch and Judy show. The smell of chives in the little garden outside the barn, and where I had the wonderful joy of growing my first daffodil.[15]

In 1951 the Family Welfare Association, as the Charity Organisation Society had been renamed, the principal tenant of the house, vacated its rooms, and when the London Probation Service left shortly afterwards, the Trust was faced with the serious problem of finding suitable tenants. Help came from an unexpected quarter.

Trade union headquarters

In July 1952 a letter was received from an official of the Association of Supervisory Staffs, Executives and Technicians (ASSET), a trade union, expressing interest in the work of the National Trust and asking for a brochure. Almost as an aside, the letter continued, 'Have you any places to let that might be used as offices or for residential purposes?' Thus began an association of the union with Sutton House that was to last for thirty years.

The Trust seized on this request as a way out of its difficulties and concluded an agreement with the union for the grant of a 21-year lease of the whole building at an annual rent of £450; the premises occupied by the caretaker, who was to continue to look after the building, and the top-floor flat which was rent-controlled, were excepted. The Trust was to be responsible for structural repairs and outside painting and the union for interior decoration, repairs and maintenance. As part of the agreement the public were to be admitted to the panelled rooms only by prior appointment, which the Trust thought unlikely to be 'at all an onerous liability'. The lease was to run from spring 1953, when the union was to take up residence.

The existing tenants were given notice in December 1952. One of them, the Mission of Help, described this as 'a very big blow' and, commenting that they had been at the house for twenty-two years, thought that the need to move would prove 'fatal to our little mission'.

One further change was necessary. The union thought that the name St John's Institute, by which the house was then still known, 'conjures up a rather grim picture to some people' and asked if it could be

Unfortunately, however, a new tenancy agreement for the yard had recently been concluded.

In 1968 ASSET merged with the Association of Scientific Workers to form the Association of Scientific, Technical and Managerial Staffs (ASTMS). The Prime Minister, Harold Wilson, wrote to the joint general secretaries of the new union, John Dutton and Clive Jenkins, to congratulate them on forming a body which was to be a powerful voice in the trade-union movement. Sutton House became the headquarters of the new union.

The union had always been prepared to sublet parts of the house. For some years the Youth Employment Committee of the London County Council was a tenant of Wenlock Barn, which had been converted into offices by the installation of temporary internal partitioning. In 1970, however, ASTMS sought to relinquish their tenancy of the main part of the house but to retain a presence there as a sub-tenant of Wenlock Barn. Arrangements were made between the union, the National Trust and Hackney Borough Council for a new lease to be granted to the Council with the union as an under-lessee. The Council adapted the main house for its Social Services Department, while the union occupied the Barn. By 1975, however, the Council decided to move offices again and assigned its lease to ASTMS which once more took over the house.

This period of uncertainty was a portent of worse to come. Early in 1981 the union announced its intention to finally move from Sutton House. After years when the fabric of the house had been subjected to little more than essential repairs and maintenance, substantial remedial work was necessary. A large bill for dilapidations was served on the union and it was not until 1984 that a settlement on a much lower figure was reached. In such circumstances the search for a new tenant was likely to prove difficult and protracted.

changed to Sutton House after Sir Thomas Sutton, who was thought to be 'the chief historical character connected with the house'. The Trust readily acquiesced, although first prudently ascertaining that the National Provincial Bank as the trustees of the Robertson bequest would not object to the change of name. Thus the name Sutton House which has come to seem indelibly associated with the house was only acquired as recently as 1953.

ASSET moved into the house in 1953 and proved to be a highly satisfactory tenant. The union's General Secretary at the time was Harry Knight. When he resigned in 1960, he was succeeded by Clive Jenkins, a charismatic, jovial and often controversial Welshman who became a noted public figure (Fig 9.3). Jenkins set up office in the linenfold room (G4) and was proud of the union's association with a historic building. He was full of plans for the house and looked beyond the end of the present lease, at one time asking if an extension of fifty years would be considered. One proposal was to acquire the car breaker's yard on the west side of the house, which met with the full approval of the Trust.

The fabric

As most of the work which was done in the house during the period covered by this chapter was basic care and maintenance which did not involve any substantial changes to the fabric, this account of the most important elements of that work proceeds on a chronological basis rather than room by room.

Even before the house was formally acquired by the National Trust in March 1938, William Weir, who had been appointed as architect to supervise repairs on the recommendation of the Society for the Protection of Ancient Buildings, surveyed the building and drew up a schedule of works. The local builders, Barrett & Power of Lyme Grove, Hackney, undertook the repairs which consisted mainly of repainting, repointing the brickwork and retiling the roofs. The thoroughness of this work doubtless helped the house to withstand the depredations of World War II.

One other repair, which may in the event have proved a little premature, was the reinstatement of the Tudor window on the ground floor of the west wing, including the replacement of some of the glass. Sir William Power was able to report that this had been 'excellently carried out and one is able to look upon something less mixed in colour than previously obtained'.

Even at the height of the war, Weir was consulted about the historic features of the house. In 1942 he examined the panelling, which had become discoloured in places, and concluded that the discolouration might have been caused by the use of soda in cleaning the panelling or removing paint in the past. He recommended that after removing the oil and stain with which the panelling had been treated, it should be 'lightly polished with beeswax dissolved in turpentine and applied with a stiff brush'.

In comparison with the destruction which was wrought upon much of east London by bombing, the house was relatively unscathed. It suffered no direct hits but blast damage from bombs and rockets that fell nearby led to several windows being blown out, the fall of plaster ceilings in a number of places and the dislodging of tiles on the roof. While the war was still underway only the most rudimentary repairs could be undertaken and even after the war the strict licensing of building work meant that only essential work could be immediately undertaken. This included the replacement of many of the damaged ceilings on the second floor with new plasterboard ceilings.

One loss during the war which could not be attributed to enemy action was the removal of the iron railings from the front of the house in a misguided salvage operation which had more to do with maintaining civilian morale than providing material which could be converted into weapons of war. The gates and overthrow of the western

entrance were retained as a historic feature, but the net effect was to add to the sense of dereliction which produced an unfavourable impression on some of the most important officials of the Trust.

In 1952 the Trust's Secretary, Jack Rathbone, while not at all well disposed to the house, thought that its appearance could be improved by the removal of the chestnut paling which had apparently replaced the railings. The paling was duly removed and the low wall which had served as a plinth for the railings was replaced by a higher wall. Part of this was rebuilt in 1961, when road widening led to the loss of the north-east corner of the forecourt, and the boundary took on its present canted configuration. The reinstatement of railings had to await the restoration of the house in the 1990s, when the wall was once more reduced to the height of a plinth (*see* Fig 8.7).

In 1948 further repairs were carried out to the Tudor window which had suffered wartime damage. Glass was broken in approximately half of the leaded lights, and this was replaced by the specialist firm of James Gibbons Ltd of Southampton Row.

During the years between 1953 and 1982 when ASSET and later ASTMS leased the building, the union was responsible for maintenance and repairs to the interior while the Trust was responsible for structural repairs and the decoration of the exterior. It appears that sometimes the union interpreted its remit rather liberally and some alterations were made which went beyond the installation of temporary partitioning and office fittings. These are not always easy to document. Some changes were made in the lavatory accommodation in room G2 and it was probably during these years that the doorway from this room into the courtyard was formed in what had previously been a window opening.

In 1960 Pamela Cunnington, who had a distinguished record in the field of conservation, was appointed by the National Trust as architect with responsibility for the house.[16] She instituted a 5-year programme of repairs but this was immediately thrown off course when the roof was found to be seriously defective. The union had reported that a series of leaks had damaged ceilings and walls on the top floor. When this was investigated, major failings were revealed which cost over £7,000 to remedy in a programme of work which lasted for a year, from 1961 until 1962. The builders were T Rider & Son of Union Street, Southwark.

During this work the roof at the front of the house was substantially renewed. A concrete ring beam was inserted at the level of the former wall plate and three new rolled steel beams were inserted to span the roof from north to south. To facilitate the repairs, the stud partition in the centre of the second floor of the hall range was dismantled and when it was replaced it was hung from one of the steel beams.

The removal of the partition enabled the central beam at second-floor level to be inspected. It was found to be failing to such an extent that the district surveyor insisted that it should be supported in the centre. Accordingly in 1962 circular steel columns, $3\frac{1}{2}$in. (89mm) in diameter, were inserted on both the first and ground floors, fixed to the beams above them by wide flange plates and supported at ground level by a concrete foundation. These intrusive features were to remain until the restoration of 1991–5 (see Figs 3.39, 3.72, 3.73 and 3.74).

In the course of repairs to the roof, three lengths of carved oak were found. These were probably the remnants of bargeboards for the original gables at the front of the house and had been reused as hip rafters in the remodelling of the roof c 1740. The two best of these were displayed in room G5 with a notice stating that they had been discovered during roof repairs in 1962, but they were stolen in the mid-1980s (see Fig 3.17).

Another problem which had been pointed out by the tenants was the penetration of damp in the west wall which had affected the stone fireplace in the west wing. This was tackled by digging a new drainage channel and other measures in the car breaker's yard next door and in 1964 the fireplace was carefully restored and repaired by New Stone and Restoration Ltd of Brentford.

In 1965 Pamela Cunnington brought in an expert, Eve Baker, to examine what remained of the wall paintings in the west wing. She cleaned and restored those that were visible and advised that more were likely to exist behind later wall coverings. Pamela Cunnington immediately cautioned that only materials which could be removed easily should be used in future for the redecoration of the west-wing staircase.

In 1969 estimates were obtained for repairs to the roof in the southern half of the east wing but before this could be put in hand Pamela Cunnington announced that ill health had forced her to give up private practice.

In 1974 Caroe and Martin were appointed as architects to the house, and among the work undertaken by them was the replacement of windows in the upper part of the main elevation. As part of this work, repairs were made to the brickwork around the sills which unfortunately proved rather obtrusive.

10

The Worst of Times and the Best of Times

The beginning of 1982 was not auspicious for Sutton House. When a stolen car crashed into the front boundary wall causing considerable damage on New Year's Eve, it was a portent of worse to come. The premature departure of its union tenants, the Association of Scientific, Technical and Managerial Staffs (ASTMS), early in the year left the house tenantless and forlorn.[1]

Decay and dereliction

The National Trust's architects, Caroe and Martin, reported that 'the building is a Pandora's box of trouble' with problems including damage to the linenfold panelling from damp penetration, a long-standing problem in the west wing; the depredations of active furniture and death-watch beetle elsewhere; and the accumulation on the premises of large amounts of flammable material gathered by a subtenant of the union, the Children's Scrap Project, which had failed to find alternative accommodation.

The risk of vandalism was ever-present while the property remained empty; the ground-floor windows were also boarded up, adding to the air of dereliction which had settled on the house. In September, during an inspection in connection with the dilapidations schedule which was being served on the union, the gruesome discovery of a decomposed body under the stairs in the west wing underlined the apparent ease with which entry could be gained to the building. Investigations by the police confirmed that there were no suspicious circumstances surrounding this incident.

Soon after this, Stan Piesse – a local resident, churchwarden and school governor – became concerned about the loose state of the security grilles to the windows on the east elevation, which he felt might attract children's attention to the empty house. Approaching the front door to check whether anyone was inside, he slipped on the mossy flagstones. In an enraged state, he wrote to the Trust to ask why it was neglecting the property in a way that could only cause future problems. The resulting exchange of correspondence led to Piesse, who had first been involved with the house when he was a member of the St John's Church Institute, becoming an invaluable keyholder for the Trust. He provided a much needed local contact in the troubled times ahead.

While the architects were itemising the work needed to repair the house, the Trust was searching for a new tenant. The London Borough of Hackney and several local organisations expressed interest, as did the property developer Kentish Homes and a transcendental meditation group called Siddha Dham, but all negotiations fell through for a variety of reasons.

In October 1984 the Trust's fears were realised when the architect, Patrick Crawford, reported that thieves had broken into the house and stolen three cast-iron fireplaces and the carved bargeboards which had been discovered during roof repairs and placed on display. They had also removed some of the oak panelling, seemingly to ascertain whether they could remove the stone fireplaces. It was the beginning of a catalogue of thefts, which continued when lead was stolen from the roof a month later.

At the beginning of 1985, three years after the union had left, two further organisations expressed interest in becoming lessees: the Community Psychiatric Research Unit from Hackney Hospital and the local adult education service. There were promising prospects that one of them would take a lease but, before any progress could be made, an event occurred which was to raise fresh problems for the Trust's management team.

The Blue House

Early in April 1985 Stan Piesse reported to the Trust that he had visited the house, only to be told by the tenant of the car breaker's yard next door that squatters had moved into the building. The new occupants, who had taken over the house on 2 April, soon announced their intentions with a letter to local residents. 'Hello!' it stated, 'As you've probably noticed, something is happening at Sutton House – several of us have moved in and are hoping to convert it into a kind of community centre.'

The original eight squatters were an articulate group of young people who proposed to establish workshops for clothes-making, leatherwork, painting, drawing, photography and other arts and activities for the young unemployed, as unemployment was then very high in Hackney. They wanted to reopen the house to the public and to set up a café and were prepared to undertake the necessary rudimentary repairs to make this possible. The squatters made it clear to the Trust that they understood the importance of the building and would respect its historic fabric. They asked for a licence to remain there temporarily and agreed to vacate the premises if a new tenant was found. The group even conducted their own investigations into the history of the building and reminded the Trust how their own aims tallied with those that had been announced for the house when it had been reopened after restoration in 1904. Finally, they renamed the house 'the Blue House'.

The squatters quickly gained support from a number of local luminaries, including councillors and the MP for the constituency, Brian Sedgemore. The Trust obtained a High Court order for the group's eviction, but its execution was delayed while negotiations were entered into to see if there was a way in which they could remain there legally. The Trust's Regional Director for Thames and Chilterns, Julian Prideaux, paid a visit to the house and talked to the group and for a while there seemed to be the genuine possibility of an accommodation between the Trust and the squatters.

However, as the year wore on, the high hopes of the squatters began to be eroded as not all of their number and their supporters appeared to share the commendable aspirations of their leaders in trying to respect the wishes of the local community and protect the historic fabric of the house. By November relations between the Blue House residents and neighbouring householders had deteriorated to an alarming extent as the noise and late-night disturbances following musical events were followed by smashed windows and attempted break-ins of nearby houses. The house, too, suffered damage. Letters of complaint were sent to

the Trust's Chairman, Lord Gibson, and sympathy with the aims of the squatters rapidly evaporated. By Christmas, all but one of them had moved out.

This colourful episode was to leave a lasting legacy. The attempt, however abortive, to utilise the house for the benefit of the community struck a strong enough chord with a number of local people that it was revived in the so-called 'community scheme' to persuade the Trust to restore the house for just such a purpose. In physical terms, besides the debris and graffiti of a normal squat, there were also several drawings on the walls, of varying degrees of artistic merit, and a number of vivid murals, some of which have been preserved on the second floor as a lasting reminder of this short-lived but striking phase in the building's history (Figs 10.1 and 10.2).

The development scheme

While the squatters had occupied the house, the Trust had continued negotiations with the health authorities over the grant of a lease, but these broke down over the latter's refusal to commit the substantial funds which would be needed for refurbishment. The Trust's agents, in some exasperation, thought that consideration now had to be given to the alternatives open to the Trust and asked 'whether it is worth one further attempt at finding, by advertising, a developer prepared to take on the building or whether you would prefer that we should immediately investigate the viability of a residential conversion to be carried out by the Trust themselves.' The response was that an advertisement should be placed making it clear that, subject to planning consent, 'any use will be entertained for the building'.

In December 1985 the house was advertised in the *Estates Gazette* as a listed building available on long lease for office use but for which institutional, community or residential use would be considered. There was a rapid response from Avanti Architects, an Islington-based practice, with a record of 'social architecture' which included the sensitive restoration and reuse of historic buildings. They had obtained the cooperation of Village Estates, a development company headed by Martin Village, aptly described by Patrick Wright as 'a developer of the 'post-hippy' variety',[2] who believed that it was possible to combine social responsibility with commercial viability.

Figure 10.1
Room S2. View to south during restoration, showing one of the murals painted by squatters in the mid-1980s.
[Ken Jacobs]

Their proposal, which the Trust received enthusiastically, was that they would convert the building into five residential units – two town houses and three flats – under a 99-year lease, in return for which they would pay for the restoration of the panelling and wall paintings by National Trust craftspeople (partly, they hoped, with the aid of a grant from English Heritage). They promised that the conversion would be handled sensitively, even though it involved the partial demolition of Wenlock Barn, and that the leases of the individual units would contain strict covenants requiring the lessees to preserve and maintain the historic fabric. Access was also to be granted to the public for a limited number of days each year, although exactly how this was going to be arranged with five separate tenants was not clear.

There is no doubt that the National Trust saw the Village Estates scheme as a way out of its difficulties. As these largely unpublicised plans matured during 1986, there were some complaints about the neglect of the house by the Trust, especially in view of the potential that it offered for the local community. The local conservation body, the Hackney Society, organised a visit early in the year and one of its members, Mike Gray, wrote to the *Hackney Gazette* berating the local council for its lack of interest and lamenting that future generations would have cause to regret the loss of

Figure 10.2
Room S3, showing another painted mural by squatters.
[Mike Gray]

the house as a public resource if it was converted into expensive private flats. But it was not until the following year, as public knowledge of the scheme grew, that murmurings of discontent swelled into a fully fledged campaign to save the house for public use.

The Save Sutton House Campaign

In February and March 1987 three local activists – Mike Gray, Julie Lafferty (who had been a former employee of ASTMS at Sutton House) and Ken Jacobs – wrote letters, unknown to each other, to the *Hackney Gazette* deploring the proposal to turn the house into residential units. They and other local residents quickly formed the Save Sutton House Campaign, which organised a petition and questionnaire for the occupants of nearby houses. The result was an overwhelming opposition to the conversion of the house for private use with only limited public access. Instead, the Campaign proposed 'as an alternative, a scheme which would preserve the essential integrity of the house and more appropriately reflect its cultural, historical and architectural merit by encouraging community involvement in its development and ensuring full public access.'[3]

Stung by this orchestrated and unexpected opposition, Village Estates and Avanti Architects agreed in April 1987 to present their plans to a largely hostile Clapton Square Area Community Development Association, whose secretary, Jane Straker, was also a founder-member of the Save Sutton House Campaign. The Association was an important catalyst for action and had earlier passed a resolution to occupy Sutton House in the event that it became empty again to ensure its protection against vandalism and further dereliction.

The fears of the Association had indeed been realised early in the year when, over a weekend during which the remaining squatter was away, thieves had broken into the house and stolen virtually all of the irreplaceable linenfold panelling. What happened next is unclear but the panelling eventually turned up at the premises of the London Architectural Salvage and Supply Company (LASSCO) in Shoreditch. The proprietor, whose knowledge of historic buildings enabled him to identify the probable source of the panelling, arranged for its return to the National Trust. This extreme situation prompted the Trust to take action and the remaining oak panelling and

fireplaces were removed to the National Trust's store at West Wycombe.

A number of Hackney councillors became interested in the campaign's objectives, and in May 1987 a meeting was arranged between officers from the Council's Planning Department, officials of the Trust, the developers, members of the campaign and representatives from local residents' associations. In July the Chairman of the National Trust, Dame Jennifer Jenkins, and its Director-General, Angus Stirling, visited Sutton House where they met Mike Gray and Martin Village. This was a recognition of the concern which was already being felt at the highest levels of the Trust over the future of the house.

By now Martin Village probably recognised that he would have difficulty in implementing his development scheme in the face of growing opposition. After a period in which he sought to accommodate the Campaign by proposing that part of the house should be adapted for community purposes while the remainder would be converted for residential use, he eventually withdrew from the scene without submitting a formal planning application to Hackney Council.

The local author, Patrick Wright – whose *On Living in an Old Country*, published in 1985, was amongst the earliest exposés of the 'heritage industry' – was an early convert to the aims of the Campaign. He has described his visit to the house in company with Mike Gray and Martin Village (*see* p 1) and, in August 1987, he wrote a long illustrated article for *The Guardian* in which he used the fate of the house as a launching pad for an attack on the policies of the National Trust and in particular the dominating influence which the Country House Scheme had had on the organisation.[4] He was later to develop those themes in a television programme, 'Visions of Britain: Brideshead and the Tower Blocks' in October 1988, and in his book, *A Journey through Ruins*, which contained an account of the campaign to save Sutton House.[5]

In the meantime, in 1987 the Campaign had also approached Julian Harrap – a conservation architect with an excellent record, particularly in the East End of London – to flesh out 'the community scheme' which had been devised by its members. The job was enthusiastically undertaken by the architect Richard Griffiths who was then an associate in Harrap's practice and had himself recently moved to Hackney.

In the autumn of 1987 the Save Sutton House Campaign, which had already achieved more than it had dared to hope for, decided to re-establish itself on a permanent and less confrontational footing by becoming the Sutton House Society. A steering committee was set up to manage the transition, with Mike Gray as Chairman, Julie Lafferty as Secretary and Ken Jacobs as Treasurer. They were to become the first elected officers of the new society. Before the significant year of 1987 had ended, the Sutton House Society was able to record another triumph when approximately 800 people turned up to visit the house at an open day on 13 December organised jointly with the National Trust (Fig 10.3).

The acceptance of the community scheme

If this event amazed the Trust, there was still understandable caution within its ranks at embracing such a radical solution to the problems posed by the house. An understanding had been reached with the Sutton House Society that some form of community use should be entertained for part of the building, but the Village Estates scheme was still on the table and there was no commitment to the wholehearted adoption of the community scheme and the expense for the Trust that it would entail.

The community scheme proposed a highly ambitious range of uses, with the intention of serving the local community in a wide variety of ways and of generating an income which would ensure the sustainability of those uses by obviating the need for excessive reliance on external revenue funding. The historic rooms, while being carefully repaired, would be discreetly provided with services to allow their use for functions; Wenlock Barn would be converted as a multi-use hall, particularly suitable for conferences and recitals of chamber music; there would be a permanent exhibition about the house as well as rooms for temporary exhibitions, education facilities and a café-bar. The west wing additions could be adapted both for the management of the house and as lettable offices to provide additional revenue. As Richard Griffiths developed his plans for the realisation of these objectives, it was agreed that the community scheme should not only repair the surviving historic fabric to the highest conservation standards but also add an appropriate layer of new design

The National Trust & SUTTON HOUSE SOCIETY
FORMERLY 'SAVE SUTTON HOUSE CAMPAIGN'
invite you to

SUTTON HOUSE

2~4 Homerton High Street, E.9
by SUTTON PLACE & HACKNEY CHURCHYARD

OPEN DAY

SUNDAY 13ᵗʰ DECEMBER
10·30am~3·30pm

BUSES TO HACKNEY CHURCH
22,22a,30,38,55,106,253
TO HOMERTON S2,236,35
B.R. Hackney Central

Including an Exhibition on the Past and Future of Hackney's most historic House ....

Built in the characteristic Tudor H plan around 1525 it is the oldest domestic building in Hackney and one of the oldest in the London area. Architectural historian John Summerson described it as "a composition of beauties welded together in the course of time"

ENQUIRIES TO :-
Julie Lafferty 32, Ickburgh Rd. E5
Tel. Day 01-267 4422 Eve 01 806 2441
or Diane Forbes Nat. Trust (0494) 28051 (day)

M.L.G. 16 Nov.'87.

to accommodate the new range of uses proposed.

A number of events gave succour to the increasing number of people within the Trust who felt goodwill towards the scheme. In February 1988 a meeting was held at English Heritage's London Region offices to discuss ways in which that body could help. Out of that meeting came the decision to offer the services of two of the authors, Andy Wittrick and Richard Bond, who would undertake a detailed study of the fabric of the building as an aid to understanding its history and to assist in formulating approaches to its restoration. Such a commitment in terms of time over a two-year period gave invaluable support to those who were pressing within the Trust for the acceptance of the community scheme.

Figure 10.3
Poster advertising the first open day event at Sutton House on 13 December 1987.

[Mike Gray]

Figure 10.4
Fiona Reynolds (right)
and Anne Blackburn
(left), *Chair and Vice-*
Chair of the Sutton House
Local Committee, during a
visit to the house in 1992.
[Ken Jacobs]

pivotal to both these commitments: its potential for use as a vehicle for the education of future generations could be built into the restoration scheme while, as a historic building in an impoverished part of an inner city, its restoration to beneficial public use could act as a potent agent of local regeneration.[6]

Support came from several other leading figures within the Trust. Robin Mills, who had taken over from Julian Prideaux as Regional Director, tirelessly sought to surmount the obstacles which inevitably appeared and was instrumental in channelling the energies and enthusiasm of local people into taking the practical steps which were necessary to implement the scheme. Other leading figures in the field of conservation gave their time and expertise, including Peter Burman, a one-time Hackney resident, who was the Secretary of the Council for the Care of Churches and later Director of the Centre for Conservation Studies, King's Manor, York; Fiona Reynolds, subsequently Director of the Council for the Protection of Rural England and now Director-General of the National Trust; and Margaret Willes, the Trust's publisher and another resident of Hackney (Fig 10.4).

Towards the end of 1988 a joint committee was set up with Isobel Watson as Chairman and composed of representatives appointed by the Trust and the Sutton House Society to develop the community scheme in greater detail. Roger Lansdown of Prometheus Ltd (Business Consultants), a firm specialising in the preparation of business plans for community-based projects, was appointed to draw up a business plan. He reported that, in view of the proposed revenue-generating activities, any deficit in the early years was likely to be modest and should be eliminated later. In the opinion of the Trust's representatives such a degree of subsidy was readily sustainable.

However, the capital cost of the scheme, involving as it did the meticulous restoration of the house to the highest standard and the provision of new work of high quality, was always going to be substantial. This was estimated at approximately £1,700,000. Originally, it was anticipated that the Trust would provide about a third of this sum, while grants from English Heritage and other bodies and fundraising would account for the remainder. However, the share that eventually fell to the Trust was over £1,000,000. Such a commitment on the

In June 1988 a study day was held which was chaired by Martin Drury, Historic Buildings Secretary of the National Trust, and Isobel Watson, a respected historian of Hackney's built environment. Reports were given on the progress made in understanding the house and the proposals for its future and a number of leading figures from the worlds of conservation and education gave lectures. Other events such as open days and concerts raised the profile of Sutton House and in November 1988 a craft fair attracted over 1,000 visitors.

While, through its committees and bureaucratic structure, the Trust moved slowly, the impetus for change came, perhaps surprisingly, from the top. The Chairman, Dame Jennifer Jenkins, and the Director-General, Angus Stirling, were both looking for a new sense of purpose as the Trust approached its centenary year of 1995. They found it in a renewed emphasis on education and in reviving the aims of Octavia Hill, one of the Trust's founders, who believed that conservation should be allied to social change. Sutton House was part of the Trust, at a time of many calls on its resources, should not be underestimated, but Sutton House had become so central to its concern to embrace those aspects of conservation which it felt it had hitherto neglected, particularly conservation in the inner cities, that the investment was considered to be worthwhile.

It was decided to implement the scheme in two phases so that parts of the house would still be available for activities and to avert the danger that local enthusiasm would be dissipated if the house were to be closed for a long period. The decision also had the practical advantage of staggering the capital cost and allowing time for fundraising. The first stage would concentrate on those parts of the house with the maximum earning potential, namely Wenlock Barn, the west wing and the west wing addition, while the restoration of the rest of the house would follow shortly afterwards.

It was on this basis that the community scheme was presented to the committee of the Thames and Chilterns Region of the National Trust on 14 July 1989 and it received unanimous approval. Endorsement by the various Head Office committees followed later in the same month.

Several months were spent in finalising details. Julian Harrap Architects were officially appointed as architects by the Trust, with Richard Griffiths as the director responsible. (He later formed his own practice, Richard Griffiths Architects, which carried the project through to completion.) A form of management which had been used earlier by the Trust – the local committee – was revived, with an equal number of members appointed by the Sutton House Society and the National Trust. The committee held its first meeting in December 1989 and was responsible for the management of the community scheme. Its first chairman was Fiona Reynolds.

A project manager, Carole Mills, was appointed in September 1990; she was later to become the property manager of the restored house. Loe & Co of Maldon, Essex, was chosen from a shortlist of contractors to undertake the work. A family business which had been founded in 1919 by the grandfather of managing director Peter Loe, the firm specialised in the high-quality restoration of historic buildings. The contractors took possession of the areas for the first phase of the restoration in January 1991 and shortly afterwards fundraiser Martin Kaufman was appointed with the daunting

task of raising £700,000, which had been set as the target of an appeal.

In the meantime, while the community scheme was being honed, activities continued at the house. A limited archaeological investigation was undertaken in the summer of 1990 by MoLAS, to be followed by a second phase in January and February 1991, in advance of the building works. Open days were held, music recitals were given and the craft fair became an annual occasion. One event which was to have lasting repercussions was a drama project conducted with local schools in May 1989 by the Young National Trust Theatre on the theme of '1789'. When the restored offices were opened in the west wing addition at the end of the first phase of work on the house, the Young National Trust Theatre became the tenant.

The implementation of the community scheme

The principles which guided the restoration of the house are described in the next chapter. Here, an outline of the timetable of the work is given.

The first phase proceeded on schedule. The enthusiasm and expertise of the team of craftsmen employed by Loe & Co was a substantial bonus. They responded with commitment and dedication to the demands of a project which changed by the day as new problems and opportunities were uncovered during the course of the opening up of the fabric (Figs 10.5–10.8). With the builders' cooperation, it proved possible to share the excitement of the process of restoring the house with the public in an open day. In this phase, conservators continued to work on the wall paintings on the staircase of the west wing and the complicated jigsaw of repairing and reinstating the linenfold panelling from G4 was executed by the National Trust's own craftspeople. They benefited greatly from the careful study of the panelling while it was at West Wycombe (see Fig 4.7).

The restored part of the house was opened to the public on 16 September 1992. New facilities included the café-bar (see Fig 11.12), and the Wenlock Barn had been refurbished as a 130-seat hall for public performances and conferences, with a new gallery at the rear for storage and extra seating (see Fig 11.13). The number of recorded visitors in the first six weeks after reopening was over 1,600.

225

Figure 10.5
Some of the people
responsible for the
implementation of the
community scheme at
Sutton House in the early
1990s. The architect,
Richard Griffiths, is at the
top right and the Property
Manager, Carole Mills, at
the centre.
[Loe & Co]

Figure 10.6
Room F3 during the
restoration. Drawing by
Martin Shortis which
formed part of an art
exhibition held at Sutton
House to mark the
implementation of the
community scheme. Since
1991, such exhibitions
have been held regularly in
room F5.
[Martin Shortis/The
National Trust]

The second phase of the restoration began shortly after the conclusion of the first, and was preceded by a further limited archaeological investigation in September 1992. Progress was delayed by a fire which broke out on 11 February 1993. Fortunately, damage was largely limited to room F2 and nothing of great architectural value was lost. By sad coincidence, Stan Piesse, who had been involved with the building since the Institute days and who had latterly been the keyholder for the National Trust in the difficult years of the mid-1980s, died on the same day.

Some six weeks were lost because of the fire but the contract, which included the rehanging of the panelling in the great chamber (F3) and the recarving of the panels with a version of the Tudor rose which had been stolen, as well as the restoration of the rooms in the east wing, was concluded in December 1993. On 2 February 1994 the newly restored parts of the house were opened to the public and the realisation of the community scheme was complete (Fig 10.9).

*Figure 10.7 (above, left)
The unblocking of the
entrance to the garderobe in
room F1.
[Ken Jacobs]*

*Figure 10.8 (left)
Conservation work to the
fire surround in room G6.
[Ken Jacobs]*

*Figure 10.9 (above, right)
Schoolchildren visiting
Sutton House after its
opening to the public on
2 February 1994.
[Chris King/National
Trust Photographic
Library]*

227

11

The Restoration of Sutton House: Principles and Practice

Sutton House is chiefly remarkable for the degree to which it was altered in all periods to reflect changing architectural fashions, new uses and the social history of the neighbourhood, and this determined the principles guiding its repair.[1] It was decided to respect all periods of its history; layers would not be stripped away to reveal earlier ones and a new layer would be added to suit the new use of the house. But it was recognised that a line had to be drawn somewhere and that while vandalism, graffiti and decay had made a valid impact on the history of the building, they could no longer be allowed to dominate. Preservation wholly 'as found' was not an option; value judgements were therefore inescapable, with different approaches adopted in different places and for different reasons.

The approaches to conservation

The linenfold parlour (G4) is the finest of the Tudor rooms and its panelling, retrieved following its theft, was carefully pieced together (Fig 11.1) and reinstated, with some missing panels and ones that had been irreparably damaged replaced by new panels meticulously carved by National Trust craftspeople. A new floor of wide oak boards

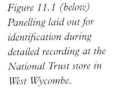

Figure 11.1 (below) Panelling laid out for identification during detailed recording at the National Trust store in West Wycombe.

Figure 11.2 (right) View into room F4 from the great chamber (F3), following the restoration in the 1990s. [© James Morris/Axiom. London]

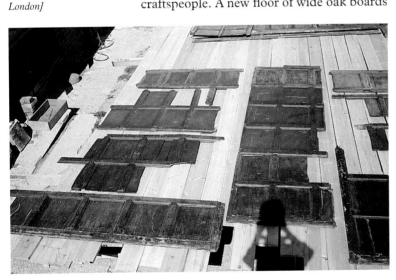

was laid and a specially-made fireback was introduced, as in some of the other historic rooms where nothing had survived inside the fireplace (*see* Fig 4.6).

Elsewhere, oak plank doors and specially made wrought-iron latches were restored to surviving Tudor door frames (Fig 11.2). A Tudor doorway and window, bricked up since at least the 18th century, were reopened since they were needed for practical reasons. New chimneys in a recognisably modern version of the Tudor idiom were built (Fig 11.3) and the problem of ensuring that Wenlock Barn was properly ventilated was solved by the erection of a prominent cupola, newly designed in a manner that was sympathetic to the Arts and Crafts style of this Edwardian addition but with the date '1991' clearly inscribed on it. In the Georgian parlour (G1), however, as the later Victorian mantelshelf had been stolen it was replaced with an entablature designed in an appropriate classical style (Fig 11.4).

This editing of history may offend some purists and indeed produced some angst among the conservation officers of the statutory authorities; however, the architect maintained that such carefully considered interventions, minor in extent and carried out for reasons of visual harmony, avoided the risk that principle should turn into dogma. By contrast, some areas were left precisely as found: for example the un-bricked Tudor privy, where the collapsing plaster ceiling was left unrepaired in order to save the cobwebs which had been accumulating since the 18th century (Fig 11.5). Even some of the finer squatters' decoration from the 1980s were left *in situ* on the second floor, which was used for an exhibition about the history of the house when the restoration was completed (*see* Figs 10.1 and 10.2).

The discovery of so many interesting surviving features of the Tudor house hidden under later surfaces posed an interesting

Figure 11.3 (above, left) Work being carried out on the chimneys at the rear of the hall range in 1992.

Figure 11.4 (above, right) Room G1, following restoration. [B000345]

Figure 11.5 View from room F1 into Tudor garderobe, deliberately left unrestored during the restoration of the 1990s. [© James Morris/Axiom. London]

problem (Figs 11.6 and 11.7). To remove them for display elsewhere would have deprived them of their historical context and significance; to reveal them behind glass panels would potentially have robbed the later surfaces of their architectural integrity; and to lose them altogether from sight would have been a great pity and a serious loss to the educational interest of the house. The problem was solved by the extensive introduction of hinged panels (forty-three in total) that can be opened to reveal the earlier fabric (Fig 11.8). In the Tudor panelling, a number of small panels open like an Advent calendar to give a surprisingly complete picture of original oak framing and plaster surfaces and of the interesting plain panels painted in *trompe l'œil* imitation of linenfold panelling. Original privy shafts exposed during the archaeological investigations can also be viewed below floor hatches, while the modern lavatories are approached through a lobby with a glass floor revealing lime-filled 18th-century cesspits (*see* Fig 7.7.).

The adaptation to new uses

The greatest challenge was to adapt the house to accommodate the extensive range of new uses without compromising its historic character and integrity. The range of proposed uses could only be made possible by compliance with modern regulations for public floor loadings, means of escape, fire compartmentation and by the introduction of a complete range of modern services.

Fortunately the Tudor house was very solidly built, with brick walls and a double-floor construction with separate systems of oak floor and ceiling joists tenoned into the 380mm square primary beams. The 150mm square oak floor joists generally complied with modern requirements for public assembly use. In the case of the primary beams across the great chamber (F3), however, reinforcement was necessary. In 1962 steel columns had been introduced on the ground and first floors to support the main beams which had been found to be failing (*see* Fig 3.74; *see also* p 218). In the interests of aesthetic harmony, particularly in the great chamber with its fine spatial proportions, it was clearly desirable to find an alternative solution to this problem, but the London Advisory Committee of English Heritage agonised for some time over whether the steel columns had become part of the historic structure and should therefore be retained. Fortunately common sense

Figure 11.6 (above) John Dobson, specialist bricklayer, in the process of revealing a four-centred arch buried in the external wall of the east wing. [Mike Gray]

Figure 11.7 (right) Conservation work being undertaken on the 16th-century fireplace in room F5. The fireplace had remained hidden from view for over three centuries. [Ken Jacobs]

prevailed and the beams were reinforced by means of steel flitches, specially designed by the structural engineers Hockley & Dawson, so that the columns could be removed.

Half-hour fire separation between floors was adequately provided by the traditional timber lath and lime plaster ceilings, but all doors on to the means of escape had to be upgraded to half-hour standard with intumescent and smoke seals and self-closers. The most heavily used doors are normally held open by magnetic catches linked to the fire-alarm system.

Services

Every void in the historic fabric was pressed into service to hide the equipment associated with a highly serviced building: pipe runs, emergency light battery packs, transformers, telephones and valves. In the historic rooms, the hot-water central-heating radiators were concealed below specially made timber grilles in the panelled window seats, the brickwork having been removed to create the necessary voids; the heating is controlled by a sophisticated control system designed by Max Fordham & Partners, the service engineers. The historic rooms are normally heated only to a low level to create suitable humidity conditions for the panelling but the heating can be boosted to create comfortable conditions for limited periods by pressing an 'occupancy switch'. In addition, the chimney flues were lined with pre-cast flue liners to allow the use of open fires in all the main Tudor rooms.

A low level of lighting is provided from electrified chandeliers in the Georgian rooms and hand-crafted brass-and-terracotta wall sconces designed and made by local

Figure 11.8
Room G1, following restoration. Above the fireplace, a hinged panel (here in an open position) reveals the stone Tudor fireplace beneath, while to the right, a section of panelling opens to reveal the timber-framed partition wall beneath.
[© James Morris/Axiom, London]

231

craftspeople in the Tudor rooms (Fig 11.9). This can be supplemented on occasion by free-standing lights plugged into sockets concealed below hinged pieces of floor-boarding. In the great and little chambers (F3 and F4), low voltage spotlights can be plugged into a system of jackplug sockets in the oak panelling. In this way these rooms can be used to display paintings hung from the top of the oak cornice moulding, which has been carefully fixed 3mm below the ceiling to allow the introduction of brass picture hooks. In the room currently used for art exhibitions (F5) (Fig 11.10) and in the shop (G3), which are both permanently in use, the lighting is by low-voltage spots resting on wires suspended clear of the ceilings; the exhibition fittings and glass shelves in the shop are similarly suspended on wires, allowing a clear view of the walls and panelling behind (*see* Fig 6.16).

Smoke detectors were required in all rooms but, in order to avoid giving them undue prominence on otherwise unrelieved flat ceilings, they were positioned near doors rather than centrally in the rooms. Emergency lighting was needed to satisfy the requirements of the public entertainment licensing authority. Too many historic buildings are ruined by bulky self-contained fittings; at Sutton House the 'EXIT' signs were painted directly on to the joinery (*see* Figs 1.8 and 3.71) and illuminated by exposed pigmy bulbs fixed in small bayonet holders to the ceilings adjacent, powered from central battery packs concealed in spaces below the staircase. Such devices minimise the intrusion of the services in the historic core and, wherever possible, the need for such intrusion was avoided by locating highly serviced areas such as the kitchen, lavatories, plant rooms and the main service ducts and risers in the 1904 additions rather than in the Tudor core.

New work

Somewhat unusually for an architect specialising in work to historic buildings, Richard Griffiths combined an interest in conservation with a keen interest in contemporary design. It was agreed from the outset that the community scheme should set out not only to repair the surviving historic fabric to the highest conservation standards but also to add an appropriate layer of new design to accommodate the new range of uses proposed for the house (Fig 11.11).

The only opportunity for a new extension on the site, required in order to create a viable café-bar, was in the area of the rear courtyard. One of the main characteristics of all the alterations made to Sutton House during its history is that they were carried out unselfconsciously in the style and materials of their time. The Tudor house was built of brick and oak with iron fittings and the Georgian alterations were in painted softwood with brass fittings. The new café-bar extension was therefore designed in the form of a conservatory to take advantage of the southerly aspect, using polished ash with bronze fittings in a contemporary architectural language (Fig 11.12). The spacing of the mullions was used as the basis of a three-dimensional grid of ash framing; this continues over the walls and roof as a treillage for supporting vines, across the bar counter and even over the floor, forming panels filled with terracotta floor tiles.

Ash, bronze and glass were used elsewhere in the house for other new additions, including the gallery in the Wenlock Barn (Fig 11.13), the offices in the west wing addition and, more controversially, for the screen across the entrance corridor. It was felt important that the heavy, oak

Figure 11.9 (facing page, top)
Room F4, following restoration and installation of modern lighting. Covering the floor is a reproduction of a traditional decorative oil cloth.
[A000037]

Figure 11.10 (facing page, bottom)
View of the art gallery (F5), looking northwards. Since restoration, Sutton House has housed a number of successful exhibitions by local artists.
[B000351]

Figure 11.11 (below)
Proposal drawing showing the alterations to the ground floor of Sutton House carried out in the early 1990s.
[Julian Harrap Architects]

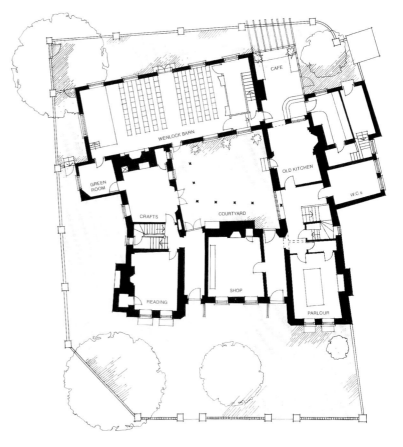

Figure 11.12 (above, left)
One particularly successful addition made to Sutton House during the restoration was the café-bar, housed partly in a new conservatory, seen here looking towards the south-west.
[B000349]

Figure 11.13 (above, right)
The west end of the Wenlock Barn, showing the gallery added during the restoration.
[© James Morris/Axiom. London]

Figure 11.14 (right)
Room G2 following restoration, displayed as the Tudor kitchen, and used for educational purposes.
[B000346]

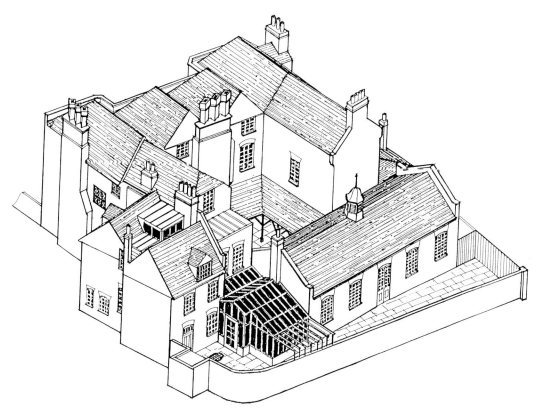

Figure 11.15
Sutton House as it appears today, from the south-west. The glass roof of the new café extension can be seen to the left of Wenlock Barn, at the bottom of the drawing.
[Grace Bryan-Brown]

Tudor front door should be kept open and welcoming when the house was open to the public and it was therefore necessary to provide an inner screen and door for reasons of security and protection against draughts. English Heritage reluctantly accepted the practical need but was opposed to a modern design in this context unless it was of plate glass. Richard Griffiths felt that the supposed transparency of such a design was an illusion. He also felt that the inner screen door had a symbolic significance as the front door to the community scheme and that the facts of the conversion and new use of Sutton House might properly be announced by a piece of new design through which visitors entered. The National Trust's architectural panel supported this approach and the architect's wishes prevailed.

The philosophy of restoration

The restoration of Sutton House was a highly ambitious and, for the National Trust, an entirely novel attempt to use one of their properties intensively for a wide range of activities, while still respecting and preserving its historic fabric. The keynotes were flexibility and inclusivity. In this spirit the community scheme was designed so that the house would be open to visitors as a traditional National Trust house (Fig 11.14) but would also be available for use by school groups on educational projects or for meetings, conferences, dinners, weddings, lectures, concerts and many other activities.

In order to allow such multiple uses, the historic rooms were lightly furnished with a few suitable pieces of permanent period furniture, supplemented by modern furniture brought in when required. The period pieces were deliberately robust and not of great value; chests and cupboards provided additional storage and 17th-century tables could be used for dinners and meetings, suitably protected with druggets. The house, rather than the contents, was to be the chief exhibit.

The experiment at Sutton House in demonstrating how a historic building can be put to modern intensive uses is certainly not applicable to all historic buildings. It is, however, of particular relevance to historic buildings in cities and it therefore provides useful lessons and experience which could be applied elsewhere. If nothing else, it is an optimistic statement of faith in the possibility that the preservation of historic buildings need not only be an end in itself but also that their creative conservation can serve the needs of present and future generations (Fig 11.15).

Endnotes

Abbreviations

APC	*Acts of the Privy Council*
APC, NS	*Acts of the Privy Council, New Series*
Arch J	*Archaeological Journal*
BL	British Library
Cal Ct Min	*Calendar of Court Minutes of the East India Company*
Cal Pat	*Calendar of Patent Rolls*
Cal S P Dom	*Calendar of State Papers, Domestic*
Cal S P E I	*Calendar of State Papers, Colonial Series, East Indies*
DNB	*Dictionary of National Biography*
GuiL	Guildhall Library
HAD	Hackney Archives Department
Harl Soc Publ	Harleian Society Publication
IGI	International Genealogical Index of the Church of Jesus Christ of Latter Day Saints
L & P Hen VIII	*Letters and Papers of the Reign of Henry VIII*
LMA	London Metropolitan Archives
PRO	Public Record Office (now National Archives)
SoL	*Survey of London*
SPAB	Society for the Protection of Ancient Buildings
VCH	*The Victoria History of the Counties of England*

Chapter 1

1   Wright 1991, 45–6.
2   Pevsner 1952, 171–2.
3   Summerson 1945, 97–102.
4   Pevsner 1952, 171–2.
5   Gray 1989, 282–4.
6   Phillpotts 1994; Phillpotts 1998, 207–12.
7   Tyers 1991.

Chapter 2

1   Gerard 1597, Vol I, 178; Vol II, 786 observed that 'The small turnep groweth by a village near London called Hackney and [is] brought to the Crosse in Cheapside by the women of that village to be sold.'
2   *VCH* 1995 *Mddx X*, 75–80, 101–3. Surviving records of Lordshold and Kingshold manors are LMA, M79/LH and M79/KH. Some records for Grumbolds survive as LMA, M79/G, but most are in the form of a Victorian translation of the court rolls in HAD, D/F/Tys/40.
3   *L & P Hen VIII*, Vol XII, 1336; Luckett 1995, 3-9; [Strype] 1720, Vol II, appdx, 122. Strype was a lecturer for 35 years at St John at Hackney, dying in Hackney in 1724 at the age of 94.
4   *DNB*, under Urswick, Christopher; Taylor 1999, 8.
5   Richardson 1952, 114–16, 160–6, 217–19 and *passim*.
6   Slavin 1966, 1–13.
7   PRO, C54/407/29.
8   Mander 1993, 7.
9   Ibid, 11.
10 Ibid, 55–6; *VCH* 1995 *Mddx X*, 120–1.
11 Mander 1993, 10; *VCH* 1995 *Mddx X*, 18, 103, 148, 153; Robinson 1989, 31–2.
12 HAD, D/F/Tys/40, 58, 78, 85–6.

13 *VCH* 1995 *Mddx X*, 18.
14 Barton 1962, 48; *VCH* 1995 *Mddx X*, 4.
15 HAD, D/F/Tys/40, 86, 89, 92, 109, 112.
16 Ibid, 68; Taylor 1999, 3–5.
17 Taylor 1999, 1, 7–10.
18 Sunnys appears as Sunnyf in records of the Haberdashers' Company (probably mistranscribed).
19 HAD, D/F/Tys/40, 49, 52, 93–4, 97; *VCH* 1995 *Mddx X*, 19.
20 HAD, D/F/Tys/40, 65; *VCH* 1995 *Mddx X*, 18, 77–8.
21 *VCH* 1995 *Mddx X*, 66; Luckett 1995, 3–9.
22 LMA, ACC/1876/D1; HAD, D/F/Tys/40.
23 HAD, D/F/Tys/40, 52, 77, 79, 82–4; PRO, C54/407/29; Bindoff 1982, Vol II, 350.
24 GuiL, MS 1594; LMA, ACC/1876/D1/926–48; Brenner 1993, 14n, 16n, 72n, 73n.
25 *DNB*, under Sutton, Thomas.
26 LMA, ACC/1876/D1.
27 *DNB*, under Peyton, Sir John; LMA, ACC/1876/D1/948.
28 Gray 1997, 3, 30.
29 HAD, D/F/Tys/1, 66.
30 GuiL, MS 1594.
31 Mann 1904, 22, 24; *SoL* 1960, *Vol XXVIII*, 80.
32 PRO, C54/2443/12.
33 Ibid; *VCH* 1995 *Mddx X*, 44, 46, 53.
34 *VCH* 1995 *Mddx X*, 53, 58, 105, 109.
35 Solman 1995.
36 *SoL* 1960, *Vol XXVIII*; *VCH* 1995 *Mddx X*, 78–9.
37 *SoL* 1960, *Vol XXVIII*, 57–8.
38 *Cal S P E I*, Vol II for 1513–1616, 115–17.

Chapter 3

1   Clifton-Taylor 1972, 297; Airs 1975, 108–9; Howard 1987, 165.

2   PRO, C54/407/29.
3   GuiL, MS 1594.
4   HAD, M820, M1045.
5   PRO, C2/JASI/M2/47.
6   Fuller 1662, 183; Clifford 1809, i–ii.
7   Slavin 1966, 3–13.
8   PRO, SP1/66, fol 47, transcribed in full in Ellis 1846, 164–5.
9   *L & P Hen VIII*, Vol V, 279.
10 Slavin 1966, 4–6.
11 BL, Cotton MS Titus B1, fol 153, transcribed in Ellis 1846, 144–6. Slavin (1966, 9–10) assumed that Henry Sadleir's wife was then living in Hackney, but the letter only refers generally to London.
12 BL, Add MS 35824.
13 There are three full-length biographies of Sadleir. Stoney (1877) was by a descendant; Drummond (1969) concentrated largely on matters relating to Scotland; Slavin (1966) concentrated on Sadleir's life and career during the reign of Henry VIII and is, for that period, by far the best. In addition there are lengthy accounts of his career in Bindoff 1982, Vol III, 249–52 and Hasler 1981, Vol III, 318–21. The spelling of the name varies, but Sadleir is used throughout this work as the variant generally preferred by his descendants.
14 PRO, C89/6/2 (a badly damaged manuscript which is transcribed, in an 18th-century hand, in BL Stowe MS 671, fols 251–66). *See also* Slavin 1966, 216–18.
15 PRO, DL42/95, fol 142v. *See also SoL* 1960, *Vol XXVIII*, 56–7.
16 *L & P Hen VIII*, Vol VIII, 1142; Vol IX, 47, 66, 105–6, 131, 172, 259, 339–40, 413–15.
17 PRO, C66/667; Colvin 1982, 124–5.
18 *L & P Hen VIII*, Vol VII, 1021 (the original is PRO, SP1/85, fol 94).
19 BL, Cotton MS Titus B1, fol 348, transcribed in Ellis 1846, 225–6.

20 Venn and Venn 1922–54, pt 1, Vol IV, 2–3.
21 Starkey 1985, 111–15, 120–1.
22 Slavin 1966, 163. Howard (1987, 35) discusses the necessity for a successful courtier to have a base in or near London.
23 *L & P Hen VIII*, Vol X, 1015 (37).
24 PRO, SP1/125, fol 116.
25 PRO, SP1/125, fol 129.
26 *L & P Hen VIII*, Vol XV, 1027 (40).
27 BL, Add MS 35824.
28 *SoL* 1960, *Vol XXVIII*, 59–60.
29 Tawney 1941, 27, 28.
30 Slavin 1966, 195–6.
31 GuiL, MS 1594.
32 HAD, M820 and M1045.
33 Slavin 1966, 84, 212–19.
34 PRO, C54/407/29; GuiL, MS 1594; BL Add MS 35824.
35 Airs 1975, 104.
36 *SoL* 1960, *Vol XXVIII*, 69–73.
37 Wight 1972, 29.
38 Tyler 1997.
39 Howard 1987, 172, 174–5.
40 Comment by W Rodwell in a lecture given at the Study Day held at Sutton House on 18 Jun 1988.
41 BL, Egerton Roll 2080.
42 Clarke 1986, 135–7.
43 Heal 1943, 108–16.
44 Slavin 1966, 13.
45 Ibid, 15.
46 Ibid, 28–9.
47 Ibid, 16.
48 Beckingsale 1978, 5.
49 Colvin 1982, 169; Beckingsale 1978, 5.
50 Colvin 1982, 125.
51 Slavin 1966, 16.
52 Colvin 1982, 127–8; Wight 1972, 207.
53 Colvin 1975, 26, 214.
54 Ibid, 10.
55 *L & P Hen VIII*, Vol V, 1442.
56 Colvin 1975, 264, 346; Colvin 1982, 303; Colvin 1975, 346.
57 Colvin 1975, 13–14; *SoL* 1960, *Vol XXVIII*, 57.
58 Slavin 1966, 16.
59 Ibid, 23.
60 Ibid, 163.
61 Colvin 1982, 193.
62 For these and other examples of brick building see the gazetteer in Wight 1972.
63 *VCH* 1998 *Mddx XI*, 22–3; Colvin 1975, 125.
64 Cooper 1999, 129.
65 Summerson 1991, 92.
66 Wight 1972, 77.
67 Schofield 1984, 129; Schofield 1995, 150–2.
68 *SoL* 1913, *Vol IV*, pt II, 18–27; Ackroyd 1998, 247–8.
69 Bond 1999.
70 Tyers 1997.

71 *See* Turner 1997.
72 Smith 1992, 57.
73 Kingsford 1921, 34; Cooper 1999, 17.
74 Gunn and Lindley 1988, 276.
75 Cooper 1999, 277.
76 Kingsford 1921, 23. At Coldharbour, there was a 'Great Chamber' listed over the 'Great Hall', as well as another 'Great Chamber' over the 'Little Hall'.
77 Thurley 1993, 114.
78 These items are taken from the 1539 inventory of Sir Adrian Fortescue's house (Fortescue 1880, 308) and the 1517 inventory of the Lovett family's house at Astwell, Northamptonshire (Anon 1873, 423–4). For other inventories, *see* Howard 1998, 14–29.
79 *See* Fortescue 1880, 307, 310 and the 1509 inventory of Edmund Dudley's London house in Kingsford 1921, 42.
80 Anon 1873, 421.
81 Kingsford 1921, 39.
82 Schofield 1995, 131.
83 Compton 1930, 310.
84 *See* Cooper 1999, 17.
85 Ibid, 288–9.
86 Kingsford 1921, 39; Fortescue 1880, 307.
87 Compton 1930, 308.
88 *L & P Hen VIII*, Vol XV, 650.
89 Cooper 1999, 17.
90 Anon 1873, 418.
91 Kingsford 1921, 40–1.
92 Cooper 1999, 305.
93 Fortescue 1880, 311.
94 Ibid, 310–11.

Chapter 4

1 *Cal Pat Edward VI*, Vol I, 140, 5 Apr 1547; *APC*, NS, Vol II, 1547–50, 235, 9 Jan 1549; Slavin 1966, 165–6.
2 Information kindly supplied by the archivist of the Clothworkers' Company; Bellasis 1886, following 466 (pedigree of the Machell family); Beavan 1908, 18, 207, 349; Beavan 1913, 34.
3 Nichols 1848, 12.
4 Sissons 1993, pedigree following 163.
5 BL, Egerton Roll 2080.
6 PRO, PROB11/58, fol 163.
7 LMA, ACC/1876/D1/926.
8 PRO, PROB11/41, fols 201v–205v; transcribed in HAD, D/F/Tys/47/6, 377–400.
9 PRO, C2/ELIZ/M2/38.
10 BL, Egerton Roll 2080; HAD, D/F/Tys/38, 4, 6, 10, D/F/Tys/40, 102–3.
11 HAD, M1045.
12 PRO, E179/142/193, transcribed in HAD, D/F/Tys/15, 115; BL, Harl MS 897, fol 24; HAD, D/F/Tys/47/1, 483.

13 *Cal Pat Eliz I*, Vol IV, 29, 21 Oct 1567; HAD, M1045.
14 *APC*, NS, Vol XXV for 1595–6, 22; *APC*, NS, Vol XXVI for 1596–7, 386–8.
15 Sissons 1993, 64–7; PRO, C24/63, Lodge *et al* v. Wytbroke, deposition of John Machell.
16 *Cal Pat Eliz I*, Vol I, 35.
17 GuiL, MS 11, 592A, list of freemen of the Grocers' Company. A search of the calendar and indexes of minutes of the Company revealed no other references to Machell.
18 Robinson 1843, Vol II, 32.
19 PRO, C3/318/37.
20 GuiL, MS 1594.
21 PRO, C2/ELIZ/M2/38.
22 PRO, C3/107/50.
23 LMA, ACC/1876/D1/942.
24 LMA, ACC/1876/D1/946.
25 LMA, ACC/1876/D1/947.
26 PRO, C2/ELIZ/M2/38.
27 PRO, C2/ELIZ/M13/61, C2/ELIZ/M6/54, C142/193/73, C142/200/46; BL, Egerton Roll 2080; *Cal Pat Eliz I*, Vol VII, 1880, 28 Jan 1577.
28 LMA, ACC/1876/D1/948.
29 LMA, ACC/1876/D1/949.
30 HAD, D/F/Tys/1, 17, 18, 23, 29, 31, 45–7, 163.
31 *VCH* 1973, *Cambs V*, 73; *VCH* 1978, *Cambs VI*, 24, 222.
32 PRO, C2/JASI/M2/47, C2/CHASI/M29/51, C54/1554, Machell to Deane.
33 Information kindly provided by the archivist of the Drapers' Company; Beavan 1908, 158; Beavan 1913, 49, 176; Povah 1894, 75–8, 265–7; *APC*, NS, Vol XXXI for 1600–1, 427.
34 PRO, PROB11/111, fol 434v.
35 Stone 1956, 274, 290–1.
36 PRO, C2/ELIZ/H22/48.
37 HAD, D/F/Tys/40, 60–1; PRO, STAC8/127/11.
38 PRO, C3/267/9.
39 PRO, C2/CHASI/M29/51.
40 House of Lords Record Office, House of Lords Papers, 19 Jun 1641, petition of John Machell.
41 PRO, STAC8/127/11.
42 HAD, D/F/Tys/1, 66; PRO, C2/CHASI/M29/51.
43 PRO, C3/318/27.
44 Sissons 1993, 33–7.
45 PRO, C2/JASI/M2/47.
46 PRO, C2/JASI/M17/28.
47 PRO, C3/318/37, C142/445/15.
48 PRO, PROB11/111, fol 435.
49 PRO, C2/CHASI/M29/51; C33/158, 533; C33/162, 445; C33/166, 167, 267, 379.
50 House of Lords Record Office, 19 Jun 1641, petition of John Machell.

Chapter 5

1   PRO, PROB11/111, fols 434v, 435.
2   Povah 1894, 75–8.
3   Armytage 1887, Vol I, 308; HAD, D/F/Tys/12/2, 5; BL, Add MS 14417, fols 5v–6.
4   PRO, PROB11/99, fols 329–31; GuiL, MS 17832, fol 55v.
5   PRO, C2/CHASI/C72/6.
6   Information kindly provided by the archivist of the Drapers' Company. Sir James Deane's will is PRO, PROB11/111, commencing on fol 427v; extracts from the will are in HAD, D/F/Tys/32/1, 290–5.
7   GuiL, MS 4097, fol 8; PRO, C2/CHASI/D61/76.
8   VCH 1911, Hants IV, 134, 200, 206; PRO, C54/2361/38.
9   PRO, C2/CHASI/D61/76, C2/CHASI/M29/51, C2/CHASI/C72/6; HAD, D/M/STE/1, 115.
10 Foster 1891–2, Vol I, 278; GuiL, MS 11592A, list of freemen of Grocers' Company; HAD, D/F/Tys/40, 59–60, 155, 157, 159.
11 HAD, D/F/Tys/40, 59–60; VCH 1911, Hants IV, 206.
12 HAD, D/F/Tys/40, 59–60, 155, 157, 159.
13 Ibid, M1527.
14 PRO, PROB11/137, fol 59.
15 HAD, D/F/Tys/1, 118; PRO, PROB11/125, fols 482–3.
16 G E C 1910–98, under Warwick; DNB, under Rich, Sir Robert, 2nd Earl of Warwick; Brenner 1993, 100; Dalton 1880, 117–47.
17 Typescript reference to deed (no. 576) in box file of notes on Hackney in possession of SoL section of English Heritage (whereabouts of deed not stated and original not found). Will of Countess of Warwick is PRO, PROB11/166, fol 95.
18 HAD, D/F/Tys/2, 75.
19 PRO, E179/142/307.
20 'Boyd's Citizens of London' nd, under Milward, Humphrey and Milward, John; Milward-Oliver 1930, 87–8; pedigree of Milward family in Howard 1883, 104; GuiL, MS 15211/1, fol 228, MS 15211/2, 27.
21 GuiL, MS 15211/2, 82, 102, 106.
22 Cal S P E I, Vol II for 1513–1616, 117; Cal Ct Min, Vol II for 1640–3, 33.
23 Bannerman 1904, 122.
24 Freshfield 1890, xlvii, 70, 82, 84–5, 86, 91.
25 Crawford 1977, 97–8, 287.
26 Raikes 1878, Vol 1, 105.
27 Cal S P E I, Vol II for 1513–1616, 238–40.
28 Ibid, Vol III for 1617–21, 230.
29 Ibid, 504; Cal S P E I, Vol VI for 1625–9, 198, 219, 224–6, 243, 245, 249, 251, 255–6, 259, 288–9, 321.
30 Cal S P E I, Vol VI for 1625–9, 157; Cal S P E I, Vol VIII for 1630–4, 32, 268; Cal Ct Min, Vol I for 1635–9, 185.
31 Cal S P E I, Vol VI for 1625–9, 477, 483.
32 Cal S P E I, Vol VIII for 1630–4, 325, 449.
33 Stern 1956, 26; Cal S P Dom Charles I, Vol IX for 1635–6, 193.
34 Cal S P Dom Charles I, Vol IX for 1635–6, 443; APC, Sep 1627–Jun 1628, 26; Ashton 1960, 105–10.
35 Cal S P E I, Vol VI for 1625–9, 601, 699; Cal S P E I, Vol VIII for 1630–4, 109, 239, 506–8.
36 LMA, Hackney marriages, 7 Jul 1631.
37 Ashton 1960, 93; pedigree of Milward family in Howard 1883, 104.
38 DNB, under Abbot, George, Archbishop of Canterbury; Abbot, Sir Morris; and Abbot, Robert, Bishop of Salisbury.
39 BL, Egerton MS 3006, fol 42v.
40 Freshfield 1890, 111, 132.
41 HAD, D/F/Tys/2, 113.
42 LMA, M/93/2, 15–17.
43 Smith 1992, 106.
44 Freshfield 1890, 123, 127.
45 Chaudhuri 1965, 56–73, 203–6.
46 Cal Ct Min, Vol I for 1635–9, 169, 173.
47 Chaudhuri 1965, 222–3; BL, Egerton MS 3006, fol 42v.
48 Cal Ct Min, Vol II for 1640–3, 20, 33, 57, 164.
49 LMA, P/79/JNI/21, fol 246; HAD, D/F/Tys/12/2, 49.
50 LMA, M93/2, 15–17.
51 'Boyd's Citizens of London' nd, under Abbot, Maurice; HAD, D/F/Tys/47/1, 1; information kindly supplied by the archivist of the Drapers' Company; PRO, SP105/148, fol 141.
52 Drapers' Company records; GuiL, MS 4457/2, fol 335v.
53 Cal Ct Min, Vol I for 1635–9, 39, 60, 185; Cal Ct Min, Vol II for 1640–3, 61.
54 PRO, PROB6/16, fol 177.
55 Fourth Report of the Royal Commission on Historical Manuscripts (1874), 62, 72, 73, 102; The Journal of the House of Lords, Vol IV, 1641, 240, 242, 271, 292, 300, 303, 304, 388, 398; Drapers' Company records; PRO, SP105/150, fol 106v, 148.
56 Cal Ct Min, Vol V for 1655–9, 9, 16, 85, 106, 141.
57 LMA, M93/2, 15–17.
58 HAD, D/F/Tys/12/2, 48; Armytage 1887, Vol II, 254; LMA, baptisms at St John at Hackney, 1545–1750.
59 Cal S P E I, Vol VIII for 1630–4, 270, 338; BL, Egerton MS 3006, fols 66, 150.
60 PRO, PROB6/20, fol 34.
61 Cal Ct Min, Vol III for 1644–9, 226–7, 243, 270; Cal Ct Min, Vol IV for 1650–4, 17, 64.
62 PRO, PROB11/250, fol 282, PROB6/31, 30 Jan 1654/5.
63 Cal Ct Min, Vol V for 1655–9, 271.
64 LMA, M93/1, 160–1, M93/2, 15–17, 57.
65 'Boyd's Citizens of London' nd, under Whittingham, Henry; PRO, PROB11/346, fols 56–8.
66 Calendar of the Proceedings of the Committee for the Advance of Money, 1642–1656, Vol 1, 494.
67 LMA, M79/LH/41.
68 LMA, M93/2, 57, M79/LH/41.
69 LMA, P79/JNI/23, 25 Feb 1656/7.
70 LMA, P/JNI/138, 26 Nov 1672, 14 Sep 1689.
71 PRO, E179/253/16, E179/143/370.
72 Quotes taken from Gardiner 1929, 211–14, 219–20.
73 LMA, P19/JNI/24, 152; PRO, PROB6/77, fol 193v.
74 PRO, PROB11/346, fols 56–8.
75 LMA, M93/90, 117, 126, M79/LH/41; 'Boyd's Citizens of London' nd, under Whittingham, Henry; Whittingham, Robert; and Wagstaffe, William; PRO, PROB11/401, fol 235.
76 PRO, PROB11/516, fols 290–1.
77 The Builders' Journal and Architectural Record, 30 Aug 1905, 116.
78 Information kindly provided by the College of Arms.
79 LMA, ACC/1876/D1/762, MP1/220.

Chapter 6

1   PRO, PROB11/516, fols 290–1.
2   LMA, M79/LH/49, courts of 6 Apr 1711, 8 Apr 1718, 3 Apr 1719.
3   LMA, M79/LH/41, M79/LH/49, courts of 2 Apr 1714, 10 Apr 1724.
4   PRO, PROB11/593, fol 190; LMA, M79/LH/49, court of 10 Apr 1724.
5   PRO, PROB11/617, fols 261–2.
6   M79/LH/50, courts of 8 Oct 1727, 26 Apr 1728, 11 Apr 1729.
7   PRO, PROB11/701, fols 31, 71.
8   LMA, M79/LH/50, courts of 12 Apr 1743, 23 Apr 1745, M79/LH/27, 86–7.
9   PRO, PROB6/77, fol 193v.
10 GuiL, MS 8674/19, fol 115; HAD, P/J/P71–9.
11 Matthews 1939, 81–2, 84.
12 LMA, P79/JNI/140, 5.
13 HAD, P/J/P81.
14 LMA, P79/JNI/141, 130, transcript of Hackney burials, 4 Mar 1740/1; HAD, P/J/P81–95, P/J/LT1–8.
15 PRO, PROB11/708, fol 202; LMA, P19/JNI/25, 20 Sep 1723.

16 LMA, TA/HACK.R/1–2; HAD, P/J/LT1–8.

17 LMA, P/JNI/142, 55, 66, 95; HAD, P/J/LT7–9.

18 A number of original court books of Lordshold manor in LMA are deemed to be unfit for consultation. Some, but not all, of the gaps are filled by draft court books in LMA and there are some abstracts in HAD, D/F/Tys/38.

19 HAD, M1049, M1055.

20 HAD, P/J/LT7–9; PRO, PROB11/855, fols 324–5.

21 HAD, D/F/Tys/48, 65; IGI; LMA, transcript of Hackney burials, 21 Oct 1751, P79/JNI/142, 11, 19, 66; Paley 1991, nos. 632, 719, 756, 996, 1028.

22 SoL 1957, Vol XXVII, 239.

23 HAD, P/J/P79, P/J/LT8.

24 LMA, M79/LH/68/6/5.

25 HAD, P/J/LT10; files in the library of the Huguenot Society; IGI; DNB, under Lethieulier, Smart.

26 The Political State of Great Britain 1711–1740, Vol XXXVIII, 494.

27 PRO, PROB11/790, fol 361.

28 HAD, P/J/P98–116; GuiL, MS 8674/81, fol 130.

29 London directories: The Intelligencer: or Merchants Assistant (1738) and A Complete Guide (1740, 1743, 1749, 1752 edns); LMA, M79/LH/51, 1 May 1753; Paley 1991, xii, nos. 1102–3; BL, Add MS 35603, fols 229–32; SoL 1957, Vol XXVII, 209; files in the library of the Huguenot Society.

30 London directories: A Complete Guide (1752, 1755, 1758, 1765 edns), Kent's Directory (1753, 1761, 1765, 1768, 1771 edns) and Mortimer's Universal Director (1763); IGI; SoL 1957, Vol XXVII, 70; HAD, P/J/P145–7; PRO, PROB11/1062, fol 28.

31 HAD, P/J/P104–14.

32 LMA, M79/LH/14, 26.

33 PRO, PROB11/855, fols 324–5.

Chapter 7

1 LMA, M79/LH/14, 192–3, 195–7, 301–3; HAD, M1055.

2 LMA, M79/LH/16, 145–52, 289, M79/LH/27, 26–35.

3 LMA, M79/LH/27, 26–35; HAD, M1049.

4 LMA, M79/LH/27, 202.

5 LMA, M79/LH/27, 196–200, M79/LH/28, 246–58.

6 HAD, M3679.

7 LMA, MDR 1865/12/528–31.

8 HAD, M3679; LMA, MDR 1895/23/726.

9 The Builder, 1 Nov 1873, 869.

10 HAD, P/J/P124/2.

11 GuiL, MS 9171/82.

12 HAD, P/J/L13, P/J/P132–9; London directories: A Complete Guide (1738, 1740, 1749, 1752 edns); Kent's Directory (1753); IGI.

13 Index to marriage licences in library of Society of Genealogists; IGI; Gentleman's Magazine, Vol LXXX, pt 2, 1800, 806; PRO, PROB11/1347, fol 142.

14 Généalogie de la famille de Coussmaker (BL, 9915 BB 13); MS notes on the de Ste Croix family in the possession of Mr Ralph de Ste Croix.

15 IGI; PRO, PROB11/910, fol 98.

16 LMA, MR/PLT5422; HAD, P/J/LT54.

17 HAD, P/J/P139–43; LMA, MR/PLT5422; SoL 1957, Vol XXVII, 221, 222.

18 HAD, P/J/P145, 210; LMA, MR/PLT5446; file at Huguenot Society library; Rothstein 1985, 134, 138.

19 HAD, M1922; The Gentleman's Magazine, Vol LXXXV, pt 2, 1816, 186, 286.

20 HAD, P/J/P208–12; LMA, MR/PLT5432, 5448.

21 MS notes on de Ste Croix family in the possession of Mr Ralph de Ste Croix.

22 BL, Add MS 38234, fols 230–2; PRO, PROB11/1342, fol 6.

23 BL, Add MS 38234, fols 230–2, 38472, 313.

24 The Gentleman's Magazine, Vol LXXXV, pt 2, 1816, 186.

25 HAD, H/E/75/2, no. B463, P/J/LT95–100; LMA, MR/PLT5481, 5491, 5493, 5495, 5497, 5503.

26 Pedigree in Huguenot Society Library; Cox 1996, 94.

27 The Hackney Magazine and Parish Reformer, Vol I, 1834, 56–9, 96, 110–12 (BL, PP 3612 k).

28 Printed and published by the author [Charles Green], Church Street, Hackney, 1834.

29 LMA, MDR1865/12/528–31.

30 The Builder, 16 May 1863, 358.

31 LMA, P79/JNI/49, 15 Dec 1864, 21 Apr 1865; General Register Office, death certificate of Charles Horton Pulley.

32 Principal Probate Registry, will of C H Pulley, proved 18 Mar 1865.

33 HAD, Hackney local directories, censuses of 1871, 1881 and 1891.

34 HAD, P/J/P124–32, 205, P/J/CW69.

35 HAD, P/J/P149, D/F/Tys48, 266; Collinge 1978, 9–10, 41, 95; PRO, PROB11/1342, fol 6.

36 Lytton 1913, 48–50.

37 Venn and Venn 1922–54, pt 2, Vol I, 458; inscriptions in the church and vestry of St James Garlickhithe; HAD, P/J/P169.

38 HAD, censuses 1841–71; Post Office directories, 1874–6.

39 HAD, census of 1991; Hackney directory, 1890.

40 LMA, M79/LH/27, 86–7.

41 RCHME 1930, 45 (Monument 2).

42 Clarke 1986, 135–6.

43 The Builders' Journal and Architectural Record, 30 Aug 1905, 116.

Chapter 8

1 LMA, MDR 1895/23/726, P79/JNI/467/1–21.

2 LMA, MDR 1896/5/282; Baldry 1970, 54.

3 Hackney and Kingsland Gazette, 9 Nov 1891, 3; 27 Nov 1891, 3; Who Was Who 1897–1916, under Hunter, Sir William Guyer.

4 Anon 1933, esp 45–58; Hackney and Kingsland Gazette, 17 Oct 1904, 3.

5 Crawford 1985, 57–66, 437 (n 85); Hobhouse 1994, 6, 29.

6 Crawford 1985, 59.

7 Correspondence in archives of SPAB.

8 Ibid, letter of 9 Jun 1903.

9 LMA, P79/JNI/399/7–9; Who's Who in Architecture, 1914 edn, under Crane, Lionel Francis; Post Office Directory, 1911 and 1913 edns; The Builders' Journal and Architectural Record, 30 Aug 1905, 116.

10 Hackney and Kingsland Gazette, 17 Oct 1904, 3; Anon 1933, 48; HAD, cuttings relating to Sutton House.

11 St John-at-Hackney Church Institute . . . Prospectus and Rules (copies available at Sutton House).

12 Information kindly provided by Mrs Barbara Cardale, daughter of Francis Vaisey.

13 St John-at-Hackney Parish Magazine, Jul 1914.

14 St John-at-Hackney Parish Magazine, illustrated souvenir edition commemorating the visit of the Prince of Wales [May 1926].

15 Letter from John Dyter to Sutton House Society.

16 HAD, local directories; Mission of Help to the Suffering Poor, Annual Report, 1932 (copy available at Sutton House).

17 The Builders' Journal, 30 Aug 1905, 116.

18 St John-at-Hackney Parish Magazine, Jul 1914.

19 Ibid.

20 Information provided by Mrs Barbara Cardale.

21 The Builders' Journal, 30 Aug 1905, 116.

22 Ibid.

23 HAD, undated cutting entitled 'St John at Hackney, November Fair, The Institute in the Past'.

Chapter 9

1 Typescript 'Report upon an Inspection by the Commissioners of HM Office of Works, Aug. 1936' (copy available at Sutton House).
2 Hobhouse 1994, 19–20.
3 *The Journal of the London Society*, Dec 1936, 179–80; Files relating to Sutton House in the possession of the National Trust; Records of the London Society; *The Times*, 10 Dec 1936, 10.
4 Wright 1991, 48–9.
5 *Journal of the London Society*, Jan 1937, 5.
6 National Trust files.
7 *The Hackney Gazette*, 4 May 1938; *The Times*, 5 Jul 1937, 21; *Who Was Who 1941–1950*, under Power, Sir William.
8 National Trust files.
9 Typescript list of donations in the records of the London Society.
10 Information in this and succeeding paragraphs, unless otherwise stated, is based on files relating to Sutton House in the possession of the National Trust.
11 *The Hackney Gazette*, 4 May 2000, 3.
12 Gaze 1988, 121, 125; Wright 1991, 54–5.
13 Lees-Milne 1984, 35.
14 Memo of 23 May 1952 found in files relating to Sutton House in the possession of the National Trust.
15 Letter of Mrs Geraldine North to the Sutton House Society.
16 Miss Pamela Cunnington, who was the National Trust's architect for Sutton House between 1960 and 1969, maintained a file of correspondence relating to her work at the house. The information in this and succeeding paragraphs is based on that file, which has been deposited at Sutton House.

Chapter 10

1 This chapter, unless a specific source is cited, is based on files relating to Sutton House in the possession of the National Trust, newsletters of the Sutton House Society and the personal recollections and files of individuals involved in the campaign for the implementation of the community scheme.
2 Wright 1991, 46.
3 'Sutton House: The Community Scheme', document issued by the Sutton House Campaign, Sep 1987 (copy available at Sutton House).
4 Wright 1987, 17.
5 Wright 1991, 45–9, 59–60, 112–15.
6 Waterson 1995, 243–6.

Chapter 11

1 Parts of this chapter have appeared in Griffiths 1995, 8–11.

Select Bibliography

Ackroyd, P 1998. *The Life of Thomas More*

Acts of the Privy Council of England, 1542–1604, NS, 32 vols, 1890–1907. Dasent, J R (ed)

Acts of the Privy Council of England, 1617–1628, 8 vols, 1929–49. Prepared by H V Lyle

Airs, M 1975. *The Making of the English Country House 1500–1640*

Anon 1873. *Stemmata Shirleiana, or the Annals of the Shirley Family*

Anon 1933. *Algy Lawley* (various authors, printed for private circulation)

Armytage, G J (ed) 1887. *Allegations for Marriage Licences Issued by the Bishop of London 1520 to 1610*, Vol I, Harl Soc Publ **25** and *...1611 to 1828*, Vol II, Harl Soc Publ **26**

Ashton, R 1960. *The Crown and the Money Market 1603–1640*

Baldry, J 1970. *The Hackney Free and Parochial Schools, A History*

Bannerman, W Bruce (ed) 1904. *The Registers of St Helen's, Bishopsgate, London.* Harl Soc Publ **31**

Barton, N J 1962. *The Lost Rivers of London*

Beavan, A B 1908. *The Aldermen of the City of London*, I

—1913. *The Aldermen of the City of London*, II

Beckingsale, B W 1978. *Thomas Cromwell: Tudor Minister*

Bellasis, E 1886. 'Machell of Crackenthorpe'. *Trans Cumberland Westmoreland Antiq Archaeol Soc* **8**, 416–66

Bindoff, S T (ed) 1982. *History of Parliament: The House of Commons 1509–1558*, 3 vols

Bond, R 1999. *Isaac Lord, Fore Street, Ipswich: A Report on the Historical Development of the Site.* English Heritage Historic Analysis and Research Team Reports and Papers **7** (unpublished)

'Boyd's Citizens of London' nd, (MS series available in library of Society of Genealogists)

Brenner, R 1993. *Merchants and Revolution: Commercial Change, Political Conflict, and London's Overseas Traders, 1550–1653*

Calendar of the Court Minutes of the East India Company, 1635–1679..., 11 vols, 1907–38. Sainsbury, E B (ed)

Calendar of the Patent Rolls Preserved in the Public Record Office. Edward VI, 1547–1553, 6 vols, 1924–9

Calendar of the Patent Rolls Preserved in the Public Record Office. Elizabeth, 1553–1582, 9 vols, 1939–86

Calendar of the Proceedings of the Committee for the Advance of Money, 1642–1656, 3 vols, 1888. Green, Mary A E (ed)

Calendar of State Papers, Colonial Series, East Indies, 6 vols, 1862–92. Sainsbury, W N (ed)

Calendar of State Papers, Domestic Series, of the Reign of Charles I..., 23 vols, 1858–97. Bruce, J and Hamilton, W D (eds)

Chaudhuri, K N 1965. *The English East India Company: The Study of an Early Joint-Stock Company 1600–1640*

Clarke, B 1986. *Glimpses of Ancient Hackney and Stoke Newington*

Clifford, A (ed) 1809. *The State Papers and Letters of Sir Ralph Sadler Knight-Banneret*

Clifton-Taylor, A 1972. *The Pattern of English Building*

Collinge, J M 1978. *Office-Holders in Modern Britain: VII: Navy Board Officials 1660–1832*

Colvin, H M (ed) 1975. *The History of the King's Works*, **3**

—1982. *The History of the King's Works*, **4**

Compton, W B 1930. *History of the Comptons of Compton Wynyates*

Cooper, N 1999. *Houses of the Gentry 1480–1680*

Cox, M 1996. *Life and Death in Spitalfields 1700 to 1850*

Crawford, Alan 1985. *C R Ashbee: Architect, Designer & Romantic Socialist*

Crawford, Anne 1977. *A History of the Vintners' Company*

Dalton, C 1880. *History of the Wrays of Glentworth 1523–1852*

Drummond, H 1969. *Our Man in Scotland: Sir Ralph Sadleir 1507–1587*

Ellis, H (ed) 1846. *Original Letters Illustrative of English History*, 3 ser, **II**

Fortescue, T, Lord Clermont 1880. *The History of the Family of Fortescue*, 2 edn

Foster, J 1891–2. *Alumni Oxonienses 1500–1714*, 4 vols

Freshfield, E (ed) 1890. *The Vestry Minute Books of the Parish of St Bartholomew Exchange in the City of London 1567–1676*

Fuller, T 1662. *A History of the Worthies of England*

Gardiner, D 1929. *English Girlhood at School: A Study of Women's Education through Twelve Centuries*

Gaze, J 1988. *Figures in a Landscape: A History of the National Trust*

G E C (Cokayne, G E (ed)) 1910–98. *The Complete Peerage of England, Scotland, Ireland, Great Britain and the United Kingdom...*, 14 vols

Gerard, J 1597. *Herbal*, 2 vols (facsim edn 1974)

Gray, M 1989. 'Sifting Sutton House'. *The Ephemerist* **64**, 282–4

—1997. *Sutton House, Hackney: An Illustrated Souvenir*

Green, C 1834. *Ideal "Horsewhipping!" Facts relating to Mr Charles Horton Pulley, (Vestry Clerk of Hackney), Mr Charles Green, (late editor of the Hackney Magazine), and The Almshouse Case*

Griffiths, R 1995. 'Sutton House: sole survivor'. *SPAB News* **16.2**, 8–11

Gunn, S J and Lindley, P J 1988. 'Charles Brandon's Westhorpe: an Early Tudor courtyard house in Suffolk'. *Arch J* **145**, 272–89

Hasler, P W (ed) 1981. *The House of Commons 1558–1601*, 3 vols

Heal, Sir A 1943. 'A great country house in 1623'. *Burlington Magazine* **82**, 108–16

Hobhouse, H 1994. *London Survey'd: The Work of the Survey of London 1894–1994*

Howard, J J (ed) 1883. *Visitation of London 1633, 1634 and 1635.* Harl Soc Publ **17**

Howard, M 1987. *The Early Tudor Country House: Architecture and Politics 1490–1550*

—1998. 'Inventories, surveys and the histories of great houses 1480–1640'. *Architect Hist* **41**, 14–29

Kingsford, C L 1921. 'On some London houses of the early Tudor period'. *Archaeologia* **71**, 17–54

Lees-Milne, J 1984. *Caves of Ice*

Letters and Papers, Foreign and Domestic, of the Reign of Henry VIII, 1862–1932. Vols 1–4 ed by Brewer, J S; vols 5–13 ed by Gairdner, J; and vols 14–21 ed by Gairdner, J and Brodie, R H

Luckett, R 1995. 'Pepys and Hackney'. *Hackney History* **1**, 3–9

Lytton, Earl of 1913. *The Life of Edward Bulwer, First Lord Lytton*, **I**

Mander, D 1993. *St John-at-Hackney: the Story of a Church*

Mann, E A 1904. *Brooke House, Hackney*. London Survey Committee Monograph **V**

Matthews, W (ed) 1939. *The Diary of Dudley Ryder 1715–1716*

Medhurst, L 1992–3. 'Sutton House wall paintings: conservation reports'. Unpublished typescript available at Sutton House

Milward-Oliver, F F 1930. *Memoirs of the Hungerford, Milward and Oliver Families*

Nichols, J G (ed) 1848. *The Diary of Henry Machyn, Citizen and Merchant Taylor of London, from AD 1550 to AD 1563*. Camden Society Publ **42**

Paley, R (ed) 1991. *Justice in Eighteenth-Century Hackney: The Justicing Notebook of Henry Norris and the Hackney Petty Sessions Book*. London Record Society Publ **29**

Pevsner, N 1952. *The Buildings of England: London except the Cities of London and Westminster*

Philpotts, C 1994. *Sutton House, 2–4 Homerton High Street, Hackney E8: an archaeological report* (unpublished, Museum of London Archaeology Service)

—1998. 'Excavations at Sutton House in Hackney 1990–92'. *London Archaeol* **8**, 207–12

Povah, A 1894. *The Annals of the Parishes of St Olave Hart Street and All Hallows Staining*

Raikes, G A 1878. *The History of the Honourable Artillery Company*, 2 vols

RCHME 1930. *An Inventory of the Historical Monuments in London, Vol V East London*

Richardson, W C 1952. *Tudor Chamber Administration 1485–1547*

Robinson, E 1989. *Lost Hackney*

Robinson, W 1843. *History and Antiquities of Hackney*

Rothstein, N 1985. 'Huguenots in the English silk industry in the eighteenth century', *in* Scouloudi, I (ed) *Huguenots in Britain and their French Background, 1550–1800*, 289–306

Schofield, J 1984. *The Building of London from the Conquest to the Great Fire*

—1995. *Medieval London Houses*

Sissons, C J (ed) 1993. *Thomas Lodge and Other Elizabethans*

Slavin, A J 1966. *Politics and Profit: A Study of Sir Ralph Sadler 1507–1547*

Smith, J T 1992. *English Houses 1200–1800: The Hertfordshire Evidence*

Solman, D 1995. *Loddiges of Hackney: The Largest Hothouse in the World*

Starkey, D 1985. *The Reign of Henry VIII: Personalities and Politics*

Stern, W 1956. 'The trade, art or mystery of silk throwers of the City of London in the seventeenth century'. *Guildhall Miscellany* **6**

Stone, L 1956. *An Elizabethan: Sir Horathio Palavicino*

Stoney, F S 1877. *A Memoir of the Life and Times of the Right Honourable Sir Ralph Sadleir*

[Strype, J] 1720. *A Survey of the Cities of London and Westminster…*, 2 vols

Summerson, J 1945. 'Town buildings', *in* Lees-Milne, J (ed) *The National Trust: A Record of Fifty Years' Achievement*, 97–102

—1991. *Architecture in Britian 1530–1830*, 8 edn

Survey of London 1913. Vol IV: *The Parish of Chelsea* (pt 2)

Survey of London 1957. Vol XXVII: *Spitalfields and Mile End New Town*

Survey of London 1960. Vol XXVIII: *The Parish of Hackney* (pt 1): *Brooke House*

Tawney, R H 1941. 'The rise of the gentry'. *Econ Hist Rev* **11**, 1–38

Taylor, M 1999. '"Naboth's vineyard": Hackney rectory in the 17th century'. *Hackney History* **5**, 3–11

Thurley, S 1993. *The Royal Palaces of Tudor England: Architecture and Court Life, 1460–1547*

Turner, R 1997. *Plas Mawr, Conwy*

Tyers, I 1991. *Sutton House: main building and panelling*. Dendrochronology Report REP02/91 (unpublished, Museum of London Archaeology Service)

—1997. *Tree ring analysis of Eastbury Manor House, Barking, Greater London*. English Heritage Ancient Monuments Laboratory Report **12/97** (unpublished)

Tyler, K 1997. *2–6 Link Street, London E9: an archaeological post-excavation assessment* (unpublished, Museum of London Archaeology Service)

Venn J and Venn, J A 1922–54. *Alumni Cantabrigienses*, 10 vols

VCH 1911. *A History of Hampshire and the Isle of Wight. Vol IV*

VCH 1973. *A History of Cambridgeshire and the Isle of Ely. Vol V*

VCH 1978. *A History of Cambridgeshire and the Isle of Ely. Vol VI*

VCH 1995. *A History of Middlesex. Vol X.*

VCH 1998. *A History of Middlesex. Vol XI.*

Waterson, M 1995. *The National Trust: The First Hundred Years*

Wight, J A 1972. *Brick Building in England from the Middle Ages to 1550*

Wittrick, A and Bond, R 1991. *Sutton House*. English Heritage report of the survey undertaken in 1988–90 (unpublished)

Wright, P 1987. 'Why the blight is stark enough', *The Guardian*, 1 August, 17

—1991. *A Journey through Ruins: The Last Days of London*

Index

Key first-floor plan (Scale 1:200)

Chapters 3, 4 and 5 (16th and 17th century)
F1 Withdrawing room/Bedchamber
F2 Inner bedchamber
F3 Great chamber
F4 Bedchamber
F5 Inner chamber
S end of F5 South-west chamber

Chapter 6 (mid-18th century)
F1 Bedchamber
F2 Inner bedchamber
F3 Great chamber
F4 North-west chamber
F5 Middle chamber
S end of F5 South-west chamber

Chapter 7 (late 18th and 19th century)
F1 Victorian parlour
F2 Inner bedchamber
F3 Great chamber
F4 North-west chamber
F5 Middle chamber
S end of F5 South-west chamber

Chapter 8 (early 20th century)
F1 Victorian parlour (Bedroom)
F2 Curate's room
F3 Great chamber (Large billiard room)
F4 North-west chamber (Small billiard room)
F5 Social room

Chapter 11 (modern)
F1 Victorian study
F2 Education room
F3 Great chamber
F4 Little chamber
F5 Gallery